Justin

The Biography

Also by Sean Smith

Robbie: The Biography
Kylie Confidential
J.K. Rowling – A Biography
Sophie's Kiss
Royal Racing
The Union Game
Stone Me!
(with Dale Lawrence)

Justin
The Biography

*'My name is Justin. I guess I should go ahead
and tell you I sing.'*
JUSTIN TIMBERLAKE, aged eleven

SEAN SMITH

**SIMON &
SCHUSTER**

London · New York · Sydney · Tokyo · Singapore · Toronto · Dublin

A VIACOM COMPANY

First published in Great Britain by Simon & Schuster UK Ltd, 2004
A Viacom Company

1 3 5 7 9 10 8 6 4 2

Simon & Schuster UK Ltd
Africa House
64-78 Kingsway
London WC2B 6AH

www.simonsays.co.uk

Simon & Schuster Australia
Sydney

A CIP catalogue record for this book is available from the British Library

ISBN 0-7432-5969-6

Photo Credits
Page 1: Dave Hogan/Getty Images; Page 2: (*top*) Stephanie Roach, (*middle & bottom*) E. E.
Jeter Elementary School; Page 3: (*top*) Sherry Yerger, (*bottom*) Blue Wave Productions; Page 4:
(*top & bottom*) Danielle Ditto; Page 5: Danielle Ditto; Page 6: (*top*) Mitchell Gerber/CORBIS,
(*bottom*) S. I. N./CORBIS; Page 7: (*top & bottom*) Veronica Finn; Page 8: (*top & bottom*) Toby
Canham/Splashnews; Page 9: RJ Capak/WireImage.com; Page 10: (*top & middle*) John
Shearer/WireImage.com, (*bottom*) Sherry Yerger; Page 11: (*top*) Kevin Mazur/WireImage.com,
(*middle right*) Mike Guastella/WireImage.com, (*bottom left*) Steve Granitz/WireImage.com;
Page 12: Reuters/CORBIS; Page 13: (*top*) Frank Trapper/CORBIS, (*middle*) Kevin Mazur/
WireImage.com, (*bottom*) MBZ/Rex Features; Page 14: (*top*) James Devaney/WireImage.com,
(*bottom*) Kurt Miller/PE/WireImage.com; Page 15: (*top*) Scott Gries/Getty Images, (*middle*)
James Devaney/WireImage.com, (*bottom*) Reuters/Corbis; Page 16: Frank Micelotta/Image-
Direct; Page 17: Getty Images; Page 18: (*top*) Kevin Mazur/WireImage.com, (*bottom*) Reuters/
Corbis; Page 19: (*top*) Albert Ferreira/Reuters/Corbis, (*middle*) Stephane Cardinale/People
Avenue/Corbis, (*bottom*) Mike Blake/Reuters/Corbis; Page 20: (*top & bottom*) Pierre
Ducharme/Reuters/Corbis; Page 21: (*top*) Gary Hershorn/Reuters/Corbis, (*bottom*) Randall
Michelson/WireImage.com; Page 22: (*top*) Kevin Mazur/WireImage.com, (*middle*) Charles
Sykes/Rex Features, (*bottom*) Vince Bucci/Getty Images; Page 23: (*top & bottom*) Kevin
Mazur/WireImage.com; Page 24: Steve Sands/New York Newswire/Corbis

Typeset by M Rules
Printed and bound in Finland
by WS Bookwell

Acknowledgements

When I complimented Justin's former headmistress Mrs Mary Ann McNeil on the courtesy with which I was being treated in Tennessee where everyone called me 'Sir', she replied, 'I bet you thought you'd been knighted by the Queen.' I would like to thank everyone who helped me on my trips to the United States to research this book. It made my work on *Justin: The Biography* an enormous pleasure.

Firstly, my sincere thanks to Danielle Ditto and Veronica Finn, former girlfriends of Justin who were generous with both their time and their memories. Good luck ladies with your careers. I am also greatly indebted to Pat Austin, Paulette Bond, Regina Castleberry, Bob Fischetti, Allison Hammett, Betty Kirk, Jacqueline Lackey, Kim Lampkins, Mary Ann McNeil, Nanci Norwood, Lou Pearlman, Betty Roach, Erika Ruch, Mike Tebbe, Karen Toombs, Beth Wendel, Bob Westbrook, and Chuck Yerger. Thanks also to Mrs Sherry Yerger and Stephanie Roach for sharing their old photos of Justin. My lasting impression is of a group of people with a great deal of admiration and affection for Justin Timberlake.

I would like to mention the waitresses of Old Timers restaurant in Millington for explaining the southern home cooking menu to me, the staff at the Admiralty Suites and Inn and John Guirl at the Neighbourhood Business Centre. The Shelby Forest General Store is well worth a visit but don't do what I did. The coffee is paid for on an honour system where you put a contribution into a cup. I had no idea what to leave so emptied the change in my pocket – a $5 cup of coffee!

My old friends Rick Sky and Gill Pringle were enormously helpful. I can't wait to read Gill's first novel. Yet again Lizzie Clachan did fantastic research for me. Adele Herson had the unenviable task of transcribing more than 100,000 words of original interview tapes.

At Simon and Schuster, my thanks to the publisher Jonathan Atkins for commissioning this book and to my brilliant editor Rumana Haider for her professionalism and encouragement. Arianne Burnette did a superb job copyediting my original manuscript. I am also indebted to Emma Noel for publicity, Barry O'Connor for production, Kate Hibbert for foreign rights, Jacky Mujico for marketing and Darren Wall for design.

I am grateful once more to Madeleine Moore for producing a fascinating birth chart for Justin. Finally, a special thank you to my wife Zoë Lawrence for being an inspirational support for the ninth book in a row.

Contents

Introduction

'Señorita', the first track of Justin Timberlake's solo album *Justified*, begins with a voice-over declaring, '. . . Justin . . . all the way from Memphis, Tennessee'. Memphis seemed like the best place to start a book about the man. After all, it is such a cool place to come from. It conjures up all the right images for association with the current 'coolest man in pop'. And it is full of kings.

To begin with there is *the* King – Elvis Presley, still the biggest-ever star of popular music. Although he was born in Tupelo, Mississippi, Elvis spent most of his life in Memphis. He was discovered there by legendary producer Sam Phillips, who made the groundbreaking early Sun recordings of Elvis. In the fifties, Elvis was for many the first white artist to sound like a black singer – a legacy Justin is continuing fifty years on. Memphis remained Elvis's home throughout his life despite his successful movie career. He died at his mansion Graceland in 1977 and since then this gaudy monument to bad taste has become the second biggest tourist attraction in America after the White House.

B. B. King is arguably the most revered figure in modern blues. The bar named after him is a popular venue in Beale Street in downtown Memphis. Since the jazz composer W. C. Handy lived in the street and immortalized it with 'Beale Street Blues', it has become one of the most famous music addresses in the world, showcasing up-and-coming talent. Justin is now a part owner of B. B. King's and was filmed there last autumn prior to giving a concert at the New Daisy Theatre down the street. Just off Beale Street is the Gibson Guitar Factory, which makes the unmistakable black 'Lucille' guitar forever associated with B. B. King. When he was a struggling musician in Mississippi in the early fifties, B. B. King played a set at a particularly rough bar. At the interval, he set his guitar down on the small stage while he went to grab some refreshment. At this point, two men standing at the bar started arguing about a lady they both knew, and before long the row degenerated into a bar-room brawl. Fists were flying, chairs were scattered and an oil lamp was knocked over, starting a fire. B. B. King watched in horror as the stage was engulfed, threatening an early cremation for his one and only guitar. He could not afford another, so unless he saved it his music career was finished. He plunged into the fire and rescued a rather charred instrument. Later he discovered that the name of the woman the men were fighting over was Lucille. From that day on, all his guitars have been called Lucille as a reminder of that evening. Now nearly eighty, the great man still carries his own guitar off stage after a performance.

The third King of Memphis is Martin Luther King, Jr, the civil rights leader and winner of the Nobel Peace Prize. His great legacy can be seen throughout the southern states of America. His policy of passive resistance and magnificent oratory inspired a generation to overcome the shameful racism that was still prevalent in the sixties. He was from Atlanta, Georgia, but became associated with Memphis for the worst of reasons when he was shot dead there in 1968. As a mark of respect for the man who 'had a dream', many states hold a national holiday in his honour. Tennessee, where the Ku Klux Klan was founded at Pulaski in 1866, is one of them.

Memphis is one of the major ports on the grey and muddy Mississippi River and is clearly a wonderful place for the new 'King of Pop' to hail from. The largest city in the State, it is rich in history and musical heritage – Jerry Lee Lewis and Aretha Franklin, the 'Queen of Soul', are just two more of the greats associated with Memphis. I had read several accounts stating that Justin had a typical Memphis childhood and looked forward to discovering more about it when I flew into the city on a blustery autumn day. The one problem with this ideal scenario is, as I quickly discovered, Justin is not actually from Memphis and has never lived in the city.

Admittedly, he was born in the St Jude Hospital, Memphis, but I had to drive forty minutes along the highway, north to the town of Millington, to pursue his true roots. This is rather like saying you're a Londoner if you come from Windsor. When I asked a local hotel if they were in the centre of town, I was told that Millington did not really have a centre. It has one long strip with tributaries darting off here and there. The main road through the town is home to Best Western, Days Inn, Kroger's Store and the usual selection of coffee and fast-food chains. On the way out of town is a giant Wal-Mart, where all the men's sizes seemed to be for local citizens who had spent too much time eating fast food or dining at exotically named restaurants, such as Big Dave's Steak and Rib Shack, Cactus Joe's Bar and Grill, Cattleman Jack's or Miss Sipps Catfish Saloon. Since 1941 Millington, or, more precisely, its outskirts, has been home to the world's largest inland naval base. It is also part of the mid South Bible belt and practically 'dry', which means it is very hard to find a drink. Just two or three restaurants in the town sell alcohol. When I asked a twentysomething woman if there were any bars in town, I was advised to avoid the few there were as they were full of 'rednecks'. It may have done them an injustice, but I decided to take her word for it. She also advised me to go to Beale Street in Memphis because it was 'really cool'.

Millington was certainly friendly enough, but by no stretch of the imagination could it be described as 'cool'. Justin's family home, I knew, was near his elementary school, E. E. Jeter, so I decided to drive out to take a look at the neighbourhood. The directions were simple. Take a right past Kroger's store and head down Shelby Road and 'you can't miss it'. This proved to be a Tennessee-style exaggeration. The drive is certainly pleasant enough, drifting easily past lines of cypress trees, immaculate one-storey houses with manicured lawns and big American flags. I noticed Glenn's Country Store proudly proclaiming the 'Best Beer Around' – not exactly a competitive category in this drink-free desert. Onwards I drove, deeper into Timberlake country, for some 10 or 12 miles, until the imposing Shelby Forest Baptist Church came into view. It is a brownstone, crazy-paving type of modern building with an air of quiet and tranquillity about it, with just the sounds of birds calling from the forest to disturb its peacefulness. Outside, a sign proclaimed: 'Jesus is coming, People get ready, Soon we'll be going home'.

Justin's grandfather used to be the preacher at the church and his father is still the choir director. The pastor is now Brother Barney Austin. I noticed some children's swings at the back, which made its immaculateness a little more welcoming, although the church door was locked. At the end of Locke Cuba Road, there is a junction where the Shelby Forest General Store sits, a neighbourhood oasis. Justin used to hang out there with his pals after school. The cheeseburgers are famous throughout Shelby County and the home-made sandwiches boast fillings as big as a fist. This is the epicentre of Shelby Forest, the true roots of Justin Timberlake. E. E. Jeter Elementary School is less than a mile away and Justin's childhood home is less than two. His home is in an exclusive road, rather like a gated community with no gate. In UK terms it might be a little bit like Sunningdale or Wentworth – Home Counties' detached houses set away from the road. His home is a million miles away from an Eminem-style trailer park. This is transparently a middle-class rural environment where, quaintly, signs declare that a Neighbourhood Watch scheme is in operation. There is barely a sound save for the birds. In the forest there are raccoons, opossums, beavers – and hunters by the dozen.

It struck me that here was an environment that people aspire to work towards all their lives: one that has peace, tranquillity, space, clean air and comfort. Ironically, Justin swapped it for the consumer creation that is Orlando, Florida, before he was out of short pants.

This is the place where the Justin Timberlake story begins. Not in Memphis, not in Millington, but here, sipping coffee outside a country store in Shelby Forest. My journey of discovery revealed a world very different from the star backgrounds I am used to. Along the way I was asked a number of questions about Justin. I propose to end this introduction by answering a selection of them.

Isn't he too young for a full-length biography?
Justin is not an overnight sensation. His relatively recent breakthrough in the United Kingdom gives a false impression, because

the UK was out of step with the rest of the world and, in particular, with the United States. It is thirteen years since he won his first talent contest, twelve years since he joined the cast of Disney's *Mickey Mouse Club*, nine years since the formation of 'N Sync and five years since he was voted the World's Most Beautiful Person. Justin is emphatically not a one-hit wonder with no story to tell.

Justin grew up in a rural community and piecing together the important components of his life – a Christian faith, academic achievement, musical influences and broken hearts – was fascinating. I hope the final portrait of a complex and talented young man does him justice.

Is the God stuff an affectation?
Definitely not. Justin believes in God and has a strong spiritual side. He grew up in the Bible belt, where it is commonplace to express your faith more readily than it is in Britain. The church is a big part of his family's life, 'N Sync were committed Christians, and his teenage girlfriends had a positive attitude towards religion. Britney Spears also has a strong faith, despite what the cynics might think. Performing is what these people do for a living and we shouldn't confuse the image with the person.

Is it *NSYNC, *N SYNC, *N Sync, NSYNC, N Sync, N*SYNC, 'NSYNC or 'N Sync?
This is a tough question that certainly had me confused at first: I have seen it spelt all these different ways and more. *NSYNC was the logo devised for the launch of their debut album in America, which was released first in Europe where they made their initial breakthrough without a US record deal. In the official book on the band, it is *NSYNC on the cover and 'N Sync in the main text. That's good enough for me, and what I decided to do for this biography. I don't want to be out of Sync.

How did he make the jump from being the naffest – 'N Sync – to the coolest man in pop?
There is nothing naff about success, and for two years 'N Sync could justifiably claim to be the world's number one band –

incredible, but true. I had absolutely no idea when I started this book that 'N Sync were so big. Artists such as Britney Spears, Pink and P Diddy opened shows for the Orlando-based boy band. They would not have made a list of the top 100 bands in the United Kingdom, but the figures in the United States do not lie. The group's first album sold more than 10 million copies; the third album, *No Strings Attached,* broke the record for the fastest selling album of all time with 2.4 million sold in the first week. Their follow-up, *Celebrity,* in 2001, came in second on the list with 1.88 million in the first seven days. In the year 2000, the total revenue for the band was $278 million (£153 million). They sold out stadiums all across America. We're not talking about the Hammersmith Palais here but venues like Shea Stadium in New York, where the Beatles once performed a legendary concert.

Justin became a solo artist from a position of great strength. He had a huge core following in the US and celebrity status across the Atlantic of the sort only David Beckham can boast of in Britain. He also had the absolute support of his record label, who recognized that he was their golden boy. Justin was an odds-on shot to make a successful transition.

Success does not guarantee respect – far from it – but Justin was shrewd in working with people who had it in bucketfuls. The Neptunes and Timbaland were revered in the music business as the hottest producers in town and here they were working with Justin Timberlake – he *must* have something. I discovered that this was not something that happened post-'N Sync. Justin sowed the seeds of solo stardom within the 'naff boy band' so mercilessly parodied by Eminem. The Neptunes, BT and Rodney Jerkins all worked on the last 'N Sync album. Justin co-wrote seven tracks on the album and co-produced five. Far from being a giant leap, the step Justin took to move from 'N Sync to solo stardom was a much smaller one than I anticipated.

How did Justin become black?
I love this question. Justin was brought up in a predominantly middle-class, white, rural neighbourhood in the southern Bible belt where they still grow cotton. His grandfather liked Johnny

Cash, and the country music tradition was strong. But Memphis, the nearest big city, has a huge legacy of fantastic black music, both blues and jazz.

More than anything else, I think Justin appreciates the magnificent voices of the all-time great black artists: Stevie Wonder, Donnie Hathaway, Marvin Gaye and Al Green to name but four he has cited as heroes. He loved the style of Michael Jackson during his classic period in the eighties, as well as the energy and exuberance of Janet Jackson. He was also influenced by the new generation of Motown artists, such as Brian McKnight and Boyz II Men. All these performers had an effect on Justin as he developed his musical talents.

The predominant culture in music today is a black one. R & B, hip hop and urban are cutting edge and commercial. Crucially, they also attract the cream of the musical talent, both in writing and in producing, and Justin is very smart in recognizing ability in others. As a result, he has formed a strong bond with producers like the Neptunes and Timbaland. When he wanted to move away from the clean-cut boy band image of 'N Sync, he merely gravitated towards the music that most interested him.

His next album will be interesting. I expect it to follow the successful formula of *Justified*, but I also don't expect Justin to stand still for long. If he hears something and likes it, he wants to work with the person responsible. That open-minded approach led to his association with the Black Eyed Peas, and there will be other innovative artists who will cross his path in the years to come. I believe he is a stayer and not a one-album wonder, especially as I was told that people in the music business genuinely enjoy working with him.

Does he know how fit he is?
Of course he does. He doesn't have to do 300 push-ups a day to keep in shape. He may protest that he doesn't think he's sexy but this is the boy who won a beauty contest when he was eleven, beating a host of girls to the title. He is very conscious of the way he looks, hence the years of agony over his terrible hair. Justin has a quiet confidence about him that is not easily thrown.

Why are there no kiss-and-tell stories about Justin?
There is still time for those, but I was told time and time again that
Justin was a one woman kind of guy and unlikely to end up in the
sack with a pair of nubile lap-dancers. He values being in love and
being faithful.

Why has Justin been unlucky in love?
I don't think he has been unlucky. Cameron Diaz is the fourth serious relationship he has had and he is only twenty-three. The
evidence suggests he expects too much of women. Amateur psy-
chologists might highlight an unhealthy obsession with his mother
combined with the strong Christian values of the community in
which he grew up. Justin himself has pointed an unnecessarily
harsh finger at his former girlfriends, claiming they cheated on
him whereas he has never cheated. Why does he reveal this in
public? What satisfaction does he gain from these unchivalrous
comments? So far no woman has been able to stay on the pedestal
on which he has placed them. The difficult problem for Justin is
that he is in a business where suspicion and gossip are albatrosses
on the shoulders of celebrities. Long absences and the temptation
of having everything presented on a plate are facts of his life and
the lives of the women he is likely to date, and he is not going to
find it getting any easier. On the positive side, Justin is a very intelligent man and may work it out for himself that he may have to
compromise to find a love that lasts.

Is he well endowed?
Britney Spears put the cat among the pigeons when she suggested
that the trousersnake wasn't all it was cracked up to be. His first
love, Danielle Ditto, immediately stuck up for him. She told me
that it wasn't true. She said, 'I don't want a lot of people thinking
he's not a man, so I had to stick up for him on that one, even
though that's something you really shouldn't say!' The likelihood
is that Britney's remark was a snippy bit of hurt manifesting itself in
a bitchy remark. Danielle has no axe to grind and no reason not to
be accurate in her assessment. Let's leave it there.

What will he be doing when he is fifty?

He will be counting his money for one thing. At the age of twenty-three, he is worth an estimated $54 million (£30 million) and that figure is increasing quickly. He has lucrative merchandising and sponsorship deals, as well as songwriting royalties from *Justified*. He would never have to work again if he fancied taking it easy, playing golf and watching sports. He could retire to Shelby Forest and become a preacher. In her fascinating birth chart, Madeleine Moore suggests he will end up behind the scenes, helping to bring out the talent in others. My feeling is that he likes to stretch himself, so he is always liable to surprise. I also think he will not give up as an actor until he has an Oscar on his mantelpiece. He may combine acting and singing in equal measure over the coming years. At fifty? Perhaps then it will finally be time for the 'N Sync reunion.

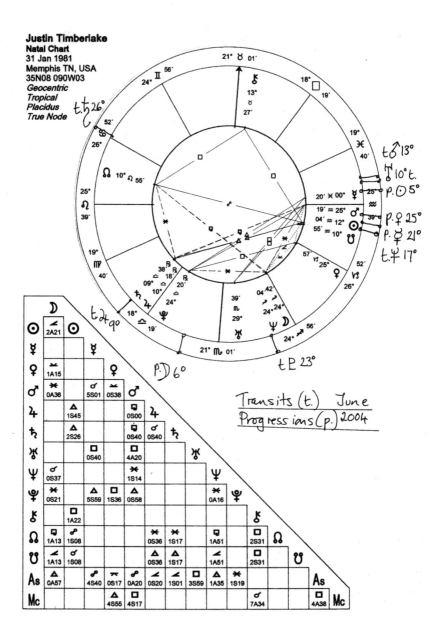

Justin Timberlake
Natal Chart
31 Jan 1981
Memphis TN, USA
35N08 090W03
Geocentric
Tropical
Placidus
True Node

Transits (t.) June
Progressions (p.) 2004

The Justin Timberlake Birth Chart

This is a gifted and compassionate man whose chart reveals an intense desire to serve humanity. In order to achieve a sense of worth and purpose in his life, he needs to feel he is giving something to others. The desire to serve is a spiritual need in which he recognises people's hunger for love and the problems of loneliness. He will drive himself hard, striving for perfection and setting himself standards that will sometimes seem ridiculously high. But he is driven by an urge to uplift, soothe, and put right past wrongs.

With the sign of Leo rising at his Birth, the ruler of Justin's chart is the Sun. The focal planet is ruled by Apollo, known as 'The Bright One'. Apollo is the master of many attributes including poetic inspiration, medicine and music - Justin is enormously creative. Placed within the area of the birth chart associated with employment (the sixth house) and forming a beautiful link to ebullient, supportive Jupiter a picture emerges of a man for whom, as Noel Coward said, 'Work is much more fun than fun.' But what direction will his work be pushed towards? This is a people person who will find himself drawn to the exploration of relationships and the bonds that exist between people. Central to his being is the impulse to communicate with precision, emotion and beauty. These are the components of his essence.

High in Justin's chart, standing clear and proud is the planet Chiron (discovered 1977), forming strong links to both the Sun and the Moon's nodes. It represents the 'Wounded Healer' and in such an elevated position in Justin's chart it indicates a man who has much to offer others in sorting out problems and pain without ever being entirely able to free himself from them. There is a degree of hurt in his life, perhaps in his upbringing, which he has had to face and which spurs him on to helping others.

Justin will have benefited in his life from someone, perhaps more than one person, who channelled his tremendous energy into disciplined, fruitful activity. The sixth house of a chart is associated with master/apprentice relationships. In Justin's chart it contains the Sun and is ruled by Saturn, strong and serious, teaching discipline and reining in runaway rebelliousness. Allied with combative Mars in this area, the signs are that Justin will have encountered a strong-willed mentor or hard taskmaster whose approval has been difficult to win. Eventually Justin will in his turn provide the honoured function of leader and mentor. The channelling of his own energies into the role of teacher is a very powerful urge. This is the chart of someone who would have made a good doctor, perhaps specialising in the field of psychoanalysis.

At the heart of the chart lies a glorious Dionysian moon, a planet powerful in its own house. This Moon is in conjunction with Neptune, the planet of imagination, creativity, illusion and chaos. It is an inspiring Moon, placed in fiery Sagittarius, needing to bring drama and excitement into Justin's daily routine, urging him to live as a gifted child of the gods. It is also a compassionate Moon, linked to Pluto and alive to the anguish of emotional disintegration and subsequent rebirth. And it is a wild Moon, at odds with the sweet reason and direction of his Apollonian Aquarius Sun.

The force of all these energies plays out in several areas of Justin's life but there is no doubt that Justin's home life, his roots and the forming of his psychological foundations (represented by the fourth house in his chart) are key to how he lives his life. The knowledge he gained about himself and others in his early life is instrumental to his mature creative success. Father would have been valued, embodying a message about independence and rationality. But the Moon, cyclical and changing, stresses the importance of family and mother. With this placement Justin's mother would have been expected to have encouraged a frank, optimistic outspokenness and independence in her son. She would have valued education in the broader sense and demonstrated an enquiring mind and spirit, which is a model her son may tend to idealise and seek in other relationships. He will be attracted to women like his mother.

The close bond of mother and son reflects an innate, empathetic understanding. Justin is fully appreciative of her naturally philosophic intelligence. The Moon's closeness to Neptune suggests that in some respect she was a victim, or experienced periods of sadness, illness or loss which may have resulted in her not always being easy to reach. This relationship will have awakened Justin's sensitivity to the emotional needs of others, drawn towards people he can help and enormously responsive to the hidden worth of those undervalued in society. The Moon symbolises his instinctive strengths – sensitivity, imaginative insights into relationships and an almost visionary creativity. Justin's home roots are surrounded by a strong matriarchal signature. Home is where he will want to return to feel nurtured and draw upon inspiration when he has given out to people and risks running dry. If he retreats, then he can be reborn, again and again.

As well as being 'The Bright One' Apollo is also the Curse Breaker and Justin will fulfil this function in terms of his family. This man's chart clearly indicates conflicting drives between instinctive needs which may be assuaged through belonging to a group or family and conscious goals which require a more self-focused independence – the conflict between selfless and selfish. As Justin matures the pull will be towards his independence and worldly achievements. He will find the power and authority to be most wholly himself through work – and work is where he will be his own boss. He will learn if life is to be better he must be the lord of it and it is up to him to break established patterns which threaten his well being and that of those close to him. It is in this way of breaking potentially destructive patterns - solving problems with drastic action - within his family that Justin will be a 'curse breaker'.

Justin has an enviable ability to fall in love. First he will consciously narrow the field, employing a degree of pragmatism and expediency before giving his heart. But when he gives himself up to it, he will surrender and readily embrace the intense and chaotic experience. The planet Mercury, ruler of Gemini, sits tightly on the

Descendant, an area associated with partnerships. It strongly indicates that Justin feels incomplete without a partner. When not in a relationship, the sense of a missing 'other', a lost companion, will never be far away. He will want to share everything with the partner, often overriding an innate need to have some space to himself. The planet Venus in ambitious, status-conscious Capricorn suggests he expects total faithfulness. As Mercury links back to Pluto in the chart area associated with siblings, it suggests issues around early family relationships resurfacing in adult bonding.

Mercury stresses the desire for mental communication and intelligent dialogue. It reveals his excellent and highly seductive negotiation skills. Justin can sweet-talk in the relationship arena but he can sharp-talk too. Links to Uranus and Mars incline him to blunt honesty, contrariness and bouts of indiscretion. He is sometimes far too ready with a cutting tongue.

Justin will make a very loving father and an inspirational one with a strong influence of the outdoors in his role. There is, however, a generation born between 1973 and 1982 for which the function of fatherhood is a thorny issue. It will concern his role in a family unit and the problem of a man feeling he is pushed off centre stage by a strong, independent woman and ignored when procreation is achieved. Justin will find his own solution to such dilemmas and there is enough to suggest, with such a strongly aspected Pluto, that if anyone can find a comfortable balance to the challenges of modern partnerships, he can.

In terms of relationships and creative projects, Justin is approaching a period of completion. There is a final passing of Neptune over his natal Sun during the last third of 2004, which will enable him to draw on his creativity and, if he so wishes, produce work which is inspirational. He will find himself more open to spiritual issues. It is a time of much sensitivity and artistry, a period of refining where, perhaps through his work, he can bring harmony and release to others. He should, however, be careful of his health, avoiding excess physical strain. He may also experience psychological fatigue. He is essentially approaching a stage where he needs to retreat, at least on the work front. From October 2004, on and off until June 2005, relationships will require serious focus and thought and may make heavy demands. Some will need to be tidied up and relegated to history. This will happen. Others will require change. His established pattern of behaviour in love affairs will be criticized and change forced upon him. This may be uncomfortable but he will have the strength to learn and move on. It is in any case, a matter of bend or break.

A major transit of Pluto occurs at the very end of 2005, its effects apparent throughout most of 2006. This planet of endings and rebirth joins both the Moon and Neptune in Justin's chart, most exactly in July and October of that year. It suggests Justin will begin a very deep process of inward transformation that will ultimately prompt changed goals in his life. This transit will affect his home life, possibly his mother and other relationships with women. It can represent a power struggle - for example, Justin may feel he needs to be more in control of his own destiny. It may indicate house moves. Endings may be symbolic or literal and are likely to involve enormous feelings. What is certain is that this transit, however uncomfortable, clears the way for rebirth and reconstruction. It is possible that this intense energy will play out in terms of Justin re-inventing himself professionally. It is of great importance to this man that he is valued not so much for his appeal and charisma, but for what he has to say.

It is interesting that the last planet to rise before the Sun at the time of his birth was Venus. This is an astrological signature frequently found in the birth charts of actors and those who wish to be judged more by their work than an assessment of their character. No matter how successful he may be, it is likely that this could be thrown overboard should he feel he is appreciated more for his popularity and image and less for his genuine ability. One would expect untiring creative work to be a feature of this man's life. Astrologically this period is one of enormous intensity. Whilst it appears to highlight issues of home and emotions most specifically, it is impossible to divorce this from Justin's creative drive. This is not an easy time, but a period of profound experience.

Madeleine Moore
2004

PART ONE

SHELBY FOREST

1

Mr Jeter

It was a disaster. Right in the middle of the E. E. Jeter Elementary School Christmas concert, the power failed. The enormous gym was plunged into darkness as bewildered parents and children wondered what they were going to do. Suddenly a voice launched forth from the gloom. It was Justin Timberlake, aged eleven, singing 'O Holy Night', unaccompanied. His friend Erika Ruch recalls, 'He didn't freak out that the lights were out, he didn't stop, he sang and it was just beautiful. The whole gym was in tears.'

Justin's school was little more than a mile from his house, but he took the bright yellow schoolbus like everyone else. It would pull into his road of superior detached homes, stop outside his driveway and wait for him to finish scoffing his morning cereal – still his favourite breakfast as a music superstar. On the bus would be his many friends from this confined country community spread around the rambling roads of Shelby Forest. It is barely an exaggeration to suggest that half the children on the bus were likely to be related.

'Our family is really close knit,' explains Allison Hammett, who believes she is Justin's fourth or fifth cousin. 'Justin's grandfather, William Bomar, is the first cousin of my grandmother, Judith Bomar. I am a year younger than Justin, so I guess I've known him since I was born.' The Timberlake and Bomar clans were so pervasive that when Justin was a boy they would hold family reunions every year in the park.

The early days of Justin Timberlake have a very homely, picture-book quality. The community of Shelby Forest, where the bus stops at everyone's home, where grandparents and parents went to school together and where families attend church on Sunday mornings is like a snapshot of fifties America, when the world was a much more wholesome place, with little crime and none of the urban tensions that bedevil big cities like nearby Memphis. The neighbourhood may not have been an exact replica of the sort that inspired *The Truman Show*, but it was predominantly middle-class, financially comfortable and white.

E. E. Jeter Elementary, which was the only school Justin ever attended, had no more than 500 pupils and provided the sort of environment where a child could flourish and make the best use of his or her talents. The name of the school is pronounced Jeeter, which led to former students being labelled 'Jeter Beaters' when they went on to high school. It was named in honour of the magnificently titled Squire Emmett Early Jeter in 1923, and is one of the oldest schools in Shelby County. Justin would barely recognize the place now if he dropped by while visiting his family. It is in the process of being completely remodelled, using money from his charitable foundation. Only the capacious gymnasium, the location of Justin's early triumphs in his twin loves of singing and basketball, remains as it was when he was there.

If Justin had been a schoolboy in England, he might well have had to bear the sobriquet of swot, spod or spanner. He was a naturally bright child for whom academic work came easily, a straight-A student with a bad haircut who, in a less forgiving environment, could easily have become the target for bullies. Unsurprisingly, he was selected as a gifted student for Jeter's Apex programme. Ten or so of the brightest children in the school would meet every Friday for special lessons that presented them with challenges aimed at broadening their intellectual horizons beyond the normal curriculum. The state of Tennessee has specific requirements a child must meet in order to be considered a gifted student, including an assessment from a qualified educational psychologist.

The Apex group would miss regular classes on Fridays and meet up in a tiny schoolroom at the back of a corridor where their teacher, Renée Earnest from New Orleans, would involve them in a series of projects, IQ tests and mind puzzles. 'She didn't teach us maths, or English skills,' recalls Erika Ruch. 'It was more along the lines of expanding our intelligence. Ms Earnest would decide who would be in the class. You would go along to the school office and take an IQ test and she would ask some questions and invite you to join the class.

'Apex was absolutely great. Justin was always amazing in class and they were some of the funniest times we had. We would make our own little commercials with Ms Earnest filming it all with a video camera she always kept in the classroom. The funniest one was when we sent up the Calgon ads which were for a lot of bath products for women. Justin acted the part of the woman consumer and would shout out the slogan, "Calgon, take me away!", and we would wheel him across in front of the camera. He had a great comedic talent and was just one of the funniest guys.' A talent for comic timing and impersonation has never left Justin and showed up well when he appeared on *Saturday Night Live* in 2003.

Ms Earnest, a very jolly woman in her thirties with a hint of a slimmer Rosanne Barr about her, proved to be very popular, not just with Justin and his friends but also with the parents, especially Justin's mother Lynn. Another classmate, Beth Wendel, recalls, 'She made everything so much fun. We would be learning stuff but we wouldn't realize because we were just enjoying it all.'

Single-handedly, Ms Earnest would organize trips for her students. The highlight of Justin's time as an Apex student was when Ms Earnest organized a stay-away to Biloxi for a marine study. Biloxi was on the Mississippi coast, west of New Orleans. All the children piled on to a huge Greyhound bus and were driven eight hours south to Ms Earnest's home territory. She took them to a marine institute, where they dissected a dogfish. Erika remembers, 'It was the coolest thing in the world for a seventh grader. And we all ate alligator. It tasted just like chicken.'

Even on a school trip Justin could not help being the entertainer. He would make up little songs about his classmates to help take their minds off a particularly scary bus driver called Eugene, who drove them the wrong way down a one-way street, and backed into a car and tried to drive off without anybody noticing. He reckoned without the good young citizens of Shelby Forest, who insisted that he stop and leave his details.

Ms Earnest devised pageants to liven up the evenings. Justin excelled when girls had to dress as boys and boys dress as girls. Ms Earnest led things off by impersonating the American cartoon character Bubba, stuffing her shirt to make her seem very fat and drawing a beard on her face. Justin threw himself into his role with great enthusiasm. He clipped back his thick curly hair with one of the girl students' clips; he borrowed a Barbie shirt from another and wore a bra stuffed with tissue paper. His cousin, Nick Bomar, who was also in Apex, dressed up too and the pair of them were voted first and second. 'They just did the best impression of girls I've ever seen in my life,' recalls Erika.

Ms Earnest's reward for being Justin's favourite teacher was to become part of Team Timberlake when his career took off in Orlando, Florida. She is now a key member of his management team and received fourth billing in his list of acknowledgements, after Lynn, Paul and his manager Johnny Wright, in the programme for his sell-out *Justified* tour. Like many pop stars, Justin likes to keep people around him whom he likes and, perhaps more importantly, trusts to have his best interests at heart. Justin and Ms Renée, as he has always called her, laugh at the same things.

They shared a fondness for Spree candies, an American sweet with a sharp taste. The problem was they both favoured the red ones. Justin would carefully open up the packet, remove all the red sweets and then meticulously put it back together before giving it to Ms Renée as a gift. Pleased, she would unwrap it to discover there were no red ones, declaring, 'Oh, Justin!'

Justin's first principal at E. E. Jeter was a larger-than-life African-American woman called Mary Ann McNeil, who encouraged affection and respect in equal measure from the children in her care: 'I first noticed Justin when he was just a little tyke at the school. I remember that he was a cute child, very charming, very polite and sweet. We didn't know at first that he had such a talent for singing as well as dancing.'

Mrs McNeil never had to have Justin in her office for any disciplinary action and never had to call his parents in for a conference involving his behaviour. Her successor, Regina Castleberry, recalls only one occasion. Children in trouble had to wait for their punishment on the 'black couch'. Justin's offence was that he and another boy plaited their hair so that they had little pigtails sticking out all over. Mrs Castleberry recalls, 'They had little rubber bands just all over their heads. All the kids were going nuts. I asked them to take them out, and his mom came up and had a talk with him, but he was a good kid. You never had to worry about Justin. If he was with children who had a tendency to misbehave, he didn't. It's like he set a goal. I don't mean he was a Mister Goody Two Shoes, but he was more mature than a lot of kids and I think they kind of picked up on that. He just didn't get into all that silly stuff.'

It speaks volumes for the perspective of this country school that Justin's mother had to make a special visit to E. E. Jeter because he tied his hair back in rubber bands. The punishment for such minor transgressions was copying out part of the dictionary. A large percentage of the students at Jeter knew how to spell 'aardvark'.

Justin's career as a potential school swot was relatively short-lived. He liked basketball too much to be very academic. He did, however, join the Algebra Club set up by his mathematics teacher Jacqueline Lackey – inevitably called Jacky Lackey by her pupils. She entered into the spirit of things by pretending she had a sister called Turkey Lurky. She still has the original sheet on which the students signed up for the class, although she had no idea how famous Justin would become. Justin was the twenty-first to join but one of the first to leave. She laughs, 'The problem was that the kids found out it really was about maths and they weren't real sure if that's what they wanted to stay after school for – especially as it interfered with basketball! Basically the Apex students were of well above average ability in maths and science. Justin was a very good student, but he did not have to work hard to attain that.'

Justin finished first in the Jeter spelling bee but, despite his success in spelling contests at E. E. Jeter, he had his come-uppance in the Memphis–Shelby County Spelling Bee when he tied for 136th place in the first round after misspelling 'wharf', a word that is unlikely to be appearing any time soon on a Justin Timberlake lyric sheet.

Surprisingly, Justin Timberlake was not the biggest thing that ever happened to E. E. Jeter. It might be different if he turned up now to sing at a graduation dance, but when he made his early breakthrough into show business he was still plain old Justin to his contemporaries. Tom Cruise, however, was the real deal. The Hollywood star stayed in a house not far from Justin's home while he was shooting the film version of the John Grisham thriller *The Firm*. Regina Castleberry observes, 'Tom Cruise was a star. Justin's one of us.' Every day the teachers would gather outside the school gates to catch a glimpse of the diminutive heart-throb as his limousine sped past. Justin's English teacher, Karen Toombs, recalls, 'One day we were all there waiting for him to pass when the crossing guard stopped the car to let somebody cross. And we were like, "Yeesss!"'

Mrs Toombs and her fellow staff members were not as lucky as a girl pupil called Scarlet Hurt, whose father owned the Shelby Forest General Store. Scarlet held up a sign outside the store one day that said 'Tom, we love you' and, to her delight, he instructed his chauffeur to stop. For days Justin and his classmates – mainly the girls – had gone to the store after school hoping he would pop in for one of the famous cheeseburgers but they had begun to lose interest. On this particular afternoon it was just Scarlet. Tom chatted with her and happily posed for a picture that had pride of place in the store until the Hurts sold up.

That was the most exciting thing that happened in this backwater of the mid South, although the afternoon there was a bomb scare ran a close second. Justin and his friends were evacuated to a nearby baseball field while the school was searched. All the parents rallied around, bringing blankets, drinks and sandwiches, turning a potentially difficult situation into a picnic and a fun day out. Mrs Toombs recalls, 'The parents were right there, any time anything was going on. It was just a little country school. The children had been together since kindergarten and everybody knew everyone. It was a very, very close-knit community.' Fortunately, the bomb scare proved to be a hoax call.

E. E. Jeter is a public school – similar to UK State schools – where, unlike in the UK, parents do not pay any fees, although they might have to help with school books and equipment or cheerleading and sports uniforms. There was no wandering aimlessly about in breaks and at lunchtime. Everyone sat down for a midday meal. Justin's favourite was the pizza they served on Apex day.

Justin's contemporaries were rather blasé about his success. He had grown up with them and was just one of the gang. Even between seasons of *The Mickey Mouse Club*, when he was back in school, he was exactly the same old Justin as far as they were concerned. Chris Kirkpatrick was an entirely different matter. After Justin joined him in 'N Sync but before they were the biggest boy band in the world, he brought Chris back to see everyone in Apex on a Friday. Chris was ten years older and, recalls Erika, a real heart-throb: 'The girls thought he was so cute because he was older. We were like, "He's a cute boy, come and sit by me, come and sit by me." We happened to be taking an IQ test that day and he came and sat at a desk in this tiny little room and said he wanted to take it with us. But he didn't know any of the answers, so he cheated off us the whole time.

'There were four girls in the class and we all thought he was very cool. Justin was just Justin.'

He may not have bowled the girls over, but Justin's first hesitant steps into the world of romance happened within the safe confines of E. E. Jeter. The kids were very young but the boyfriend–girlfriend scenario was taken very seriously and conducted properly and with great courtesy. After he had given Mindy Mabry an uncertain kiss at the age of ten, he presented her with a bracelet. Mindy was a year older, which quite surprised Jacky Lackey when she saw them together on a sofa at Jeter, because usually in student couples the girl was younger.

This was very much kid's stuff; boyfriends and girlfriends saw each other every day in class and talked all evening on the telephone. A striking, tall dark-haired girl called Deanna Dooley was the first girl Justin dated properly but not seriously. Deanna played a mean game of basketball, which immediately endeared her to Justin. Like the Timberlakes and the Bomars, the Dooleys could have filled the park with all their family members. Erika Ruch observes, 'Deanna had a vibrant personality and, like Justin, was very funny. '

At the time, Justin was fourteen, and in the eighth grade at school. He kissed Deanna for the first time in the back of a friend's car on her birthday. It was not a resounding success: 'I went really red and turned away in embarrassment.' Justin displayed a romantic streak far beyond his years. When he took Deanna to the E. E. Jeter Homecoming Dance, he hired a white limousine and gave her a gold bracelet and perfume. It was an early example of the sort of slushiness that has characterized Justin's behaviour towards the opposite sex. Deanna looked lovely in a black dress and bore a passing resemblance to the teenage Marie Osmond. Justin was dressed more appropriately for a wedding in a grey double-breasted jacket, dark trousers, white shirt and stripy tie with a white carnation in his buttonhole. He looked far from comfortable when posing for a formal picture. He looked more at ease on the dance floor with Deanna after he had changed into jeans.

Justin and Deanna were so popular that they were given the titles of Mr Jeter and Miss Jeter, an honour voted on by the other pupils. They did a photo shoot for the school yearbook that consisted of them posing innocently, if a little self-consciously, in the woods near the school. The yearbook is a fascinating social document in the US in which students write messages to their classmates and teachers, and parents publicly congratulate their offspring for being so great. Justin's mother and stepfather were no exception:

> Justin Timberlake – our Superstar! Always aim high and go for what you want! We're so proud of you. We love you! . . . Mom & Dad

The sentiments, sincerely felt, reveal the enormous level of support Justin has always received from his mother Lynn and his stepfather Paul Harless, whom he has always called 'Dad'. At least Justin's message did not reach the embarrassing depths of classmate Patrick Walker, who chose to write about his headmistress: 'Mrs McNeil – Thank you for your excellent leadership during my years at Jeter.'

There is a more poignant tribute among all the others to a girl called Kera Bolgeo whom Justin dated a few times. Shelby Forest is not exactly the crime capital of the South, so it was a deep shock to the community when Kera was shot dead. It was a few years later, after she had left high school and fallen in with a drugs-connected crowd in Memphis. Two men broke into the home she shared with her boyfriend and she ended up being shot in the back as she made for the front door. A friend from school confides, 'Kera had gone down a bad road.'

'Justin was highly intelligent. He could have probably taught himself.'

2

God's Country

When Justin was nine he was asked to perform at a school carnival in Millington in front of an audience of 300 people. The organizer, Debbie Welch, was concerned about how some of the older residents in this Christian corner of Tennessee might respond to the moves Justin made on stage, so she studied a video of him performing a Garth Brooks song. She was worried that the youngster's hip-grinding dancing might offend. In the end, she let him go ahead. 'He did a great job,' she recalls.

Justin is very open and candid in his appreciation of God. In his contribution to the sleeve notes on the 'N Sync album *Celebrity*, he writes that he thanks GOD (in capital letters) every day for watching over him and that there is 'no greater power than that of His love'. In these godless times such sentiments might be derided as, at best, cheesy southern patter or, at worse, hypocrisy from a man enjoying the fruits of the bacchanalian world of show business. But there is nothing flip, born-again or 'hallelujah' in Justin's appreciation of God in his life. He was born into a family and a community in which the church is the fundamental bedrock of day-to-day life.

Shelby Forest is Bible-belt country – a legitimate term for describing the Protestant South, but one that verges on pastiche because of the histrionic performances of some TV ministers. When Justin was born, his grandfather, Charles Timberlake, was the pastor of the Shelby Forest Baptist Church and a greatly respected local figure. Justin has always had to be on his best behaviour when visiting Brother Timberlake and his wife Bobbie. One girlfriend recalls, 'There was no crap, no this, no that, don't say these words. I had to be careful. His family are real religious.' The first Baptist church in the United States was established in 1639 in Providence, Rhode Island, but the faith spread rapidly throughout the South in the late eighteenth and nineteenth centuries, when it took a firm grip on the black population. The black Baptist churches of the South played an important role in the quest for civil rights, a movement spearheaded by the Reverend Martin Luther King, Jr, in the sixties. King had himself been the son of a Baptist minister. In Justin's area of Tennessee, the emphasis in church was on music and on resolute preaching from biblical texts. The Timberlakes originally settled in the US at the beginning of the eighteenth century, having sailed from England. Justin's most colourful ancestor was a Lt Henry Timberlake, who married the daughter of a Cherokee Indian chief after he was sent to negotiate a peace treaty with the tribe.

Justin grew up fully understanding the importance of his faith and the correct way to behave in front of adults. It is the southern way, in which courtesy rules; the grossly misused word 'respect' really does apply here, where men are 'sir' and women are 'ma'am' or 'ms'. His tutor as a teenager, Chuck Yerger, recalls the time he and his wife Sherry visited Justin at his home. They went in to the lounge, where Justin greeted them in a casual and friendly manner, "Hi, Mr Yerger. Hi, Sherry.' Chuck recalls, 'His mother heard it from the back of the house and yelled at him, "Justin", in a way only a mother can. Without Lynn having to say another word, Justin, getting all apologetic and turning red, quickly corrected himself and said, "I'm sorry, Ms Sherry."'

Sadly, a strong faith is not necessarily a recipe for a perfect marriage. Justin's parents were young when they married in 1978. Randall Timberlake, who was in the building trade, was twenty and Lynn Bomar a mere seventeen. She was just twenty when Justin was born in the maternity ward of St Jude Hospital in Memphis on 31 January 1981. Randy and Lynn separated within two years and divorced when Justin was only three. The most noticeable effect within the local community was that Lynn moved churches. It would have been too raw and embarrassing for her to listen to her estranged husband singing every Sunday, especially in such a small church. So she joined the much larger First Baptist Church, next to the high school in Millington. Despite living most of his life no more than 2 miles from the Shelby Forest Baptist Church, Justin was a rare visitor there, although he did sometimes stay over and sleep in the small back bedroom of his grandfather's house.

Randy Timberlake has a fine singing voice, slightly deeper than his son's. His father has since moved to take charge of another parish, but Randy retains close links with Shelby Forest and is now the musical director – 'minister of music' – of the church under the stewardship of Brother Barney Austin. Members of his congregation confirm that he can 'really belt it out'. Beth Wendel, who still lives locally, recalls, 'I used to go to the church there and I remember Justin's dad would get up there every night, playing his guitar, and we'd all sing.'

Her friend Allison Hammett adds, 'Randy is very talented musically. That's where Justin gets a lot of his musical ability.'

Justin's boyhood singing coach, Bob Westbrook, confirms, 'I would imagine Justin got more of his vocal talent from his dad than from Lynn, although she's got a real good feel for music. Randy is a very good soloist.' Even Lynn has been prone to comment, tongue-in-cheek, that the only thing Justin got from his daddy was his beautiful singing voice. Superficially, there is little physical resemblance between Randy and his son. Whereas Justin has always been athletic and rangy, Randy is built more for comfort than for speed. Erika Ruch, whose parents live across the street from Randy, puts it succinctly: 'Justin's always been this real skinny kid, while Randy is pretty stocky.'

Both Randy and Lynn remarried when Justin was still a young boy and both have found long-lasting, happy relationships. While Lynn has continued to devote all her maternal energy to Justin, Randy and his second wife Lisa have two sons, Jonathan and Stephen. Justin has always been their 'big bubba', a sibling bond that has brought the two families closer together. Friends acknowledge that Justin and his father did have 'some issues' when he was younger, but they now enjoy each other's company. If you see them out together, perhaps playing golf, it is easy to see they are related as they laugh and joke their way around the course. Erika, who was Jonathan and Stephen's babysitter when she was younger, observes, 'I think they're such good buddies. Randy is such a fun person. He is always making goofy little faces, which is something Justin definitely gets from him. Randy is one of my favourite people.'

Randy has been careful not to court publicity in the wake of his son's rise to fame and fortune. Instead, he has studiously kept a low profile, preferring life as a quiet family man, combining a job at the Lebonheur Children's Hospital in Memphis with his musical work at the church. He has to bear a great deal of rubbish being written about him, including the myth that he was once in Elvis Presley's backing band, but he has always remained silent. His reward is that he is included in Justin's life and his eldest son still calls him 'Daddy'. But he does have some regrets about the quality time he has missed with Justin, admitting that they hadn't been as close as he would have liked, particularly in Justin's early years. The family concedes that Randy was probably too young to settle down when he married for the first time.

In the space of just one generation Justin's family has extended along the byways of Shelby Forest. Randy still lives in a very quiet neighbourhood not far from Justin. He and Lisa share a house with her father, Mack Perry, a popular character and a substitute teacher at Millington High School. 'Pa Mack', as Justin calls him, is a great devotee of the old-style southern gospel music and would love his step-grandson to devote an entire album to this kind of music. He, too, has a renowned singing voice and was part of a quartet that performed regularly at the Shelby Forest Baptist Church.

Justin's stepmother Lisa is a pharmacist, an accomplished pianist and a superb horsewoman. Justin has paid her the compliment of describing her as a 'great mother'. She once won the Tennessee High School Rodeo Association Breakaway Roping and

Goat Tying Championship and regularly competed in the Intercollegiate Rodeo Association. Riding runs in the family. Her elder sister Sue Lynn is a past holder of the Miss Rodeo Tennessee title and her mother Mimi runs an indoor riding school across the state line in Harrisburg, Arkansas. Mimi taught Justin to ride on a lovely little pony called Molly, which she gave him as a present on his eighth birthday. Justin used to show the pony at his local Woodstock Saddle Club in Shelby Forest. Sadly, Molly later developed founder, a condition affecting horses and livestock that restricts movement, but by then Justin's time was almost exclusively taken up with singing and basketball.

Justin dotes on his two younger half-brothers. Jonathan, Justin's junior by twelve years, has become a superb hip-hop dancer, appearing in contests and sporting events. He performed at half-time at a Grizzlies football game in Memphis – coincidentally, the same game that began with Justin and Isaac Hayes performing 'The Star-Spangled Banner'. Stephen is the baby of the family, seventeen years younger than Justin. He arrived after a family tragedy had disrupted the happy family idyll and tested their Christian faith to the fullest extent. This was the death of Justin's sister. The world first had an inkling of the trauma from the dedication on the debut 'N Sync album on which, on a list of the special people he wanted to thank, he included: 'My Angel in Heaven, my sister Laura Katherine'. For many years it baffled Justin's fans, because it was well known he was an only child. Nobody realized that she was his baby half-sister, who survived for only an hour after birth.

At the time, Justin was sixteen and living in Orlando, where 'N Sync were based and where they were gaining a strong footing in the music business. He was deeply upset by the news. A stark funeral notice appeared in the local Memphis paper, the *Commercial Appeal*, in May 1997: 'Laura Katherine Timberlake, new-born daughter of Randy and Lisa Timberlake, died Tuesday at Methodist Hospital North of complications following birth.' A simple memorial plaque in the Memory Gardens in Millington reads: 'Laura Katherine Timberlake in the arms of Jesus'. The grave is well tended and has a bunch of silk flowers and a winged cherub on it.

This was Justin's first real experience of death, certainly of a death in the family, and friends admit that it was on his mind the whole time, rendering his then teenage love troubles insignificant. It brought Justin and his father closer than they had probably ever been. Erika Ruch recalls, 'It was a hard time for the family. I know it hit Justin hard. She was a girl and all boys have a soft spot for girls. And Justin is great with kids.'

Randy and Lisa decided to try for another baby and Stephen was the happy result. 'Justin thinks a great deal of his brothers,' confirms Pat Austin, the local preacher's wife. Perhaps naturally, the loss of Laura has led Justin to appreciate his family even more than before. In his dedication on 'N Sync's album *Celebrity*, he takes the opportunity to recognize specially one of his favourite people, his grandfather and buddy, William S. Bomar. Justin writes, 'You're a man's man and I will never forget your smile as long as I live.' It is a very poignant tribute, because few outside of Justin's immediate family realized that Bill Bomar was seriously ill at the time and was not expected to live. Although frailer than he used to be, he has survived to witness the enormous success of his grandson as a solo performer, although he would prefer it if he sounded more like Johnny Cash. 'I am trying to persuade Justin to do a country album before I die,' he has confided to friends.

Justin never fails to mention his family in interviews, both verbally and in print. He also always includes God, repeating time and time again that he is blessed. It is as if God himself is part of this large Timberlake clan. Saying grace to thank God at mealtimes is something that Justin grew up with and is almost second nature to him. Obviously, it is not easy to reconcile the church with every aspect of a life in rock 'n' roll, but more than anything else it has helped to keep Justin's size 12 feet firmly on the ground. It helps if you believe in a munificent God who will forgive you your sins. His Christian faith did not prevent Justin from enjoying sex as a young teenager. It might, however, have made him feel guilty about doing so.

The church in this small part of the Bible belt is the nearest thing to a singles bar in the neighbourhood. Justin's mother met his father when her family started attending the Shelby Forest

Baptist Church. Justin would also meet his first serious girlfriend at a church do. The church and school are the social centres of such a close-knit community.

Surprisingly, the teachings of church and school seldom intersect. Religious instruction is not part of the curriculum in American public schools; it is considered to be the responsibility of the child's parents. Headmistress Mary Ann McNeil explains, 'Character education is what we do in our curriculum – honesty, trustworthiness and respect. It's our southern heritage. When we ask you, "How do you feel?", we really want to know and, if you're feeling fine, we're happy for you. If you express that you're not, we want to know what we can do to help you.' E. E. Jeter Elementary School was slightly different in holding religious Christmas programmes and Justin would sing at those. 'O Holy Night' and 'Away in a Manger' were two particularly memorable Timberlake solos. 'Jeter was so unique because of the close-knit family feeling here. It's such a small community. I know that Christian faith was a real strong area for Justin's family.'

When Justin was an Apex student, the class prepared a play based on *The Twelve Days of Christmas*. Justin practised his part for weeks. He was playing the father of the girl lead and everyone agreed he displayed a talent for elderly voices. Alas, the big night in front of the whole school clashed with a singing performance he had to give, and Lynn decided he had to save his voice. Renée Earnest stepped in and played Justin's part to general disappointment. Even at this stage of Justin's career, Lynn always had her eye on the ball.

Every single Justin Timberlake recording thanks God first and foremost. An appreciation of the character of Justin as a boy and as a man must include this vital part of his life and the role that it had to play in the development of his character. He does not belong to the 'God squad', but he is mindful of the church's importance not just in his own life but also in the world of those he loves. The preacher's wife, Pat Austin, who is also a student counsellor at Millington High School, explains, 'You may put the church on the back burner, but you can always come back to it. The church is so much part of his life – the values it instils remain and it forms a background for everything children like Justin who grew up here do for the rest of their lives.'

Justin is not spending every waking moment as a superstar reading the Bible or attending a church on Sunset Strip. Over the past few years he hasn't had time for church and it does not fit into his lifestyle. He has adapted his Christian beliefs to a modern life, preferring, he has said, to make his decisions based on a love of God rather than regular church-going. But that does not mean he has forsaken his spirituality. He says, 'My thing is that God is all around us in everything we say, everything we do, everything we feel. I really believe that.'

And he believes in angels.

'He's a very spiritual young man.'

3

Mom

When Justin was little, his mother Lynn used to joke, 'Some day when you get rich and famous, will you buy me a Harley?' After he received his first bumper pay cheque from 'N Sync, he gave her a jewellery box for Chrismas. Inside were a set of motorcycle keys.

Justin's mother Lynn cut his hair. The pictures of Justin with 'poufy' hair, as an early girlfriend described it, were a result of his home haircuts. It is hardly surprising that Justin has always been less than confident where his hair is concerned. Can you imagine any self-respecting teenager letting mum come within a million miles of him or her with a pair of scissors? It is a recipe for disaster. But Justin has always had an exceptionally close relationship with his mother. She remains the most important woman in his life and the person most responsible for him fulfilling his dream. She is also the reason Justin has a 'Venus complex', and persistently puts women on pedestals. The problem for Justin has always been that no flesh-and-blood woman can match his extraordinarily high standards and his idealistic view of falling and being in love. He once observed, 'You keep searching for someone as good as your mother, and that's a losing battle.'

Superficially, Lynn Harless is everything one might expect a pushy showbiz mother to be – a lioness protecting her cub as she smashes through the jungle. While Lynn has devoted a great deal of energy to her only child, she did not turn him into an obnoxious spoilt brat. Friends agree that she has 'indulged' Justin to the extent of allowing him to spend time and energy pursuing his personal dreams. But they are *his* dreams; he is not living out *her* dreams.

Lynn's philosophy in raising Justin was disarmingly simple: if he was having fun, then it was OK and she would work with his interests. Justin alluded to that approach in a documentary filmed in 2003 when he announced: 'I'm still having fun, Mother.' Hers was an example that met with the approval of Mary Ann McNeil: 'Justin has a marvellous mother, who is alive and alert and very actively involved. I believe entertainers need that kind of mother.'

At an age when many girls are finishing up college and considering how to pursue a career, Lynn Timberlake was contemplating life as a single mother. With 20:20 hindsight, it is easy to conclude that she married a (then) rather feckless young man too soon. Randy Timberlake was not ready to settle down. He would become a responsible father later in his life, but when Lynn divorced him on the grounds of irreconcilable differences he was giving her just $45 (£25) a week in child support for little Justin. In any community other than Shelby Forest it might have been a desperate struggle for her, but there she had the support of her family and the close-knit community. It is not a place where a single mother is a social leper who has to queue up for a meagre welfare cheque.

Lynn's parents, Bill and Sadie Bomar, were a well-loved and respected couple who rallied round, even though they had tried to talk their daughter out of marrying so young. They had wanted her to go to college – she had won a scholarship – but like any stubborn teenager Lynn was determined on her own course of action. Missing out on her education has always rankled with Lynn and, as a result, she has put education at the forefront of Justin's life. The biggest ambition she harboured for her son was not that he became the 'new King of Pop' but that he graduated from college. She insisted that he study even when he was a bona fide star. Justin's first love, Danielle Ditto, recalls the times she phoned up 'N Sync House, where the boys lived in Orlando, only to be told by Lynn to call back because Justin was 'at school'. 'His mom was real stern about it,' she remembers. 'It worked because he got some really good grades. Even when I was visiting we would be separated until he got all his work done.'

In her mother Sadie, Lynn was fortunate to find someone who was happy to play a very active role. Her father Bill actually built both his own house and the one next door, which Justin has called his home for twenty years. With her parents' help, Lynn was able to take a job as a clerk at the First Tennessee National Corporation bank in Millington. There she met and fell in love with the man who has been the most influential male figure in Justin's life and the one he calls 'Dad'.

When Paul Harless met Lynn, he was totally smitten by her vivaciousness and good looks. They married when Justin was five, and since then Paul has treated Justin like his own son. Sadie Bomar has acknowledged that Justin 'idolizes' Paul. Every day Paul would kiss Justin on the forehead and say, 'You have a good day, son. I love you.' It was just the security a young boy, inevitably upset by his parents' divorce, needed. The home became a happy place to be for Justin, and he has always sought to emulate Paul in the way he conducts himself. Tellingly, he wrote in appreciation in the notes for *Justified*: 'More and more each day I understand what being a "man" is all about because of you.' That paternal standard of behaviour includes the immaculate and romantic way he behaves towards Lynn. Danielle Ditto explains, 'Justin is a total romantic because his stepdad is like that. When he surprised me one Valentine's Day by cooking a lovely dinner, I realized that was exactly the sort of thing Paul would have done for Lynn.'

Outwardly, Paul might not appear a likely candidate for a role model for someone cool and cutting edge. He is resolutely conservative, and wears a button-down shirt for all occasions; he drove a sports car when Justin was younger but ruined the effect by listening to the Doobie Brothers on the stereo. Justin's infamous 'geography teacher' look at the 2004 Brit Awards, where he appeared strangely middle-aged in a shirt, tie and preppy jacket, was more the style of a certain banker from Millington, Tennessee. Danielle observes, 'I don't think I've ever seen Paul in a T-shirt – always a shirt and tie. He was totally conservative and prissy, but I really liked him. Justin had some issues with his father – they weren't as close as he wanted to be – so Paul was his real father. He was the main man in his life. It was Paul who taught him stuff like how to play basketball.'

Paul Harless gave Justin and Lynn the security they needed to exploit Justin's full potential as an entertainer. Paul may be conservative in outlook, but he is not a bore or a man of limited horizons. When he and Lynn are at home in Shelby Forest, he is likely to whisk her off for a night out, perhaps to the casino. Their Bible-belt county does not have any gambling, but half an hour away across the Mississippi state line is Tunica, where Tennessee residents can let their hair down. These days, he and Lynn divide their time between Shelby Forest and Bay Hill, Orlando, where they have a beautiful home in the sun and where they help run Justin's company 'Just-in-Time'. Paul is able to spend more time on Justin's career and is now formally acknowledged with Lynn as part of Justin's management team.

While Paul was conservative and a little cautious during Justin's childhood, Lynn was the type of young mother who becomes a friend to her child. She explained, 'I had Justin when I was twenty and he seemed about twenty when he was born, so we've pretty much shared everything.' Justin has described his mother on many occasions as his 'best friend' and 'a very special woman'. They speak on the telephone every day, whether Justin is at his new home in the Hollywood Hills of Los Angeles or in some far-flung hotel on tour. Lynn has always been a young spirit, the type of mother who will still be enjoying herself at a party after her son has called it a night. Not many mothers can boast of giving their son a love of motorbikes and the open road. Justin loves the freedom of cruising around the roads of Shelby Forest on a Harley. These days it's more likely to be the Pacific Coast Highway, but the principle of 'easy riding' remains the same. Lynn is now surrounded by Harleys wherever she stays. She and Paul have two at home in Shelby Forest and three at their house in Orlando, and Justin has two in Los Angeles. She is resolutely 'fun'. Paul will sit there in a shirt and tie while Lynn bounces around in a sweatshirt with the words 'Be Naughty' emblazoned across her chest. Justin's second 'love', Veronica Finn, observes, 'Paul is a really intelligent man, while Lynn is a little more carefree and bouncy about things. Together they were really cool.'

Justin's best friend was another boy from Shelby Forest, Trace Ayala. Justin may have had enough cousins to fill a park, but Trace has been like a brother to him: many people have taken them to be brothers when they have been out together. Their story is broadly similar to that of those other famous pals, Robbie Williams and Jonathan Wilkes. They, too, had mothers who were best friends and grew up together in a relatively small neighbourhood, took holidays together, and continued their friendship into adulthood. Trace and Justin used to go four-wheeling along the roads of Shelby Forest. Legally, they were not allowed to because they were too young, but there were not too many police officers in the neighbourhood. Justin has always been a very fast driver, and honed his skills on those mini quad bikes. Erika Ruch recalls, 'He was always going too fast. He would press the throttle too hard and go flying.'

Jonathan Wilkes has carved out his own showbiz career independently of Robbie, whereas Trace works for Justin. On the *Justified* tour, he had the title of 'Personal Assistant to Mr Timberlake'. Personal assistant basically means opponent in all forms of games and relaxation. He is the fall guy on the pinball machine or the Halo game. Justin plays to win so Trace, who is much smaller and less athletic, is the perfect foil when shooting hoops, snowboarding or playing pool. Friends comment that the two friends share a very similar sense of humour and are always laughing together. Justin lightens up around Trace and becomes less intense. The other way Trace has acted as 'personal assistant' is in playing matchmaker for Justin. Not only did he date Danielle Ditto before Justin, but he was also the guy who introduced him to Veronica Finn because he thought they would get on really well. He was absolutely right about that.

Trace has never had the desire for a pop career, realizing that there is room for only one superstar in their friendship, but he is keen to carve out a career as an actor. So far he has appeared with Justin in a film called *Jack of All Trades*, in which they had bit parts playing valet parkers. Justin tossed some car keys to Trace and that was it.

Growing up, Justin enjoyed the trimmings of middle-class life in America, which were especially noticeable in the quality of the holidays the family were able to take – not every boy has the chance to enjoy holidays skiing or taking in the warm waters of Hawaii. Justin's home was stylishly furnished in a modern way and boasted a pool table in the games room upstairs and a piano in the drawing room. Veronica Finn says, 'It was very welcoming and homely.' She recalls that Justin would often be tinkering away on the piano.

Justin's room, which was painted his favourite shade of blue, was full to overflowing with 'stuff' – primarily his clothes and, in particular, his shoes. He has always had an obsession with every kind of footwear, especially sneakers. Lynn says that as a boy Justin could never stand any marks on his shoes. They had to be perfect. 'He was a shoe fanatic,' laughs Danielle. 'They always had to match his clothes!'

Justin shared his home with assorted pets. The apple of Lynn's eye was a cairn terrier called Ozzie because he was the image of Toto from the film *The Wizard of Oz*. When Lynn went with Justin to forward his career in Orlando, Ozzie went too. Justin's tutor, Chuck Yerger, remembers the dog racing around everybody's feet: 'Lynn was so proud of the dog – she would say, "Chuck, you don't know how smart this dog is." She had these toys in the shape of vegetables and she'd say, "Watch this, Ozzie go and get me the broccoli", and he'd race out and come back with the chewed-up toy in the shape of the broccoli. And then she'd ask for the carrot and the same thing would happen.' Lynn had no idea that Justin and her cherished pooch did not get on. Ozzie was forever nipping at Justin's ankles when Lynn had left the house. One afternoon Justin decided to take action and tossed Ozzie down a flight of stairs: 'He limped for a couple of weeks, but he respected me after that.'

Justin had his own dog, Scooter, a cute 'mutt' he had fallen in love with when she licked his face on a visit to the local pound when he was six. Sadly, she ran off when Justin was in his last year at E. E. Jeter and accidentally ate some poison. Justin had to make the difficult and sad decision to have his dog put down: 'It was really tough on me, because she was my dog, you know?'

The overall impression of Justin's home life was that it was 'homely'. He used to dress up as Batman at Halloween and head off with Trace and the other members of his young 'posse', Kyle Davenport and Nick Bomar, for some serious trick or treating and return home with a year's supply of sweets. Lynn would cook him his favourite meals, such as Philly cheesesteak sandwiches with home-cooked fries, or he would pop round the corner to his grandmother Sadie's kitchen for some of her locally renowned peach cobbler. He also enjoyed it when the family went out to eat Italian, when he would invariably order lasagne. Justin's number one food, however, is breakfast cereal. At any time of the day, he is liable to disappear into the pantry and reappear with an enormous Tupperware bowl of Apple Jacks. Unlike Robbie Williams's mother Jan, Lynn has not had to deal with her son falling into a downward spiral of drink, drugs and depression. He always got out of bed on the wrong side, however, and he is a legend in his own household for being completely antisocial for the first hour of the day and ready to bite Lynn's head off if she talked to him.

If Hollywood ever produced the Justin Timberlake story, it would be hard to avoid it brimming with saccharine and being a throwback to the world of Mickey Rooney musicals, where enthusiasm, hard work and good old-fashioned family values lead to a precociously talented youngster's triumph. It is desperately hard to avoid clichés when describing the talents of a child. Proud parents will inevitably tell you that their little treasure started tapping a foot to a Sinatra 45 and they immediately realized they had a superstar in the making. In Justin's case, he had a toy guitar that he carried everywhere. His grandfather, Bill Bomar, was an excellent guitarist and little Justin would copy him – a premier air guitarist in nappies. One of his own earliest memories is as a 2-year-old, sitting in the living room at home, singing the theme tune from *Cheers*, 'Where Everybody Knows Your Name': 'I used to sit there and sing that every night.'

Justin was very fortunate that he had such a musical family, because the musical programme at E. E. Jeter was practically non-existent when he was there. Encouraged by Lynn, Justin set up the 'Giving Back Foundation' to help fund local projects that he thinks are worthwhile. Robbie Williams has done something broadly similar with his 'Give It Sum' charity based in Stoke-on-Trent. Robbie's first donation was arts funding for his old school. Justin, likewise, donated $50,000 (£27,500) to be used specifically for the music programme at E. E. Jeter. As a result, his old school has purchased a programme called 'Music in Education', which consists of about sixteen keyboards, all computerized and hooked up to one main computer. The grant has also bought numerous other wind and percussion instruments. In addition, an oversized music room is being built that will house all the state-of-the-art equipment. For a country school, E. E. Jeter is going to be unusually well placed to encourage its pupils' musical talents. The present headmistress, Paulette Bond, is delighted that, thanks to Justin, the school can now offer free piano lessons to the community at large – not just to the pupils at E. E. Jeter. Lynn is much more able to keep an eye on things than Justin, and keeps him informed about how his money is being spent. He has now built a studio at the house in Shelby Forest, so if a local child were to show any ability there is a place nearby to make a demo.

Other than early signs of his musical talent, Justin was so quiet as a child that his worried mother was forever having to check that he was all right. Although he could not have started in show business so young without that essential quality of extrovertism mixed with a dash of narcissism, Justin has always been happy in his own company. As a small child, he would disappear to his room for hours at a time to play by himself. The only drawback of that ability to enjoy 'quiet time' is a tendency to over-reflect on things and to analyse them to death. Justin is very self-critical and seeks perfection at all times, whether in his music or in his relationships with girls. Few people could live up to the exacting standards he sets for himself. He also chooses his words very carefully, which is why no interviewer has really got to the bottom of what makes him tick.

The search for perfection is something that Lynn instilled in him from an early age by encouraging him to 'Never do anything half-assed.' And so, when Justin decided he was going to be a singer, she was the one who fixed up lessons so he could do it properly; when he decided to enter talent contests, she worked on his programme and his appearance and went to cheer him on. When he won the talent contest in Nashville, she charged on stage like a demented bronco, fiercely proud, and hugged her diminutive son so hard she half squeezed him to death. Her pleasure was not the least restrained or modest – it was hollering triumph. At every single stage of Justin's life and career, Lynn has been right behind him, especially on the relatively few occasions when he has been at a low ebb.

Justin has the intelligence and the self-awareness to realize that his obsession with perfection comes with an unsettling side effect – difficulty forgiving people. He has never been a boy or a man who has found it easy to forgive and forget. This is most evident in the termination of the first three serious relationships in his life. Coincidentally, it was during Justin's first sexual relationship that Lynn changed from being dearest mommie to more like 'mommie dearest'. She did not want him to make the same teenage mistakes she did.

The overriding impression from people who have known Lynn is a positive one. She is hardly fazed by the prestige and enormous wealth she has indirectly gained through her son. The local residents report that she is little changed. Allison Hammett confirms, 'She is not smarmy at all and never thinks she is better than you.' Lynn Harless is still only forty-four and her energy and ambition for her son show no signs of diminishing. Sometimes she looks more like his big sister than his mother. She still has 'big' hair – at least this is one area where Justin has been able to distance himself from his mother.

'He's always been a momma's boy.'

4

Talent

One December afternoon, social studies teacher Karen Toombs asked her class of 11-year-olds to write their own mini-biography. Justin wrote, 'I guess I should go ahead and tell you I sing. In fact, I just won $16,000 worth of savings bonds in a contest in Nashville. Okay, enough about singing. Let's talk about my childhood. I have a pretty easy temper when it comes to sport, my favorite ice cream is chocolate chip and I love basketball! Well, that pretty much wraps it up. Gotta Go. Excitedly, Justin.'

Justin's first taste of the audience frenzy that now accompanies his every move on stage came in the third grade at E. E. Jeter when he was eight years old. He and his 'posse' of four pals decided that they would perform as New Kids on the Block at a school concert. In the early nineties, New Kids were the teen sensation of the world. They set records that would remain until another boy band, 'N Sync, eclipsed them a decade later. The Boston band formed the template for the modern boy band and were the inspiration behind Take That, the premier British group of the nineties. New Kids had a very short shelf life – little more than three years – but in 1990 alone they grossed $861 million (£473 million). Pictures of Jordan, John, Danny, Donnie and Joey adorned the walls of millions of bedrooms across the country. It was not surprising that Justin, Kyle, Trace, Nick and Wade thought it would be fun to imitate them. These guys were Justin's basketball buddies.

Justin was Jordan, mainly because he was the only one with any aptitude for singing. They mimed, or lip-synched mostly, to million-selling hits 'Hangin' Tough' and 'Step by Step', although Justin did sing on a couple of songs, most notably 'Please Don't Go Girl'. The reaction of the schoolgirls watching was startling. Wade Horton could not believe that girls were screaming as if they were the real New Kids, not 8-year-old kids: 'The girls started chasing us, and some parents had to block the door so that we could make our escape.' Erika Ruch, who was one of those girls, recalls, 'New Kids were absolutely huge at the time. I was a Jordan fan and so was Justin. They did all the dance moves and were so good. It was one of the great performances. The girls went crazy. We thought they were so cute.'

The most important person in the audience that day was Justin's mother Lynn. She may not have chased after her son in teeny-bopper fashion, but she was impressed enough with the reaction to his performance to want to do something about it. She already knew singing teacher Bob Westbrook. She had taken piano lessons from him when she was growing up and thought he would be the perfect person to teach her talented son the rudiments of singing properly. Armed with the video that she had shot of Justin performing at school, she visited Bob's house in Germantown, one of the more attractive Memphis suburbs. She played him the video and asked, 'Don't you think we ought to start giving him some lessons?'

Bob had seen enough to agree: 'There wasn't much technique to what he did, but there was this charisma on stage and good movement. The girls were screaming so hard you could hardly hear him singing anyway!'

And so, at the age of eight, Justin Timberlake started taking singing seriously. He had not exactly been singing since birth, but he was born into an environment where it was regarded as positive and uplifting, particularly in church. His family, especially his father Randy, were fine singers and, like any child, Justin was keen to copy the adults. Lynn had always found him rather a quiet boy, but Justin was one of those children who would go unnoticed until they had an audience. Then they would be transformed, lit up by the thrill of performance.

Bob Westbrook's first task was to slow Justin down and take him back to the basics: 'Kids like Justin can get put out real quick because they want to do things this fast and you have to go over and over some things. I told him to quit pouting, because we were going to go over it time and time again until we got it right.' Bob is always careful not to be too critical at the beginning, especially with youngsters: 'You don't want to hurt their ego. If you tear them down completely, you can never build them up quickly enough.'

Learning to breathe properly is key. A child who has not been taught the basic techniques but thinks he can sing like Elvis is going to end up doing his voice irreparable harm. 'You teach children exactly as you would an adult. It's the same technique, but you word it a little bit differently,' explains Bob. 'When you or I breathe to live, we breathe from the chest. Breathing to sing is totally different and Justin had to learn that. I told him to fill up like a balloon. Some teachers say that you shouldn't give a kid a singing lesson until they're fifteen. That seems to be the magic number. The idea is that by then the voice is mature enough to handle tuition. What are you going to do about a kid who wants to sing anyway? Are you going to let them wreck their voice? I was very pleased Lynn brought Justin here when she did. Justin was already singing and he was going to be singing no matter what.'

Justin had to fit his weekly $30 (£16.50) an hour singing lesson in around his basketball practice and schoolwork. When Bob helped to find him venues to appear in public, the pressures on his time were even greater. Justin was never one of those children who slope back home after school and turn on the television. He took his singing ambitions very seriously. Bob explains, 'Justin was here to learn. I knew that Justin could perform before his first lesson because of what I had seen on the video. But when he was here, I didn't see the performance side because he was being taught. Even when he was using the mirror to work on his technique, he wasn't thinking about performing. Every once in a while, being a kid, he'd get to moving around and I had to slow him down a bit. You can't teach technique if your student is dancing all over the room.' Ironically, the ability to sing while dancing all over the stage is exactly what Justin would later have to perfect in his professional career.

Over the next two or three years, Justin's reputation as a young singer spread in his local community. Justin brought two key ingredients to the table as a child singer. First, he had confidence, a quality he has always had and equally admires in others. Mrs McNeil, who witnessed many of his early performances, recalls, 'Even at eight, nine and ten, he had such poise about him. He didn't show any fear. It was fun for him, never a chore – as if it were the most natural thing in the world.' Secondly, he had superb pitch. 'He's got a great ear,' observes Bob. Justin and the four other 'New Kids' did a couple of other school 'shows', but it soon became clear that Justin had loftier ambitions than being the star-turn in the classroom. Bob Westbrook encouraged him to sing in public at every opportunity, whether it was in school, in church or in a shopping mall.

Bob put together a group of his pupils to form the Bob Westbrook Singers and they gained invaluable experience at local events. Justin was younger and smaller than the others, and the only boy among six girls. They used to make innocent fun of Justin, calling him 'afro' because of his wild and curly hair. It was a learning process for Justin. Bob used to video the shows and thus could monitor the progress of his star pupil. This was especially apparent in Justin's movement on stage, which changed from being a little tentative and stiff to much more rhythmic. At first he would shuffle out apprehensively and declare to the watching shoppers: 'Good afternoon, everybody. My name is Justin Timberlake and I am going to sing for you "Please Don't Go Girl".'

Justin soon grew more confident. Bob recalls him performing a storming version of Elvis Presley's 'Heartbreak Hotel', displaying a sureness that made him realize how far his young charge had progressed since his uncertain early days. Another highlight was when the girls performed 'Leader Of The Pack', the old Shangri-Las hit from the sixties. Justin was centre stage, wearing a black leather jacket, looking cool on a Harley Davidson, his favourite make of motorcycle.

Justin decided to try his hand in the competitive world of

junior talent contests. Bob Westbrook had paired him up with another of his pupils, a girl called Holly Gaines, who had a lovely high soprano voice like Charlotte Church's. Together they made the finals of the Mid South State Fair, singing the Christian song 'More Than Wonderful', originally a hit in the US for Sandy Patti and Lauradale Harris. Most of the time Justin would have a very clear idea of the songs he wanted to practise and polish with Bob. Occasionally, Lynn would come in and they would talk through ideas together. Justin was very chart-oriented but Bob searched for tracks that would suit his vocal range and, at the same time, stretch his ability. Justin has acknowledged that it was this world of talent contests and singing in malls that made him fully realize that it was his destiny to become a performer. He loved the applause and thrived on it. When he was ten, he appeared on the Grand Ole Opry in Nashville and won a talent contest in Houston, Texas.

Holly wanted to try her hand at a talent contest in Nashville called the Universal Charm Pageant on 8 August 1992. Justin decided to have a go as well, but not just as a singer. Justin went the whole nine yards, entering the modelling and the sportswear sections too. Bob recalls, 'He was the only guy in the whole pageant, but he won the lot, including talent, of course.' The first prize was a car or, more precisely, $16,000 (£8,800) worth of savings bonds, the value of the vehicle. In addition to the accolade for singing, Justin's clean sweep at the pageant was as Best Model, Best Dressed, Best Sportswear, Most Handsome and Supreme Winner. The whole thing sounded more like Cruft's Dog Show than a prestigious contest for young hopefuls, and Justin certainly looked like a dog's dinner. He resembled a junior Elvis in one of those ghastly white outfits. The pageant director, Darlene Burgess, gushed, 'He's the most incredible thing I've seen for his age. He's got the showmanship. He's got the talent.'

The singing part of Justin's appearance seemed strangely overshadowed by his catwalk capabilities, but he had, in fact, performed a powerful version – for an 11-year-old – of the all-time soul classic 'When A Man Loves A Woman'. Mercifully, Justin chose to copy the great Percy Sledge original and not the tepid Michael

Bolton cover. Justin may have had big hair, but he always had taste in music.

Back in Memphis, the *Commercial Appeal* was suitably impressed at the local boy made good: 'His baby-blue eyes beam. His mound of golden blond hair sweeps back. His wide, pearly smile flashes. His trained soprano voice rolls, trills, yodels and twangs . . . Justin Randall Timberlake, eleven, may be just another kid in the legions who dream about becoming a singing star. But this sixth grader from Shelby Forest who sings country and pop has bolted out of the chute towards his dream.'

That dream gained momentum almost immediately when Justin was booked to appear in Memphis the following month at a charity evening of country artists, including Billy Jo Spears and Curtis Walker. One of the judges in Nashville was a record executive, who suggested Justin put together a demo. The Ardent Studios in Memphis were an obvious choice for Justin's first recording because of a useful family connection – his stepmother Lisa's sister, Sue Lynn Perry, worked there. Wearing a dodgy pair of purple shorts, the superstar of the future sang 'When A Man Loves A Woman' and the Garth Brooks song 'Two Of A Kind' – complete with the Brooks trademark yodelling. Lynn was there to urge him on, but a sinus problem meant Justin was not on his best form.

He provided the engineer, Andy Black, with an early taste of the Timberlake perfectionism. 'Did that sound scratchy?' asked Justin through the mike.

'In a few places,' said Andy. 'But how did you think you did overall?'

'I can do better.'

Lynn was very keen for Justin to make the most of this exposure, and they decided 'the young singing sensation of North Shelby County' should try for a 'national breakthrough'. At this stage of his fledgling career, Lynn was concerned about Justin's stage name. They tried several variations. He was Justin Randall Timberlake when he joined 500 other young hopefuls at the Oak Court Mall in Memphis to audition for the two available spots on *Star Search*, the great American talent show. In an early blueprint for *Pop Idol* and *American Idol*, Justin had a mere thirty seconds to impress the judges with his rendition of 'Two Of A Kind'. Fortunately, there was no sarcastic Simon Cowell figure to dent the young boy's confidence and Justin went through to the national programme, filmed in Orlando, Florida. At the time, Justin had no idea that the land of Disney was going to become his second home.

One of the myths about Justin's career is that he started off as a country singer and might have turned into a spangled Kenny Rogers if it hadn't been for 'N Sync. According to Bob Westbrook, Justin only ever performed this one classic country song. The confusion over Justin's musical roots occurred because this was the song he sang in his first bid for stardom and clips of him singing it are still shown on national TV as the first failure for the pop star with the Midas touch. The junior section of *Star Search* was a showcase for precocious, slightly objectionable kids wanting a taste of show business. The late Lena Zavaroni famously won the UK talent contest *Opportunity Knocks* as a precocious youngster. Imagine a show full of little Lenas and you have a picture of *Star Search*, which was presented by Ed McMahon, best known as Johnny Carson's sidekick on *The Tonight Show*.

The *Star Search* gimmick was that it was a straight contest between two contestants. You were either eliminated after a two-minute spot or you lived to fight another day. The future stars who cut their showbiz teeth on the show included Britney Spears, Beyoncé, Christina Aguilera, LeAnn Rimes, Alanis Morissette and Rosie O'Donnell. Justin had been practising his Garth Brooks at every opportunity. Karen Toombs recalls when she went to Jeter's school talent contest for the first time. She had no idea that Justin Timberlake was Jeter's star-turn: 'I wasn't teaching him then and all the children were doing their best, but it was definitely a school thing. Suddenly this little kid comes out in his jeans and a button-down shirt and black cowboy hat and starts belting out this country song. I was blown away.'

Bob went through the performance tirelessly with Justin, right down to the little move when he flips the hat up and down his arm like a Las Vegas professional. Despite all the hard work, Justin surprisingly lost his first round to a 10-year-old girl called Anna

Nardona, who warbled a winsome version of Crystal Gayle's hit 'Don't It Make My Brown Eyes Blue'. He was naturally gutted and it required a lot of encouragement from Lynn to get him to pick himself up again for the next challenge – a hug from Ed McMahon. It could have been worse. His conqueror was subsequently beaten by a cute 5-year-old, which she found so embarrassing that she lost all heart for a show business career. Justin was in good company, because Britney and Christina, whom he had not met by this stage, were also knocked out early when they appeared on the show.

Like his two young female contemporaries, Justin Timberlake had the capacity to bounce back, and the opportunity came much sooner than he expected. It was a classic case of getting back on a contrary horse the minute after you have fallen off. Justin was grumpy and fed up, and wanted to get home to Shelby Forest, but Lynn persuaded him to try out for one more programme.

While in Orlando for *Star Search,* she had heard from another mother about some auditions for a Disney kids' show in Hendersonville, near Nashville. Justin sailed through the first open audition and was told to return for the serious audition a few weeks later. The irony is that if he had made it through to another round of Star Search he would never have joined *The Mickey Mouse Club.*

Ambition, talent and a capacity for hard work are all important in turning a promising child performer into a star, but they can count for nothing without some luck. This was Justin's lucky card and he took it. Kylie Minogue, for instance, might not have auditioned for *Neighbours* if she had not been written out of the second series of a dire Australian daytime drama called *The Henderson Kids.* Justin acknowledges that it was a fluke: 'It's funny. If I had won on *Star Search* just one time, I would not have made the audition. I think God has his master plan and he'll lay it out for you. But *you* have to walk that road.'

'He sang as if it were effortless.'

5

The Mouseketeer

Justin took a break from filming to hang out with his old Apex friends from Jeter and join them on some rides at Disney World. 'Hey, watch what I can do,' he announced, taking off his cap and placing it on the ground. He started humming the opening bars of a familiar tune, 'New York New York', and then, to the surprise of his pals, began singing: 'Start spreading the news . . .'. A tourist walked by and threw a couple of dollars into the hat.

At the big audition, Justin was appraised by Gary Spatz, the acting coach on *The Mickey Mouse Club* (MMC). By coincidence, Justin was in the same group as both Britney Spears and Christina Aguilera. They had to prepare a routine that consisted of singing, dancing and a speech. Gary gave them marks out of ten in six categories. Justin's scores were: vocals 8–8½; acting 7½–8; camera persona 8; dance 7½–8; personality 8; appearance 8¼. Gary's overall comment on Justin Randall, as he was calling himself at this audition, was: 'Raw but good.' Britney, whose hair was mousy brown as a girl, scored better than Justin, although neither of them was told this at the time. She scored 8½ across the board, except for appearance, where she slipped to an 8. Britney's total mark was the highest at the auditions, although everyone was outscored in the singing category by Christina, whose voice was always exceptional. Gary gave her 9 for singing.

All three were recommended for the sixth season of the show, which would start the following spring. Justin's achievement in winning a spot on the show should not be underestimated. More than 20,000 youngsters across America had set out hoping to take this important step on the road to fame. Gary recalls that he was struck, even then, by how extraordinarily focused both Justin and Britney were: 'They had this absolute passion for their work.'

Back in Shelby Forest, there was plenty for Justin's mother to think about. There was never any question of Justin not accepting the Disney offer. It was what she had dreamed of for her son. But it meant going to live in Orlando for six months, leaving her comfortable home, her friends, not to mention her husband Paul. This was a giant leap for the family, albeit an exciting one. *The Mickey Mouse Club* had been on television for five years, so Justin and his friends had grown up watching it. Only Justin entertained serious hopes of joining the cast who, to his youthful eyes, seemed to be having the time of their lives.

The *Mickey Mouse* season was going to run from April until September 1993, so one of the first tasks for Lynn was to make sure Mrs McNeil at E. E. Jeter was happy about Justin opting out of school for six months. Lynn was a very active parent at the school and was already on very good terms with the teachers. Mrs McNeil recalls, 'She came and saw me and explained what they had told her at Disney – he would have so many hours of practice, so many hours performing and so many hours of schooling. She absolutely understood that he needed his education and it wasn't just about entertaining. I knew that she would not have supported the venture if it was going to be at all detrimental to Justin. I thought it would be a wonderful experience for him, especially as he would be with other children who had similar talents and he would get an opportunity to perform.'

The Mickey Mouse Club provided Justin with what Gary Spatz calls a 'million-dollar education' in singing, dancing and acting. For someone so purposeful in his pursuit of his ambitions, it was priceless. Justin, quite naturally, could not wait to be a star of the small screen. His mind was certainly not on schoolwork as the new intake of child stars and their parents or chaperones gathered in a meeting room at the Disney/MGM Studios in Orlando for the first time. They did not know it then, but these seven 'New Kids on the Lot' would be the last intake of children to *The Mickey Mouse Club*, which was going through a period of restyling. The feeling at Disney was that the old *Mickey Mouse Club* was looking a little dated and square. Blue Wave Productions, who made the show for Disney, were looking for a slightly older, hipper approach. They started downplaying the name *The Mickey Mouse Club*, preferring to call it *MMC* and making it sound more like a vaccine than a cool show for kids.

On the first day, the seven new 'Mouseketeers' and their parents, who were wondering what they had let themselves into, sat around a big table. Everyone was naturally excited to be there, so it came as a shock when they discovered that the most important person they would meet that morning was their head tutor. Back to school! His name was Chuck Yerger and he would be a very significant figure during Justin's teenage years. Chuck had moved down to Florida from Pennsylvania and found a job working for On Location Education, which specializes in teaching child actors and performers while they were filming. His first job was to tutor Macauley Culkin's younger brother Shane, while the *Home Alone* star was filming *My Girl* in Orlando. From there Chuck moved on to *The Mickey Mouse Club*, which was then in its third season. He proved so adept at dealing with its fledgling stars that by the time Justin showed up he was the principal of the school, responsible for hiring, firing and scheduling, as well as teaching. He also taught for Nickelodeon in Orlando, where he encountered one of his favourite students, Melissa Joan Hart, who would later become famous as Sabrina, the Teenage Witch. 'I taught her for six hours every Sunday,' recalls Chuck. 'She was a marvellous young lady.'

At the first meeting, the executive producer of *The Mickey Mouse Club*, Dennis Steinmetz, talked about the production schedules and drew attention to the amount of schooling the children would have in order to meet statutory requirements. The Screen Actors Guild (SAG) and the American Federation of Television and Radio Actors (AFTRA) required all children to be in school for three hours a day, a total of fifteen hours a week. The teaching could not be from any old textbook they had lying around; a recognized curriculum had to be approved by the child's home school – E. E. Jeter in Justin's case. The young actors could bank some hours if they were taught for more than three hours in a day, but there was a limit of thirty hours to prevent an unscrupulous company from putting children in school for ten hours a day for a month and then shipping them off to Mexico to shoot a film with no schooling whatsoever.

Disney took their educational obligations seriously, because if the inspectors came in and discovered just one child who fell short in his schooling requirements, it would be a serious breach of contract. Justin, Britney, Christina *et al.* were told in no uncertain terms by Dennis Steinmetz when he introduced Chuck Yerger: 'This man will tell me if you are allowed to perform.'

Chuck was surprised when he surveyed his new charges that first morning. He knew the producers of *MMC* were trying for an older approach, so he was not prepared for the new cast that greeted him; 'I was dumbfounded. These were little kids. I was expecting to see teenagers with an "I'm with it" attitude. But these were rugrats – that's a teachers' term for little kids who play on rugs.' Chuck was particularly unimpressed by his first encounter with Justin Timberlake: 'He was wearing a leather brace on his left wrist. I didn't know it at the time but he had sprained it playing basketball. I thought to myself, "Oh, here's a prima donna who's always going to be injured. Look at me, I'm injured. What did he do – hurt his wrist tap dancing?" I thought I was going to have somebody who was going to be a problem. I had no idea what an athlete he was.'

Lynn was still worried about what Justin's professional name should be. She needed to make a decision. Chuck recalls hearing her on the first day talking it over with another parent: ' I didn't know her at all then, but she was concerned because whatever he was at *The Mickey Mouse Club* would be his billing for the rest of his life: Justin Randall Timberlake, Justin Timberlake or Justin Randall or Randall Timberlake. Which was the coolest name?' By coincidence JC Chasez (pronounced Sha-say), who would later join Justin in 'N Sync had also agonized over his name. *The Mickey Mouse Club* already had a Joshua when he joined in the fourth season, so he opted for what would become famous initials. After much agonizing and taking advice from everyone from Disney executives to the pizza delivery man, Lynn left it up to Justin, who opted for Justin Timberlake, because it was his name and it was what he was used to.

The *Mickey Mouse* life was perhaps not as glamorous as it might have appeared. The world for the 'nearly-bes' revolved around four bungalows at the back of the Disney/MGM lot. One of them was the 'school', while the others were used either for filming or for practising and rehearsing. Disney provided the youngsters and their families with apartments in a complex they owned in Orlando. In Justin's case, it was just him and Lynn, although Paul would fly in some weekends to be with them. The Timberlake family had no financial worries. Justin's winnings from talent contests had been carefully set aside to help with his expenses on the road to the top. He was not going to become a millionaire on his Disney salary, although he would still be a teenager when he achieved that goal. The Mouseketeers were paid about $15,000 (£8,250) for a six-month season, although perks, including free rent, meant that most of that money could be banked. It was a very good wage for a 12-year-old boy.

The transformation in the new intake brought about by the 'million-dollar education' was a rapid one. The little 'rugrats', understandably apprehensive that first day, acquired the precious commodity of confidence. When Justin started, a typical day would be three hours of schooling in the morning followed by rehearsals and taping. Although there was no recognized sports programme, the cast would have at least an hour's dance class every day. They were filming most days, even though the show, billed as the *All New Mickey Mouse Club*, was not scheduled to start its new season until October. The show was put together in pieces and then edited into separate programmes. Sometimes Justin would film openings, another day it would be dance numbers or sketches. It kept everyone on their toes. By the time they were ready to leave Orlando at the end of October, the 20-strong cast, ranging in age from eleven to eighteen – Britney, the youngest, would not be twelve until December – had filmed thirty-five episodes.

Justin particularly enjoyed the little comedy scenes in which he and Britney displayed an early empathy. It was all very homely, confined to a set that would not have looked out of place in Ramsey Street, home to the top-rated Australian soap, *Neighbours*. One of the most noticeable changes in Justin was in his 'stage' clothes. Gone were the dubious Grand Ole Opry white suits and, in their place, were cool teenage clothes, jeans and tops. Chuck Yerger noticed Justin growing up: 'When I first met him he had an "Oh, gee whizz" country boy kind of feel to him. But he was very respectful and definitely an above average student, very much up to speed academically for a boy of his age.' Surrounded by so much young talent, Justin did not particularly stand out; he was more of a good all-rounder. Christina Aguilera had the voice that everyone noticed and acquired the nickname 'Diva'. Even Chuck, who was too busy to spend much time watching his students perform, observes, 'Christina had the most beautiful voice I think I've ever heard. She was a tiny girl who a puff of wind would blow away, but when she opened her mouth to sing she filled any room she was in.'

The youngsters were encouraged to stick together, work together and play together to promote a family atmosphere. Britney and Christina tended to stick together at first because they were the smallest and the scrawniest. Justin and the very pretty Nikki DeLoach were a little bigger and were called 'Weenies' by the adults because they were between the little kids and the older teenagers. Nikki would spend a great deal of time with Justin when she, too, was trying to make it as a pop star. While Britney Spears and Justin were destined to become the most famous ex-*Mickey Mouse* couple, Nikki and JC Chasez also dated for a while when they were older. Justin was particularly friendly with a mouseketeer called Matt Morris, who would later forge a successful career in the music business as a songwriter; Matt co-wrote several of the tracks on Christina's phenomenally successful *Stripped* album.

The older children tended to become role models for the youngest. Britney and Christina looked up to Keri Russell, who, at sixteen, was an old *Mickey Mouse Club* hand and had a boyfriend. It was typical hero worship. Christina, who loved her time on *MMC*, said of Keri, 'She had the car. She had the boyfriend. She was more

developed. We totally looked up to her as to what we wanted to be.'
The heart-throb was Tony Lucca, a good-looking, clean-cut 17-year-
old from Detroit, who would go on to become a popular recording
artist. It was rare for the older children to mix with the younger
ones, simply because when you are a teenager there is a huge difference between thirteen and seventeen, although Justin did get
on well with JC Chasez, the *MMC* host.

Mostly, on their time off, the youngest children would hang out
together and go for ice cream, or take advantage of their 'Silver
Passports', special free passes to the theme park. Sometimes they
would go dancing at Pleasure Island and show off the moves they
had learned in rehearsals.

At the end of every show, all the mouseketeers would gather
round to join hands and sing the MMC theme song, a wonderful
slice of Americana:

'And now it's time to say goodbye
To all our company
M-I-C, See you real soon! K-E-Y
Why? Because we like you! M-O-U-S-E!'

Cue lots of hugs and spontaneous dancing. One of the behind-the-
scenes jokes on the show was the alternative goodbye that Justin
soon learned:

'M-I-C, See you real soon! K-E-Y
Why? Because we get paid to! M-O-U-S-E!'

The arrival of the seven newcomers was announced by Disney in
July with a little titbit to whet the anticipation of devotees of the
show, which was screened on the Disney cable channel at 5.30p.m.
daily from Monday to Thursday. They were: Justin Timberlake
(likes chocolate chip ice cream); Britney Spears (favourite actor:
Tom Cruise); Christina Aguilera (favourite colours: turquoise and
purple); Ryan Gosling (nickname: 'Trouble'); Tate Lynche
(favourite sport: tennis); Nikki DeLoach (favourite actress: Meg
Ryan); and TJ Fantini (favourite singer: Michael Jackson). Justin

would have to get used to the insatiable appetite fans have for little profile pieces, a staple diet of teen magazines. They nearly always consisted of age, height, eye colour, nicknames and any number of assorted 'favourites'.

His Disney biography was very dull: 'Justin Timberlake is a loyal, creative, and extremely conscientious 12-year-old, who has put everything he has into being a great performer . . . Academically, Justin is very conscientious, achieving a straight-A average and enjoying such subjects as maths and science . . .' The image of Justin as a school spod was not one he could shake off easily.

Justin was particularly fortunate that when his voice broke his tone and pitch altered very little. He had been a high tenor, but acquired what his old voice coach Bob Westbrook calls 'bottom end'. Almost the entire club went through puberty while on the show. It made things difficult for Chuck Yerger, who was trying to keep a sense of discipline about schoolwork: 'Kids will have bad days when they are going through adolescence. I had to be tough. If a kid came in and said, "I'm tired, I was dancing. Can't I just read a book?", I would have to say, "No", because I would tell them I could not clock them in. Sometimes I would have to threaten them with going to tell Production. The ultimate sanction was the words, "Do I need to tell your mother?"' The saving grace for the cast was that when their own schools broke up for the summer holiday so did they.

At the end of October, Justin returned home to Shelby Forest. When he went back to E. E. Jeter, Mrs McNeil had moved to start up a new school in Collierville, a suburb of Memphis. The new principal, Mrs Regina Castleberry, proved to be one of Justin's biggest fans. She had never heard of Justin Timberlake until, by coincidence, she had gone to a fellow teacher's house the night he was on *Star Search*: 'He was wearing that big cowboy hat that was bigger than he was and he was so cute.'

Mrs Castleberry was concerned that Justin would have a big head: 'I expected to meet a child kind of filled up with himself. But Justin never ever presented himself in that way, which is one of the reasons he was so liked at the school. He never went round saying, "Look who I am", or "Look what I did". When he came back here he was just another kid on the block and you would never have been able to pick him out if you didn't know who he was, except when we had musical events at the school because he was always handed the solo parts.'

Mrs Castleberry was so impressed by his talent that she persuaded him on two occasions to sing at her sorority evenings during the holidays. The ADK sorority was a social club for women teachers in the Memphis area and they would meet for dinner, discussion and entertainment. Justin was an enormous hit with the ladies. Regina would pick him up from home, they would go to collect the food they were taking, usually chicken, and Justin would be introduced to the club: 'He would appear to be shy, but you put a mike in his hand and he was a different person.'

At one dinner Justin sang 'All I Want For Christmas Is A Kiss From Santa Claus'. He was wearing black trousers, a white shirt and red waistcoat with pockets in which he had stuffed little paper kisses. As he sang, he handed them out to the ladies. 'They just drooled over him', recalls Mrs Castleberry. 'He was such a doll.'

Justin never pushed himself forward as the great singer at Jeter. But on the last day of his eighth-grade year, he treated the audience to a sensational version of the Seal hit 'A Kiss From A Rose', which those lucky enough to be there still talk about.

Some changes were in place when Justin returned to Orlando the following April for his second season of *The Mickey Mouse Club*. The studio had abandoned the three hours' standard tuition in the morning for a more flexible approach. The director, Jack Seifert, decided they were wasting half a day and that the young stars should fit in their schooling when they were not required on set. It was a logistical nightmare for Chuck Yerger, who had to keep track of every student's hours: 'It was hard for the kids as well. Justin was now thirteen and he might have to perform a comedy routine or a song-and-dance number and walk off stage to hear the stage manager saying, "OK, Justin, you've got school for the next ninety minutes." He would have to walk out of there in full make-up, change out of his costume, come over to the schoolroom, sit down and do double geography! All he wanted to do, naturally, was talk about what he had just done on the show.'

61

The producers tried to introduce some more *Grange Hill*-style topics into the show, including eating disorders, teenage depression and racism, but the problem for *The Mickey Mouse Club* was that it was a Disney brand. Disney is great all-American escapism, a world of make-believe populated by happy kids with great teeth. All the talent in the world and a repositioning of its place in the marketplace could not make *The Mickey Mouse Club* cutting edge.

At the end of Justin's second season, in October 1994, none of the cast had the slightest idea that the show would be cancelled. The ratings were still respectable. Chuck Yerger recalls, 'Disney was very coy about not bringing it back. Even as late as Christmas they were talking about bringing the *Mouse Club* back, but no announcement was made until the February. So there were no big tearful goodbyes, because all the children were scattered by the time it happened.' Instead there was a big wrap party. Justin gave Chuck Yerger a special teacher sweater, which had maths sums on it and the dreaded words 'Spelling Test Tomorrow'. He also wrote his teacher a touching note:

Chuck – Thanx for everything.
You're like a second Dad to me.
Thanx again.
Sincerely – Justin

If they had known it was going to be the last wrap party, there would have been many tears, because *The Mickey Mouse Club* was an exclusive *Fame Academy* that brought together a relatively small bunch of kids for an intense, very close crash course in show business. They formed a bond much closer than the usual 'Friends Reunited'. Justin and Britney, in particular, may have garnered most of the headlines over the following eight years for their high-profile romance, but many of the cast have formed a network that supports an MMC member if they are performing in a play or at a concert.

The most obvious question was who, if any, of the Mouseketeers would go on to greater things. They used to joke off set that if the show was ever cancelled they would all go off and become stars.

They had undeniable talent, but now they were a bunch of unem-
ployed teenagers facing the prospect of going back to school in
their home towns. The success rate in the ten years since the last
season has, in such a cut-throat business, been nothing short of a
phenomenon. Britney and Christina are pop superstars; JC Chasez
and Tony Lucca are not far behind; Keri Russell won an award for
her role in the popular television series *Felicity*, while Ryan Gosling
is a much in demand actor as the star of *Young Hercules*. Others are
living in Los Angeles waiting for a break into the big-time. How
would Justin Timberlake fare at home in Shelby Forest? He was
going to fall in love for the first time.

'They were all kind of giggly and nervous.'

6

Love-struck

It was Justin's fifteenth birthday and he was disconsolate. He had asked his girlfriend, Danielle, to come to Orlando to celebrate with him, but she had told him she had to stay in Millington for school and would have to miss it. He was moping around the house when his mother arrived home and told him to unload the groceries from the trunk of her white Lexus. He went out to the driveway, opened the boot and his eyes popped out of their sockets. There was Danielle, surrounded by flowers, balloons and brightly wrapped presents. 'Happy Birthday,' she shouted. 'I got here!'

Danielle Ditto was a popular girl among the adolescent boys of Millington. Petite but shapely with honey blonde hair and blue eyes, she had the look of a traditional southern belle about her. She also had cheekbones chiselled as if out of the finest marble. Unsurprisingly, she caught the eye of the young Justin Timberlake, home from the bright lights of Orlando and eager to display his newly acquired *Mickey Mouse* sophistication.

By coincidence, Danielle had been out a few times with Justin's best friend, Trace Ayala, but, at the time, Justin had been in Florida, so she had never really hung out with him before they both pitched up to a youth evening at the Lucy Church. That night they were part of a group that went to a local pizza parlour called Madio's on nearby Navy Road, Millington's main street. While Danielle was seated at a table with her best friend Stacey, Justin made his move. He slipped up to Danielle and handed her his card, but it failed to have the desired impressive effect: 'It was this little comic card and he had signed his autograph on it with some words like "Justin's into peace and harmony". I thought, "Who *is* this weirdo?" My friend told me, "He's Justin Timberlake and he's on *The Mickey Mouse Club.*" I didn't even know what *The Mickey Mouse Club* was. I was like, "Whooah, somebody get satellite television out here." So I just took a restaurant card, flipped it over, wrote my name on it and sent it back over to him. He was dumbstruck.'

Justin was not a commanding presence at the tender age of thirteen. He was small for his age and had to suffer an afro hairdo. Danielle observes, 'His mom used to put so much stuff in his hair to tame it. She used to poop it up so that it was like a wave. It was terrible. So, me and my friend pretty much laughed at him. I was a kid, so thought it was OK to make fun of boys. I was like, "Who is this person?"'

The saga of how Justin and Danielle became first loves owes more to *When Harry Met Sally* than *Romeo and Juliet.* It would be a year before she spoke to him properly, this time at the baseball field close to E. E. Jeter. She had seen him coming out of school from time to time: 'Stacey would always point to him and say, "Look at Justin, how big he's gotten." He had really shot up over the summer and I was surprised that the same person from the pizza restaurant now had a face that was really cute but it had broken out with acne.' Justin's acne was so bad that Lynn had to seek medical help for the complaint, and Justin took an intensive course of tablets that cleared it up after a few months. It was certainly better when he invited Danielle and some friends back to his house to shoot pool after the ball-game. It was a short walk from the ballpark to his house. They did not get the opportunity to talk much that day, but at least it had broken the ice.

Soon after, at another ball-game, they had the chance to talk by themselves. Justin showed up on a motorcycle and sparked off a conversation by showing Danielle the finer points of the machine. At fourteen, Justin was too young to ride a motorcycle legally, but as Danielle explains, 'Everyone in the country rides bikes young.'

They got along like the proverbial house on fire, discovering that they shared a teenage obsession with the latest fashions. Danielle noticed that Justin was wearing Lucky's, a brand of jeans that nobody really knew about in Shelby Forest, which was in the Ice Age where the latest trends were concerned: 'I couldn't believe that someone out in Millington knew what that name brand was. It was weird. We just clicked about everything. I remember we would finish each other's sentences. We were telling jokes back and forth and he was very funny. He had these goofy facial expressions. You never really get to talk to someone when you are with your girl-friend, but this time it was like, "Wow!".'

The backwater nature of Millington and Shelby Forest is aptly demonstrated in Danielle's appreciation of the latest trends simply because she often stayed with her mother, Shawn, in the Memphis suburb of Germantown, a journey of just half an hour but a world away from the less sophisticated country. She and Justin discovered that their family circumstances were similar. Their mothers had given birth young – Danielle's was eighteen and Justin's was twenty. They had also divorced while their children were still in nappies and had subsequently remarried. Danielle's father John was in the Navy before he set up his own gym business. Danielle, nearly five months older than her prospective suitor, spent most of her time growing up at the home of her grandparents, not far from Justin's house, although not in such a prosperous neighbourhood. They both shared an enormous respect for their grandparents and rec-ognized the importance of the church in their respective families. 'My family would rather be in church than anywhere else, 'explains Danielle. 'I had a very strict curfew growing up. I had to be in at nine o'clock. Some weekends I could come in at twelve, but if I was a minute late . . .'

Justin forgot to ask for Danielle's phone number at the ballpark, much to her disappointment, but remedied the situation by get-ting it from Trace and calling her that night. In the best tradition of teenage romance, they talked until four in the morning. Another thing they discovered they had in common was singing. Justin was obviously accomplished and already successful, but Danielle entered talent contests both locally and out of state. She also sang regularly at the Casper Creek Country Club near Millington. The club did not serve any alcohol, so it was popular with parents who felt reassured that their children would be safe there. Danielle told Justin that she would be singing there the next night, but they didn't arrange to see each other. Imagine her surprise when Justin walked in while she was on stage – a surprise made especially intense because her boyfriend was in the back room playing pool!

Danielle was distraught: 'I was so shocked and it was like, "Oh, no!" This guy was there and I thought, "Oh Lord, I'm in trouble now." I went up to Justin and said, "You shouldn't have come here. You don't understand; I'm dating this guy and he'll beat you up. You need to go home." And Justin said, "I really like you, I want to start dating you." And I was like, "Well, not tonight. I don't think that would be a very good idea." The other guy was bigger and just had one of those personalities . . .'

The boyfriend left, so Danielle walked Justin to his friend's car. It was an opportunity and Justin took it: 'He just plants a kiss on me. It was a good one – a swooner! It was scary how good we got along. You know how you meet somebody and sometimes you think, "I think I like him", and then other times you think, "I really like him", and sometimes you think, "Oh, my God, this is unbelievable!" That's about how it was with Justin. It was like lightning.'

For the moment, however, Danielle's primary concern was her boyfriend and her desire for Justin to get the hell out of there, especially when the boy in question drove back into the car park. 'I was shouting, "Leave, leave, leave! Get in the car. Go now, please. You just don't understand." Justin was saying that he wanted to stay, but eventually I managed to shove him in the car.'

Later, when Danielle returned home, Justin was on the phone before she had taken the key out of the lock. He favoured direct action and wanted to speak to the boyfriend that very night and tell him what was going on. Danielle was trying to dissuade him when the boy in question started beeping in to Justin's phone as an incoming call. Justin had already left a message for him to ring. Danielle recalls, 'Justin said he was going to go ahead and take care of it now. He told him that he liked me a whole lot and that it was special and that he wanted to give it a shot. He said, "If you don't understand, you know where I live." But they talked and that guy never spoke to me again – not ever.'

Now that the inconvenience of another guy on the scene had been decisively dealt with, it was time for Justin to sweep Danielle off her feet with a real date. He took her to a basketball game with his parents. Fortunately, Danielle loves basketball and so was thrilled at the invitation to the annual Penny Hardaway Classic in Memphis. Danielle had to deal not just with first date nerves but with the ordeal of meeting the folks as well. She wore a green and white button-down sleeveless blouse with blue Levi's and boots. Justin, however, was a vision in white. A white, V-neck, sleeveless vest, white trousers and summer shoes all topped off with a gold necklace. He had started doing his own hair, putting mousse in it and using a menthol-scented styling shampoo called Ice Cap to help keep everything in place. On the way to the game, Lynn made Justin squirm by playing tapes on the car stereo of him singing a Glen Campbell song. 'He went so red,' laughs Danielle.

After the game, the four of them went for a meal at Wendy's but, to Danielle's relief, Lynn and Paul sat at another table to give the teenagers some privacy. They talked mainly about basketball and afterwards went back to his house for a cold drink before Paul took her back to her grandmother's home before the curfew. The important thing at the end of her first date with Justin Timberlake was that Danielle wanted a second. This time Justin suggested the Oscar-winning film *Braveheart*, starring Mel Gibson. Millington did not have a cinema, so they had to be ferried to a theatre in Memphis, but at least, on this occasion, Justin's parents did not join them for the film. Danielle might have been able to relax and enjoy the movie but for the fact that her now ex-boyfriend was sitting a couple of rows in front of them: 'I couldn't believe it. We picked exactly the same movie. I was so embarrassed the whole time I was in there. But he never saw us, not once. Justin and I didn't care much for the movie – we just talked the whole time.'

Justin and Danielle were now officially dating. It was a hot summer in Tennessee. Justin was feeling at a bit of a loose end because of the unexpected cancellation of *The Mickey Mouse Club*.

At this stage, 'N Sync was still in the future, so Lynn was trying to decide what the best move for her son would be. Justin told Danielle that his mother was thinking that they should move to California and try to break in to acting and the movies. He was still taking his singing very seriously, having lessons with Bob Westbrook and travelling to Nashville to record some demos. Those trips were the longest time he and Danielle were apart that summer. When they were together, they preferred their own company, watching television or just hanging out in each other's homes, to spending time with a group of friends – a sure sign in a teenage romance that it was serious.

By the time Justin and Lynn moved back to Orlando, taking a chance on 'N Sync, Danielle realized she was in love. Justin did not subscribe to the 'treat 'em mean, keep 'em keen' philosophy. He always called Danielle 'Baby'. When she was involved in a nasty car crash and needed stitches in a cut on her face, he sent her a dozen roses. For her birthday in September, he bought her a cream sundress with brown and blue petalled flowers on it: 'I never wore it. It's so ugly. I never told Justin that I hated it.'

The relationship became more intense when Justin left Shelby Forest behind him. He and Lynn moved into what became known as ''N Sync House' on Doctor Phillips Boulevard in Orlando. Fellow band members Chris Kirkpatrick and JC Chasez were living there too. Danielle would fly down at weekends and sometimes stayed weeks at a time: 'My parents and his parents were very understanding. We were so love-struck, I would have died if I couldn't have seen him. I think my mom kind of knew that I would probably have locked myself in my room and never come out. She would probably have never heard from me again. It was Romeo and Juliet, if you know what I mean. So they were all good about it and talked it through between them. My mom was like, "Please watch my baby", and that kind of thing, and I would sleep in my own room at the house. Everybody was living at that house! I think mom figured that if anything happened she would find out.'

They had some laughs, including the time they took an old boat out on to the Mississippi with a group of friends and family. Danielle recalls that Justin was obsessed by 'The Turkey Song', which the actor and comedian Adam Sandler, star of *The Water Boy* and *The Wedding Singer*, used to perform. Justin wouldn't stop singing it that particular afternoon. There were thirteen of them, which proved to be a particularly unlucky number when the boat started sinking and they were left stranded on an island in the middle of the river. Danielle will never forget that afternoon because one boy ended up with a 'big old leech' on his back. Fortunately, 'The Turkey Song' did not become the special song for Justin and Danielle; that was the classic soul track 'Still In Love' by Brian McKnight.

Justin and Danielle started to talk about making love for the first time. This was not something either of them took lightly. In fact, they talked about it for eight months before planning it like a military exercise. The problem for both of them was the strong sense of morality instilled in them by their religious upbringing. In these days when sex is treated so lightly in our culture and media, here were two young people trying to take their responsibilities seriously. Danielle explains, 'Justin's grandfather was a preacher and I was still singing in church, so we were both from religious families. But when you're with somebody for so long, you keep on taking it to the next level. I think a lot of it had to do with him living in Florida and me being back in Millington. We were spending so much time away from each other and missing each other like crazy that everything became a little more extreme.'

While they agonized about sex, their declarations of love became more intense. Danielle bought Justin a big, chunky gold necklace and a gold nugget ring with grooves in it. Justin insisted on wearing the ring on his engagement finger. In return, he bought Danielle a 'promise' ring, which she, too, wore on the third finger of her left hand. She enjoyed Justin's displays of affection, admitting that she is attracted to 'incurable romantics', but she was worried that the ring might become a millstone: 'He got down on one knee and gave it to me, almost like a proposal. He said, "I love you; we'll be together for ever." I was like, "No, take that thing back!".'

Justin revealed a predilection for going completely over the top where women are concerned when he planned Danielle's

Valentine surprise. She was 'bad sick' and wanted to curl up and die at her grandparents' house. Her grandfather was out of town and she had no idea that her grandmother was in cahoots with Justin. She got in a tub filled with bath salts and treated herself to a long, sleepy soak. Meanwhile, Justin had sneaked into the house and set up a candlelit dinner complete with non-alcoholic champagne, flowers, cards and a teddy bear. He had made brownies and blinis, which he knew were Danielle's favourites. Danielle came out of the bathroom, feeling wretched, and there was Justin beaming, 'Happy Valentine's Day, Baby.' Danielle was overwhelmed and started to cry: 'I had no make-up on, my hair was like, "Eew!" And I had on this ugly blue nightdress. It was a long flannel blue shirt and something only your grandmother should see you in.'

Eventually, the following September, just after Danielle's fifteenth birthday, Justin was due to fly back home to Shelby Forest and they decided it would be the perfect time to make love for the first time. Friday night was a football game, Saturday was Danielle's homecoming dance at high school and Sunday was the day they planned to do the deed. They went shopping for condoms together in Memphis on the Saturday morning, giggling as they read the backs of the packets in the pharmacy. They did not want to run the risk of being seen buying protection in such a small town as Millington, especially since Justin's stepmother was the pharmacist at one of the biggest drug stores there. Danielle refuses to identify the place they had chosen to make love, revealing only that it was quiet and preferring to keep the memory of that place a precious secret.

'Making love to Justin was romantic and sweet. But I could have died of nerves and he was really nervous too. We were both embarrassed and shy. It's good that I can look back on it and know that I was in love. Justin said, "If nothing else, we'll always have this."'

Afterwards, Justin took Danielle home on the back of his motorcycle, and the next morning he flew back to Orlando to resume his quest for fame. They continued their love affair as before, but now they shared a special secret. 'I had absolutely no regrets we made love,' says Danielle. Justin showered her with cards and little notes declaring his affection. She still keeps a card he designed on his computer that says simply, 'Justin *adores* Danielle.' Another is addressed to 'Danielle, the woman I love'. Perhaps sweetest of all are the lines he wrote from the heart:

You are constantly in my thoughts
Falling for you
Is the greatest thing
That has happened to me.

Danielle started calling Justin by the pet name 'Stud Muffin', an indication that she was more than satisfied by his lovemaking abilities. On her visits to Florida, they became far less circumspect in snatching moments for sex: 'Kids are good at hiding stuff from their parents. We were definitely sneaky and always found a way. Maybe there was a little rebellion in there because everyone wanted me to be so perfect. It was a growing-up kind of thing.' 'N Sync House was supposed to be a celibate area, but the young lovers managed to break that particular rule.

The first problems began to threaten their idyllic situation when Danielle confided in her mother's younger sister. Her aunt Micki was still in her twenties and probably more of a sister than an aunt figure to Danielle. It was a couple of months later and they were sharing a 'couch evening' at home, talking about life and love. Danielle was reading Micki's old love letters and decided in the spirit of female camaraderie to share something very personal with her. So she told her aunt that she and Justin were lovers. Micki was alarmed when Danielle told her the details because she could see that the youngsters were getting careless and were being cavalier about sex: 'She was really afraid I was going to get caught and that something bad would happen, especially with me in school and Justin trying to do his career stuff. She told my mom because we were getting really serious and she was concerned for us.'

Micki's concerns proved to be justified when Danielle was in Orlando and joined Justin at the recording studio where he was doing some work that day. Overcome with lust, they disappeared into the bathroom for a quickie, but were discovered in the throes of passion by a girl they knew, who told the studio manager. 'I

Mr JT takes to the stage on the first night of his *Justified* tour in Sheffield, May 2003

An early sighting of the million-dollar smile and the big hair: Justin poses with schoolfriends Stephanie Roach, Amber Donovan and Kelley Thompson (standing); Crystal Highfill, Trey Schweitzer (kneeling)

Mr Jeter and Miss Jeter – Justin Timberlake and Deanna Dooley pictured casually in the forest

Justin said he would rather play basketball than be a singer. He is wearing the number 12 shirt, fourth from the left in this school team photo from 1995, just before he left to join 'N Sync

The Mouseketeers. Justin has his arm round Britney Spears who is already displaying a bare midriff. A waif like Christina Aguilera is seated in front of Justin

The last photo of *The Mickey Mouse Club* before the show was cancelled. Justin is holding the MMC card, Christina Aguilera wearing a blue denim jacket is on his left beside Britney Spears in a black top

Come Dancing: Justin and his first serious girlfriend Danielle Ditto became lovers the day after attending her homecoming dance together in September 1995

Justin and Danielle are all smiles before the cracks start to appear in their teenage romance

Another year, another homecoming dance. At last Justin has pensioned off the white suit

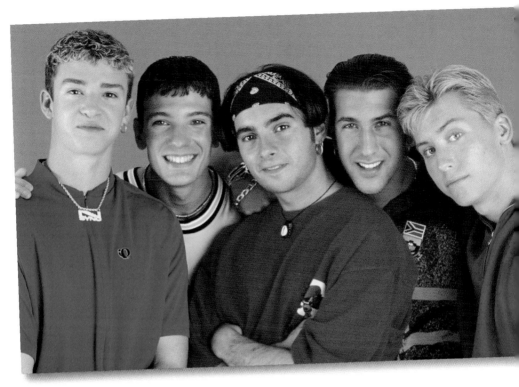

Justin, JC, Chris, Joey and Lance are in sync

Justin performs with 'N Sync on stage in New York. They were always proud
of their abilities as singers

Veronica Finn gets to grips with Justin during a break in the Bahamas in June 1998

Coming up for air, Justin shows off his bleached-blond look

Justin remains close to all his family. He is standing next to his cousins Amy, Nick and Matthew while his grandparents Sadie and Bill Bomar are seated and cousin Heather sits on the floor

Justin with his father Randy Timberlake's family – stepmother Lisa, and brothers Jonathan and Stephen. Justin is immensely proud of his younger brothers

Justin unveils his look-a-like marionette as part of the merchandising for the *No Strings Attached* album and tour in July 2000. The hair was perfect

The 'N Sync concerts were always spectacular shows.

On stage in Oakland, California, during the *PopOdyssey* tour in July 2001

'N Sync of the dead – the band are back at the Oakland Arena for the *Celebrity* tour in March 2002

Justin and 'N Sync always had time for 'tutor', Chuck Yerger. Chuck's daughter Stephanie is in front while at the back, her husband Tim Carmody pretends he's in the group

Justin's closest pals in 'N Sync were former Mouseketeer JC Chasez and group founder Chris Kirkpatrick, with whom he shared a wacky sense of humour

Justin's career throughout 'N Sync and, now, as a solo star has been guided by manager Johnny Wright

Innosense were planned as the female equivalent of 'N Sync. Justin's girlfriend Veronica Finn is second from left

Justin and Britney Spears provide the half time entertainment during the 2001 Super Bowl in Tampa, Florida. They had worked well together ever since The *Mickey Mouse Club* when they were only twelve

Cowboy and cowgirl, Justin and Britney arrive at the American Music Awards in Los Angeles in January 2001

Justin and Britney reveal their pet names for each other during a basketball game in 2001

Britney breaks down when talking about Justin on American television in November 2003

Nelly was one of the guests at the fourth annual 'N Sync Challenge for the Children basketball game in Orlando in July 2002. Justin featured on Nelly's hit 'Work It' in 2003

Justin loves golf almost as much as basketball and displays one hundred per cent concentration – and style – at the Bob Hope Chrysler Desert Classic in January 2002

The 'coolest man in pop'
at MTV's TRL studios in
New York in October 2003

Justin owes a huge
musical debt to singer
Brian McKnight

The Neptunes' Pharrell
Williams teaches Justin
the rudiments of Star Trek
hand gestures

Justin's 'Michael Jackson' performance was not greeted with universal approval at the 2002 MTV Video Music Awards in August 2002

think she had bad motives. She wanted to get closer to Justin. She was a fan of his from *Mickey Mouse* days and wanted to be in his gang. We got kicked out of the studio, which was one of the most embarrassing things of my life. It was seriously a terrible moment.'

Worse was to come when they had to face Justin's mother. She called the teenage lovers into the living room and sat them down for a serious heart to heart. Danielle recalls, 'She told us she knew it was occurring and that we had to be careful. She said, "I want you to stop this right now. I don't want to see you hanging around and holding hands and kissing. Don't go messing up your lives." She didn't want *us* to ruin *his* life.'

Danielle's mother Shawn favoured a more direct approach and hurled a large box of condoms at her daughter. Perhaps the two mothers were haunted by their own mistakes in their reaction to their offspring's sexual activity. Shawn had been about to start nursing college when she fell pregnant and had to postpone her career. Lynn was barely out of teens when her marriage to Justin's father fell apart and she was left to start again as a single mother. They both had other plans for their children.

All might have settled down at this point if it hadn't been for the night that everything blew up. It was not long after the incident in the recording studio when Danielle paid her next visit to Orlando to see Justin. The pair were getting hot and steamy in 'N Sync House when Lynn walked in and caught them. They were not having sex when she walked in, but they might have been ten minutes later. All hell broke loose and, in Danielle's mind, that night marked the beginning of the end for her and Justin.

Danielle recalls that dreadful night: 'Lynn was crying hysterically. I was crying. Justin was crying hysterically. Lynn called my grandmother, she called my mom, and she called his dad Randy as well as Paul. I was heartbroken. I will probably never, ever have a moment that embarrassing. I think Justin was upset because he was trying to be the perfect kid. I could understand that. I wanted my own parents to keep the image they had of me as their daughter. I didn't want them thinking I was a bad kid. I knew my mom was going to cry a river . . .'

At first Lynn demanded that Danielle take the next plane home, but after she had calmed down a little, they talked, and Lynn seemed more understanding of the fact that Danielle and Justin loved each other. The problem for the young lovers was all too apparent when Danielle flew back to Memphis. How were they going to see each other if their parents were not making the arrangements for Danielle to visit Orlando regularly? 'We basically got split up by our parents,' confirms Danielle. It did not help that Lynn and Danielle's mother fell out in a big way: 'Things were getting difficult between our families. My mom was thinking that his mom was a terrible mother because it was her kid that had done this. His mom was thinking, "That girl, she's terrible, and it's her mom's fault." Our parents really didn't like each other at all. They were just trying to protect us.'

Justin was about to discover the truism for all celebrities: absence does not make the heart grow fonder; instead, it plants the seeds of doubt and anguish that ultimately create a fissure through a great many relationships. Justin and Danielle spoke to each other on the telephone for hours at a time until Danielle's grandmother discovered to her horror that the bill for the long-distance calls was more than $600 (£330) and promptly blocked them. In any case, phone calls are no substitute for the real thing. Justin and Danielle did their best, sneaking off to make love on his increasingly rare visits home to Shelby Forest. He sent her a heart-felt letter with a tear on it: 'I love you and I know that our love is strong enough to last these trying times.' But they were not confiding in one another as much as they once had. Justin got upset when he thought Danielle was not sharing personal feelings about her family and about growing up. 'It was one of the reasons we grew apart, but I had never learned to talk about those things.' Danielle became increasingly difficult and stroppy at home and was falling behind at school. 'I hated everybody,' she declares.

It took a further six months for the crack in their relationship to become a canyon. They were seeing less and less of one another with fewer and fewer plane tickets for Danielle. There was little Justin could do; even though he was earning money of his own, Lynn took care of financial matters. If he saw a pair of sneakers he wanted that cost $100, she would give him that amount. He could not very well ask for the plane fare for Danielle. The inevitable happened. Danielle was popular with the teenage guys at her school and frequently got asked out on dates. One afternoon after school she let a boy she liked and knew well escort her home. 'He kissed me,' she recalls. 'I came home and I cried for two days. I wouldn't answer the phone when Justin called. It was just a constant stream of tears. I was scared to tell him. I'm not a good liar and I can't stand to hold something back. If I was dating somebody and they were with me all the time I would have just said, "This guy kissed me, can you believe that!", but Justin was so far away . . .'

Eventually Danielle confessed to Justin on the telephone and told him what had happened. He 'freaked out' and they broke up for two weeks: 'But we talked every day and he was like, "I don't want not to be with you. I want to be together."' A week or so later, Justin was flying back home and Danielle was thrilled that everything was going to be sorted out. She had reckoned without a close 'friend' of Justin, who dripped poison into their relationship. 'He told Justin that it was more than just a kiss, if you understand my meaning.'

Justin was totally devastated. He adored Danielle and felt completely betrayed. He sped over to her high school and confronted her in the courtyard in front of her friends. 'He came up to me and he was crying and said, "I can't believe you'd do this to me. How could you do this?" I said, "What are you talking about?", but he shouted, "I know something more happened." I tried to tell him to calm down and that nothing more had happened. I think when he saw me he realized that everything was OK and he believed me. You can tell, and he just knew there was nothing more than a kiss and so we dropped it. But it was the end of us really, or the beginning of the end.'

Justin went back to Orlando, but the irony of what had happened was that Danielle was starting to be eaten away by what Justin may or may not have been getting up to away from her. She feared that in some way she had given him the green light to cheat on her. After another couple of months of this absence and torture, it was Danielle who took decisive action: 'We were technically still together until I called him one day and said, "I'm in high school. I don't see you. I haven't seen you in a month and I want to date people and have a high school life." That's when it ended.'

Typically, despite their new-found freedom, neither of them felt like dating. Danielle observes, 'We had the worst break-up. I don't think we dated anybody for a year. I broke up with him to date people and I didn't. We both just sat around and drank coffee. I was pathetic.' Eventually Danielle started to pull herself together, leaving high school to take a home-teaching course to try to catch up from her 'lost' Justin year.

There was a twist in the tale of young love. Danielle weakened one night and rang Justin in Orlando only to discover that he had been on a date with a lovely blonde called Veronica Finn. Danielle laughs, 'I had the luck of calling when they had been out together and she was over there with him. I said, "I can't believe you're dating somebody", and we fought back and forth. I had actually called him because he had invited me to an 'N Sync concert in Memphis. I told him I didn't want to see his ugly face and he was saying I would need a pass to see him in concert. I said, "You're a prick", and that was it.'

And that really was it. Danielle pulled the 'promise' ring off her finger and hurled it against a wall with such force that she broke it in two: 'It snapped right in half and, when I finally went to look for it, I could only find half. I probably wore it out. It had three diamonds on it but I've got only two left.'

Danielle keeps the broken ring in her 'Justin memory box', along with her tickets to the Penny Hardaway Classic and to *Braveheart* and various airline tickets between Memphis and Orlando. She has also kept some personal mementoes from him, such as the note in which he beseeched her, 'Be My Little Love Monkey'. On her nineteenth birthday, she had a small blue tattoo of a treble clef inked on to her ankle – a musical memento of her time with Justin. She explains, 'I decided to get something I'll remember for ever – a private reminder of my past like a rest in peace – a reminder never to be that stupid again!' Looking back on a most traumatic time for her granddaughter, Betty Kirk says, 'It was one of the most hurtful break-ups of young people I've ever seen.'

Danielle's life is back on track. Justin turned out to be as near as she wanted to get to the show business world. She still sings occasionally, but she decided against a singing career after she won a talent contest in Florida when she was eighteen. The prize was a recording contract, but she decided not to do it: 'That was the point where I decided I could get on with my life.' Instead, she decided to follow the course her mother had chosen. She attends nursing college with the hope of eventually becoming a doctor. She is in a grown-up relationship with a doctor, of whom her family whole-heartedly approve.

The nearest Danielle has got to Justin since their split was when he almost knocked her down on a road near her house. She has seen him occasionally driving around the roads of Millington and Shelby Forest, but they never speak or even wave. She did go to an 'N Sync concert in Memphis, but did not see Justin. She did, however, have the misfortune to bump into the poisonous friend, who was there with his girlfriend. Danielle could not understand why the girl was so cool to her until she blurted out that she knew the guy had lost his virginity to Danielle. This was a blatant lie and one Danielle was not prepared to let go. She confronted the fantasy merchant and demanded that he retract this smear, which, in the end, he sheepishly did. He is certainly not on Danielle's Christmas card list, but she has moved on, even if he hasn't. Universally described as a local 'character', he still lives in the Millington area.

For her part, Danielle became the blueprint for the type of girl Justin goes for. She explains, 'I could describe his type very easily – kind of short, big booty, long, long hair, preferably blue eyes, but he would probably take brown, and very pretty.' Justin may not have been scarred by the deeply upsetting break-up with Danielle, but it has coloured his attitude. It has not stopped him from falling head over heels in love, but it has eroded his trust. Subsequently, his most serious relationships have ended with allegations that he was cheated on and a perception that he is a victim where women are concerned.

'Don't ever forget that I'll never stop loving you.'

PART TWO

*NSYNC

7

Getting in Sync

Justin decided it was time to start playing the guitar more, because he wanted to write songs. One night at 'N Sync House with Danielle Ditto he composed his first 'hit'. He called it 'Just Another Lonely Night'.

The original line-up of the band that became known as 'N Sync was: Chris Kirkpatrick, Charles Edwards, Justin Timberlake, Joey Fatone (pronounced Fa-*tone* not Fat one) and JC Chasez. The odd man out is easy to spot: Charles Edwards never features in any of the histories of the phenomenally successful boy band. He is one of two amazing revelations that have been airbrushed out of the official 'N Sync biographies in favour of more convenient fan fodder. As the first 'N Sync record boss Lou Pearlman observes, 'Charles is a great story. He is a two-time Pete Best.'

Pete Best achieved an unwanted slice of rock 'n' roll fame by being the first drummer in the Beatles. He was replaced by Ringo Starr, and missed out on untold riches and legendary status. Charles Edwards is the unlucky singer who came within touching distance of glory, first with Backstreet Boys and then with 'N Sync. The musical success of 'N Sync and, ultimately, the artist Justin Timberlake owed a great deal to following in the footsteps of Backstreet Boys and to the regard in which Lou Pearlman held Charles Edwards.

Lou Pearlman, aka Big Poppa, is one of the moguls of pop for whom the cliché 'larger than life' actually rings true. He is a massive presence both physically and in the aura he has aquired as the multimillionaire boss of the Trans Continental conglomerate. His reputation is controversial, to say the least, especially in the wake of bad-tempered lawsuits involving Backstreet Boys and 'N Sync. But he is held in the highest regard by those who recognize his loyalty and enthusiasm for the projects in which he becomes involved. As a risk-taking entrepreneur, he has few peers in the music business. He sits behind an enormous desk at his Orlando offices while a succession of business folk try to interest him in their latest money-making scheme. Occasionally, he will open a drawer to reveal not important files and papers but a galaxy of chocolate bars.

Although he has made his home surrounded by the sunshine and the palm trees of Orlando, Lou is proud to be a native New Yorker. He grew up in a one-bedroom apartment in a working-class area in the borough of Queens, not far from the home of the US tennis championships in Flushing Meadow. His father ran a small dry-cleaning business and his mother was the milk lady at his school. His parents followed a blueprint for raising their only child that was similar to the one Lynn and Paul Harless used for Justin: 'I got so much support from my parents that I felt good about myself. They loved me so much, they made me believe in myself and in the potential for great things in my life.'

His entrepreneurial skills saw him graduate from running a lemonade stand and making deliveries of newspapers and doughnuts to getting a foothold in the aviation industry by recognizing the potential in airship marketing (airships are the blimps that dominate the skies at sporting and tourist events). His was a simple strategy of spotting a demand and supplying it, and one that would serve him well with Backstreet Boys and 'N Sync. In an earlier association with the world of music, he had supplied a spectacular airship for Pink Floyd's 1985 tour of the US. The blimp landed in the Rose Bowl car park in Pasadena, California, to launch publicity for the tour and then flew a step ahead of the band, helping to generate huge ticket sales in the cities where they would be performing

Lou has referred to his dalliance with music as a midlife crisis, but it is one that has so far brought in $2 billion (£1.1 billion) in gross worldwide sales. He did have one important musical contact to turn to for advice – Art Garfunkel is his cousin, the son of Lou's father's sister. Simon and Garfunkel were not, however, the inspiration for Lou going into the music business. His was another head that was turned by the phenomenal success of New Kids on the Block. It was not the talents of the New Kids that caught Lou's attention but the fact that they had been 'put together' by Maurice Starr who, starting from scratch, had turned them into a multi-million-dollar money-making machine. Lou's cousin 'Artie' was on the same record label and told him that Starr had masterminded a brilliant promotional and marketing campaign for the teen market. Lou was hooked. He wanted to find an alternative to New Kids in Florida, starting from scratch.

Backstreet Boys was the result. The band was hugely significant for Justin and 'N Sync because Lou would adopt the maxim that if it worked well once, it could work again. A series of newspaper ads followed by auditions led to him finding five promising guys. They included Charles Edwards and a 12-year-old boy, Nick Carter. Nick set a precedent for a young teenage lead singer in a band of young men – a Justin prototype. Coincidentally, Nick, a seasoned young pro like everyone breaking into Florida show business seemed to be, had been set to join *The Mickey Mouse Club* before deciding to take a chance on a pop career. The irony is that if he had joined *MMC* as Justin's contemporary, he might well have ended up in 'N Sync rather than in Backstreet Boys. The coincidences surrounding Justin and Backstreet Boys did not end there. Backstreet's AJ McLean won $1,000 (£550) in a Miami talent contest, in which he sang, danced and performed a puppet show. The only thing he did not do was parade up and down the catwalk in sportswear.

Charles Edwards was a young singer who seemed to fit in perfectly at the auditions that Lou held in a warehouse in Tampa where he stocked parts for his aircraft. Unfortunately, it soon became apparent to everyone that Charles was not up to the required vocal standard. Lou recalls that a difficult decision needed to be made: 'He wasn't singing powerfully enough, and his voice wasn't blending with the others. Nick, AJ and Howie felt kind of sad when Charles left. It was a very emotional time for a group just starting out.'

Nobody enjoys telling anyone they're out and Lou liked Charles, so he told him his door would remain open if he went away, took some lessons and improved his voice. Lou said he would help him in the future if he could – luckily for Justin and 'N Sync. Charles did come back and see Lou two years later with a friend, Chris Kirkpatrick, with whom he was hoping to put together a boy band that could sing *a cappella*. Backstreet Boys had yet to make it really big, but they were well on the way. They were following the path 'N Sync would soon tread by going to Europe to hone their skills and to find a fanbase to start building a brand.

Chris Kirkpatrick is probably due the most credit in the formation of 'N Sync. He never lost faith and he displayed admirable determination. He deserved some good fortune. He had dragged himself up from a poverty-stricken childhood in Pennsylvania. His father had left the family when Chris was a year old and money was at such a premium that at one time he, his mother and four younger half-sisters were homeless and living in a Chevy Suburban. He told the *New York Times*, 'We went a lot without food. It was almost an everyday thing. All the money we had would go on bills and stuff like that. We didn't have a phone. We didn't have a car.' There was no *Mickey Mouse Club* for Chris when he was thirteen. Instead, he could be found shovelling sheep dung on a farm near Pittsburgh trying to earn some extra money for the family while he went to high school. The family moved to Dayton, Ohio, where Chris attended high school. He concentrated most of his energies on music: he took roles in the classic musicals *Oliver* and *South Pacific*, and learned to play trombone, guitar and keyboards. When he was sixteen, he worked in an all-night grocery store from 4 a.m. to 8 a.m., when he went off to school.

Perhaps to compensate for the grim times at home, as well as to stop getting bullied at school, Chris became a joker, the proverbial class clown, always doing crazy things and acting spontaneously. His manic sense of humour, almost Monty Pythonesque, was one of the reasons he became such good friends with Justin even though there was a ten-year difference in their ages. Chris made Justin laugh by inventing a pet tree that he took for walks. He even pretended the tree peed on passing dogs.

After finishing high school, Chris went on to graduate from Valencia College with an arts degree before starting a psychology degree at Rollins College in Orlando. He was much more interested in a music career and had wanted to audition for Backstreet Boys. Unfortunately, he had the wrong colour hair – brown; Lou needed a blond to complete his picture of how the group should look. Chris had to take peripheral showbiz jobs to help pay the bills and to stay on the edge of the entertainment fraternity. He worked as a waiter at an Outback steakhouse in Orlando and, more significantly as a member of the Hollywood Hi-Tones, an *a cappella* group, consisting of three guys and a girl, who entertained people outside the fifties diner at Universal Studios. Chris had to do six shows a day – a tough introduction to the world of showbiz. At least it meant that Chris met like-minded people such as Charles Edwards and Joey Fatone. He did not meet Justin Timberlake then, but he had heard on the music grapevine that Justin was a very talented young performer on *The Mickey Mouse Club*.

When Chris met Lou Pearlman with Charles, he was hungry for success. Already twenty-four, he was quite old to be involved in a boy band, but Lou could appreciate his talent as a singer. Lou was also very impressed with the improvement in the voice of Charles Edwards: 'He sounded phenomenal.' Lou and the boys discussed the possibility of starting up a group. Lou's philosophy was a sound business one. He didn't want another talented bunch of guys signing to a rival record company and stealing Backstreet Boys' thunder.

'First up I told them, "You've got to have an anchor – someone with a very strong voice who could take the lead." Chris knew of someone who had mentioned a Justin Timberlake, who was living at home with his folks in Memphis, Tennessee, and had a fine high tenor voice. We knew he had been on the *Mickey Mouse* TV show but was now going to school and leading a normal kid's life. I watched an early tape of him on *Mickey* and was so impressed I decided to call him up at his parents' house. This person answered the phone and I said, "Can I speak to Justin?" and this deep voice said, "This is Justin." I had thought it was his dad! I told him, "You're speaking kind of deep, Justin." He said, "Yes, my voice changed. It got lower." We had a laugh about that and I invited him and his folks to come down to Orlando for an audition and to talk about our plans for a group.'

Justin flew down with Lynn and Paul, and Lou took them to a Mexican restaurant called Chevy's, where he, Charles and Chris outlined their plans. Lou recalls that Lynn, who had been agonizing over Justin's future after *The Mickey Mouse Club* was cancelled, thought it all sounded great. Lynn's management career would take shape in these early days of starting the band.

Despite the name, Trans Continental Records was not a record company. It was a production company, a grooming company, where Lou would invest in acts and, with luck, mould them into something so successful his investment would be repaid tenfold and more. Lou quickly recognized that Justin was perfect boy band material, claiming that he had his first vision of Justin's face on the cover of all the teen magazines within a few minutes of meeting him. The 'N Sync history books never said it but, in Lou's mind, Justin was clearly recruited as the figurehead of the band – the Ronan Keating or Gary Barlow figure who would go on to bigger things.

Five was the magic number, so Justin, Chris and Charles needed to look for two more guys to join them. It was at Chevy's – now a regular hangout – that Justin first mentioned JC Chasez. After the demise of *The Mickey Mouse Club*, the two had kept in touch, meeting up in Nashville, where JC helped Justin record some demos that ultimately he did not need. Justin convinced everyone that JC was superb at harmonies. JC was working at a restaurant in Baltimore, Maryland, when he received the invitation to go to Orlando. Lou Pearlman's first impression was of his hair: 'He had grown it real long. I told him he should cut it, because we've got to make this boy band pay.' (One of the differences between JC and Justin was that the former liked his hair while the latter hated his.) By the time the band was up and running, JC's hair and general look was a cross between George Chakiris in *West Side Story* and jockey Frankie Dettori.

Joshua Chasez was born in Washington, DC, but was brought up in Maryland. He was yet another precocious youngster who decided to pursue a show business career after he won a talent contest in his home state – this time as a dancer. The influence of the curious American phenomenon of junior talent contests is so pronounced that it is hard to find one of the current crop of young entertainers in the US who did not win one. JC is nearly five years older than Justin and was a veteran of five seasons of *The Mickey Mouse Club*, including a spell as presenter. JC had been very shy about performing as a young teenager. After winning a number of competitions as a dancer, he signed up for the vocal contest on a whim. His family knew he had a superb tenor voice, but they were the only ones who did. Even his dance teacher, who paid his entrance fee for the vocal part of the talent contest, had never heard him sing. She heard him for the first time when he performed the Richard Marx ballad 'Right Here Waiting'. He won, despite the cheesiness of the song.

JC later claimed that his shyness was more his desire for perfection: he did not want to perform unless he was sure he could do it in the very best way. Perfectionism is something he shares with Justin. Although they are two very different characters, Justin and JC probably had the most in common musically in the band. Sometimes fans would have trouble telling the two fine tenor voices apart, and it is no coincidence that they are the two band members who have released solo albums.

Orlando seemed to be overrun with teenage wannabes – a sort of Hollywood for kids who haven't started shaving. Joey Fatone was another familiar face looking for a break. His ambitions lay more towards becoming an actor than a singer, but in show business you must grasp any opportunity. His family had moved from New York to Florida when he was thirteen, and he had tried his hardest to break into *The Mickey Mouse Club* with no success. He did get to know the cast though, especially JC, who was the same age. After he left school, Joey found work at Universal Studios, which is where he met Chris Kirkpatrick. Joey was playing a werewolf called Wolfie in a show called *The Beetlejuice Graveyard Revue* – not exactly the first place one might have looked for a potential boy band member. Lou Pearlman recalls that they all went over to see Joey perform and thought he was great.

Joey was a ladies' man, full of twinkle and sparkle. He loved to flirt, a quality that would prove invaluable in the band's stage act. Bob Fischetti, Lou's right-hand man, observes, 'All the guys had different personalities, but Joey was the Italian lover.'

Unlike the others, he had grown up with a background in the music business. His father Joe, Sr., had been the singer in a Brooklyn doo-wop group called The Orions, who specialized in fifties and sixties songs. Joey puts his father's group as his number one musical influence, just ahead of Boyz II Men.

The whole 'selection' process was much less complicated and painful than it had been for Backstreet Boys, when Lou had sat through more than 100 auditions to try to find the right five boys. This was different. The boys had found each other just by talking and remembering people who might fit in. Nothing is that easy though, and Charles Edwards was about to drop a bombshell. Lou recalls, 'We were all feeling really good and then, out of the blue, Charles announces that he has met a young girl and wants to get married. I was shocked when he left.' Lou later heard that Charles did not have his heart in the group, which was a shame after all the hard work he had put into improving his vocals. Enthusiasm is a vital ingredient during the long hours of rehearsal and the weeks and years waiting to be discovered by the record-buying public. Charles Edwards is divorced now, but still speaks to Lou on the telephone every so often. It would be a miracle if fate came knocking on his door a third time.

So Justin, JC, Chris and Joey had to rack their brains for someone to fill Charles's shoes. Joey, who had lived full time in Orlando for longer than the others and who went to high school in the city, recommended a guy he knew who worked at Flipper's Pizza. His name was Jason Galasso, a friendly, easygoing guy who everyone thought would fit in well. At this stage, the principal occupation of the band was talking about what they were going to do. Lou was hinting that he might arrange for them to go to Germany at some stage, because that had worked so well for Backstreet Boys. Paul and Lynn joined them all for a meal at Chevy's one day when the pressing matter of the band's name came up. As Lou remembers it, 'Lynn was talking and said, "You know, these guys just sound so tight together, they sound very much in sync."' It was an Archimedes moment and, while no one jumped up and shouted, 'Eureka!', 'In Sync' was picked as a promising name.

There are two versions of what happened next. In one, it was Lou Pearlman who noticed that you could spell 'N Sync' using the last letters of the band's first names. In the second version, it was Justin's mother who was playing around with the names and noticed you could get 'N Sync from JustiN, ChriS, JoeY, JasoN and JC. This really was the Eureka! moment, because the name 'N Sync had a little extra edge to it.

It was all systems go for 'N Sync, or at least it would have been, if Jason hadn't announced that he wanted to leave. 'Are you mad?' blasted Lou Pearlman. 'This can blow up huge.' But Jason was adamant, and responded, 'I don't think 'N Sync is happening.' Jason Galasso has now followed Charles Edwards into the delete file of 'N Sync history, although over the years he has amused friends in Orlando with how he nearly made it big. Although his departure was a disappointment to the remaining four, it was far better for these hiccups to happen before the band started making deals and records.

The four remaining members of 'N Sync had to take stock. They needed to get it right the next time. There was a feeling that what they were lacking was a clear bass voice. Joey could sing baritone, but the group needed some 'bottom end'. Justin decided to ring Bob Westbrook, his old vocal coach. Bob was teaching a young man who instantly came to mind: 'Justin called me, and he said, "Bob, I need you to give me some of the students' names, because we have to try to get a bass for the group." So I gave him Lance's name. Lance's second name was Bass, so it was kind of a sign. Justin rang off, but then his mother Lynn phoned and said, "I need some more names." I told her, "I'll give you some more names if Lance doesn't work out. Go and get him down there and we'll pay his plane fare. Just get him down there and audition him, and if for some reason it doesn't work out, I've got some more names I can give you." But I felt that Lance would be the guy.'

Lance did not have the show business credentials that Justin and the rest of the boys had. The nearest he had come to Disney was carrying around a Mickey Mouse toy until he was five – this was one of those nuggets of information fed to the teen magazines. He was a southern boy like Justin, from a small town in Mississippi. His mother was a teacher and his father worked for the local phone company. He had enjoyed a very solid and stable Christian child-hood, rather like Justin's: 'I was born in a really small town [Laurel] in southern Mississippi, where you didn't have to keep your doors locked and you didn't have to worry about murders and things like that. As a kid I was very secure. I wasn't scared of anything.'

His boyhood ambition was not to dress up in a white suit and be Elvis but to don a space suit and be Neil Armstrong. He belonged to a successful state touring choir, but was not bitten by the show-biz bug until he was fourteen and went to see Garth Brooks in concert. It inspired him, although he expected to finish high school and go on to university. Then he took the call inviting him to Orlando to try out for a band. His mother Diane was far from happy at the prospect. Lance was only sixteen and still a home-body, a million miles away from the relatively experienced Justin Timberlake, despite being two years older. For a 14-year-old, Justin was an old hand.

Diane Bass sought out Bob Westbrook, who did his best to allay her concerns: 'She was on the point of tears over the phone because she just didn't want to think about Lance going down there. I told her, "Lynn knows what she is doing and you can trust that these guys will be good. Don't worry about it, please go down and do the audition. Nobody's committing you to anything."'

Lance and Diane made the trip to Orlando and it changed their lives. Lance sang 'The Star-Spangled Banner' for everyone and then all the guys sang it to see how their voices sounded together. By this time, Lou had brought in a musical coordinator and voice coach called Robin Wiley: 'She was great because she helped us audition with the guys and gave them the sound. She met with Lance and thought he was fantastic. We all did. We liked him and we decided to put it all together. Lance helped the sound of the band and Lance Bass was a really cool name!' Robin was a vital figure in the development of Justin's career and, more specifically, his sound. He immortalized her in a vote of thanks on the first 'N Sync album with a dedication to Robin Wiley Coyote.

Lynn and Lou's powers of persuasion were such that within a short space of time Diane Bass moved from being uneasy about her son's trip to Orlando to quitting her job and moving into a house about a mile from where Lou had rented one for the boys on Doctor Phillips Boulevard. Her husband Jim joined her soon afterwards and Lance was able to continue living at home while treading the path to success with 'N Sync. Lance was the closest in age to Justin, but they were not very similar. Lance was less exuberant and more practical, particularly when it came to business.

Back in Memphis, Bob Westbrook was delighted his matchmaking had been such an instant success. 'Lance worked out fine. But so far, I haven't got my Mercedes,' he jokes. The boys generously put 'Thanks for Lance!' on their first album sleeve.

One thorny problem remained. What were they going to do about the name of the band now that Lance had replaced Jason? They could not very well call themselves 'E Sync'. Lou recalls, 'Lynn just said, "We're going to call you Lansten" and we all laughed. We had LansteN and we kept it 'N Sync.' It was one of those wonderful rock 'n' roll moments in which a myth is created in a casual conversation. The true story of how 'N Sync came about has become blurred over the years. The parts played by Charles Edwards and Jason Galasso have been lost in the image building on which the pop business thrives. Instead, an unassuming teenager from Mississippi suddenly acquired a new first name.

'Let's call it *NSYNC.'

8

Pop Central

Justin came off stage with his thumb throbbing and swollen. Lynn asked him what had happened. 'I landed on it the wrong way,' he replied. An X-ray showed that he had broken his thumb. It happened during the first number, 'I Want You Back', but he had soldiered on for the rest of the gig. Lou Pearlman was impressed: 'We knew from early on that nothing was going to stop this guy.'

Five young men stood on the verge of something. Or maybe of nothing. They had not even signed a deal with Lou Pearlman yet. That did not happen formally until April 1996, although Lou had seen the potential and was keen to have the band on his books. Neither Lou Pearlman nor Justin's infectiously driven mother Lynn Harless could guarantee success. You cannot force a young teenager to part with their – or their parents' – money to buy a record. 'N Sync had some big advantages when they entered the game. Crucially, they were from the same stable as Backstreet Boys, who were acting as minesweepers, slowly picking out the best route to success. 'N Sync could follow the flags Backstreet Boys left in the pop minefield. Bob Fischetti observes, ''N Sync stepped right into the format.' They also had sound financial backing. Money was not a concern for this fledgling band, as Lou was paying for everything. It always sounds romantic if a band has to scrape together the few dollars for a tank of petrol to travel to a gig in a broken-down van. The reality is that sort of struggle for fame is an unwelcome distraction and can sap morale. 'N Sync were also, relatively speaking, old hands. They had already confronted the twin impostors of triumph and disaster. Justin had put the disappointment of losing ignominiously on *Star Search* behind him to achieve a childhood ambition with *The Mickey Mouse Club*. That, too, had led to nothing when it was cancelled, but he was ready to have another go.

The 'N Sync image machine wanted to project Justin, Lance, Joey, JC and Chris as regular guys and 'not as a pre-packaged rent-a-band assembled by big-time music promoters'. The reality was slightly different. While it is true that 'N Sync were not put together as a result of a ten-week television show like pop disasters Hear'say or One True Voice, the band was a show business unit in which the boys shared the common bond of a thirst for fame. The band members were not discovered playing blues or jazz in Greenwich Village bars. They were basically wannabes trying to get a break in the Hollywood of Florida. It is no coincidence that Orlando has Disney, Universal, Sea World and other Californian favourites. These young men were not postmen or plumbers or people with 'regular' jobs. They were two former *Mickey Mouse Club* performers, Wolfie in *The Beetlejuice Graveyard Revue*, a singer with the Hollywood Hi-Tones and, in Lance's case, a young man who had been a member of the Mississippi Show Stoppers. One thing they all knew about show business was that you don't get anywhere without a great deal of hard work and your fair share of luck.

'N Sync House, aka The Compound, was a house Lou rented for the boys – and Lynn – near the marketplace on Doctor Phillips Boulevard. Lance and Joey would continue to live mainly with their parents, but this would be Justin's home for the next few years; although, when touring began in earnest, home became whatever hotel room he was in at the time. Lou had put Backstreet Boys in one house and it had worked well for them, so he adopted the same practical strategy with 'N Sync. He explains, 'The house idea was a place that they could live in and do their own thing, be able to practise and play in and no one would disturb them – and it was just cheaper than getting a hotel.'

It was late 1995 and 'N Sync were some time away from reaching the consciousness of teenage girls, so the hordes of young fans encamped outside the house were still to come. Lou knew all about that side of fame from the attention his house in the affluent suburb of Windermere received from girls hoping to catch a glimpse of the members of Backstreet Boys. He made sure 'N Sync House was set back from the road and had a long driveway.

Justin has never suffered from the kid-in-the-candy-store syndrome where girl fans are concerned. He prefers to be involved in a relationship. At this early stage of 'N Sync's development he was in love with Danielle Ditto. She remembers Lou coming round to check on things at the house: 'He would come over to make sure they were doing everything right – like, "I'm not paying you to sit around" and stuff. He was like a father to them. We went over to Lou's house one evening because Justin wanted me to see it. It was amazing. You pressed a button and the TV came down from the ceiling. I walked into the kitchen and there was a couch in it – a couch in the kitchen! I was looking for the bathroom and I saw this guy asleep on the bed and I realized he was a Chippendale. I had to call my mom and tell her, "I saw a Chippendale!"'

A familiar face was another early visitor to 'N Sync House. Justin was then fourteen. At the end of the summer vacation, he would normally have been starting high school. Enter Chuck Yerger. Lynn was keen for Chuck to take charge of Justin's further education. Danielle recalls Chuck being quite hard on Justin at this stage, perhaps realizing that the finer points of Shakespeare might not be the number one priority for a boy set on becoming a superstar. Chuck brought in a colleague from On Location Education, Brenda Crenshaw, to share the load, and between them they set about making sure Justin received the education Lynn wanted him to have. Lou's company, Trans Continental, picked up the bill for 'tutoring expenses'. Lynn enrolled Justin in the University of Nebraska Home School Programme, which was basically like an Open University course leading to graduation but for students of school age.

Chuck would drive up to the house whenever the boys were in town and spend a few hours teaching Justin. At the beginning it was relatively easy to keep this routine, but it became more difficult as their careers accelerated. Later on he would teach Lance too, but his primary reason for turning on to Doctor Phillips on a Sunday morning was to try to get Justin out of bed. Justin is not at his best in the mornings in any case, but especially not when Chris and JC were having an easy time. Justin would sit at the dining table, munching a huge bowl of cereal, while Chuck outlined the plan for the lesson. Chuck recalls, 'That kid loves cereal more than anyone I know. His cereal bowl would be the kind you use to make a cake in.'

It may seem a little hard to comprehend but Justin Timberlake, heart throb of 'N Sync was really a schoolboy. His age was never an issue within the group and the other four did not take advantage or patronise him because he was the baby of the band. Justin was an athletic, well built teenager who never appeared on stage as a gawky kid. He had always been a good dancer, learning moves watching MTV at home in Shelby Forest. The physical side of performing came more easily to him than the others although they were all spurred on by a common desire to succeed. They spent long hours working on singing and harmony with Robin Wiley as well as improving their dancing skills with choreographer Robert Jacquez. He had a very difficult job to do, helping to come up with routines that the boys could perform while singing. Justin recognised the importance of his own personal fitness level. You are not going to be at your best if you are wheezing and spluttering after two minutes of leaping around on stage. It is no coincidence that Justin would adopt a regime of 300 push ups a day when he was preparing to tour.

While the boys were putting in the hours of song and sweat, Johnny Wright, the manager of Backstreet Boys, became involved in the development of 'N Sync. He was a very experienced music industry figure who had started out on the pop road by driving a van for the New Kids on the Block manager Maurice Starr. He became the tour manager. At the height of 'N Sync's success, Maurice wryly commented, 'He was under my wing, and right now I'd like to be under his.' Wright was to become one of the most influential figures in the career of Justin Timberlake. He possesses a vital asset – Justin's trust. He was just turning thirty when he was hired by Lou Pearlman to take charge of turning Backstreet Boys into stars. Johnny proved to be the pop brains, whereas Lou was the business brains. Together they formed a formidable partnership until relations became more strained when 'N Sync grew massively successful. Johnny observed, 'Lou's very good at writing cheques. I'm the artist-development person.'

Wright, whose mild manner conceals a hard edge, had moved to Orlando in the early nineties for the weather. He was from Cape Cod but had grown sick of the harsh New England winters. He was managing the chart band Snap when Pearlman contacted him to ask if he would take on Backstreet Boys. He was not interested until his wife Donna checked them out and reported that she was impressed. Crucially for his later dealings with Justin and the boys, he shared the same long-standing Christian values. He used to wear a baseball cap emblazoned with the letters WWJD – 'What Would Jesus Do'.

At first Backstreet Boys were not too pleased that their manager was trying to copy their success with another boy band. Johnny acknowledged, 'I won't say we didn't go through that phase. But there's no animosity. The more vocal groups there are, the better it is.' This may have been wishful thinking by Johnny, because within a couple of years he had parted company with Backstreet Boys. For his part, Justin had never even heard of Backstreet Boys when the idea of being in a boy band first presented itself.

Lou Pearlman's number one tip for creating a pop brand – and that is how he saw 'N Sync – is to the get the word out there 'any way you can'. In his book *Bands, Brands & Billions*, he describes the problems he had securing a record deal for Backstreet Boys. The record companies seemed to think boy bands had died with the demise of New Kids on the Block. So he and Johnny sent Backstreet Boys out to high schools and malls to try to build the word on the street and develop a fanbase. It is a strategy that has been proven to work, and one that Justin and the boys would follow too. 'N Sync produced a showcase video that they filmed at the Rock 'N' Roll Beach Club on Pleasure Island, Orlando. It was the basis for their first stage act aimed at school-age children. They did a set at the Doctor Phillips High School; Joey had graduated from there the summer before. Justin was an experienced performer in these sorts of locations from his early days with the Bob Westbrook Singers, singing at malls, schools and sporting events. Each mini concert was a showcase for the boys' talents. The idea was to get out there and try to reach as many people as possible: one new fan would be money in the bank at a later date.

Meanwhile, Johnny Wright was in Europe putting together the first 'N Sync record deal. The career of Backstreet Boys continued to be of enormous importance to 'N Sync. The Backstreet breakthrough happened across the Atlantic, specifically in Germany, after their first single, 'We've Got It Goin' On', flopped in the US. For good measure, it failed to break the top fifty in the UK, but in Germany it went into the top ten and the band were up and running. A six-month tour of Europe cemented their popularity. Armed with that success for their first group, Lou Pearlman and Johnny Wright were much better placed to help 'N Sync. It was business opportunism that secured the deal. The music business was a labyrinthine network of contracts and agreements, as Justin would later discover. Backstreet Boys were on Jive Records, but were distributed in Europe by the giant German record conglomerate BMG. When Jive decided to handle the distribution themselves, the BMG executive in charge of the German, Swiss and Austrian territories, Thomas Stein, spoke to Lou and said, 'I can't believe that we blew up Backstreet Boys and now they're famous we're losing them.' Lou, before you could blink, responded, 'We have another group you might be interested in.' After some discussions, two senior BMG representatives flew to Orlando to take a look at 'N Sync for themselves. Lou recalls, 'They thought the group was great, but they weren't hit by Lance. They thought Lance was a little slow with the dancing, but we insisted he would be fine with some more good practice. So in the end they said, "Great." We stuck up for Lance and kept the group as it was.' On 4 August 1996, 'N Sync signed with RCA, under the BMG corporate umbrella. Six days later they were in Munich to perform a couple of *a capella* songs at a summer pop party so the BMG executives could see their latest signings. In an untimely reminder of the concert night at E. E. Jeter, the power failed. It was dark, but, just as Justin had done in the school gym, the boys calmly sang as if nothing had happened. It probably did them good, because Lou enthuses, 'They were fantastic.' It also proved conclusively right from the start that 'N Sync could sing – not previously perceived as a prerequisite for boy and girl bands.

When he returned to Orlando, Justin could barely contain his excitement at the band's progress. When Chuck Yerger came over to the 'N Sync House to give him a lesson, Justin exclaimed, 'Mr Yerger, we blew them away. We came in from the back, because we wanted to prove to them we could really sing and then we jumped into a high-tech dance number.'

Justin and the boys had boarded the rollercoaster, but it would be another nineteen months before they released an album in the US. During the early live shows in Europe, Justin began to blossom as a performer. Lou Pearlman observes, 'Justin was already the heart-throb, the young kid that people loved. The young girls thought he was definitely the one.' And while Justin was moving towards the spotlight within the group, Lynn was becoming the power off stage. Justin was still very young and for the first eighteen months of his career with 'N Sync, Lynn would travel everywhere with him as his chaperone. She and Diane Bass both went to Europe and were in the wings every night, enthusiastically applauding and urging on their sons.

Lynn's determination that Justin was going to be a success perhaps explains her strong reaction to the Danielle Ditto affair. She did not want any distractions when he was within touching distance of that goal. She was prepared to make sacrifices in her own life. She cried when she gave up the family cat Millé, a beautiful white, fluffy pedigree Persian who had been Justin's cat when he was growing up. In all she had seven names and was very posh, but everybody called her Millie. The huge amount of time the boys were to spend in Europe over the next year meant it became increasingly difficult to look after Millé. Paul's work meant he was travelling more than in previous years and he saw Millé only one day a week. Justin's grandmother popped in every day to feed her, but Lynn reluctantly decided that a year of this lonely existence was enough for Millé and she deserved a new home.

By lucky chance, Lynn was at Chuck and Sherry Yerger's house on Thanksgiving and noticed they had a sleek Siamese cat. She explained about Millé and asked them if they might consider looking after her. 'She said they thought it was unfair to the cat,' recalls Chuck. 'So we agreed and they brought her round at Christmas – this big old white thing. I remember that both Sherry and Lynn were crying. Whenever Lynn spoke to Sherry afterwards, she would ask, "How's my Millie?"'

Timing is crucial in the music business. 'N Sync's shadowing of Backstreet Boys was like Burger King opening up a franchise next to McDonald's. At the beginning of October 1996, 'N Sync's first single, 'I Want You Back', was released in Germany. They had recorded it at the Cheiron Studios of Swedish DJ and producer Denniz PoP in Stockholm. Denniz, whose real name was Dag Volle, and his songwriting partner and friend Max Martin had written early Backstreet songs, including 'Quit Playing Games With My Heart' and 'Nobody But You'. Backstreet Boys had a string of massive European hits that year, and the timing was perfect for 'N Sync to cash in on reflected glory. A week before its release, 'I Want You Back' was played 103 times on German radio. A week after its release, it was in the German charts. The song was catchy but formulaic and not a patch on the band's later work. It was described by *Bop* magazine as 'Oh so sweet'. That did not worry the teenagers of Sweden, where it raced to number one.

Denniz PoP was a hugely influential music figure of the nineties, responsible not just for the boy band sounds of Backstreet Boys and 'N Sync but also for Britney Spears. In the eighties he was a DJ who became one of the most sought after remixers in the business. His treatments of Michael Jackson's 'Billie Jean' and Donna Summer's 'Love To Love You Baby' breathed fresh life into those classic numbers. He reached a wider audience in the early nineties when he wrote and produced a song for a new Swedish band called Ace of Base. The song, 'All That She Wants', reached number one in the UK, where it sold more than 600,000 copies. The group's debut album, *The Sign*, sold 22 million copies worldwide – a figure that made Lou and Johnny sit up and take notice in Orlando.

Although Denniz was more influential in the career of

Backstreet Boys, he was the driving force behind the dance sound of the nineties that dominated the charts worldwide in the same way that Stock, Aitken and Waterman had in the late eighties. He became affectionately known as the 'Dancemeister'. Although it was written by Max Martin, no song captures that sound better than 'Baby One More Time', the song that launched Britney Spears to superstardom. Britney was particularly upset when Denniz was struck down by cancer at the age of thirty-five. He died in August 1998. At the MTV Europe Music Awards in 1999, 'Baby One More Time' won Best Song and Britney dedicated the award to the memory of Denniz PoP. Her first album also contains the dedication: 'To Denniz PoP: Your memory lives on in the beautiful music you wrote for me. Thank you.'

His legacy to 'N Sync was the song that put them on the pop music map. It was time for the publicity machine to explode into action. When a record company decides to get behind a band, media raids are practically continuous. The first news story about 'N Sync appeared on Bravo, claiming they would be the next Backstreet Boys. Eventually their rivals got more than a little fed up with 'N Sync. Justin and the boys followed a routine of interviews, photo sessions and performances throughout Germany in the coming weeks. They were the opening act on the German tour of DJ Bobo – not exactly a household name in the UK. Frequent playing of their video on MTV helped generate excitement among young female German fans. In Munich, girls threw cuddly toys and knickers on to the stage. Even better, they chased the tour bus after the show, which meant the band was an hour late for a reception with record company executives to celebrate the end of their first promo-tour. The tour could hardly have gone better. It set a standard of relentless engagements creating maximum exposure that few bands have ever attained. Between 7 October, when the single was released, and 9 November in Munich, they had one day off. It was time to return to Orlando, recharge the batteries and think about the first 'N Sync album.

Debut albums for boy bands and assorted one-hit chart acts tend to be all about speed and product rather than music. The overriding impression of the first 'N Sync album, *'N Sync*, is that it doesn't do them justice. They sang nicely but one could not help feeling there was so much more to come – as turned out to be the case. The idea at this stage was to get material into the shops, perform the album at gigs, sell merchandise and build up the brand. Some of the lyrics were distinctly of the moon and June rhyming variety, particularly on the dire 'Here We Go . . . Feel the Flow . . .'. One of the problems with European pop is that the lyrics, written in English as a second language, tend to be simplistic, classroom stuff. Abba set the standard with 'Waterloo' and 'Super Trouper'. Justin's best moments on the album came on the ballads 'For The Girl Who Has Everything', for which he recorded additional vocals in Munich, and '(God Must Have Spent) A Little Time On You'. His soulful tenor provided an early indication that he was going to become a superb slow singer by the time he was ready to go solo.

Inevitably on a boy band debut, there were a couple of covers: the syrupy David Gates song 'Everything I Own' and the equally saccharine Christopher Cross hit 'Sailing'. The album also featured their second single, 'Tearin' Up My Heart', written by Max Martin and Kristian Lundin, another Backstreet Boys producer, and recorded at the Cheiron Studios. The boys flew to Stockholm and recorded the song in a day. The schedule was breathtaking – Warsaw, Munich, Stockholm, Frankfurt, Hanover, Zurich, in a whirlwind of interviews and TV shows. The hard work soon started to pay off, with an award from a German magazine for Best Newcomer of the Year and the news on 16 December that 'I Want You Back' had chalked up sales of 250,000 in Germany alone.

'N Sync would never have dreamed of saying so at this exciting time, but Lance Bass later revealed that they did not like a lot of the songs: 'We don't sing techno, but we had to put it on the album because of Germany.'

'Where there's a Coke, there's a Pepsi; where there's a Backstreet Boys, there's an 'N Sync.'

9

Huckleberry Finn

Justin and Veronica were kidding around and playfully wrestling at his home when out of the blue she blurted out, 'I love you.' She was so embarrassed: 'I was so shocked that it came out that I covered my mouth because I hadn't premeditated it at all and he started cracking up laughing and he said, "I love you too, calm down, and don't be shy." That was the first time he told me.'

Justin is one of the great thank-you men of pop. The dedications on his records are always personal and heartfelt. On the first 'N Sync album he gives a special 'shout-out' to his 'Huckleberry Finn'. It was not much of a clue tucked away in hard-to-read small print. Huckleberry Finn was Justin's second serious girlfriend, the second girl to whom he would declare his love. In the world of boy bands, an admission that you have a girlfriend is the ultimate publicity sin. The perceived wisdom is that you have to be seen to be available to all the young female fans who kiss your poster good-night before they turn off the light. The idea that the youngest and best looking member of 'N Sync was already attached would have sent millions reaching for the smelling salts. Veronica Finn was the object of Justin's affection, although it would have been impossible to have deduced that Huckleberry was a girl unless you were in the know.

Lou Pearlman professes to being relaxed about the boys being involved in relationships. That had certainly not been the case across the Atlantic with the premier British boy band Take That. Their strict and disciplined regime was partly responsible for the rebellious behaviour of Robbie Williams. But, crucially, 'N Sync chose to live their lives in a relatively responsible way. They did not embrace the debauchery of rock 'n' roll. Instead, Lance, Chris and Joey chose to thank God first and foremost in their dedications on *'N Sync,* while Justin thanked his saviour Jesus Christ. This is not bogus claptrap cynically promoting a Christian image. As Lance Bass confirmed to Larry King, 'God has been a huge part of our career.' One of the reasons the boys were so close was that they shared many of the same moral values. Justin's own moral code is simple. He asks himself the question: 'Would my parents approve of what I am doing?' This did not mean the band behaved like monks looking for the local 'kirke' every night when they were on the autobahn driving from one gig to the next.

'N Sync were so squeaky clean they were like pieces of chalk screeching down a blackboard, but Lou Pearlman maintains they never lied about girlfriends: 'We always said the boys dated and they did.' Justin's 'date' was a bubbly blonde girl from Memphis who was introduced to Justin by Trace Ayala. Veronica Finn had never heard Justin's name before Trace mentioned him. Justin was home for Christmas and Trace thought it was time his pal put Danielle Ditto behind him and met somebody new and fun. Veronica recalls, 'Trace had been telling me there was somebody I *had* to meet because he was certain we would hit it off. I went out with him to Justin's house and he just said, "This is Justin", and we took it from there.'

Veronica's parents had split when she was two and – just like Justin and Danielle – she had grown up very close to her grand-parents, who lived in Raleigh, a Memphis suburb. She also had a kid sister the same age as Justin's half-brother Jonathan, so from the outset they had family things in common. Veronica was living with her mother in Boulder, Colorado and, like Justin, had come home to Tennessee for Christmas when she first met him. 'I thought he was a really funny guy and he entertained me a lot. He was making me laugh. It was kind of strange because Trace had said, "This is a great girl" and "This is a great guy", but once we sat down and got talking we just had a good time. I met Lynn and Paul, and they made me feel comfortable.'

That first meeting was not really a date. They never even kissed before Veronica flew back to Colorado and Justin returned to Orlando to prepare for another assault on Europe. They had enjoyed a laugh together but nothing more than that – except Justin was smitten. Despite the opportunities presented by hordes of girls across the Atlantic who were prepared to throw themselves at him, this particular teenager preferred to spend his evenings on the telephone to a girl in Colorado he had met only once. 'He called me a lot,' she laughs.

About six months later, in mid 1997, Veronica was tired of Colorado and moved back to Memphis, where she ran into 16-year-old Justin again and, just as importantly, his mother Lynn. Justin was relaxing after the gruelling '*I Want You Back*' tour across Germany, but Lynn was busy putting together the female equivalent of 'N Sync. Her experiences with the band had inspired her to have a shot at management, with the financial backing of Lou Pearlman. The Spice Girls had exploded on to the music scene the previous year and Lynn thought there was a gap for a US equivalent, although her idea was for something a little more wholesome than the 'girl power' British band. The name she had chosen, Innosense, did not suggest these were girls who were going to get down and dirty.

By a twist of fate, Veronica was in the right place when Britney Spears decided not to become part of Lynn's group because she had been offered a solo opportunity – although there is the suspicion Britney's interest may have been exaggerated to gain Innosense a little publicity. Lynn thought Veronica would be perfect for the band. She was taller than Britney, with curly blonde hair that was more like Justin's. 'I don't think they were trying to emulate her when they replaced Britney with me. I think they just wanted to find someone that everyone got along with – that was the most important thing.' By this time Veronica was dating Justin and forging a lasting friendship with Lynn. Veronica asked Justin what he thought she should do: 'I said to him, "Would you care?", and he was like, "You're perfect for it." He was really encouraging.'

Although Veronica and Justin were dating, it was very young dating. Justin was not old enough to drive, so a friend would be behind the wheel when he picked Veronica up at her grandparents' house, and they would go to a party or just hang out. Their relationship did not move to another level until they were in Orlando together.

Veronica agonized about what to do. She knew her family were keen for her to finish high school and continue with the 'girl' things she enjoyed doing, like cheerleading. They did not want her to grow up too quickly. She had never dreamt of being the next Mariah Carey: 'I never wanted to be the most amazing singer in the world at all, but I did feel comfortable performing and I loved entertaining people. I had also been dancing all my life. Cheerleading is really good for dancing.'

One of the girls already signed up for Innosense was Nikki DeLoach, Justin's old friend from *The Mickey Mouse Club* who was JC Chasez's girlfriend at the time. 'Nikki had a big influence on me', says Veronica. 'She really pushed for me to be in the group. She was like "Come on, girl." We really clicked.' The other members of the group were Danay Ferrer, Mandy Ashford and Amanda Latona.

Eventually Veronica decided to take a chance on Innosense, but she had to do some serious coaxing where her family were concerned. 'My mom, grandma and grandfather all liked Justin. He came over to the house and hung out. But they wanted me to finish school and I was saying, "You don't understand! We're going to be famous." It was really childish dreaming. I was too young, but eventually they said, "Fine, see you later", and I got myself down to Orlando. I like Memphis, but when I came down to Florida I loved it. I felt like I was living in a fantasy world. I always wanted to be around palm trees.'

Justin himself has commented that his teenage friendships became intimate very quickly and that certainly happened with Veronica. He admits to being a 'hopeless romantic', who, when he falls, falls hard. Even Veronica's grandfather, Davie Lawrence, noticed it: 'He was in love. But Veronica cared a lot about him.'

Veronica appreciated being put on a pedestal by Justin: 'I was his girl and he treated me very respectfully. I know most girls want the bad boys kind of thing, but at the time it was just right. He wasn't overwhelming and it was never too much. I think Justin does like being in love, most definitely. I think he can get engulfed in that. He is very romantic and I loved that.'

Veronica, a little shyly, praises Justin as a very considerate lover, an unusual quality in a boy of his tender years: 'Oh yeah, I've dated since then!' laughs Veronica. 'We were very young, but Justin was very gentle and caring and did his best to make sure I was comfortable.'

The romantic idyll for Justin and Veronica was about to be broken up by that scourge of show business relationships – long absences. Instead of holding your lover in your arms, you are left holding the telephone night after night. Justin had to go back to Germany for the next phase of his bid for fame, and Veronica moved into 'N Sync House with the rest of Innosense to train hard for her chance to ride the rollercoaster. Lynn followed almost exactly the same rigorous pattern that had worked for Justin and the boys. Robin Wiley was brought in to be their vocal coach and arranger, and Brenda Crenshaw took care of Veronica's schooling with a little help from Diane Bass. Soon Lynn was able to cut down on her chaperoning duties.

It was about this time that Lynn persuaded her great friend Renée Earnest to join her as her right-hand woman. Renée has never lost the precious ability to make Justin laugh she has had since her days as his Apex teacher. 'Renée and Justin were always joking around together,' says Veronica.

Meanwhile, Justin telephoned Veronica from Europe. 'He was calling two or three times a day,' she recalls. 'He was very sweet. But he couldn't call when they were busy. I didn't like being in a long-distance relationship. At first it wasn't too bad because we were both having a great time. The trouble is if someone's not around me, I'm always wondering what they're doing. I just can't accept that they're being totally faithful.' The fact that Justin professes never to cheat because he doesn't believe in it is small consolation to a girl stuck thousands of miles away from her boyfriend.

Justin was too exhausted to have much fun. 'N Sync were doing well in Europe but nobody had heard of them in the US. Joey Fatone later explained the situation on *The Larry King Show*. 'We would get on a plane and there would be thousands of girls just waiting for us to get off the plane. We'd come home and our parents would be picking us up from the airport.' The reality for the fledgling pop stars was that they spent most of their days on a bus. Eventually they had a lucky break when Johnny and Lou persuaded some executives from RCA in America to watch the band perform in Budapest. A & R Director Vince Degiorgio told *Entertainment Weekly*, 'It was me, 11,000 girls and the band. I thought, I get this so much.' By this time, 'N Sync were experienced, seasoned pros who needed next to no grooming money from a US record label – an important consideration. RCA decided to take them on. At last!

Justin was understandably exhilarated when he returned home to Orlando. He immediately whisked Veronica off for an idyllic holiday in the Bahamas with JC and Nikki. Justin looked every inch the young pop star, with bleached blond hair and two gold earrings, but, for the moment, he could walk down the street unrecognized. Veronica recalls, 'Justin and I got along great. We got a hotel room and went on a cruise and I had my hair braided and got a tan. We had a really great time.' Veronica also discovered that waking up with Justin was not that easy. 'It took him a minute to wake up,' she confides.

That good time continued in Orlando while Justin and the boys re-recorded a video for 'I Want You Back' at Universal Studios and prepared for the release of their first US single with some promotional work. The first European video had a spaceship theme, but the new version had a more athletic, outdoors feel. More immediately, Justin celebrated his seventeenth birthday by taking delivery of a brand new, bright red Mercedes. Justin loves cars and this was the first of many. Veronica observes, 'He drives fast and I don't like it when people drive fast. But he likes nice, new cars. I remember that first car – it was a really groovy colour but he drove it so fast. I think he likes the excitement.'

Justin was growing up 'on the road' and enjoying having some money for the first time. He brought home a watch that he had specially picked out for Paul while 'N Sync were on tour in the Far East. He also bought a special pair of Buffalo shoes for Veronica. They were not yet available in Orlando and she was absolutely thrilled with the gift.

When the boys came back, Veronica and the girls had to move out of 'N Sync House and find their own House of Innosense nearby. Although they were living apart, Justin and Veronica were able to spend some time as a regular couple, going to the movies, eating in restaurants, going downtown and hanging out at Disney. They even had school lessons together just like a normal high school boyfriend and girlfriend. Like Justin, Veronica was the youngest member of her group: 'We actually thought it was cool being the youngest.' He kept up a constant stream of banter with the rest of 'N Sync. 'They're all big jokers!' says Veronica. Justin's best impression, according to Veronica, was of the rapper Mase, an early collaborator with Puff Daddy on hits such as 'Mo Money, Mo Problems' and 'Feel So Good'. Justin could also do some of the alien creatures from *Men in Black* and the other members of 'N Sync. These were happy, carefree times for Justin, who was very much in love and happy to tell Veronica how he felt. One of her favourite memories is of them dancing and singing in the rain outside the 'N Sync House.

The first 'N Sync album was released in the US on 24 March 1998. It had been a long road to the American record stores. The album had been repackaged for the US market, complete with a new 'N Sync logo. This was the first time *NSYNC was seen. Despite all the anticipation, success wasn't instant like it had been in Germany. Lou recalls that they had a lot of trouble persuading MTV to play the video of 'I Want You Back' because of a general feeling that Backstreet Boys were a fluke and there was no market for a new band like 'N Sync. 'I said, "Let me tell you something. I know exactly when this boy band business is over – when God stops making little girls", and they all laughed and said, "Yeah, you might have a point there."'

After the euphoria of a US break, it was a huge disappointment for Justin to realize the break was not necessarily the breakthrough. Instead the group concentrated their attentions on Canada – at least they were getting nearer! In his book, Lou Pearlman calls it: *If You Can't Get To Your Target Audience Through the Front Door Then Try the Back.* Once again Backstreet Boys had been the guinea pigs for the strategy. The idea was that if Canadian radio stations played the record as the band toured the country, the sound would cross the border, leading to requests being phoned in to American stations. If you were lucky, all the months of hard work would pay off when you were declared an 'overnight sensation'.

If Backstreet Boys were getting a little irked at the attention 'N Sync were attracting, then what happened next hit them like a thunderbolt. Disney wanted Backstreet for their first venture into pop broadcasting but, inexplicably, they turned it down. They were lined up to do the special when they told Johnny Wright they did not want to do it. According to Lou Pearlman, the band said they were too tired after a relentless bout of touring. It left Lou and Johnny with egg on their faces when they had to tell Disney that they could not deliver the band. Tina Treadwell of Disney was distraught, because this was to be the first-ever Disney Concert Special. Lou and Johnny grasped their opportunity. 'We said we had another group that's pretty big in Europe and were going to be coming back to the US with a name,' recalls Lou.

'She said, "Who's that?"

"'N Sync."

"I've never heard of them."

"Well, you will!"'

Tina reviewed her options and, with time running out, realized she did not have that many. She decided to take a chance on 'N Sync. On 18 July 1998 'N Sync got the biggest break any band could hope for.

Ironically, the concert was at the MGM studios where Justin and JC had spent so many days filming *The Mickey Mouse Club*. Even more of a coincidence was the location of the green room where friends and family gathered to wish them all luck. Lynn and Paul were there, as well as Randy Timberlake. It was the only time Chuck Yerger met Justin's real father. Justin came in and picked up his little half-brother Jonathan and gave him a hug. He did not realize where he was until Chuck said, 'Justin, you slacker, get to work!' He was in the old schoolroom. Both Justin and JC went to the spots where they used to sit and started talking about old times, which, if nothing else, helped to soothe the nerves.

Chuck Yerger says: 'I honestly don't think Disney knew there were two former Mouseketeers in the band. When the concert was shown, I don't think Disney was in any way, shape or form ready for the positive results they achieved. They must have shown the concert nine or ten times over the next six months. Obviously tens of thousands of people would have recognized Justin and JC, but they never made a point of it in the concert. I don't expect they could believe that two of the tootsy mouseketeers were now hip teenagers. 'N Sync tapped in to a national audience there and then.'

The band was unprepared for the response. Chris Kirkpatrick told *Entertainment Weekly*, 'Even after we filmed it, we just thought it was a little concert. I was like, "That was cool. Now we gotta go work on our careers."' Lou Pearlman, with a practised eye on the ball, saw dollar signs. The debut album *'N Sync* entered the Billboard chart at number nine and stayed in the top ten for several months to come, selling a million copies within a couple of months of the Disney special being transmitted. 'Record sales went through the roof,' he enthusiastically recalls. 'Wow, this TV stuff was pretty cool!' The album eventually produced an impressive four number one singles: 'I Want You Back', 'Tearin' Up My Heart', '(God Must Have Spent) A Little More Time On You' and 'Drive Myself Crazy'.

While 'N Sync were hitting the big-time, their female equivalent set off for Germany on the first leg of the now well-trodden path. This time the enforced absence was going to be more serious for Veronica and Justin. 'We were in Munich and they were starting their tour in the States. Britney was opening for them. I don't know what happened. I didn't feel like we were happening any more and I don't think he did either. It's a trust issue. At the time it could have been my own insecurity.'

Doubt became the cancer in their relationship. Both knew the other would have the opportunity to stray. Veronica calls it 'miscommunication', but the long-distance phone calls were no longer the fun, jokey conversations they used to be. Instead, they were fraught with unspoken insecurities. 'Justin never said, "Are you seeing someone else?", but he just thought I might have while they were gone. I'm sure he thought, like I did, there were possibilities.'

Justin's second love affair went the same way as the first; it was ended by telephone. Veronica left a message on his answerphone telling him not to call back. 'Eventually I did speak to him and we came to the mutual conclusion that we weren't going to mess with it any more. Once it gets to that kind of "Did you do this?" . . . I was ready to stop and I guess he was too.' Justin's mother was still the manager of Innosense, so it was important that the fallout wasn't too acrimonious. Veronica remains on very good terms with Lynn and Paul. She also gets on well with Justin and sees him as a friend. When she came back from Germany in late 1998, he had already embarked on a high-profile relationship with Britney Spears. It was uncomfortable for her at first, but she says, 'That was for a very short amount of time and then I didn't care at all. Once I saw that they were happy together it wasn't a big deal because I had started seeing someone.' Ironically, Innosense opened for two of Britney's tours, so it was just as well there was no hatchet that needed burying.

There was a sting in the tale for Veronica, however, when Justin, who clearly has a fixation with fidelity, claimed his first three girlfriends had cheated on him. He told *Rolling Stone*, 'They've all gone down the same way. All of them. Three strikes. I'm out.' Danielle Ditto admits to a kiss. Veronica Finn says she is totally innocent of any charge: 'We could have both been seeing other people. But I wasn't and, I don't know, even to this day . . . he *says* he wasn't.'

'Justin can be very dramatic.'

10

No Strings

The first time Justin played the Pyramid in Memphis he showed off to his friends from home. They were chatting on the bus surrounded by screaming girls. 'Watch this,' he said. He turned round, held up his hand and mouthed, 'Ssshhh!' The crowd fell silent, waiting for him to speak. He simply turned back round and carried on talking to his friends, and the screaming instantly began again.

Just when it seemed Justin had put the cheese back in the refrigerator, up popped the ultimate career Stilton, the 'N Sync Christmas album *Home for Christmas*. The year 1998 had been brilliant. The band's foothold in the US had been strengthened by their appearances as the opening act for Janet Jackson's *Velvet Rope* tour which, for the first time, took them to Memphis and gave Justin a chance to show his family and friends how far he had come. The highlight was an *a capella* version of the Stevie Wonder song 'Overjoyed', which 'N Sync performed with Janet. Somehow they had found time in September to dash in to the Trans Continental studios in Orlando to whizz through a new album. The product was a Christmas album that smacked of the desire to make a fast buck from the seasonal shopping mall market. It was nicely sung, but what on earth was the point? Cliff Richard, after a zillion years in the business, might get away with including 'The First Noel' on an album, but a newly discovered teenage band?

Justin did get the chance to sing 'O Holy Night', a song of many triumphs for him. Of more significance was that he was the first group member to be pictured in the sleeve booklet – all spiky blond hair and teeth. On the first album there was no sign of the Timberlake molars, but there seemed to be at least twenty on show here. Trans Continental Vice-President Bob Fischetti remains dazzled, 'The biggest thing that ever stays in my mind with that kid is his million-dollar smile. It could be mischievous; it could be innocent or smirky, or whatever kids wanted, but it always had a kind of cocky confidence, reflecting who he was, not in a bad way, but in a 100 per cent great way. It gave him an aura.

'I used to see him at parties we had and I'd always say, "You've got a million-dollar smile. That will take you places."'

Justin was subtly being pushed to the forefront of 'N Sync. When they shot the all-important Disney special, it was clear that Justin and JC, with their experience of *The Mickey Mouse Club*, were most aware of how to use the camera. Chuck Yerger, who had watched them on *MMC* years before, noticed it: 'Justin and JC knew how to play the cameras. They had watched themselves so often on tape that they instinctively knew what was a good move for the camera. As you watched the group progress, it was obvious Justin and JC were the centrepieces.'

There was never any question, however, of 'N Sync being Justin Timberlake's band. The boys all had equal billing, but Justin was the one with a little extra portion of star quality. Vocally, Justin shared the limelight with JC, and Veronica confesses even she had trouble telling their voices apart: 'They sounded very similar a lot of times, especially in the concerts. But they all have great voices in different ways. But I thought Justin had the best voice – because I was dating him!'

Home for Christmas is not exactly the highlight of the 'coolest man in pop's' CV, but it is balanced by other achievements. The band won Best Dance Clip and Best New Artist at the Billboard Music Video Awards for 'I Want You Back'. They also began their first US headlining tour in Orlando with Britney Spears as their opening act. It was the start of a colossal tour programme that made 'N Sync probably bigger as a touring band than they were as a recording band. *Home for Christmas* was the only new 'N Sync

113

album available to fans until March 2000. It reached number nine and sold 153,000 copies in the first week of December 1998. Undoubtedly, it was a commercial success and made a lot of money. The only problem for Justin and the boys was that it made Lou Pearlman significantly more money than it made them.

A good juicy lawsuit with copious amounts of mud-slinging is practically de rigeur for any self-respecting top-selling music artist. Lawyers do very nicely out of the minefield of pop contracts. It is not a new phenomenon by any means. The Rolling Stones had a protracted legal argument with their former manager Allen Klein. George Michael had a well-documented falling out with Sony. Robbie Williams fell foul of three managers and a record company before he was able to embark on a serious bid for solo stardom. 'N Sync, managed by a multimillionaire entrepreneur, were litigation waiting to happen. Pragmatism where legal action is involved is, however, something acquired with experience. For Justin, who was still a teenager, the perceived threat to his dreams was very real, especially when figures like $150 million (£82.5 million) were being tossed into the ring.

Justin was shattered by the whole experience with Lou Pearlman and BMG. He told *Face* magazine after the matter was resolved: 'It was horrible and my biggest low point. It's the one time I honestly said, "I don't want to do this any more." I thought our careers were over.' The dispute was, of course, about money, although it would be comforting to think it was for artistic integrity after *Home for Christmas*. Lou Pearlman had a draconian hold on the finances of 'N Sync. Flushed with the success of *'N Sync*, which had by then sold an astounding 7 million copies, the boys and their mothers wanted a better deal, but they were unable to agree new terms with Lou.

The band claimed that Lou Pearlman and Trans Continental Records had not fulfilled the terms of their contract with 'N Sync when they were signed to an American record label. As a result, they were free agents no longer signed to RCA. In an exceptionally bold move, they announced in the summer of 1999 that they had signed with Jive Records, home of Backstreet Boys and Britney Spears. Jive was run by South African-born record mogul Clive

Calder, a former bass guitarist who had once worked as a talent scout for EMI. Calder was particularly astute at recognising talent and by 2004 was estimated to have a net worth of $2.3 billion (£1.28 billion) making him the richest man in the whole of the music business. Justin holds him in the highest regard.

'N Sync already had their next album ready and waiting for release in November. Backstreet Boys, meanwhile were reportedly very unhappy at this news and, faced yet again with the spectre of 'N Sync, tried to extricate themselves from Jive. They had parted company with Johnny Wright the year before, allegedly because of the amount of time he was devoting to their rivals. A lawsuit – the first of many – involving Lou Pearlman and Backstreet Boys had been settled out of court. The squeaky clean boy band business was turning dirty.

The reaction from BMG, RCA's parent company, and Lou Pearlman to 'N Sync's defection was predictable: a massive lawsuit. When the media got hold of the story, it focused on Lou Pearlman because that was the personal angle. He was portrayed as a pop Svengali, an unscrupulous character running the equivalent of a sweatshop employing child labour. It made for a colourful story but tended to obscure the fact that big business was involved. A company as powerful as BMG were hardly likely to pat 'N Sync on the back, wish them luck and allow them simply to waltz over to a competitor. Millions and millions of dollars were at stake in royalties and the future earning potential of Justin and the band.

The complaint from BMG and Lou Pearlman, which was filed in the New York Superior Court in October 1999, sought to ban Justin, Joey, Lance, Chris and JC from recording or performing under the name 'N Sync. BMG also required the recordings for the new 'N Sync album so that it could be released on RCA Records. Lou's lawyers fanned the flames of controversy. Michael Friedman announced to the *Daily Variety*: 'It is absurd to think that now the members of 'N Sync have been made rich and famous, they can just turn their backs on Mr Pearlman . . . and go some place else.' Trial counsel J. Cheney Mason was even more outspoken: 'We're going to shut them down,' he declared. 'We believe there will be no tours, no performances, no rehearsal or recordings.'

This was scary stuff, even if it was mostly legal bluster. The threat of not being able to perform as 'N Sync was considerably more worrying than the financial aspects of the lawsuit, which in themselves were mind-boggling. BMG and Lou Pearlman were seeking $100 million (£55 million) in damages and $50 million (£27.5 million) in punitive damages. There was a lot at stake. The first album had been on the Billboard charts for eighty weeks, so the next album stood a good chance of being one of the most lucrative releases of the year.

Justin's response was to give the media a good soundbite, declaring that the lawsuit would not hold 'N Sync back, 'as long as I'm with my four friends and we stick together'. He told the *Toronto Star* that while he loved making music, he hated the music business. 'It's a screwball business and there are a lot of players who will straight up lie to you,' he declared.

The situation was further complicated by two other factors. 'N Sync were caught in the middle of an entirely separate renegotiation of BMG's distribution deal with Jive's parent company, Zomba, which could involve anything up to $1 billion (£550 million). Secondly, Johnny Wright decided to cut his ties with Lou Pearlman and hitch his wagon to Justin and the boys. They had become firm friends and continue to be.

The time had come for the rather dry legal battle to become much more personal. 'N Sync filed a counter-claim for $25 million (nearly £14 million) aimed specifically at Lou Pearlman and Trans Continental. The defence papers included statements from Johnny Wright – leaving no doubt where his loyalties now lay – Diane Bass and Lynn Harless. The most outspoken statement, gleefully reported in the press, was from JC Chasez. He claimed that Pearlman was an 'unscrupulous, greedy' businessman, who 'while hugging us and calling us "family" was picking our pockets, robbing us of our future and even endangering our health.'

The language may have been dramatic, but JC's affidavit raised the thorny question of who exactly had contributed what to the success of 'N Sync. Just how important was Lou Pearlman in the history of 'N Sync? The answer probably lies somewhere between both camps – less than he claimed and more than they thought. The band maintained that Lynn was more responsible for creating 'N Sync than Lou. Describing a multimillionaire tycoon as 'unscrupulous' and 'greedy' almost begs the response, 'And your point is . . . ?' It is more a badge of honour than a condemnation. At the end of the day, it was more important that Johnny Wright was still with them as manager. That he would later move on to manage Justin's solo career leaves no doubt as to the esteem in which he is held. Johnny is a full-time manager, whereas Lou Pearlman is the boss of a company with a number of projects to keep an eye on. By the time the legal row broke out, 'N Sync were long past needing someone to write their cheques for them.

The lawsuit was settled by Christmas. The court was not that impressed by the bickering and told both parties to go to 'settling conferences'. They were told in no uncertain terms to reach an out-of-court settlement. Judge Anne Conway heard seventy minutes of arguments before declining to issue an injunction banning the release of a new 'N Sync album. One question remains tantalizingly unanswered in the court proceedings: how much money had Lou Pearlman earned from 'N Sync? The eventual settlement was a welcome Christmas present for Justin. As is always the case in these matters, nobody is allowed to reveal any details.

So who won? Lou Pearlman continues to receive royalties from 'N Sync records but has no personal involvement with the band. He gives the impression of getting most satisfaction from making something out of nothing, from taking a risk. If he were a ladies' man, he would enjoy the chase. He says relations between him and Justin, Lynn and Paul are very cordial: 'This was about renegotiating a deal. It was never to sue or hurt anyone or to have a dragged-out battle in court. It was just to do things in the proper way and it's done. All the issues were resolved and I am still earning money from 'N Sync.

'I put my money where my mouth is and, in doing so, I could have lost a couple of million bucks.

'I saw Justin not too long ago in Roy's restaurant in Orlando and, of course, we talk and it's "How are you doing?"'

The legal outcome was an enormous success for Justin and of great importance in the furtherance of his career. The vast fortune he now enjoys is a direct result of the better deal that 'N Sync negotiated. But, at the end of the day, nobody was forcing five ambitious young men to sign a bad contract. It was a terrible deal, but they were hungry for success. Certainly every young pop hopeful would bite his own arm off to try to secure a deal, any deal. But there comes a time when that initial contract is no longer in the artist's best interest. Justin explained, 'He [Lou] said he would back us financially. It was a big rush. But we were the ones who sat around till three in the morning singing together and hanging out together and doing the things friends do. The money Lou dished out he got back within the first six months of our success and the first record. A few records had gone by since then, and we were still in the same situation.'

Once the future of 'N Sync had been secured, it was time for Justin to ensure the album that had caused so much anguish would not be an anticlimax. Despite all the problems of the previous couple of months, the boys never stopped working. They honoured 100 tour dates throughout the year, ending 1999 as the third biggest concert act, with receipts of more than $44 million (just over £24 million). The reported postponement of the new album because of the court action was not strictly accurate. Everyone had hoped it would be ready for Christmas but, in truth, there was still work to be done. The chief sticking-point was Justin's increasing perfectionism. Lance Bass observed, 'He has to have everything so perfect. He is the biggest stickler.'

Eventually even Justin was happy and the long-awaited third album from 'N Sync, *No Strings Attached*, was ready for release. The media immediately picked up on the title, claiming it was an unsubtle reference to the successful outcome of the legal action. The reality was that 'No Strings Attached' was a track from the album co-written by JC about a guy giving a girl his heart with 'no strings attached'. It was, nevertheless, a timely title.

The intriguing thing about the public perception of 'N Sync at this time was how grown up and established they had become.

They had released only one album – and *Home for Christmas* – but they had the profile of superstars. In the buildup to the release of *No Strings Attached*, they were nominated for three Grammys, they presented a Grammy to Sting for Best Male Pop Vocal Performance, they performed two sketches on *Saturday Night Live* and they made the cover of *Rolling Stone* magazine. The *'N Sync* album was certified diamond when sales reached 10 million.

Justin's personal profile was gaining substance all the time. He was the principal target of interviewers, not least because of his liaison with Britney Spears. His standing in relation to the other members of 'N Sync was revealed in a trivial way when they appeared on *Rosie O'Donnell*. After the show, the chairs they were sitting in were auctioned for charity on eBay. The figures reached were: Justin, $3,100; JC, $2,250; Lance, $1,775; Joey, $1,325; and Chris, $1,175. The perception that Justin was now the 'leader' of 'N Sync was reinforced when he was voted *People* magazine's Most Beautiful Person in the World. By then he had forsaken the bleached-blond look in favour of a more natural brown, although he was still very curly-haired.

All this would have been an anticlimax if *No Strings Attached* hadn't lived up to the hype and the huge level of anticipation. It was finally released on 21 March 2000. The first single from the album, 'Bye Bye Bye' had already reached number one.

Tickets for the accompanying 52-date US tour went on sale and the demand broke all records for a single day. Close to a million were sold, generating ticket receipts of more than $40 million (£22 million).

After one week of record sales it was clear that nobody need have worried about *No Strings Attached*. It sold 2.4 million copies in one week, more than twice the previous record, which was held by their old rivals Backstreet Boys for the album *Millennium*. Poor old Backstreet Boys – there was no escape. *No Strings Attached* was the number one album on the Billboard chart for eight weeks and was eventually to sell more than 11 million units.

All these figures are mind-boggling. In two years 'N Sync had gone from being a bunch of nobodies flogging around Europe trying to get a deal to being the biggest teen band in the world. In the United Kingdom, no one had any idea. There was so much competition. 'N Sync were nowhere near as popular as Backstreet Boys and could not be mentioned in the same breath as Westlife. 'N Sync were like Robbie Williams in reverse: the biggest stars in their home country but nobody across the Atlantic.

Justin was very proud of *No Strings Attached*. It showed he was becoming more mature and more musically aware. At the time, his enthusiasm was infectious, but the album was probably not the 'masterpiece' he thought it was. Escaping the Europop origins of 'N Sync was going to take a little time and this was a move in the right direction. Reviewers suggested that 'N Sync were 'reborn' as serious artists. Perhaps it was a pity that 'Bye Bye Bye' was the album flagship, because it was a Cheiron production like their first singles. It was hugely popular and had an almost anthemic quality, but it was also strangely synthetic. The lyrics were at least a refreshing change from the hearts and flowers of the usual boy band fodder – in this case showing a girl the door for making a fool of the boy. *No Strings Attached* was trying to be too many things. 'We have a very broad sound,' explained Justin. 'There are different directions we can take it, so we did as much of that as we could on this album. That's why we called the album *No Strings Attached*. We have no strings to hold us down. We're ready to show the world that.'

The incomparable Moby commented on the record in *Spin*: 'So much effort has gone into this you almost have to like it . . . It's the craft element like looking at a well put-together cabinet. You may not want to buy the cabinet, but you can be impressed by how well the doors open.' The production cast helped to lace the record with this highly professional and slick feel. Diane Warren, writer of mega ballads 'How Do I Live' and 'Unbreak My Heart', contributed 'That's When I'll Stop Loving You', on which Justin began to fashion the singing style that would carry him forward into his solo career. Richard Marx, a consistent chart-topper in the US, produced and arranged 'This I Promise You', another strings-heavy ballad that showcased Justin's soulful voice. There was even a guest spot for the late lamented Lisa 'Left-Eye' Lopes, who featured on the track 'Space Cowboy'. Lopes had been a member of the hugely successful and influential all-girl vocal group TLC – only The Supremes had more US number ones. She was killed instantly, aged thirty, in a head-on collision in Honduras in April 2002.

JC Chasez had four songwriting credits on the album, whereas Justin had only one on 'I'll Be Good For You'. But Justin had taken a very active role in the mixing and final arrival of this new 'N Sync sound.

A dedication on *No Strings Attached* quietly reveals how Justin and the boys felt about the release of this album: '*NSYNC would like to thank the following people and companies for all their love and support: Judge Anne Conway . . .'

'It was a challenge.'

11

The Graduate

After he and Justin hugged on stage, Chuck Yerger could not understand why a procession of young girls wanted to embrace him. He asked one of them the reason. 'Because you have Justin's sweat on you,' she replied.

Lynn Harless had always wanted her son to graduate from high school. Justin was a gifted, intelligent student who could have achieved any academic ambition he chose to pursue. Being in *The Mickey Mouse Club* or 'N Sync was not exactly rocket science, so throughout his early career as a fledgling star Lynn made sure he wrote his essays. More precisely, she made sure Chuck Yerger or Brenda Crenshaw harried him to do his homework. 'He hated writing essays,' recalls Chuck. 'It was OK once he had started writing. He took a typing class so that he could do them on a keyboard. One-on-one discussion was much better for Justin. When we did history or language, I would try to make it relevant to his own life. I knew so much about him, which helped. I was always trying to make connections with something that had happened to him to try to breathe life into something that might otherwise seem boring and dry.'

Justin grew up quickly during the golden years of 'N Sync. He became a well-travelled young man, mixing on a daily basis with people a good deal older. Chuck Yerger noticed how he dropped the rose-tinted view of show business after he started on *MMC*. 'Justin would talk about the business of entertainment in a much more sophisticated way.'

Life on the road prolonged Justin's 'schooldays' by about a year. He finished his home school programme with the University of Nebraska in September 1999 and his diploma arrived in the post the following month, but Lynn decided not to tell him. She was already plotting a special graduation. In the United States, graduating from high school is an important rite of passage, a gateway to adulthood. It is an occasion when parents can be proud of a job well done. Britain does not have an equivalent, and allows children to slide away from their schooling. The rite of passage in the UK is passing your driving test or getting drunk for the first time and throwing up. The university graduation is an entirely different affair for twentysomethings who have had the privilege of further education.

'Lynn insisted that she wanted closure to Justin's high school education,' Chuck explains. 'She wanted him to have something as close as possible to a normal ending. She wanted a speech, she wanted him to get his diploma and she wanted him to wear a cap and gown.' Lynn had formed the idea for Justin's graduation five years before, when she had witnessed a special ceremony Chuck had performed for the older children on *The Mickey Mouse Club*. In the end, there was nothing normal about Justin Timberlake's graduation.

Lynn decided Justin would graduate on stage during the 'N Sync concert at the Pinnacle, the leading venue in Memphis, on 12 May 2000. She particularly wanted it to be a 'home town' event and set about planning it with her partner in crime Renée Earnest. It would need to be run like a military operation. First of all, Lynn called Chuck and told him firmly, 'I want you to do this. I'm flying you to Memphis and you're going to do this. I have tickets for you and your wife and Brenda; I have booked your hotel. This is a top secret thing. Do not be seen by the boys!'

Neither Chuck nor Brenda needed any persuading. They were both great admirers of their famous student and happy to participate, even if it meant walking out in front of 20,000 people. By coincidence, Chuck had been in the limelight nine days before the Pinnacle concert, when Lance Bass appeared on a celebrity charity edition of *Who Wants to Be a Millionaire?* Chuck was Lance's phone-a-friend for $125,000 (£68,750). Lance did not know the name of the airfield from which Lindbergh took off for his historic non-stop flight from New York to Paris in the *Spirit of St Louis*. Fortunately for everyone, Chuck knew that the correct answer was Roosevelt Field. He might not have been too keen to walk out in front of 20,000 people if he had messed up.

On 'graduation day', Chuck, Brenda and Sherry flew up from Orlando to Memphis and checked in to their hotel. They had to duck in to a side room when Justin and the boys arrived with their entourage. Justin had spent part of the day at E. E. Jeter announcing his sponsorship of a musical programme for his old school. Lynn had wanted everything to be formal, so Chuck wore a suit and Brenda a fine red dress for their stage debuts. After they found their seats near the right-hand side of the stage, Renée Earnest came out to give them 'precise' instructions: 'When this guy comes out and waves, you guys go down.' Sure enough, halfway through the concert, they were beckoned down while 'N Sync were off stage doing a costume change. Joey, Chris, JC and Lance had been told what was going to happen in the next section of the show, but Justin had absolutely no idea. Chuck and Brenda, who had donned caps and gowns, had to hide behind some rigging while the boys rushed about getting ready. They were then ushered up behind a curtain in the middle of the set.

It was catch-your-breath time in the show. The boys lounged around on a big sofa and chatted with the audience and sang a couple of the slow numbers from *No Strings Attached*. Justin didn't know that Lance was about to change the script. 'Do you remember how you couldn't hang out with us because you had to go tutoring?' Justin looked at Lance as if he had turned mad and said, 'What are you talking about?' That was the cue for Brenda to walk on stage. Justin could not believe his eyes and staggered back in shock. 'That's my tutor. That's my real tutor!' he announced to the audience, his voice high with incredulity. Brenda, microphone in hand, delivered her lines: 'Justin, we've been trying to catch up with you, but you've been so busy on the road that we haven't been able to give you your diploma. So we finally came here tonight to do that and I've brought along your favourite tutor in the world and Lance's 125,000-dollar man!' Chuck stepped out on to the stage and was handed a microphone by Joey Fatone, who said, 'Please remember to give this back to me when you leave', because there was only one spare mike and Brenda was clutching it.

Justin was overwhelmed. He bounded across the stage and gave his old tutor a huge bearhug and whispered, 'Mr Yerger, I am terribly sorry, I'm soaking wet and I probably stink.' Chuck had to stop himself from laughing: 'This thought flashed through my mind that there were 20,000 girls in the audience who would like to be where I was and would never believe that what he actually said to me was that he was worried about being wet and smelly.' Chuck had a speech to give at Lynn's instruction. She had warned him to limit it to three minutes. Someone brought a cap and gown out for Justin – in his favourite baby blue – and the rest of the boys were given white caps so they could throw them in the air as if it were a real high school graduation.

Chuck pulled the speech from his pocket and read: 'Members of 'N Sync, tonight's production staff, honoured guests, family members and more especially you, Justin this is a special night – graduation.

'Justin, education shows us, if we look hard enough, that there are rational patterns to the world. In one pattern we can view life's experiences as an ever expanding series of circles that touch each other at one key point as they grow farther from each other at the opposite point.

'Here tonight we bring two circles back to that key point where they touch other circles.

'First, your public school education, which started in the great state of Tennessee, is concluded in the state which nourished you.

'Second, JC and Lance, whom you watched graduate, are here to honour you.

'Justin, it is impossible to tell where a circle begins or ends, so please watch where these ever larger circles of your life touch each other. When you have doubts, concerns or fears, that connecting spot will bring you back to the knowledge, skills and values that you have learned from family, community, and to some extent from us, your educators. That spot where ever larger circles meet will be your touchstone and foundation.

'Now, as these circles connect with the earlier patterns of your life, our hope for you, and for Joey, Chris, JC and Lance, is that the ever expanding future circles of all your lives will encompass memorable achievement. There are NO STRINGS ATTACHED to your potential.

'Thank you, and Godspeed.'

Whether Justin or the 20,000 fans were able to take in these well-meaning if slightly portentous sentiments did not matter. The crowd roared, the caps were thrown into the air and Justin gave Chuck another hug of appreciation. And that was it – Justin Timberlake had graduated at the age of nineteen years and three months.

Chuck and Brenda resumed their seats next to Sherry, who had been taking pictures. Chuck laughs, 'At least now the fans understood what this old guy was doing there.' The teachers were given a rare insight in to what it was like to be part of the mad world of superstars on their way back to the hotel, which was only a couple of streets away. Amid all the top secret arrangements, it had never occurred to anyone that they might need security to cope with the army of fans hanging around after the show. One girl went up to Chuck and put her hand inside his jacket to try to grab the speech that he had put back in his pocket. She even offered him $50 (nearly £28) for the handwritten paper. 'The fact that this all happened to me after just five minutes on stage gave me a much better appreciation of what Justin faced all the time and the kind of microscope they're all under. Even I had to sign autographs and I am just the teacher.'

In the cynical world of media manipulation by artists, many people thought the graduation was a publicity stunt rather than the genuine article. They did not know how much it meant to Justin and, even more, to Lynn. Some radio stations hinted that Justin had bought his diploma. Brenda Crenshaw was so indignant at one station suggesting the whole thing was staged that she phoned to give them a piece of her mind live on air and tell them how hard Justin had worked to achieve his diploma. Those suggesting that it was a publicity stunt should have asked themselves why 'N Sync needed any more publicity. They already had the fastest selling album in history and had sold a million concert tickets in a day, so they were not exactly struggling for public attention.

Fans can be an unexpected problem. They are an everyday fact of life for celebrities. The bigger you are, the more protection you need and the more careful you have to be. An extraordinary incident that allegedly took place after the 'N Sync concert in St Louis, Missouri, on 19 November 2000, threatened to derail Justin's nice guy image. Far from being Mr Cool, he was revealed to be Mr Hot Head. A month after the concert took place, the mother of a 15-year-old fan filed a lawsuit against Justin, claiming he had harassed and verbally assaulted her daughter at the group's hotel.

The girl, Danielle McGuire, claimed that she was one of a throng of fans who gathered in the lobby of the Chase Park Plaza Hotel hoping to catch sight of the group as they returned from the concert. All the boys stopped to greet and acknowledge the fans except Justin, the heart-throb and the most popular; he allegedly ignored them in his rush to get upstairs. Danielle shouted out, 'I like JC better anyway; he's cuter!'

One of the 'N Sync bodyguards allegedly singled out Danielle and asked her if she had made that comment. When she admitted she had, he told her to follow him upstairs. She said he would not let her tell her mother that she was leaving the lobby. Danielle then claimed Justin marched up, backed her against a wall and berated her for several minutes. According to her lawsuit, the incident left her suffering from 'fright, shock, intimidation, severe emotional distress, bodily harm, embarrassment, humiliation and distress'.

The impression given by Danielle in her lawsuit is that Justin bawled her out like a drill sergeant dealing with a slovenly new recruit. Meanwhile, her concerned mother was trying to get upstairs to find out what was going on but was prevented from doing so. A family friend, Randy Jackson, was able to gain access and apparently witnessed the scene. Mr Jackson was no ordinary witness. He was the news anchor with the local NBC-affiliated television station and a respected and well-known figure in St Louis – imagine Trevor McDonald witnessing an incident. When Justin saw the broadcaster, he allegedly limped away, moaning that his leg hurt.

The suit also alleged that security guards 'laid hands upon' Danielle. The specific allegations in the suit stated that the Chase Park Plaza Hotel allowed Justin Timberlake, Wright Entertainment and Zeeks Entertainment ('N Sync's company) to 'take over security and control the lobby area and control members of the public located in the lobby. It charged all defendants with six counts, including false imprisonment of a minor, assault, battery and intentional infliction of emotional distress.' The damages sought were in excess of $25,000 (£13,750), which in terms of an American lawsuit were tiny.

Money, however, was not the issue. The lawsuit was totally at odds with the image of 'N Sync and Justin in particular. His persona is one of control and of a laidback approach to life. He is certainly not recognized as a candidate for anger management. His former girlfriend Veronica Finn confirms, 'I've never actually seen him get upset. The only thing that drove him crazy was being a perfectionist with himself. So if he did less than he expected to do, or thought he could have potentially done more, that really got to him. He just wasn't rude walking around.'

Veronica is not alone in the view that Justin has a very equitable temperament. This makes the McGuire allegation even more surprising. A source close to the case observes, 'At the time, 'N Sync could do no wrong. Justin was a young guy who was treated as if he could do anything. He just acted immaturely.' As so often seems to happen in cases involving celebrities, the case never came to court. Danielle's trial attorney, John S. Wallach, said she chose to drop the case because 'it was personally difficult to go forward. She wanted no more publicity regarding the case.' Justin was probably very fortunate that she decided not to proceed, because it could have had a serious impact on his image.

Mr Wallach, a lawyer with twenty-five years' experience, believes, on reflection, that he would have won the case. 'The eyewitness,

Mr Jackson, would have clinched it, because he is such a respected person in this town. He had absolutely zero to gain by making up the story. If he had been found to have done so, it would have had serious consequences for his career. I have every confidence that what Danielle told me happened was true. She was a typical, pleasant, Middle-American 15-year-old. She wasn't flashy or showy or trying to get attention.'

Intriguingly, after the case was filed, Mr Wallach received a number of calls from around the country alleging problems with the 'N Sync bodyguards, including one from the wife of a New York lawyer who claimed to have suffered an injury in a scuffle. One observer of these guys in action described them as being 'sides of beef with heads'.

The case was dropped just before 'N Sync were scheduled to return to St Louis for another concert, which was a shame for Mr Wallach, who had been looking forward to taking Justin's deposition when he was in town. He can neither confirm nor deny that there was any secret settlement between the McGuire family and 'N Sync, although he personally was not involved in any private negotiation. He did reveal that Danielle was having a horrid time at school: 'She was getting a really tough time from 'N Sync fans at school. One girl was even suspended for making threats, I believe.'

The incident remains one of the most controversial of Justin's career and is unlikely to find its way into any official 'N Sync history. He has sensibly kept quiet about it all. Something clearly happened to Danielle McGuire that evening, which may or may not have involved him acting like a brat. It is unlikely that it will come back to haunt him, although under Missouri law Danielle has until her twenty-sixth birthday to refile her complaint.

The threat of legal action was one of the few black spots in 2000, a year of unalloyed success for Justin and 'N Sync. The *No Strings Attached* tour carved a triumphant path across America. It was, the critics agreed, a highly polished, slick, accomplished show. It took twenty-seven trucks and twelve buses – practically a small invasion force – to transport the tour around the country.

The tone had been set the moment Justin, Lance, JC, Joey and Chris took to the stage in Biloxi – the town where a younger Justin had dissected a dogfish on a school trip – on 9 May. They opened with the title track 'No Strings Attached'; dressed as marionettes, they were lowered on to the stage by cables. It was a mirror image of the cover of the album. Many critics carp at describing a boy group like 'N Sync as a band because they are singers and don't play any instruments. But they are a 'band' in their live show, appearing with superb musicians like keyboardist David Cook, a jazz pianist discovered by 'N Sync playing in a bar next to their hotel in Detroit during the 1999 tour. He explained the professional approach: 'Before the tour, we had two months of rehearsals to figure out the arrangements for each song. As a band, we could add to the songs as they were produced for the record and make them sound live. The rest is up to 'N Sync. They really are five regular guys who this just kind of happened to, and they know that. They're enjoying it as much as the rest of us. I'm rooting for them.'

The first number ended with fireworks, which created the only noise louder than the screaming fans (the band were advised during the tour that the high-pitched screams were damaging their hearing and that they should wear earpieces to block out the sound of the girls). They were not five guys coming on, singing their new album and then heading off to a bar. The show was a precisely rehearsed equivalent of a Vegas spectacle on wheels. It was a heady, over-the-top mix of pyrotechnics, nimble choreography and harmonies. And there was Justin's hair to think about. The blond curls were replaced by cornrows. Justin's hair in the US garners as much attention as David Beckham's does in the UK. They performed only thirteen numbers, but the audience got their money's worth with five supporting acts – the first of which was Pink, now a sell-out star herself. An indication of the status Justin and 'N Sync enjoyed in the States is that on various tours they had Britney Spears and Pink warming up the audience. Pink was memorably described in one review as a 'one-hit wonder with wacky hair-colour'.

Profits from each gig were reported to be in excess of $1 million (£550,000). The merchandise sales alone were astronomical, with T-shirts at $32 (nearly £18) and 'N Sync necklaces a steal at $15 (over £8) – an 'N Sync concert came with purse-strings attached.

There were fringe benefits, such as the reported fee of $1 million they were paid to sing at a 12-year-old girl's bat mitzvah in Potomac, Maryland. All the time, 'N Sync were gaining credibility, playing the sort of venues like the Rose Bowl in Pasadena and Madison Square Garden in New York, which were the preserve of rock gods like U2 and the Rolling Stones. Coincidentally, Keith Richards was spotted backstage at the Madison Square Garden concert. Further proof of their status came when Eminem started to pay them attention. He made a video in which he was a super-hero aiming to wipe out 'N Sync. He also featured a song in his show that was a parody of their early hit 'Tearin' Up My Heart'. Eminem's version was the catchily titled 'Tearin' Up My Ass'. Justin and 'N Sync had become the epitome of establishment respectabil-ity, although they were definitely a band for the girls. When they sang the national anthem at the opening of a World Series baseball game, they were booed by a predominantly male crowd.

The vital statistics for 'N Sync at the end of 2000 make breath-taking reading: they were the world's highest earning group, making a reported $267 million (nearly £147 million) in American album sales and tour revenues. They ranked first on the VH1/Money Rock Star Index, one of the spurious rich lists that takes account of CD sales, tour revenue, 'money power' – includ-ing merchandise, endorsements and licensing – and 'star power', which encompasses fan loyalty and crossover appeal. The *No Strings Attached* album was the biggest selling CD; the tour was the second highest grossing, taking in $90.2 million (£49.6 million); and the video *Live at Madison Square Garden* ended the year at number one with 207,000 copies sold.

Many multinational companies would like to boast figures like these. Even more surprising was that the group were not particu-larly big in Britain. They managed only four top ten singles in the UK charts in four years with 'Bye Bye Bye' performing best, when it reached number three in March 2000. One of the problems was that 'N Sync made a false start through events completely out of their control. 'Tearin' Up My Heart' might have reached number one in the States but in Britain it came out as the nation mourned the Princess of Wales. The death of Diana caused a thoroughly weird few weeks in the record industry. Elton John's mawkish 'Candle In The Wind' tribute single gathered 80 per cent of all sales in the week of its release. Nothing could compete. 'N Sync's lightweight pop debut did not fit the mood in the slightest and stayed only two weeks on the chart, peaking at a miserable number forty. That was one week more than 'I Want You Back', which scraped in at number forty-two in November. It would be another two years before the tracks were reissued and made the top ten. As a result, 'N Sync never built up a strong fanbase in the United Kingdom. They were the American boy band who weren't Backstreet Boys. Rick Sky, music journalist and boy band expert, having written *The Take That Fact File*, was unimpressed when he interviewed 'N Sync in London: 'They made no impact on me whatsoever,' he recalls. 'Their American people were very precious about them. They were being treated as huge stars but they meant f*** all in Britain.'

Justin's profile continued to rise in his homeland. He and Lance Bass spent Easter as guests of Vice-President Al Gore at the White House and took part in the annual Easter egg hunt there. In April he was back at the White House at a reception to spotlight his charity work with the Justin Timberlake Foundation, providing musical opportunities in schools. He also practised his hosting skills at *Teen People's 25 Hottest Stars Under 25 Special*, when he told the audience he had received a speeding ticket in his new BMW roadster. Justin is a natural when it comes to presenting, able to be funny and goofy but still get the job done in an articulate and relaxed way. On the night Justin tied for first place with Brian Litrell of Backstreet Boys. Justin was also in the gossip columns whenever he was seen in the company of beautiful girls, whether it was taking tea at the Plaza Hotel in New York or admiring some well-toned physiques at the fashionable Club Level on South Beach, Miami.

More significantly, Justin was already experimenting on the *No Strings Attached* tour with some of the techniques and styles that would be blended together to create his solo persona. Critics noted the group were trying for a more raw, hip-hop feel. Justin did what was to become a trademark human beatbox sequence. One critic wrote, 'His mouthwork was actually fairly impressive.'

The British audience did not have the opportunity to study Justin's musical development. He was practically an institution in the United States – certainly 'N Sync were – by his twentieth birthday in January 2001, but across the Atlantic he was best known as the boyfriend of a very famous female star.

'Do you believe what's happened to these kids?'

PART THREE

JUSTIN TIMBERLAKE

12

Britney

The visit of Britney Spears caused great excitement in Shelby Forest. Justin's grandfather, Bill Bomar, was chatting to a friend who told him that his grandson was a great fan of Britney. Bill paused for a second and smiled: 'My grandson is too.'

Britney Spears was always in love with Justin. He has been the love of her life for the past ten years. The tears she shed during a Diane Sawyer interview in November 2003 were the real thing and revealed how much she regrets the ending of their relationship, which began when they were both little kids on *The Mickey Mouse Club*. She kissed him for the first time during a game of truth or dare when they were new faces at Disney. Justin was so smitten with his scrawny co-star that he told his grandfather that he would marry the girl one day.

When she was twelve, Britney took singing lessons from Bob Westbrook in McComb, Mississippi to practise some of the songs she had to perform for *MMC*. She had no idea Bob also taught Justin back in Memphis. One day she took a tape out of her bag and excitedly put it in the recorder. 'I want you to hear something,' she said. It was a duet with Justin; Bob recognized him at once.

'Oh, that's Justin,' said Bob, to Britney's amazement. He recalls, 'She whipped round and asked, "Do you know him?" and I said, "Sure, I'm his teacher", and her jaw just dropped. They had both talked about their singing teachers, but it had not clicked they were the same person because of the different locations. I could tell she was enamoured of him already. She had a childhood crush on him. Don't kid yourself, I could tell!'

Justin was booked to sing 'The Star-Spangled Banner' at the start of an ice hockey game involving the local Memphis team, the River Kings. 'Would you like to go up there and sing it with him?' Bob asked Britney, who could hardly believe her luck. 'She was asking, "Could I really do that? Could you work that out for me?" So I just smiled and told her, "All I've got to do is make a phone call." Two phone calls later and she was on her way to Millington. I like to tease people that I was the first one to match that love. I wasn't, but it sounds funny.'

Britney made her first trip to Shelby Forest then and stayed with Sadie and Bill Bomar just round the corner from Justin. It was the first of many chances to sample Sadie's legendary peach cobbler, which still lures Justin back home. The quiet backwater of Shelby Forest was not a million miles away from the sort of rural country where Britney had been raised in Louisiana. The similarities between the early life of both Justin and Britney as they set out on the childhood road to fame are almost uncanny. Britney was from the small town of Kentwood, which boasted a population of little more than 2,000 and was about an hour's drive along Highway 51 north of New Orleans. Like Justin, she had family practically on her doorstep. Her grandmother lived next door and her aunt nearby. Her mother's name is Lynne, although she spells her version with an 'e' at the end. While both showbiz mothers have put an impressive amount of time and energy into their offspring's futures, they are very different people. Justin's mother Lynn waited for her son to make the choice about what he wanted to do and then she went for it 110 per cent. If he had wanted to be a bricklayer, one could easily imagine his mother setting up lessons on how to mix cement so that he would be a master of his chosen craft.

Britney's mother, a schoolteacher by profession, decided that Britney was going to be a star before she could barely walk. She enrolled her daughter in the Renee Donewar School of Dance at the age of two. Britney thus became enamoured of spangly costumes and basked in the applause of enthusiastic adults at an age when most little girls are mastering potty-training. She sang in public for the first time, aged five, when she performed 'What Child Is This' at the First Baptist Church in Kentwood. She won her first talent contest at the age of six. Britney was like a little plasticine doll being moulded into a precocious all-singing, all-dancing talented toy. She was just eight years old when her mother entered her for *The Mickey Mouse Club* auditions. She was far too young in a crowd of older wannabes and was not accepted. It speaks volumes for Britney's inner determination – and that of her mother – that she never gave up on that particular programme.

Lynne Spears was made of stern stuff where her daughter was concerned. In another similarity to the Harlesses, the Spears family split up to pursue the dream of stardom. In this case, mother and daughter left their small-town community to try their luck in New York. Kentwood is as much a part of the Bible belt as Shelby Forest. A local high school near Britney's family home boasted a sign outside that declared: 'Drive Carefully, Live Prayerfully'. Consequently, it was a bold move to take young Britney out of that environment. She went to a private Christian academy run by nuns and, armed with hindsight, it is easy to see how she has been affected by a desire to please authority as represented by adults and by the guilt when she rebels against it. Her public declaration of her virginity was just one indication of this.

Britney was an understudy for a child actor in *Ruthless*, an off-Broadway show, but she was homesick. After six months, she and her mother returned to Louisiana, but she did not resume a normal childhood. She and Justin were reading from the same child star textbook. Britney won the Miss Talent USA competition – and a $1,000 (£550) prize – when she was eleven. She also won a place on *Star Search* and was an early departure from that show – just like Justin. Like her future love, she hated losing. She sang the Naomi Judd power ballad 'Love Can Build A Bridge', but lost by a quarter of a point to a young New York boy, Marty Thomas, who sounded terrible. Afterwards Britney was inconsolable, until her mother suggested she have another try for *The Mickey Mouse Club*. She was accepted at the same time as Justin. The producers called to let her know the good news: 'When they said,

"You're going to be a Mouseketeer", I just started jumping up and down and screaming, "I'm so excited, I'm so excited."'

And so Britney, a tiny slip of a girl, found herself next to Justin Timberlake in Bungalow Four at the MGM/Disney Studios as parents and the new mouseketeers gathered that first day to discover more about their new life. Chuck Yerger remembers her well: 'Justin, Britney and Christina were sitting side by side and I swear that Britney's feet didn't even touch the floor yet. She wore little crucifix earrings as someone might if they had come from a Christian school.'

Most of all Chuck retains his impression of Britney as being a girl who respected authority and not one who questioned it. She was no rebel. 'It struck me that she had an unshakeable faith that adults would never steer you wrong and that you should do as you were told. If the teachers from her Christian school had told her to write her name a certain way on a sheet of paper, or to write in blue rather than black ink or that her margins should be exactly three-quarters of an inch on the right-hand side, then her entire self was invested in making sure she did exactly that. When she came here, everything had worked for her. She had always been successful, so she never needed to question the right way to do something. No one had ever steered her wrong.'

Chuck's opinion is an interesting one in the light of Britney's future public fall from grace, a change from good girl to bad girl. He observes, 'Britney was the sweetest, most wholesome, most innocent person that you'd ever want to meet.' His observation is not an isolated one; it is repeated time and time again by people who later met her with Justin. The public, whose first image of Britney was as a schoolgirl nymphette on the video for her debut number one 'Baby One More Time', have little idea of the true nature of a girl universally liked.

Growing up, Britney did not enjoy the financial advantages that Justin did. Her father Jamie's building contractor business collapsed when she was nine and money became very tight. The home telephone was cut off and there was no central heating or log fire to keep everyone warm in the cold winters. Her mother gave up her job to chaperone Britney and was even prepared to share a New

York studio apartment with the family of Marty Thomas, the boy who beat her daughter in *Star Search*. Britney's first New York agent, Nancy Carson, observed, 'It was a real sacrifice for them. It was tight.' Britney had to succeed to repay those family sacrifices. 'I don't think people realize how hard it was on my family to have me do this,' she once commented. 'It wasn't overnight.'

The parallel lines of her and Justin's careers continued at *The Mickey Mouse Club*. They were talented all-rounders. They were not given many solos to do – that privilege was reserved for the powerfully voiced Chrisitina Aguilera or the older Rhona Barrett, an African-American girl with an outstandingly soulful voice. Both Britney and Justin were considered to be talented, athletic dancers. Britney had been a very promising young gymnast before she became a full-time child star. Justin's obsession with basketball meant he was a very fit and sporty boy. The two of them gelled perfectly together in the acting department, when they performed the sketches that gave the show its variety. Britney also shared his goofy sense of humour, a prerequisite needed to join the Timberlake inner circle. She was nothing like the grade-A student that Justin was, but she made up for it in determination and a willingness to please.

Britney lacked a little of Justin's charisma as a kid. Bob Westbrook recalls, 'I didn't spot the charisma, but I spotted the work ethic, because during the lessons she took she stared in the mirror the whole time.' Most of the children who turned up for lessons treated them as an extension of their schoolwork in a place where they were taught a subject in a relaxed, easy way – not Britney. She treated the whole thing as a performance. 'She was so intense,' Bob remembers. 'If I sweated for any student, I sweated for her. She was so driven. She paid for her own lessons out of the money she got from the Disney kids. We're not talking about a big star here; we're talking about a kid the other kids like, and she'd already been in *Ruthless* and she'd done some national commercials. The Disney thing had begun to give her a name with the younger kids and a lot of my students knew who she was and wanted to see her when she came in for lessons. She'd give autographs – that sort of thing.

'I thought she was mature for her age in her attitude, probably because of working on the show. It was an hour's lesson and she was going to get her money's worth. I could tell right away that she was very career-minded. She bounced in the door and didn't want to do much social talking.'

The Britney Spears we know today is nothing like the Britney who took her singing lessons with Bob Westbrook. Britney, the top-selling teenage artist of all time, is all about stylized vocals within a very limited range. The *Mickey Mouse* Britney was a young girl with a big voice. Bob describes it: 'She had a big belt voice as a kid. I don't understand why she doesn't use any of that now.'

All the children on *The Mickey Mouse Club* grew up fast. Britney was the youngest and the difference in her appearance and demeanour between the first and second seasons she was in *MMC* was pronounced. Both she and the other new kid, Christina Aguilera, gained poise. Britney and Christina were best friends on the set, bonded by their age and circumstance. They would hang out with Justin, but he was a boy. Later the rivalry between Britney and Christina would fill many column inches, but that animosity was good for the image and business.

When *The Mickey Mouse Club* was abruptly cancelled, Britney found herself in the same boat as Justin – back home in a small town, wondering what to do and desperate to get out. They were both pros, both accomplished young entertainers set on following their path to stardom. They might never have clapped eyes on one another again, but fate had already decreed that the lives of Britney Spears and Justin Timberlake were inexorably entwined. They were almost two halves of the same chromosome. In Kentwood, Britney was voted Most Beautiful at her school around the time that Justin was basking in the title of Mr Jeter. When Justin was back in Orlando pursuing his dream with 'N Sync, Britney turned down the chance to join his mother's girl group Innosense – in retrospect a very wise move. All-girl groups in pop have a very brief shelflife – Spice Girls, All Saints and Atomic Kitten – and Innosense – all imploded. Britney had ambitions as a solo star and secured a probationary deal with Jive, later the recording label of 'N Sync and Justin Timberlake.

Despite turning down Innosense, Britney was on very good terms with Justin's mother and kept in touch with her. When 'N Sync finally broke in the US, Britney was able to cling to their coat tails until she could fly solo. Ironically, the roles of Britney and Justin were reversed in the US and the UK. In the States, Justin and 'N Sync were superstars giving Britney a helping hand by agreeing that she could be the opening act on their first tour. In Britain, 'N Sync were nowhere and Justin's original notoriety was as Britney's boyfriend.

The romance between Justin and Britney was one of those celebrity affairs that blossomed amid denials that they were an item. In many ways, it mirrored the relationship of Kylie Minogue and Jason Donovan. They had been child actors together on a forgettable Australian series before meeting again on the set of *Neighbours*. They agreed to keep their relationship under wraps in order not to upset fans of the popular soap.

Before Justin, Britney had had only one proper boyfriend, a gangly young man called Reg, who had taken her to the prom. She was happy to admit to Reg but not to Justin when the gossip about the identity of her boyfriend became frenzied in early 1999. She told one interviewer: 'Overseas, it's Nick Carter of Backstreet Boys. I have no feelings at all', she fibbed, declaring that she preferred to concentrate on her work. This is a common game among stars not wanting to let the public know what is really going on in their lives. The Britney image was one of teasing availability, pure as the driven slush. A true love relationship would have spoilt it.

Britney says she cannot recall when she and Justin first became boyfriend and girlfriend. Their first official date was dinner for two at a quiet restaurant in Los Angeles where, away from prying camera lenses, they were able to reminisce and talk about their current hopes. She was the opening act on 'N Sync's first US headlining *Second II None* tour, which started in Orlando on 17 November 1998. Justin was seventeen; Britney's seventeenth birthday was still a month away. The close proximity of touring together gave them the opportunity to rekindle their friendship – or, in Britney's case, to reignite her crush – and to help each other unwind from the hard grind of concert life. Britney understood the stresses a performer faces every single day. Justin described it memorably: 'Even when she doesn't understand, she understands that she doesn't understand, because she has such a big heart.'

Britney's life was about to explode because of the success of her debut single and the notorious video that accompanied the track. It was her idea to dress as a schoolgirl sexpot while cooing, 'Ooh bay-bee, bay-bee.' The record was a phenomenal hit on both sides of the Atlantic. She and Justin were able to embrace true fame at the same time. Her debut album *Baby One More Time* reached number one in the US album charts at the end of January, keeping 'N Sync's debut off the top spot. The major difference between the two was that Britney, assisted by MTV relentlessly playing the video, took off in Britain. The single was released in the UK in February and broke the record for the first week sales of a debut act with 464,000. From that week on, Justin was doomed to several years as Mr Britney as far as the UK media were concerned.

Britney gave one of those Faustian interviews that seem to doom relationships in the long run: 'No, I don't have a boyfriend. I wish I could have time for a boyfriend. I don't want a boyfriend because I hate talking on the phone. Long-distance relationships just aren't for me.'

The trials of a long-distance relationship were already taxing Justin and his girlfriend Veronica Finn – so much so that they split up. Sadly, celebrity relationships that survive the endless separations that differing schedules inevitably bring are as rare as a five-leafed clover. In many ways Britney and Justin were a match made in heaven – shared ambitions, shared experiences and shared background. If you had programmed a computer to devise the perfect celebrity partner for Justin, it would surely have been Britney. She is talented, goofy and confident, with the looks and physique that are definitely to his taste. The camera loves her and does not reveal just how small she is. She is one of the tiniest pop stars. Kylie and Geri Halliwell are the only superstar females who are shorter than Britney. Britney is, however, athletic, well-toned and sporty. Despite her lack of inches, she was always a keen basketball player, and the quickest way to Justin's heart is to accompany him shooting hoops. Britney had matured from a little

Justin's Celtic cross tattoo is one of seven, at the last count, that he has

Christina Aguilera and her dad – sorry, that's Justin, modelling the latest designs for geography teachers backstage at Radio City Musical Hall in August 2003

Justin boldly goes where all men would like to go: the famous groping of Kylie's bum at the 2003 Brit Awards

Awards come in all shapes and sizes and the best policy is to grin and hold it even if you have no idea what it is. Justin clutches *(above)* Showman of the Year at the annual GQ Man of the Year Awards *(right)* three MTV Europe Music Awards and *(below)* the greatest prize in music – his two Grammys from 2004

Single Exposure: Justin demonstrates the two steps of the controversial 'wardrobe malfunction' with Janet Jackson at the 2004 Super Bowl

Step One: Now you don't

Step Two: Now you see it

Justin on stage with two of his favourite groups. Above, performing 'Where Is The Love' with the Black Eyed Peas at the 2004 Grammy Awards. Below, on stage with N*E*R*D featuring Pharrell Williams at the Wiltern Theatre, LA, in March 2004

Justin was obviously delighted to meet Cameron Diaz backstage at the Nickelodeon Kids' Choice Awards in April 2003

The dating game for celebrity couples involves disguising yourself under a hat. Justin's is more discreet than Cameron's lampshade

Justin is so smitten with Cameron that for once he even ignores what's going on in the game between the LA Lakers basketball team and the Mavericks in October 2003

Justin takes his mother, the most important woman in his life, to the 2002 MTV Video Music Awards *(above)* and the 2004 Grammy Awards *(below)*. She looks more like his big sister than his mom

The new 'King of Pop'

mouseketeer to a very beautiful young woman. Along the way, she had become blonde, had her teeth fixed and had to deal with rumours that she had a boob job while recovering from a knee injury incurred while dancing. Justin took the breasts questions good-naturedly: 'I don't know about her breasts, I was too busy staring at her butt.'

Britney drew unwanted attention to her relationship with Justin by declaring that she intended to remain a virgin until her wedding night. Britney was simply reaffirming her strong belief in God and Christian values. 'I want sex just like any other 19-year-old girl does, but I want to have it in a committed marriage,' she explained. Unfortunately, the virginity question would become a millstone around her neck. Nobody believed it except possibly Justin's grandmother, Sadie Bomar, who was quoted in *heat* magazine reportedly claiming that Justin and Britney were still virgins and that Justin did not believe in sex before marriage because 'Justin has high moral values and has not slept with anyone.' The remarks were well meaning and well intentioned from a loving grandmother with strong values of her own, but they did not take into account the fact that Justin and Danielle Ditto had been at it like rabbits when Justin was fourteen.

Sadie very nearly had it right as far as the sentiment was concerned. The question of how to reconcile strong faith with the sexual freedom of modern times is an agonizing one for Bible-belt youngsters. If they lapse, it does not mean they were lying about their beliefs. The controversial radio host Howard Stern did not take the question of Britney's purity very seriously: 'Can't he [Justin] just get her high and bang her?' he asked on air. He also questioned whether Britney was really a virgin, especially if she had had her nipples pierced. On the other side of the coin, Britney received unexpected praise from a Church of England publication, *Celebrate*, which declared her a 'great ambassador for virginity'. Eventually, Justin and Britney both admitted they had made love during their relationship but had not rushed into it. 'Just because I've admitted to having sex doesn't make me a bad person,' insisted Britney.

When Justin took Britney home to Shelby Forest, she proved to be very popular. She fitted in seamlessly. Despite her public image and legendary shopping extravagances, she revealed her true self as a home town girl. The local preacher, Brother Barney Austin, and his wife Pat went to visit the home of the Bomars when Justin was there with Britney. 'She had a peaches-and-cream skin,' recalls Pat. 'She didn't wear much make-up. She wasn't overly made up like some stars. Justin remembered us and got up and came over and gave us a huge hug. He was like that, a very down-to-earth, friendly young man. She was very nice.'

The local residents in Millington loved having such a famous person staying in the area. Justin was still ol' Justin, but Britney Spears was the hottest star around. At Christmas it was announced on local radio that Britney was shopping at Wal-Mart with Justin's mother. Within minutes, it was bedlam, with cars jamming the approach road trying to get in to the overflowing car park. Shopping in cut-price Wal-Mart was a long way from Beverley Hills, where Britney once spent $100,000 (£55,000) on Christmas presents for Justin. American gossip journalist Janet Charlton says Britney hit the famous boutiques and bought her beloved an array of leather jackets, leather coats, leather trousers, cashmere sweaters and jewellery. Justin was a little less ostentatious but, typically, more soppy. His first gift to her was a gold ring for her seventeenth birthday. On her nineteenth birthday in 2000, at the height of their love affair, he ordered twenty-six dozen roses to be placed in her suite at a Palm Springs hotel. To top it off, he arranged for the petals of another ten dozen roses to be scattered on the carpet and on the bed. It was a wildly romantic gesture, following a pattern that had begun a few years earlier with Danielle Ditto. The roses were for 'Pinky', his pet name for Britney and the one he used on *Celebrity* to say that he could not breathe without her.

Erika Ruch met Britney and Justin together several times, including at concerts in Nashville and Chattanooga: 'She's beautiful – a girl who would turn a head when she walked down the street, but also when she walked into a room you wanted to be around her because she has one of those vibrant personalities. She and Justin seemed to have a lot in common. I most noticed what good friends they were. They were comfortable together – you could tell by the way they kept criticizing one another.'

These were the happiest of times. They shared a love of fast cars and fabulous holidays. Eventually, more than a year after they started dating properly, they were comfortable enough to let the public know they were a couple. Britney told *Rolling Stone* in May 2000 that they had enjoyed a kiss and then theatrically exclaimed, 'Oh my gosh, my manager is going to kill me,' giving the impression that her comment had slipped out accidentally.

The stark reality of their relationship was that they spent much of the time apart. Sadie Bomar revealed that they were seeing each other only about once a month. Britney said that when she was touring Australia her phone bill to Justin was costing more than the hotel suite. As so often happens, just when the press goes into a frenzy about the possibility of marriage and babies, the relationship develops difficulties. It is true that Justin bought Britney a $100,000 (£55,000) ring, but he had done the same, if less extravagantly, for girls before. It is one of the sweet things he does when he is in love, but it is a gesture not a proposal.

The public love a fairy-tale couple – Posh and Becks, Brad and Jen, Charles and Diana, Ben and J-Lo – and it is incredibly difficult to live up to the public's expectations. The gifts get more and more extravagant, the declarations of love more ostentatious, one cannot be mentioned without the other. When Justin won *People* magazine's online poll of The Most Beautiful Person in the World, it was almost inevitable that his other half, Britney, was runner-up. They became Team Timberspears. They linked up with Yahoo to promote online shopping. An interactive video, sponsored by Pepsi, showed the young lovebirds shopping in New York and gave the audience the chance to buy the products Britney and Justin found 'cool' from the comfort of their own homes. They were also the faces of an online educational campaign entitled MathNMusic Club for Youth, which aimed to raise funds for music education programmes – a very important cause for Justin. The only maths the couple needed were for counting the number of noughts on the end of their bank statements. They were both multimillionaires while they were still teenagers.

They were expected to behave in a very showbiz way. When Britney celebrated her nineteenth birthday in California, she slipped on stage during the 'N Sync concert in San Diego wearing a wig and glasses. Justin encouraged the crowd to sing 'Happy Birthday' to his girlfriend, although there was a hearty round of good-natured booing from the girls who wanted Justin for themselves. When they attended the Rock in Rio festival in January 2001 they reportedly shared a suite and spent three days and nights locked away, eating fried chicken and chips and drinking cans of cola. Britney loves chicken and chips. Intriguingly, not long afterwards, Britney confided to a magazine that she was finding it hard to stay a virgin. There was talk of them buying a $4 million (£2.2 million) home together in the Hollywood Hills: although sex was one taboo for a young Christian couple, cohabiting while unmarried was quite another. They did not spend enough time with one another for their relationship ever to justify the expression 'living together'. In the end, the house they looked at was bought by Britney alone. Justin also helped her pick out an oceanfront property in Florida. He would use Britney's house as a base when he was in LA, but it was rare that they were both in town at the same time.

The low point of the publicity glare came when hackers placed a hoax announcement on the Internet that Britney and Justin had been killed in a car crash. The whole thing had started as a joke, but it quickly got out of hand when fans started to panic that it was true that they had collided with a pretzel delivery truck. The source turned out to be two DJs. It was a cruel joke that had to be officially denied. After the death of Princess Diana in a car crash in a Paris tunnel, any such far-fetched story might turn out to be true and upsetting.

A few months later, the couple were enjoying a break in a mansion in Destin, Florida, when thieves broke in and stole video equipment and personal items, including clothes, belonging to the couple. Worryingly, they also grabbed a videotape that allegedly contained footage of Britney and Justin making out. The exact nature of the content remains a secret, because police arrested a gang of teenagers before they had the chance to post the film on the Internet. The blueness of the home movie was probably greatly exaggerated.

Less shocking was a report that they were secretly married. It was rubbish, of course, but more and more often Britney was suggesting they would get married in the future. She told *Big Brother* winner Brian Dowling on the Saturday morning show *CD:UK* that it would happen 'some time in the future'. Five months later, in March 2002, she was denying claims that they had split up. At times like these, it is a good idea to examine the official statements and then believe the opposite. A 'spokeswoman' said the reports were 'just a rumour'. She also denied 'N Sync were splitting up and were, in fact, taking 'a little hiatus' of about eight months. That was more than two years ago.

Britney was trying to cope with promoting her feature film debut, *Crossroads*, while coming to terms with a break-up that had devastated her hopes and dreams. At the London premiere she was lambasted by the press for being late and ignoring her fans when she arrived. When she appeared on the balcony to wave, she was roundly booed and jeered. It was a difficult time, even though Britney had been brought up on the clichéd mantra 'The show must go on'.

Friends reveal that she had truly expected to marry Justin and had believed the fairy tale she was living. Justin had plans for world solo domination and considered himself too young to marry. He was only twenty-one, much the same age as his parents Lynn and Randy were when they married too hastily. Lynn admitted that her son and Britney were having problems and had 'hit a rough spot'. She revealed, 'They are two kids who have intense feelings for one another.' Lynn recognized how difficult it was to repair a punctured relationship from a distance down a phone line.

After the break-up, the recriminations began: who did what and who dumped whom? At first there were reports that Justin had been seen with a busty brunette at a bar in Los Angeles, but it seemed something of nothing and not enough to cause a bust-up. Much more believable as a cause of a big row was the accusation that it was, in fact, Britney who had been unfaithful to Justin. He had certainly become very emotional when he thought Danielle Ditto had cheated on him and went to confront her in the schoolyard. It was becoming an all too familiar bleat from Justin that his first three girlfriends were unfaithful. While Danielle and Veronica Finn both refute the idea, Britney has never dwelled on it. That has only increased speculation about the identity of the man who led her astray. First in the frame was Justin's Australian-born songwriting partner and choreographer Wade Robson, who always denied the gossip. He and Justin wrote four songs together for the 'N Sync album *Celebrity* but, noticeably, none on Justin's solo debut *Justified*. They had been such big buddies, going skydiving and riding scooters. On the *Celebrity* sleeve, Justin gushes, 'Wade – never in my life have I clicked with someone creatively like I do with you.' On the *Justified* sleeve there is a big fat zero where Wade is concerned. Robson later attracted more publicity when he revealed that as a boy he had once shared a bed with Michael Jackson. A brilliant dancer as a kid, he appeared in the videos for 'Black Or White', 'Jam' and 'Heal The World' by the time he was nine. Robson said nothing inappropriate happened between him and Jackson.

Another 'culprit' fingered in print was Ben Affleck, who, it was alleged, had a fling with Britney before he embarked on his famed relationship with Jennifer Lopez. Whatever the truth, Britney was heartbroken over the split. The problem was, of course, that it was enough for Justin to believe she had cheated on him, making it immaterial whether she actually had or not. He told *Rolling Stone*, 'She has a beautiful heart, but if I've lost my trust in someone, I don't think it's right for me to be with them.' Justin has admitted that he has a problem with forgiveness and he reportedly rejected a plea from Britney to try again. They were both utterly devastated at the split, but did not have the opportunity normal couples have to try to work out the hurt and anger. Justin told *People* magazine, 'I honestly know what it's like to have a broken heart now. You get to a point where you're crying yourself to sleep at night.'

Britney Spears wanted to get married. She maintains she gave her virginity to Justin because she honestly believed she would end up as Mrs Justin Timberlake. Perhaps Britney's later behaviour was just trying to get his attention, but if that was the case, she played a bad hand because infidelity is unacceptable to Justin.

They have both moved on in interesting ways. Justin had a surge of creative energy that fuelled his songwriting for his first solo project, and he set about conquering the world as a free agent. Once more girls could think they stood a chance with the world's most eligible man. He dated Jenna Dewan, a dancer with 'N Sync, who turned out to be the mystery brunette who had so excited the tabloid press, but it was a brief and uncharacteristic fling for Justin. He seems happier in settled, more serious relationships. He did, however, put the boot in with his hit 'Cry Me A River' which seemed to transparently reflect his feelings about Britney. He compounded that impression by casting a Britney look-alike in the video in which Justin is a man wronged by a cheating girlfriend. He takes his revenge by filming himself with another woman on his girlfriend's bed and leaving the video for her to watch on her return. When she saw it Britney came out with the slightly less than ladylike comment, 'I was shocked to s**t.' Including a song about a former girlfriend always spices up an album. He went on the Barbara Walters show and, according to Britney, 'sold her out' by talking about their sex life. He also went on a radio show and talked about giving Britney oral sex, but later claimed it was a joke.

For her part, Britney seems to have gone completely off the rails. She had an ill-judged fling with Fred Durst, the crude singer of Limp Bizkit, who told the world in graphic terms that he had slept with her, claiming she was 'forward and aggressive' in bed. She was linked with Irish hell-raiser Colin Farrell; she called him a 'bad boy'. She snogged Madonna at the MTV Video Music Awards, which genuinely outraged the Bible-belt matrons who had so shaped her moral outlook on life. Most controversially, she married a man called Jason Alexander, a nobody from Kentwood, after a night of partying in Las Vegas. The marriage was annulled fifty-five hours later. All good rock 'n' roll behaviour, although it was her interview with Diane Sawyer, which many felt revealed the true Britney. She refused to confirm that she was unfaithful, as Justin had implied. 'I'm not technically saying he's wrong, but I'm not technically saying he's right either', she said, sounding like Bill Clinton. She also told Sawyer that she had thought she would be with Justin for the rest of her life. It was when she was asked what it felt like to lose him that she began to cry, sniffling, 'It was pretty rough. It was kind of weird. Hello. Um, oh my goodness.' She then had to ask Sawyer to stop the interview while she regained her composure. It would have been hard to fake.

Justin probably gained more in terms of his career from the relationship than Britney did. He was one of five guys in 'N Sync, but he was the only one going out with one of the biggest female stars in the world. Britney's career has taken an upward turn after a spell in the relative doldrums with a number one album, *In the Zone*, in the US and 'Toxic' becoming her fourth British number one single in March 2004. Everything about Britney and Justin was too good to be true. They had been the perfect celebrity couple. The break-up was a wake-up call to Justin that all matters of the heart would be very high profile from now on.

'I love Britney, and I'll always love her.'

13

Celebrity

The last time Justin saw his cousin Allison Hammett at home in Shelby Forest, he took her aside and told her, 'Coz, if anybody ever breaks your heart, you just let me know and I'll take care of it.' She recalls, 'He was so sweet.'

The new 'King of Pop' did not just emerge from the unpromising cocoon of a naff boy band to become a respected artist overnight. The seeds of solo stardom can be found some time before 'N Sync took a sabbatical. They are planted both in Justin's work on the fourth 'N Sync album *Celebrity* and in the development of his star persona as one half of one of pop's most famous couples. Justin Timberlake may have burst onto the scene in Britain, but what we saw and heard had been a work in progress for some time. Going solo from a successful group, especially one relying heavily on image, is notoriously difficult. In the eighties, George Michael managed it, but Wham was really George Michael under a different name. In the nineties, Robbie Williams surprised the music business by breaking through after Take That, although he needed a total reinvention to do it. They are the ones who successfully managed to eclipse their boy band fame. The list of those that didn't is a much longer one, and includes: Matt Goss, Stephen Gateley, anyone from New Kids on the Block, anyone from Backstreet Boys, anyone from Boyz II Men, Gary Barlow and Mark Owen, H from Steps, that bloke from 5ive and the podgy guy who used to go out with Jordan. Even Ronan Keating of Boyzone has not achieved the international stardom that might have been expected, although he is a solid British chart act. There are also the female flops: Shaznay from All Saints, anyone from the Spice Girls and anyone from Eternal. It could turn into a party game trying to identify the big successes. In the new millennium, Justin Timberlake, and his female equivalent, Beyoncé, made the leap seem like a piece of cake.

The birth of Justin Timberlake the artist can be traced back to the triumph of *No Strings Attached*, both the album of that name and the astonishingly successful tour. Financially, Justin was more than secure for life; the new contract ensured that he wasn't just a millionaire but a multimillionaire able to indulge his love of cars, clothes and jewellery to his heart's content. Justin had moved to the front of 'N Sync as the heart-throb of the group, a powerful and athletic dancer and the most soulful singer. It was time to take that prestige and influence a step further and make more of an impact on the music. Success is the most attractive commodity in music and at the end of 2000 you could not find a bigger success than 'N Sync. Who wouldn't want to work with the boys? They had good reputations. Only Justin was known as a hard man to please in the studio, but the opportunity to sell millions of records was going to ensure writers and producers queued up to work with him. He, in turn, was desperate for credibility, an elusive commodity that 'N Sync did not possess despite their record-breaking success.

Musically, Justin had matured hugely over the past five years. He had developed from a teenage kid with a vague ambition to be a famous pop star into an accomplished musical performer about to wave his teens goodbye. He may have been the baby of the group in age, but he was about to move ahead of the rest in his artistic range and ability, although JC fans might dispute that. Chuck Yerger noticed the change in Justin during the 'N Sync years: 'While he was a Mouseketeer, I didn't see a great deal of evidence of verbal creativity. But when I was tutoring him with 'N Sync, I noticed the change as words became his business. We began to look at the American poets, the transcendentalists like Emerson and Thoreau, as well as fooling around with the form of the

Shakespearean and Petrarchan sonnets. We would look at rhythms and rhyme schemes and stuff like that and it was then that I began to sense that there's something here with this boy. I could see that Justin was somebody who was beginning to see what you can do with language, what you can do with words and what you can do with rhythm.' Justin was applying his natural intelligence to his creative world. The rhythm of language was crucial to the R 'n' B direction his music began to take.

By the time 'N Sync were ready to go into the studio to start recording a new album in January 2001, Justin had co-written seven tracks which would form the nucleus of a developing sound. He would also co-produce five tracks as part of his blossoming all round musical ability. 'N Sync was riding the crest of a wave with two New Year Grammy nominations, including Record of the Year for 'Bye Bye Bye'. Even more important, perhaps, than his song-writing, was the introduction of front-line producers the Neptunes and BT, aka Brian Transeau (not British Telecom). BT is based in California and has a very laidback attitude to recording.

BT's 2000 album *Movement in Still Life* was critically acclaimed and light years away from the pop world of 'N Sync. Both JC and Justin were firm fans, and Justin, searching for credibility, tele-phoned BT and told him they wanted to record a track like 'Hip-Hop Phenomenon', his favourite from the album. BT was amazed: 'I was like, "Are you serious?"' The track they asked him to work on was called 'Pop', a Justin song in which he rejected the trivia of the music business – cars, clothes, jewellery – asserting that it was only the music that mattered. He was also making the point that 'pop' need not be a dirty word, that it could incorporate a kaleidoscope of styles. That was what 'N Sync was all about. By chance, it was BT who utilized what has become one of Justin's trademarks – the human beatbox. They were in the studio laying down the vocal track and BT was listening to one of the takes when he heard Justin beatboxing under his breath. BT was transfixed: 'That is bad-ass. We got to record that,' he exclaimed. At this stage, it was just an experiment to see how it sounded, and BT did no more than prepare a mix for Justin to listen to in private. Justin played it in his car and the more he listened to it, the better he liked it; the rest of 'N Sync liked it as well. Before they started recording *Celebrity*, JC had said they were looking for a funkier sound, and 'Pop' was a move in that direction after *No Strings Attached*.

At this time, Justin and Britney were very much an item and their work was surprisingly closely linked. After the success of 'Pop', BT moved on to work with Britney on her third album, imaginatively entitled *Britney*. He worked with her on a song piquantly called 'Before The Goodbye'. A more notable collaboration on Britney's albums was with arguably the hottest producers currently working in music, the Neptunes. They wrote and produced the track 'I'm A Slave 4 U' for Britney but, more significantly, they worked on the best track on *Celebrity*, 'Girlfriend', which could easily have been a song on *Justified*.

Justin thought the Neptunes' work was exceptional and it was the start of a mutual admiration society. The Neptunes, Pharrell Williams and Chad Hugo, were in high school in Virginia when they sold their first song. Their involvement with 'N Sync was part of a concerted effort by the boys to improve their sound. Justin was keen to do as much producing as he could, but he is also shrewd enough to surround himself with the best in the business. The Neptunes started their own Star Trak label, a breeding ground for top-line R 'n' B stars, including Kelis, as well as newcomers like The Clipse and Vanessa Marquez, who would later work with Justin. Their mainstream reputation owed more to their collaborations with No Doubt, Nelly, 'N Sync and Britney Spears. It was all very 'in-house'. Star Trak began as a subsidiary of Arista, which was also the parent label of Jive, home of Britney, Justin and 'N Sync.

The Neptunes shared Justin's spiritual belief that their music was a gift from God. Pharrell Williams, a drummer before he became a keyboard maestro, once had a bizarre radio conversation with Michael Jackson, whom he insisted on calling 'Sir' throughout the interview.

Jacko: 'The different forms of music that the black race has been responsible for bringing in, from jazz to pop to rock 'n' roll to hip hop, you name it, what do you think all that is about? Is it given from God?'

Pharrell: 'I think all music is a gift from God.'

Jacko: 'Blues, rock 'n' roll, all the different forms of popular music were invented by Chuck Berry, Little Richard, Fats Domino.'

Pharrell: 'Absolutely.'

Jacko: 'Even the dances from the cakewalk to the Charleston, the popping, the breaking, the locking. Don't you think they're a gift from God?'

Pharrell: 'Absolutely. God gave us that gift when He gave us the gift of interpretation.'

The exchange, complete with a fair bit of toadying from Williams, is significant in that it demonstrates the influence Michael Jackson had on the music of the Neptunes and, through them, on the solo sound of Justin Timberlake. For the moment, 'Girlfriend' would represent the sound; it was a track that could have been on any Michael Jackson album. It is the key linking track between the Justin of 'N Sync and Justin Timberlake, cool dude.

Justin was investing a lot of creative energy in *Celebrity* and what he was seeking could be summed up in one word: respect. His ire was mostly directed at critics of 'N Sync, although he took a protective stance where his girlfriend Britney was concerned. He exclaimed, 'It's gonna suck for the next Nirvana . . . the next generation of critics are being raised on 'N Sync, Britney Spears and Backstreet Boys. Their measurement of quality is going to be different.' His point that unashamed pop acts should not be sneered at just because they were pop is a valid one. Is *Harry Potter* a less good book because it is written for children and sells millions of copies? Perhaps comparing rock gods Nirvana with Britney was a little misjudged. Justin was also a little precipitate in building up *Celebrity*, which, in the end, was unable to throw off the shackles of the Europop sound that had first ensnared the group in Stockholm. Tellingly, Kristian Lundin, who had worked on the first album, was the writer–producer on two tracks and Max Martin 'pops' up on another. One critic derided the songs for 'flirting with hip hop and electronica, but in the kind of accessible teen-friendly way you would expect from 'N Sync.'

Celebrity was probably more interesting lyrically than musically with Justin's use of language – as Chuck Yerger had spotted – becoming more accomplished and much more self-aware. This was no moon and June stuff. The title track 'Celebrity' focused on the problems of finding true love as a celebrity. Justin has had to face the fact that he could have practically any girl in the world on a plate but only if they were lured by the image and the fame and not by the real person. Justin has always tried to be normal and not believe the hype that he was in some way better or more important than anyone else, but it was becoming increasingly difficult to be normal, even in Shelby Forest and Millington. He would attract a well-meaning crowd wherever he went. He turned up to watch a high school basketball game in Millington, queued and bought his ticket like everyone else, but inside he was unable to enjoy the game because he was so hassled by rubberneckers and autograph-hunters. In the end, he had to leave and hasn't been back to watch another game. He can no longer easily pop down to the Shelby Forest General Store for a cheeseburger and conversation without the word that he is there spreading faster than a bushfire. Instead, he prefers to order take-out and stays at home while Trace goes to pick it up.

Justin has always hated being regarded as a piece of meat by members of the fairer sex who don't know him. He was, for instance, less than delighted when a girl fan made a grab for his 'trousersnake' during a gig in Foxborough, Massachusetts. His music, meanwhile, highlighted his other pet hate – infidelity. 'See Right Through Me' was about a man who thought his girl loved him but was in fact played for a fool. 'Gone' was an amusingly titled song inspired by Britney Spears – amusing because when he wrote it they were still very much in love. He was inspired by Britney taking a trip to a hair salon and telling him she would be a couple of hours: 'When she got there she decided to get a manicure and a pedicure and wasn't back for five hours or so.' If Justin missed her that much after five hours, one can only imagine how he felt when they eventually split for good and she really was 'Gone'.

Evidence that the critics thought Justin was maturing came in the NME review, which declared, '*Celebrity* fails to disappoint on virtually every level.' It awarded it ten out of ten for six tracks, including 'Pop', which was the first single. This was a golden time for 'N Sync and Justin, who were becoming the darlings of award ceremonies. Justin was in Los Angeles after the New Year, spending some time with Britney. He stayed at her new house in the Hollywood Hills and the two of them behaved like any other couple, except that they were pursued constantly by photographers and video cameramen. A smoochy, tender moment they enjoyed when out shopping one afternoon appeared on the news. At the People's Choice Awards in Pasadena, 'N Sync won Favourite Musical Group or Band. The following day they collected Internet Artist of the Year at the American Music Awards. They had also been nominated for Best Band and Best Album. They didn't collect a Grammy, but they did win Favourite CD, Favourite Single ('Bye Bye Bye') and Favourite Pop Group at the Blockbuster Awards. Justin told the audience, 'I hope everyone's not sick of us.'

'N Sync had to begin their tour two months before the album was ready for release, because they were bringing an enormous Pink Floyd-style extravaganza to the large stadiums around the country. The dates were etched in stone before the football season resumed and the stadiums became unavailable. When the album took longer than expected to finish, the boys still had to go out on the road and present material that was unfamiliar to the audience, except for a couple of tracks and the already released 'Pop'. When the tour began in Jacksonville, Florida, on 23 May 2001, there were three openings acts: Lil Romeo, BB Mak and 3LW.

Moby, who saw the show when it powered into Shea Stadium, New York, was impressed: 'I went for the same reason my father went to see the Beatles at Shea Stadium in 1964, to see the teen phenomenon up close, and what a phenomenon it was. I have to say the concert was one of the most technically impressive I have ever seen.' Justin had even had a crewcut for the landmark concert. The *Star Ledger*, the local newspaper, described the excitement, 'The five members of 'N Sync flew on wires from the main stage to a ramp in the middle of the stadium floor. They bucked futuristic mechanical bulls and aired a computer-animated video made especially for the tour. Fireworks lit up the sky, geysers of sparks gushed from the stage' – and that was during just one song, 'Space Cowboy'. It harked back to the supergroup extravaganzas of the eighties, when battalions of trucks would bring Genesis, Pink Floyd and Led Zeppelin into town – although the thought of Phil Collins popping up and down through a trap-door like a demented mole defies imagination. It was lucky Justin and the boys were so fit. The stage set-up had such a network of tunnels, escape hatches and trap-doors that the audience risked neck injury as they tried to follow where the boys were going to pop up next.

More than fifty trucks and twenty-four buses shipped the production from city to city. It took three days to set up the huge steel construction and two days to take it down. It was hugely ambitious and, financially, very rewarding with Justin and the boys reportedly pocketing close to $1 million (£550,000) for every performance. The most amazing aspect of it all was that this was 'N Sync, mocked in Britain as a footling boy band.

Justin was searching for a more mature audience. The trick at these massive concerts was to capture the attention of the moms and dads, not their screaming, fickle kids. Critics generally agreed that both Justin and JC were solo artists waiting to happen. Justin will always have a following of pre-pubescent girls, but longevity in the music business requires an audience with more financial muscle than the girls' pocket money. It usually also requires continual reinvention. The Rolling Stones could get away with being the same for forty years, but Madonna, Kylie, Robbie and even Britney were examples of artists who reworked their image to keep appearing fresh to the public. If you idolize a band at twelve, you will probably have forgotten all about them at seventeen. But if you still love them at twenty, you will be buying their records for the rest of your life. The perceived wisdom is that the chart shelflife of a 'boy band' (and a girl band) is roughly five years, which is a generation in musical terms. Take, for instance: the Osmonds, 1972–6; Wham, 1982–6; New Kids on the Block, 1989–94; Boyzone, 1994–9; Take That, 1991–6; Spice Girls, 1996–2000; Atomic Kitten 1999–2004. Westlife had their first hit in 1999, so it will be intriguing to see if they survive Bryan McFadden leaving the group in 2004.

In 2001, 'N Sync were approaching that five-year watershed with nothing more to achieve collectively. All 'N Sync could do now was break their own records. Would *Celebrity* eclipse the first week sales of *No Strings Attached?* In the end, it didn't quite make it, selling 1.88 million copies in the first seven days compared to the 2.4 million of their previous album. It still gave 'N Sync the first two places in the list of the fastest selling albums of all time. When the stadium tour finished in August 2001, it was time for a break. How could they top one of the biggest willy-waving tours of all time? It was announced that the group wanted to pursue individual projects. Chris was pushing thirty, bus pass age for a boy band member; Lance and Joey were pursuing acting; and JC harboured similar musical ambitions to Justin. There was talk that they would all appear in a new version of the musical *Grease* and they even showed up at the Cannes Film Festival, which suggested plans for a movie were a priority. So far Joey has had the most movie success with a minor role in the huge box office hit *My Big Fat Greek Wedding*.

Justin was busy spending the year as a fully fledged celebrity, coming to terms with the fact that anything he did either by himself or with Britney was going to be news – good or bad. Something as minor as Justin hurting his ankle made the press, especially as Britney flew 1,200 miles to cheer him up. He was also an official 'celebrity' in Millington, Tennessee, when he made the front cover of the phone book arm in arm with soul legend Al Green, the only other famous local artist, who still lives in the Shelby Forest area. The Millington telephone company printed 29,000 copies, but demand was so high that they had to limit the issue to one copy per phone line.

Justin still had to fulfil all the tour dates with 'N Sync before he could turn his full attention to a solo album. Behind the scenes, Johnny Wright and Lynn were working out his solo deal with Jive Records. The *2001 PopOdyssey* tour became the *Celebrity* tour in 2002, with a raft of dates that finished in Orlando on 28 April. Three days later, Justin's solo deal was finalized. He was determined to press on straight away.

'N Sync have never split up. They are under contact to produce at least one, probably two more albums. There is no indication when or if that will ever happen. Justin's solo success has made it extremely difficult to go backwards, however rewarding it might be financially. *'N Sync's Greatest Hits* and *'N Sync Farewell Live* anyone?

'Talented, intense and just a little full of himself . . .'

14

The Point Guard

Jacqueline Lackey, Justin's mathematics teacher, asked her star pupil one afternoon after class if he would prefer to be famous in basketball or music. He thought for a second before replying, 'Basketball!'

Pride of place in Justin Timberlake's childhood bedroom was a poster of his sporting hero, Michael Jordan. If you take the wealth and fame of David Beckham and then multiply it by ten, you get a rough idea of the esteem with which 'Air Jordan' is held in the US. Only Tiger Woods comes close to the now retired Chicago Bulls star and double Olympic gold medal winner. Jordan was the highest earning sports star in the world in the nineties. He made millions from his Nike endorsements, including those for the 'Air Jordan' sneaker. Justin did his bit for the athlete's bank balance by buying every model of Air Jordans ever made. Justin is not a nervous person by nature, but meeting this sporting god in person reduced him to jelly: 'It put me out of my shoes for a second to be shaking hands with somebody that great.'

Justin was once asked what trade secrets he would swap with Michael Jordan. He replied, 'I saw him dance one time in a Michael Jackson video. He's an awesome basketball player, but he needs a couple of dance lessons.'

Basketball is the abiding passion of Justin's life. Through a common love for the game, he has forged lifetime friendships. Every day after school, he and his friends would play and practise for three hours. It was only after basketball had finished for the day that Justin would turn his attention to other less important matters like homework, singing or dancing lessons. His coach, teacher Kim Lampkins, recalls, 'He loved it and he was a good little basketball player. All the friends he had were right there with him. As point guard, he got to handle the ball a lot and he was a good catcher. We had two games a week, one home and one away and the rest of the time we just practised. He didn't seek attention in a game, always wanting to be number one. He just wanted to blend in and have fun. He was most definitely not a show-off!'

Justin's team at E. E. Jeter won the county competition for sixth graders – one of his proudest achievements. The school yearbook recorded the famous victory: 'Congratulations to Brian, Bucky, Casey, Jeremy, Justin, Kyle, RJ, Rob, Roy, Tim and Wade for such a great year. Shelby Forest Sixth Graders. What a team!'

Understandably, Justin followed the Chicago Bulls because of Michael Jordan, but they were never his favourite team. He was a big fan of a college team called the North Carolina Tar Heels primarily on account of their colours: they played in baby blue, which has always been Justin's favourite colour. When Justin graduated on stage in Memphis, he was handed a gown trimmed in the Carolina colours. He had no geographical or family connection with the team; it was a childhood whim that stayed with him, rather like a Manchester United fan secretly preferring Burnley because of their attractive claret and blue strip. 'He wore that light blue shade constantly,' recalls his first love, Danielle Ditto. Although the rest of the world knows it as baby blue, Justin has always called it Carolina Blue. In a bit of a saddo way he has collected Carolina sports gear all his life.

Shelby Forest is not particularly renowned as sporting country. The game at which many locals, including Justin, are proficient is called frisbee golf. There's a course in Shelby Forest. The basic idea is to throw your frisbee into a basket but, in order to get it there, the thrower has to deal with hazards like dangling chains and poles. The game is hard and requires a great deal of skill. Justin would pop out from his house to play with his buddies when he could find the time in between basketball, golf and riding horses. There was the added distraction of the pool table at home. Justin had a very sporty upbringing, although he never bothered with baseball, despite there being a field just across the road. Occasionally, he would play softball there when he was going out with Danielle.

Justin's love affair with basketball reached new heights when he decided to write a novel based around the sport. He was following in the footsteps of his girlfriend Britney, who had published a book with her mother entitled *A Mother's Gift*, a rags-to-riches tale of a young girl, Holly Faye Lovell, and her mother. Critics generally agreed it was a sugar-coated pill of a book. Justin's effort was called *Inside Drive: A Novel of Basketball, Life and Love*. The hero was a brilliant pro-basketball player called Justin Taylor – no prizes for guessing who provided the basis for the character – who was desperate to reach the play-offs with his team, the Tampa Stingrays. The problem he faced was that the rest of his team were not up to his standard. He needed a point guard to 'assist' him. He knew the perfect player, an old schoolfriend playing for another team. The main drawback was that she was a girl, Teresa Brunson, and women were not allowed on professional men's teams.

Justin grew up with some fine female basketball players who might have been the inspiration for Teresa. One of the first girls he dated, Deanna Dooley, played well, as did Randi Morgan, who played college ball at the University of Tennessee. She lived next door to Trace Ayala and gave some of the best parties in the neighbourhood. The girls would practise in the gym at the opposite end to the boys and did well in their competitive matches. Erika Ruch, who played in the girls' team, recalls, 'The cheerleaders were only interested in the boys because they were cute, but we were good. Everybody in Apex wanted to be a basketball player. My ambition back then was to be the first woman in the NBA.' The publicity blurb for *Inside Drive* – a basketball term – was decidedly cheesy: 'Justin Timberlake pours his passions and beliefs into this intense, exciting story about the game that he loves and a relationship that defies all boundaries.' The book was published in the UK in March 2003 but failed to make waves, perhaps because basketball is such a minority sport here. In the fictionalized story, Justin and Teresa fall in love. It would make a cracking plot for a film, a romantic comedy starring a basketball-mad singer, perhaps, and a tall, rangy popular actress – say, Cameron Diaz?

In real life a love of basketball is an essential ingredient of any romance for Justin Timberlake: 'I really dig girls who are into basketball.' Danielle Ditto fortunately loved the game and still follows it assiduously. Justin took her to a game on their first date and, subsequently, spent dinner afterwards discussing the finer points of the sport with her. They watched many games together. Veronica Finn admits that she doesn't 'really like basketball at all', and prefers American football, one sport Justin has never particularly followed. Britney Spears, however, is a great fan and loves to shoot hoops and play as well. She may be short, but she, too, could play point guard, so perhaps she was the principal inspiration for the Teresa character after all. She would play in charity games with Justin. Both had special shirts: hers had Pinky on the back; his had 'Stinky', which may or may not have been a reference to his legendary belching ability.

Britney and Justin used to play basketball together during *The Mickey Mouse Club* days. Tutor Chuck Yerger recalls, 'All the kids were basketball crazy. They would get an hour off for lunch and they would all go out and play basketball. There was a basket outside of production in one of the big driveways and it was their favourite thing to go down there.' Chuck would get in on the act himself later when he visited 'N Sync House to teach Justin. If he arrived early, he would shoot hoops into the basket they had put up outside until the time reached 8a.m. and he could hammer on the front door until Justin woke up. Veronica Finn, despite not being that interested in the game, recalls the boys would always set up a basketball hoop at venues and unwind by shooting hoops before the gig.

Justin is keen on most sports. If he were British, he would be a soccer fan but one able to hold down a conversation at the bar about any sporting topic. Bob Fischetti at Trans Continental used to throw a big Super Bowl party every year and Justin and the rest of 'N Sync would attend: 'He was a fan of anything sports-related. Not all the guys in the group were the best athletes; some excelled more than others. Justin definitely excelled. One or two may have had a tough time playing basketball with him, but at least it helped them bond.' Justin proved to be the driving force for 'N Sync's annual charity basketball games. These were huge extravaganzas. The first game in the summer of 1999 was played at Georgia State University in Atlanta and raised $50,000 (£27,500). The thrill for Justin was that one of the most famous basketball stars, Kobe Bryant, turned out for it. A year later and the money raised had multiplied tenfold. The 2000 game at St John's University in New York paraded stars including Pink, Queen Latifah and Jordan Knight, formerly of New Kids on the Block, and raised $550,000 (£302,200) for charities including the Justin Timberlake Foundation. Ironically Jordan, the star Justin copied at school, was a support act on the *No Strings Attached* tour.

Justin's team won. He is competitive when it comes to sports, and does not subscribe to the old cliché that taking part is the most important thing. He plays to win at all times, whether at basketball, golf or a board-game in a hotel room on the road. A former basketball friend explains, 'Justin is different when he is playing sports. I guess you have to be mean. But I don't ever recall him losing his temper.'

In 2003 Justin linked up with Turner Sports, covering the events that most interested him. Executive Producer Mike Pearl said, 'We are excited at what this unique marriage between the worlds of sport and entertainment can bring to our high-profile sports properties. Justin's interest and enthusiasm not only in the NBA [National Basketball Association] but in all sports should help provide our broadcasts with a new, fresh approach.'

It was the next best thing to having a professional sports career himself. For one of his first assignments, Justin hooked up with legendary player Magic Johnson for a report called *The NBA Playoffs . . . Justified.* Justin described the modern stars, while Magic compared them to the old-style greats. They shot some hoops together 'one on one'. Justin acquitted himself well, although he admitted that Magic 'took it easy on me'.

One of the other sports that Justin has become progressively more interested in over the years is golf. Surprisingly, two of the biggest modern pop stars in the world, Justin and Robbie Williams, are both very keen golfers – not a pastime that generally promotes street cred. Robbie was junior captain at his local club, but Justin trumped that by playing in the prestigious Bob Hope pro–celebrity tournament at Pebble Beach alongside film stars Samuel L. Jackson and Joe Pesci. The three celebrity golfers played the first round with Ryder Cup hero Justin Leonard; the second alongside the legendary Arnold Palmer; the third with John Daly, arguably the most popular golfer in the world; and the fourth with David Duval, who won The Open in 2001. Justin was thrilled to be in the company of these greats. The Arnold Palmer Hospital was one of the beneficiaries of the 'N Sync annual basketball fundraiser and the previous year had received a cheque for $100,000 (£55,000) from the group. The all-time great lives in the Bay Hill area of Florida not far from where Lynn has set up home.

Justin has been a regular golfer on the courses around Shelby Forest over the years, and enjoys a game with Lynn or his father Randy. He said, 'I love golf because of my situation with work, all over the place all of the time. Playing golf, you're in one place for four and a half or five hours. I can be by myself.'

The disappointment for Justin is that, in basketball terms, at a shade over 6 feet he is just not tall enough. This is a game played professionally by the inhabitants of Jonathan Swift's Brobdingnag, the country of giants. The minimum height requirement seems to be 7 feet tall. For golf, he has the perfect athletic physique, one very similar in terms of height and weight to Tiger Woods.

Justin has continued to play basketball at every opportunity over the years, whether shooting hoops with the 'N Sync guys on tour or, more recently, playing for a Hollywood team. He is one of a group of 130 or so celebrities who belong to the NBA Entertainment League, a 12-team league in which stars such as Tobey Maguire, Leonardo DiCaprio, Woody Harrelson and David Arquette can act out their fantasy of being a pro-basketball player. The idea was excellent publicity for the NBA, especially when wives and girlfriends turned up to cheer on their men: Britney Spears sat in the audience as well as former *Mickey Mouse* chum Keri Russell, who was dating the actor Scott Speedman.

These games have provided a neat link for Justin with the sport he loves and the music that has probably had the most effect on him. The MVP (Most Valuable Player) in the league in 1999 was Brian McKnight, arguably the single biggest musical influence on the career of Justin Timberlake. Brian, who is 6ft 4in, is as passionate about basketball as Justin, and once sang the national anthem at a championship American football game in New Jersey, then caught a plane straight back across to the West Coast so he could play in that evening's championship game in the NBA Entertainment League – he was on the winning team.

From the very beginning, Justin adored the music of Brian McKnight, a hugely influential figure in the US music scene but one who has barely caused a ripple in the UK, where he has never had a top 20 single. Brian is at the forefront of the new Motown era. He is a wonderfully smooth singer with a crooning style that can be seen as a benchmark for the way Justin sings ballads. He was also the favourite singer of Lance Bass and JC Chasez. In the first official 'N Sync book, Justin admitted he looked up to Brian McKnight and would love to work with him one day.

Justin had first met his vocal idol when Brian made a guest appearance on *The Mickey Mouse Club*. Justin was thirteen and in awe of McKnight. Listening to Brian's vocal style on albums such as *Back at One* and *Superhero*, the sound of Justin Timberlake jumps out so obviously. You could be forgiven for thinking it was Justin singing on the track 'Stay'. Imitation is, of course, the sincerest form of flattery. Justin seems to breathe, phrase and project the same tone as Brian. Perhaps it is just as well that Brian is still relatively unknown in the UK. Fortunately for Justin, Brian became a big admirer of his when they finally worked together. Their first collaboration was a duet called 'My Kinda Girl' for Brian's album *Superhero*. They had become friends after mixing in the same circles when 'N Sync was the biggest group in the US. Brian told journalist Lisa Elder, 'I think every time Justin and I work together, I'm amazed at how truly talented he is. I think that coming up in a "boy band" gave him a bad rap of not being talented.'

As well as their love of basketball, Justin and Brian share the same spirituality. The dedication on *Back at One* begins, 'First, Oh Lord, you have placed inside me the ability to touch others through the gift of music.' The words could so easily have graced any of the Justin albums. They are the sentiments Justin expresses to the letter. The two worked together for one track on *Justified*, the timeless 'Never Again', an exquisite ballad representing the very best of Brian McKnight. The 35-year-old R 'n' B heart-throb grew up playing music in church in his home town of Buffalo, New York. He is not a Baptist like Justin; he describes himself as a fifth generation Seventh Day Adventist: 'I learned to sing at age four, seated on my mother's lap in the alto section of the choir.' His musical career began when he was the youngest of the McKnight Brothers, a gospel quartet with a mighty reputation. Elder brother Claude went on to form Take 6, another huge influence on the music of Justin Timberlake. Outside church, the brothers were listening to jazz. Brian became a gifted jazz pianist before he was in his teens.

In another curious parallel with Justin, Brian moved to Orlando when he was a kid. He did not try for *The Mickey Mouse Club*, however, preferring to concentrate on his skills as a musician. He signed a solo record deal when he was nineteen and admits that he was an arrogant young man who had a lot of growing up to do. He also had to contend with a reputation as a sex symbol for much of his twenties, just as Justin has had to learn to do. Brian's major musical influence was Stevie Wonder, one of the seminal influences on the young Justin Timberlake. The musical circle from which the sound of *Justified* grew is a surprisingly small one. Brian aspired to equal the music of Stevie Wonder. He counts himself fortunate to have been Stevie's eyes on more than one occasion, leading him on stage and helping him during concerts. He acknowledged, 'If I had an idol, which I don't because I don't like the word, then he would be it.'

Justin had one of the biggest thrills of his career when Stevie agreed to play harmonica on the song 'Something Like You', written by Justin with Robin Wiley for the *Celebrity* album. Justin also produced the track and had the embarrassing task of telling the great man that his harmonica was out of tune. Justin admits that it was the great work of Stevie Wonder that taught him to sing, as does Brian McKnight. They form a formidable trio of soulful singers.

Brian McKnight's description of Stevie Wonder is one above all others that Justin Timberlake could appreciate. 'For me' says Brian, 'Stevie Wonder is the Michael Jordan of music.'

'I'm a decent golfer, I can shoot some hoops.'

15

Mr JT

Justin was telling Brian McKnight what was going on in his life and how he felt about his split with Britney. Brian started picking out a melody on the piano and Justin, without thinking, began singing a few lines. Before long, they had composed the wounded soul number 'Never Again', which closes the *Justified* album. 'The best songs are the ones you don't have to labour over,' says Brian.

A month before he began recording his first solo album, Justin was spotted buying three albums in the Chicago Virgin Megastore. They were the *Donny Hathaway Collection, The Very Best of Otis Redding* and Marvin Gaye's *What's Going On*. Black music, incorporating R 'n' B and rap, currently dominates the music business. The rebirth of Justin Timberlake, ex-boy band member, as an authentic 'black' artist is one of the more fascinating pop stories of the past couple of years. He is not alone among white stars hitching their wagon to black trends – Eminem and Christina Aguilera are just two examples of white artists hanging on to the coat tails of best-selling black artists, such as 50 Cent, R Kelly, Usher and Beyoncé. The Best Album at the 2004 Grammy Awards was the brilliant *Speakerboxxx/The Love Below* by Outkast, an album that brought together so many of the best aspects of modern black music – rap, jazz, dance and a lyrical content far more sophisticated than the urban chants of the nineties. It is groundbreaking music. The question asked of Mr JT is whether he is a genuine black man inside a white skin, as his friend Brian McKnight has said, or is he a musical opportunist?

Justin did not immediately embrace black culture when he walked off stage for the last time as one-fifth of the most successful boy band in recording history. He did not sit down with Lynn and Johnny Wright and decide that he was going to be a black artist. The roots of Mr JT go all the way back to Shelby Forest, when he had a poster of Michael Jordan on his wall and when his favourite actress was Halle Berry. School friend Erika Ruch remembers him talking about the beautiful actress: 'Halle was his favourite. He loved her. I think he's always had a kind of thing for older women.' Danielle Ditto recalls that when she and Justin were together, their favourite album was by the British artist Sade: 'We used to listen to Sade all the time. The three people we listened to the most were The Fugees – we loved Lauryn Hill – Brian McKnight and Sade. She's so beautiful. We thought Brian McKnight had the voice of an angel. He's so good.'

Justin tends to shuffle the pack of black superstars who are his 'idols'. Many are dead now but remain legends of music; the colour of their skin is incidental. Donny Hathaway is one of the most interesting, and is little known today except among aficionados like Justin. His tenor singing style was one of the most influential of the past thirty years: smooth yet from the heart, plaintive and emotional. His legacy can be heard throughout R 'n' B, particularly in ballads by artists such as Boyz II Men and R Kelly who so dominated the charts of the nineties.

Hathaway was born in St Louis, Missouri, and inevitably received his musical grounding in the church. Like his contemporary, Stevie Wonder, and in the next generation, Brian McKnight, he was an accomplished keyboardist and songwriter as well as a gospel singer. His career as a major recording artist was tragically short. He made his recording debut with the album *Everything is Everything* which contained his own version of 'Young Gifted And Black'. His abilities as a musician came to the fore with his own arrangements. This was the start of a golden age for black music, with Stevie Wonder and Marvin Gaye releasing albums to great critical acclaim in the early seventies.

Hathaway's reputation today rests on his work with the velvet-voiced Roberta Flack, the first black female soloist to top the US album charts with *First Take* in 1972. That was the year she recorded an album of duets with Hathaway that included the classic 'Where Is The Love'. For many, the highlight was Hathaway's solo version of the standard 'For All We Know'. Sadly, fame coincided with bouts of depression. His final solo album, *Extensions of a Man*, released in 1973, includes what is generally regarded as his seminal work, 'Someday We'll All Be Free', which Alicia Keys sang in the 9/11 concert special. Alicia cites Hathaway as one of her main musical influences. It is no coincidence that she was one of the musicians who helped Justin on *Justified*.

Hathaway collaborated with Roberta Flack in 1977 to record 'The Closer I Get To You' and 'Back Together Again'. The former was recently a hit for Luther Vandross and Beyoncé. The two tracks were the only ones he finished for another planned album of duets before his apparent suicide. Hathaway died three years before Justin was born, but the music Mr JT loves has his influence running through it. It was only a matter of time before someone who loved black music was going to discover one of the greats. 'I'm a big fan of Donny Hathaway,' he admits. 'I think it's a shock to people that I even know who Donny Hathaway is.'

Motown has been a strong influence throughout Justin's career. Hathaway, who was signed to Atlantic, was one of Justin's few musical heroes who was not on the legendary Detroit label. Marvin Gaye was the possessor of a high tenor voice that many aspire to but nobody can match. His dance tracks of the sixties, including the party hit 'I Heard It Through The Grapevine', helped shape the Motown sound, but it was his groundbreaking album *What's Going On*, the first R 'n' B concept album of any note, which gave him the status of a music great. The title track and 'Mercy Mercy Me' are just two examples of a changing sound in black popular music. The year after Justin was born, Marvin Gaye won two Grammys for the exceptional 'Sexual Healing'. Two years later, Gaye was shot dead by his father, an ordained minister.

Marvin Gaye and Donny Hathaway were not great chart stars of Justin's youth, but their music did not pass him by because Lynn, recognizing Justin's love of soul, would buy records that she thought would interest him. There are two music capitals in Tennessee: Nashville, home of country music, Kenny Rogers, Glen Campbell and Garth Brooks; and Memphis, home to blues and jazz and a great black music heritage. Fortunately, Justin liked Memphis and it helped that the Reverend Al Green had settled in his own neighbourhood. Like practically every other great black singer of the past, Al Green started his career singing in a gospel group. His first two hit singles 'Tired Of Being Alone', and, particularly, 'Let's Stay Together', would have fitted easily on to the *Justified* album.

After a personal tragedy in the early seventies, Green became a preacher at the Full Gospel Tabernacle in Memphis and bought a house in Shelby Forest, not far from Justin's family home, where he still lives. He continues to preach at the church, even though he has long since resumed a mainstream music career. He joined Justin on stage at a concert at the New Daisy Theatre in Memphis to sing 'Let's Stay Together'. Justin was not overshadowed – a tribute to how much his voice has matured since 'I Want You Back'.

As a young boy, Justin was not obsessed by these black music greats. He grew into them in his teenage years by mixing with like-minded people. His singing coach Bob Westbrook remembers, 'He liked the charts. That's what he wanted to sing when he came to lessons.' Unsurprisingly, it was imitating New Kids on the Block, a very white boy band, that first got him singing seriously. In Shelby Forest, the kids in the playground were not singing 'Where Is The Love'; they knew the lyrics to 'Please Don't Go Girl'.

The Motown act that bridged the gap between the charts and classic soul for Justin was Boyz II Men, four young black men from Philadelphia who recorded some of the biggest hits of the early nineties. They were the kings of the sweet, soulful *a capella* ballad and a great influence on the non-techno side of 'N Sync. They released three of the biggest records of the decade about the time that Justin was in *The Mickey Mouse Club*: 'End Of The Road', 'I'll Make Love To You' and the collaboration with Mariah Carey, 'One Sweet Day', which holds the US record for most weeks at number one with sixteen. All the members of 'N Sync would quote Boyz II Men as a big influence on their music.

Justin would be very unusual if he had honed his musical tastes by the end of his teenage years, but his love of black music is genuine. His desire to incorporate that heritage into his music seems perfectly honest and natural. If he had begun his solo career by dressing up in a white suit, dusting off a big ol' cowboy hat and offering a version of 'Rhinestone Cowboy' . . . that would have been a fraud. He explained, 'I grew up on Stevie, Marvin, Michael and Donny. At the same time, I love hip hop. I love to rock to the Beatles and Elvis. I love James Brown and Prince. I have so many inspirations and I take all of that and I turn them into things that are my own.'

Justin's agonizing break-up with Britney was the best thing that could have happened to his solo career. When they were happy and in love, he came up with 'Pop' and 'Celebrity'. After the split, when his mood was dark and introspective, he fashioned passionate and much more mature tracks, 'Cry Me A River' and 'Never Again'. They became instant classics. Brian McKnight observed that Justin had been spurred on by the first-love situation that Britney had represented for him: 'He had such a great story to tell that it was easy.' In a way, they are the letters he never wrote to Britney but perhaps should have done. In 'Cry Me A River', he reveals his inner bitterness, suggesting that it was Britney (not named in the song of course) who had burned her bridges and it was now her turn to cry, while in 'Never Again' he tells her that all she had to do was apologize and mean it. The video for 'Cry Me A River' would subsequently confirm that the bridge-burning Justin refers to was, in fact, being unfaithful and that the crying was as a result of Justin taking the opportunity to move on to another sexual relationship.

When it came to his first solo album, Justin was a man with a purpose. Besides Brian, he enlisted the help of Timbaland, real name Tim Mosely, a well-respected R 'n' B producer who is at the cutting edge of new music, producing an urban sound for artists like Missy Elliott and Jay-Z. Timbaland was one man Justin had not worked with at 'N Sync, and he was not easily persuaded that a white, boy band heart-throb was the best person with whom to collaborate. 'At first I was like, "He's coming from 'N Sync. I'm coming from my urban world. How we gonna mesh?" But when we got together everything was perfect. It's hard coming from 10 million sales to switch up some styles and do something different, but he's just being him. I'm down with taking chances 'cos I'm a chance-taker myself.'

Timbaland and his songwriting partner, clarinet-playing Scott Storch were the team behind the haunting melody for 'Cry Me A River', but it was Justin's lyrics that gave the song its status as the best on the album. It was restrained, even mysterious, and more powerful for it. Justin is a great learner, a product of his strong academic upbringing, and he enjoyed watching the differing styles of these influential producers. Timbaland was very intuitive and spontaneous, breezing into the studio with a 'What shall we do today?' attitude and creating something original in a ten-minute whirlwind. Justin enthused, 'I'm blown away every time, because you see him just sit there and punch buttons. He says, "You like this beat", and I'm like, "You kidding?"'

The Neptunes, however, were responsible for the overall production feel on the record. Justin lost no time in recruiting Chad 'Hip Hop' Hugo and Pharrell Williams after he had so enjoyed working with them on their song 'Girlfriend' for the 'N Sync *Celebrity* album. Justin put it succinctly, 'We had such a connection that it was a no-brainer to work with them again.' The charismatic Pharrell Williams, in particular, has become one of Justin's best friends, sharing a similar sense of fun, spirituality and musical direction.

There was no messing about because Justin wanted to hit the ground running while 'N Sync was still perched at the top of the tree. Six weeks after pitching up at the East Coast Virginia Beach studios of the Neptunes, he was playing the album to Johnny Wright who, for the first time, could hear confirmation of what he already knew: Justin Timberlake was going to be a major solo artist. There was a sexuality to the music that the clean-cut image of 'N Sync could never allow. Johnny was convinced the timing was right.

He told *Entertainment Weekly*, 'The traditional five-member, male pop group is starting to fizzle. As your musical tastes open up, at some point what you personally like and want to do might not be in the best interest of the group. So when you have that passion, you have to step out and present it, and that's what Justin did . . . This is all about the passion and the music that's inside of him.'

Justin's creativity had a growth spurt. He co-wrote all thirteen tracks on the album. At least the same number again never made it past initial recording. Pharrell Williams summed it up: 'This is not Justin from 'N Sync's solo album; this is Justin Timberlake's first album.' The man Justin put in charge of the production coordination responsible for pulling *Justified* together is Silas White, the A & R consultant, who says Justin knew what he wanted from day one: 'He wanted to stretch himself.' Silas is best described as an R 'n' B impresario. He is also the manager of Brian McKnight, strengthening the 'family' environment that Justin created for his first solo project. Silas is a one-man Justin fan club: 'This kid is one of those special artists who comes along every so often and changes everything.'

Justin's good fortune and good management allow him to surround himself with talent that is going to bring out the best in him – not just great producers and musicians but also carefully selected artists who are going to give him something extra. At first Justin wanted to do everything himself, but as the sound began to emerge, new ideas came easily. He also has the clout to hook up with the artists he admires. On *Justified,* for instance, Bubba Sparxxx provides the rap on 'Right For Me'. Bubba is a larger-than-life white rapper from Georgia. Like Justin, he was born into a Bible-belt community but one a great deal more rural – some might say redneck – than Shelby Forest. While Justin brings a soulful style to hip hop, Bubba brings country roots. Bubba is another white artist to benefit from hitching his wagon to Timbaland, releasing his debut album on the producer's Beat Club label. The album *Dark Days, Bright Nights* entered the US album charts at number three on its release in 2001. Bubba was a natural choice to provide the southern drawl rap on 'Right For Me', although the collaboration was an accident. Bubba was in the studio to see

Timbaland and told Justin he really liked one of the beats they were laying down. The two southern boys hit it off and Justin suggested he should be on the track, so Bubba popped outside for a couple of hours and wrote a 16-bar rap for the end of the song. 'Right For Me' was one of the best received tracks on the album. Justin told the *New York Post*, 'It's raw. It's just a beatbox, vocal percussion groove. If you listen closely to the melody, then it's really honky-tonk. I think it stands out.'

Overall, these collaborations promote the idea that Justin Timberlake is a legitimate artist because of the quality and the credibility of the people who will work with him. Hip-hop artists The Clipse and the dreamy-voiced Vanessa Marquez augmented that impression on 'Like I Love You' and 'Rock Your Body' respectively. Justin wrote Vanessa's part especially for her because he loved her voice. He also said, 'She's hot and she's beautiful.' Justin purposefully eschewed a big-name rapper for 'Like I Love You', believing a new start for him should have a relatively new collaborating act to give the project freshness.

Justified was released on 5 November 2002. Justin explained that he thought of the title after a dancer had come up to him and used the expression. It was apt, because Justin was now 'justified' as a proper grown-up artiste. The working title had been *Out of the Blue*, which had double meaning as an unexpected sound from the 'N Sync singer and as a tribute to his favourite colour. *Justified* was a much stronger choice with street cred, in addition to its nominal association with Justin. He gave an impetus to launch day by performing two of the strongest tracks, 'Like I Love You' and 'Cry Me A River', live in Times Square, New York, for MTV's TRL (Total Request Live). First week sales in the US were a very respectable 445,000, but the album was kept off the number one slot by Eminem's brilliant soundtrack to his film *8 Mile*. The Timberlake competitive streak rose to the surface when he declared, 'Nobody does an album and says, "I hope this goes straight to number two." I have goals and big plans.' By coincidence, Justin's album was released the week after the solo debut of Nick Carter, the pin-up singer from Backstreet Boys. Justin has since waved Nick goodbye in the solo popularity stakes.

Significantly, Justin and Johnny Wright had decided to target the UK as well. The first single from the album, 'Like I Love You', had reached number two in the British charts the week before the album was released in the States. In October 2002, Justin crossed the Atlantic to perform on *Top of the Pops* and in guest spots on Radio One and Capital Radio in a PR blitz aimed at getting his name and music out there. He did not want to fall into the trap that had snared 'N Sync in thinking their enormous American success guaranteed them prestige in Britain. Justin very nearly had a blank canvas to work on in a Britain untainted by the techno pop and terrible haircuts of 'N Sync days. Rick Sky observes, 'He was not going to make the same mistakes that 'N Sync did in Britain. The hype in music is so much quicker than it was five or ten years ago. You don't have four albums to establish yourself these days. You have one chance and that's it.' The prospect of 'N Sync ever winning a Brit Award were nil, but in 2004 Justin won two, indicating that he had 'cracked' Britain. Rick Sky adds, 'Obviously there is a musical talent there with Justin.'

The promotional campaign for *Justified* came to a shuddering halt when Justin broke his foot rehearsing for the tour. He soon found himself back at the family home in Shelby Forest being fussed over by Lynn. He was home for three weeks – the longest time he had been at home since he was fifteen and left to find fame and fortune with 'N Sync. For those three weeks, he was able to live a normal, everyday life. His immobility cast him in the unlikely role of couch potato. He would play Halo with Trace for hours. His mother fed him his favourite foods, which did no favours whatsoever to his six-pack stomach. His grandmother Sadie made him peach cobbler. He went to an Aerosmith concert in Memphis and hobbled out to dinner with old friends. He put his bodyguards up at the best local motel – it may have been home but he still needed security.

He also had plenty of time to read the reviews. Not everyone was impressed. *NME* accused Justin of 'poncing off black talent', although the review by Alex Needham also recognized that commercially it was a very savvy thing to do. Intriguingly, the respect the album went on to garner in the music world seems to have bypassed it initially, when it received a distinctly lukewarm reaction. *UK Launch* complained it was a collection of 'sounds, textures and atmospheres desperately seeking a tune' and there was 'little of substance'.

Many of the critics concentrated on the influence of Michael Jackson on the album. One wrote: '"Like I Love You" doesn't recall a Michael Jackson song so much as the feeling of dancing to a Michael Jackson song in front of the mirror.' Justin exacerbated the situation when he appeared on the MTV Music Awards in an apparent homage to Jackson. Justin protested that he never contemplated that people would think he was copying Michael Jackson. Justin wore black leather trousers, a red T-shirt, a black long-sleeved shirt, and topped off the whole ensemble with a black fedora, which he flipped around his head just like Jacko in his videos from the early eighties. Justin ingenuously claimed it was in homage to Frank Sinatra, Fred Astaire and Gene Kelly. That suggestion was undermined by him wearing two black gloves, indisputably a Jackson trademark. Justin has been adept at using his hat as a prop ever since he rolled one down his arm when he sang Garth Brooks' 'Two Of A Kind' as a child. The inevitable comparison was not helped by Jackson being at the event to receive an award from Britney Spears.

Justin was desperate to distance himself from any allegation that he was a Michael Jackson copycat. He wanted to be the first Justin Timberlake not the second Jacko. His difficulty was that the Neptunes' sound on his album was so in thrall to Michael Jackson that, in parts, *Justified* sounded like the offcuts from the legendary *Off the Wall* album, which Jackson released in 1979. 'Rock Your Body', in particular, was chiselled from the same musical block as 'Rock With You' or even the earlier Jacksons' number one, 'Show You The Way To Go'. Hugo and Williams had actually written some of the tracks with Jackson not Timberlake in mind. To be able to stand comparison with the best of Michael Jackson at the height of his fame and creativity is no mean achievement. The Jackson influence the Neptunes impressed on *Justified* gives it a smooth, stylish and sexy feel – so much so that many felt *Justified* was an album Michael Jackson should have made.

Much was also made of Justin's vocals, particularly that his falsetto was a rip-off of Michael Jackson's, but that is less than fair. Justin is a vocal magpie but he is not alone in that regard. Even the very greatest singers are influenced by others. Elvis Presley, for instance, forged his unique style from his love of the black artists of the fifties. Neither Elvis nor Justin are copycats. Justin's vocals may be influenced by Jackson but no more so than by Stevie Wonder and, in particular, by Brian McKnight. Having absorbed the styles he likes, Justin could find his own original voice. Unfortunately, the first single taken from the album, 'Like I Love You', is the most Jacko-like vocally and set the tone of critical opinion. In Justin's defence, Michael Jackson had probably experienced his best days by the time young Master Timberlake was compiling his record collection.

The 'blackness' of Mr JT does not find universal favour, and it's not just *NME* who noticed it. A music business insider in Los Angeles confides, 'If Michael Jackson is a black man who dyes his skin white, then Justin is a white boy who thinks he's black. He's got the rhythm and he's got all the moves, but he's still a white boy and a lot of the hard-core blacks are sick of him making out like he's one of them, because he will never be.' Justin may be laughing all the way to the bank, but there is growing resentment in the music industry of black music being appropriated by white artists. Justin even won the honour for Best Video at the MOBO (Music of Black Origin) Awards. The debate will continue to rage about white stars sounding like black stars. Is it still black music if it is sung by a white artist?

Despite all the hype, the sales of more than 7 million and the awards, *Justified* is only one album. The crunch for Justin will come when album number two is released. Although top producers and musicians are forming an orderly queue to work with him, he will, for the most part, stick with his friend Pharrell Williams. Lauren Christy from the LA-based hit songwriting team The Matrix, explains why the music business loves Justin: 'He is incredibly loyal to those people in his tight circle. People in this business aren't exactly known for their loyalty so it's refreshing to see someone so young making such good decisions. That's why Justin will never be a flash in the pan. Apart from his obvious talent and good looks, people have a lot of respect for him and he's going to be around for many years to come.

'Everyone would love to work with Justin but he is going to stick with the Neptunes. They helped launch his solo career and he's not going to simply forget that overnight. He's very smart. You've got to admire him for that.'

'I wrote these songs from my heart.'

16

I'm Sorry, Miss Jackson

Justin had two favourite posters on his bedroom wall at home in Shelby Forest. One was of his basketball hero Michael Jordan. The other was of Janet Jackson.

Much has been made of Michael Jackson's influence on Justin's music, but he is only one of a number of influential black artists who have shaped the musical style of Mr JT, and he is not even the most influential member of the Jackson clan. That accolade firmly belongs to Janet Jackson, who may not have shared the high profile of her brother but is still one of the most successful artists of the last twenty years.

Janet Jackson was one of the world's major recording artists at a time when Justin was hopping on the school bus or admiring her poster on his bedroom wall. He was just five years old when she broke into the UK top ten for the first time in March 1986 with 'What Have You Done For Me Lately'. How many young boys with a picture of a dream girl on their bedroom wall are going to end up snogging the object of their desire and having their nose an inch away from an exposed right breast? Janet also sang backing vocals on *Justified*. Justin's former girlfriend Veronica Finn observes, 'He was always into Janet.'

Justin first saw her perform live when her 1990 *Rhythm Nation* tour came to the Mid-South Coliseum in Memphis. Her energetic and daring dance routines and the way she worked the stage made a deep impression on the 9-year-old. He would later observe, 'She didn't just stand there and sing her song.' They first became friendly when 'N Sync were the opening act on her *Velvet Rope* tour in 1998. At a special MTV tribute to Janet Jackson, 'N Sync sang a version of her American number one, 'That's The Way Love Goes'. In *The Billboard Book of Top 40 Hits*, the track comes in at number thirty in the top 100 US hits from 1955 to 1999, which reveals just what a huge star Janet is in the States. Her brother Michael's biggest hit, 'Billie Jean', comes in at number fifty-one. She was also rated the second biggest artist in the US during the nineties, beaten only by Mariah Carey and ahead of Madonna, Whitney Houston and Celine Dion.

The first suggestion that Justin and Janet were anything more than friends came soon after he split up with Britney. There are two opinions about the extent of their relationship: the first is that they enjoyed a mild flirtation; the second is that they were good friends putting on a little show to gain some publicity. The press were excited about the possibility that they were the next showbiz mega-couple, enjoying the fact that she was thirty-six and corrupting a boy of twenty-one. They were first spotted dancing in a bump-and-grind fashion at an LA nightclub. Janet was going 'buck wild' said an anonymous source. Then another 'anonymous' eyewitness said they were 'making out' at a birthday party for Missy Elliott. They had, according to this prudish voyeur, locked lips brazenly.

The basic rule of thumb to follow with celebrity 'affairs' is that if the pages of the gossip columns or the glossy weekly magazines reveal all before you can say 'Boo', then it's not real. Justin is very private and discreet about his few real love affairs. He kept his relationship with Britney secret for more than a year before going public. His subsequent true love affair with Cameron Diaz is also being conducted, as far as possible, away from prying eyes. Yet we are expected to believe that this is the same man who let the world know about his tonsil hockey games with a fellow musical artist.

All celebrities play this game because it works. The media are happy to go along with it because it fills pages, provides headlines and sells copies. The public are happy to be duped because it's fun to read. The giveaway is that it is all hot and steamy for a nanosecond, then the trail goes as cold as a winter's night in Siberia. A classic example was Robbie Williams and Nicole Kidman's trysts at a London hotel when there was a single to promote. How many times has Robbie been linked with Nicole since? Answer: nil. Even more ludicrous was Chris Evans and Geri Halliwell's 'lurve' match when she had a single coming out. It's part of what being a star is all about – promoting an image and publicizing a product. Justin Timberlake is a product just as Robbie Williams, Kylie Minogue or David Beckham are. They have a public face to project that makes them a good living and pays the wages of a great many people attached to them. This is business and if it means having to lock lips with a beautiful member of the opposite sex, then that is not exactly hard labour. The only time a relationship might be real is if it is flatly denied, as in 'Britney, are you going out with Justin?', 'No, I'm not.'

Justin's sex life post-Britney became a matter of daily interest to the gossip columnists. It was so unusual to see Justin out with anyone other than Britney that every time he was seen in the company of a young woman it became an item of monumental importance. One report said he licked whipped cream off the belly and other areas of some young women in a New York bar. On a more personal level, Justin was seen out with Alyssa Milano, the star of the hit US series *Charmed*, about young witches, as well as with Jenna Dewan. Both women were seen hanging out in Justin's trailer while he was filming the video for 'Like I Love You' in Los Angeles. Alyssa, at twenty-nine, was an 'older' woman and a portent of a more serious love affair just around the corner. The relationship petered out apparently because Alyssa wanted to take things more seriously.

Best of all for the gossip columnists was the occasion when Justin and Britney ran into each other at The Lounge in Los Angeles. Justin was with the shapely Jenna Dewan, which did not exactly please Britney. The ex-couple allegedly got into a slanging match in which Britney accused Justin of using various women to get media attention. The prickly situation ended with the pair dancing up a storm in a *West Side Story*-style dance-off. Justin would do a move, then Britney would do one. It was all good fun for the onlookers, but there is nothing worse than bumping into your ex on a night out, and it would not be the last time this happened. The problem with the city of Los Angeles is that it really is a small town.

Amusingly, Justin, who has won so many awards in the past few years, was handed a spoof one from a television station that gave him 'The Aspiring Love Rat Award.' A whirlwind tour of London saw him out clubbing every night and drinking champagne while watching the Super Bowl in a West End bar. This is the whole point of a publicity tour – to get publicity. Justin is not going to get many mentions in the tabloids if he orders room service and tucks up early with a good book every night. His profile in Britain continued to rise with the news that *Justified* became number one on the album chart in January 2003.

Justin is a trained and polished actor and performer. When it's your life from the age of twelve onwards, you know how to handle yourself in an interview, to give away only what you want and to keep to an agenda. The listening or watching public don't always realize that the interviewer is briefed on what is allowed. No Britney, no Cameron, no Christina are three taboos Justin has been known to insist upon. The unconfirmed report was that Cameron Diaz and Miss Aguilera are not exactly the best of friends. Naturally, Justin's name had been linked with Christina's when there was a tour to promote.

Justin is at his media-savvy best in his handling of the British press. He seems to know instinctively how to push their buttons – and nothing pushed the right buttons more than the affair of Kylie's derrière. Kylie Minogue is not a big star in America. Only recently, since the success of the hypnotic 'Can't Get You Out Of My Head', has she been able to shake off the label of being the 'Locomotion' girl, a hangover from her biggest stateside hit, the murderous Stock, Aitken, Waterman version of the Little Eva classic. She failed to permeate the consciousness of Shelby Forest or *The Mickey Mouse Club*, although physically a young Britney would have been perfect casting for the younger sister of Charlene on *Neighbours*.

Kylie is no stranger when it comes to generating a little mischief with a handsome male star, as she had done with Robbie Williams.

They were put together by her record company EMI in 2000, when he was the biggest male artist in the country and she was fashioning her big comeback. He gave her timely street cred with their duet 'Kids', which revealed they could make the sparks fly between them in performance. There was some jokey banter about a possible relationship, with Robbie enquiring, 'Do you reckon she'd shag me?' The alliance worked well for both of them. She made him look sexy and he made her look cool. The formula worked well, so why not try it again? This time Kylie was paired with Justin. She could give him exposure in the UK, where he was only just beginning to break free of the chains of being Mr Britney Spears, and he could give her artist credibility in the United States, where his star totally eclipsed hers.

The result was a publicist's dream. The occasion was the Brit Awards night at Earls Court, London, on 20 February 2003. Kylie and Justin agreed to perform a duet together, a version of the Blondie song 'Rapture'. It had been a top ten hit in the UK the week Justin was born. The group fronted by Debbie Harry had also been number one in the US in January 1981 with 'The Tide Is High'. The double act was sizzling, with Justin as smooth as Sinatra, especially when he made his now famous move on Kylie's bottom. The great British public have enjoyed a healthy obsession with Kylie's rear ever since she squeezed into the tiniest pair of gold hot pants for the video of her number one, 'Spinning Around'. The reports that he 'grabbed' her bum were a little over the top, as the number was thoroughly rehearsed. But the petite Australian did look sensational in a little black mini-dress and Justin, in his favourite white and silver hip-hop gear, seemed to linger over his public grope. The performance blew every other act off the stage at the Brits that year. Robbie sensibly accepted his award by satellite. The next day the papers had only one highlight from the most prestigious music ceremony in the UK.

Justin, who has always been a connoisseur of the butt and proudly declares himself an ass man, said all the right things afterwards: 'She's got the hottest ass I've ever seen. I didn't just touch it. I copped a feel. On a scale of one to ten it was a fifty-eight.' After the event, Justin played a diverting game of musical Minogues. He joined Kylie and her sparrow-like sister Dannii for a cosy dinner 'à douze' – the three stars with assorted minders and hangers-on – at the Montpeliano restaurant in Knightsbridge. Then they moved on to an EMI reception at the Sanderson hotel just off Oxford Street, where they were joined by Justin's good friend Janet Jackson. Dannii left the party with Justin and they drove back to Knightsbridge, to the Mandarin Oriental Hotel, where he had a suite for his stay. This was the jumping-off point for a suggestion that Dannii had spent the night in his room – not true. Dannii later confessed, 'I caught a ride home in his car . . . I didn't go to his hotel room at all. I fancy Justin when he's singing – I love it when he's doing his dancing thing. But when I was chatting to him, it was like, "It's just Justin" . . . It was the best one-night stand I never had.'

Dannii had gone straight back to her Battersea home, leaving the stage clear for Kylie to slip into the hotel entirely unnoticed except by a tabloid journalist, who reported a night of passion while her soon-to-be ex-boyfriend James Gooding banged on the door of her flat in Chelsea. They were in the middle of an acrimonious break-up, which culminated in him selling his story. It was hardly a night of passion. Kylie clocked in at 3.53 and clocked out of the back entrance at 6a.m. The whole thing was practically a carbon copy of Nicole Kidman and Robbie Williams. Robbie was spotted by a *News of the World* journalist arriving at Nicole's hotel at 9.30 p.m. after she had recorded an interview with Michael Parkinson. He was clocked leaving at 2.55 a.m. precisely. Robbie has not been spotted any time since at Nicole Kidman's hotel nor has Kylie been spied at Justin's. All Justin would say is that he had been phoned by Kylie and that he had invited her over for a drink: that was probably the truth of it.

After the Brits, it was time for the Grammys and, perhaps, the master plan became clearer. Kylie flew to New York to present an award on stage with Justin, who quipped, 'Can I grab your ass again?' She had provided him with publicity gold in the UK and now he was returning the favour in the US. It was clearly a case of 'You scratch my bum and I'll scratch yours'.

A more intriguing dalliance, but not necessarily one with any more substance, involved Justin and Emma Bunton. The rumours that they had enjoyed a fling first surfaced the month before the Brits, when it was boldly reported that Justin had secretly bedded the former Spice Girl. Emma does fit Justin's preferred type – blonde with a big booty – but there was no real evidence that they had done anything more than dance to Christina Aguilera's hit 'Dirrty'. They had a laugh together at a couple of celebrity events. Emma is an accomplished and confident entertainer who, like Justin, was a child performer. The innuendoes resurfaced when they were together at the Rex Cinema and Bar in London in May. Emma revealed, 'I am a very private person. We had a bit of a kiss.' The true extent of their 'relationship' was a chat, a laugh and a snog.

However much the papers want to believe that Justin is a red-blooded one-night stand sort of guy, there is absolutely no evidence that he is anything of the kind. Unlike Robbie Williams, no lap-dancer or curvaceous blonde has come out of the wood-work to provide a voracious press with a kiss-and-tell story. Justin, in more honest moments, admits that he is quite shy with women and is a 'loving, caring person', which hardly makes the grade in the Bill Wyman–Mick Jagger school of serial shagging. Four serious relationships of more than one year's duration by the age of twenty-three are the proof. He admits that one-night stands are not really his forte, saying, 'I'm not smooth when it comes to stuff like that.' There is a world of difference between being a notch on a groupie's garter belt and enjoying some canoodling in a Chicago nightclub. Being seen in the company of beautiful women or vis-iting strip clubs, pole-dancing joints or even the Playboy Mansion is not exactly 'over-the-top' rock 'n' roll behaviour for a young man in his early twenties. In the US, it is known as harmless 'jock' behaviour. Justin claims to find strip clubs 'so funny'.

Justin is always willing to play the media game for publicity. At the 2004 Brits, the chase was not for a famous woman like Kylie, but for an 'unknown' blonde spotted sneaking into his hotel. A very attractive young blonde woman was photographed with a naked left breast hanging out of her cocktail dress as she was escorted into Justin's hotel. Her identity became a great tabloid mystery for a day or two until she was exposed as a secretary from Birmingham called Jodie Foley. She gave an interview to the press in which she came across as a level-headed girl – not on the make – who said she was dating one of Justin's bodyguards: 'Justin is loyal to his girlfriend. He never talks about his relationship with Cameron Diaz, but I think it is serious. He is just a friend – although a gorgeous one.' Justin has said on more than occasion, and with pride, that he has never cheated on a girlfriend. So why would he start now when he was involved in a steady relationship with Cameron?

He scooped all the newspapers headlines at the Brit Awards for the second year running. He won two Brits – for Best International Male Solo Artist and Best International Album for *Justified* – but that tended to be forgotten in the hunt for the mystery blonde. As for The Darkness, who practically swept the board with three top awards, nobody could have cared less after catching sight of Jodie's breast.

Jodie's breast was not the most notorious boob of Justin's year – not by a long way. That accolade belonged to Janet Jackson and the case of the mysterious 'wardrobe malfunction'. The occasion was the half-time duet of Janet and Justin at the biggest US sporting event of the year, the Super Bowl. The TV audience for this glamorous and glitzy occasion is estimated at more than 140 million. What fantastic publicity it would be if you could pull something off – like the leather cup covering Janet's right breast, which, by chance, had been decorated with a sun-shaped silver nipple piercing. Exactly why Janet was wearing such an ostentatious piece of jewellery if it was never going to be seen has never been properly explained. The timing was perfect. They were performing 'Rock Your Body' and just as Justin sings the immortal line 'Bet I'll have you nekkid by the end of this song', hey presto, out pops Janet's bap.

Afterwards there were protestations of innocence all round. Janet's spokesman said the incident 'was a malfunction of the wardrobe'. The implication was that Justin had pulled too hard. Justin joined in: 'I am sorry if anyone was offended by the wardrobe malfunction during the half-time performance at the Super Bowl. It was not intentional and is regrettable.' He hinted that his family back in Shelby Forest were among those offended by the incident. Janet was also contrite: 'The decision to have a costume reveal at the end of my half-time show was made after final rehearsals. It was not my intention for it to go as far as it did. I apologize to anyone offended – including the audience, MTV, CBS and the NFL.' Further apologies came from MTV, which produced the half-time show, and from the NFL (National Football League).

The Federal Communications Commission Chairman, Michael Powell, the television head moral watchdog, was slightly less convinced by all the hand-wringing. 'Clearly somebody had knowledge of it. Clearly it was something that was planned by someone. She probably got what she was looking for.' He promptly ordered an investigation. For good measure, he called it a 'classless, crass and deplorable stunt. Our nation's children, parents and citizens deserve better.'

The moral majority in the US were apparently up in arms over the incident. In Britain it was looked upon with a great deal of healthy cynicism. 'Oh Janet, you look a right t**' exclaimed the *Daily Mirror.* If it was a stunt, it was a very tired one, but it received an enormous amount of coverage. Once again Justin blew coverage of the main event off the newspaper pages. And Janet? Her new single 'Just A Little While' was, with amazingly fortuitous timing, released the following day. The album *Damita Jo* was ready to hit the shops the following month. The problem for the apologists was that an item (hastily removed) on the MTV website had promised 'shocking moments' from Jackson during the performance. Janet was still apologizing two months later when she appeared on *David Letterman* to plug the album, insisting it was an accident: 'It was very embarrassing for me to have so many people see this little breast.'

The shock was not peak-time viewing of Janet Jackson's nipple but the fact that the 'stunt' was so naff. It made groping Kylie's bum seem like fine art. At least two expressions have now found their way into common usage: 'wardrobe malfunction' and 'costume reveal'. For once Justin did not come out of it smelling entirely of roses. Some commentators took the opportunity to have as go at Justin for what they perceived as 'shifting the blame' on to Janet.

The problem is that Britney snogging Madonna worked so well that the shock factor became essential. *Advertising Age* reported a senior executive as saying the Jackson episode was 'extremely successful'. It re-enforced Janet Jackson as a 'product', even if she was a little past her sell-by date. For Justin, it was just another piece of publicity, although he did maintain that a stunt was not his style and he had no reason to do this – no reason at all except to do a good turn for an old friend whose poster he used to have on his bedroom wall.

'I like the way the small of a woman's back forms a nice onion.'

17

Justified and Stripped

The line-up for the SARS concert in Toronto was a rocker's dream: the Rolling Stones, AC/DC, the Guess Who, Rush and . . . Justin Timberlake. During Justin's three-song set, the Canadian rock fans booed and pelted him with water bottles. 'It messed with my head for two weeks,' said Mr JT.

The stage show for *Justified* exploded into action on 7 May 2003, in Sheffield of all places, when he was riding high in the UK charts with 'Rock Your Body', which opened the set. Justin chose the Yorkshire city to launch the tour that would become one of the most successful arena tours ever. Justin's strategy was to trial the show in the United Kingdom before making it bigger and better in the US. It would be impossible to top the latter-day 'N Sync tours, but Justin wanted something interesting and innovative. He achieved this in America by teaming up with Christina Aguilera, whose second album *Stripped* had been released to terrific reviews. It contained a record-rack of number one hits. Christina is always going to be the subject of good media copy. She demands attention and makes Justin seem very conservative in comparison to her outrageous dress, demeanour and behaviour. She has the persona of a Minnie Mouse who grew up to be Jessica Rabbit. Justin's team knew that she would help get kids in their seats. Only teaming up with Britney could have grabbed more attention. Justin observed, 'I think we were at similar stages of our career where we wanted to break the mould of what people looked on as teen pop.'

Justin was the bigger star, certainly in America, and Christina took the stage first, even if the billing was shared in the *Justified/Stripped* tour. The 'N Sync formula of putting on a spectacular was ingrained in Justin's approach to his solo stage show, which utilized a posse of brilliant dancers, a band of excellent, primarily black musicians, including a three-piece horn section, and a hatful of pyrotechnic tricks, including Justin tap-dancing on a grand piano before disappearing with a bang and a puff of smoke.

The show was, physically, very demanding for Justin, but he was used to the all-singing, all-dancing routines. Somehow the rumour began that he had an obsession with changing his underwear after practically every number. He allegedly had a whole box of briefs ready to slip on and off whenever there was a lull. All Justin admits to is changing his underwear after he has showered on the bus. Initially, it was strange not being one of five guys on the road hanging out together. But Justin's best friend Trace and Renée Earnest were often on hand to play Cranium or charades. Touring is an exceptionally tedious exercise in all aspects except the actual performance. Justin's best defence against the monotony is that although he is a very sociable man, he does not hate his own company nor does he do anything to excess – the sex, drugs and rock 'n' roll lifestyle is to be enjoyed only in moderation.

Justin was in for a shock when the tour hit Orlando. After Christina had done her half, he came strutting out to work the audience. He moved across the stage to where it jutted into the audience in a L-shape. Looking down at the two seats closest to him, he almost dropped the microphone in surprise. There, beaming up at him, were Sherry and Chuck Yerger, looking more than slightly out of place among the screaming young women. Chuck recalls, 'His mouth dropped wide open and his eyes got wide in surprise. He missed his dance step right there. Three more times during the concert he came over and mouthed these words very clearly: "Don't you ever do that again!", meaning come to a concert and surprise him like that.'

Chuck hadn't intended to cause a problem. He did not want to ask for free tickets and decided on the spur of the moment to ask for the best tickets they had, not realizing that they would be right under Justin's nose. Christina saw Chuck during the opening half; it was the first time she had laid eyes on her tutor in nearly ten years. She recognized the bald head immediately, and gave him a thumbs-up, but she forgot to pass a message to Justin about who was sitting in the front. He was happily waving at the friends he was expecting to see, but the Yergers knocked him dead. After the encore a mother and her two daughters clambered over five rows to get to Chuck and Sherry. 'Are you Justin's grandparents?' they asked, autograph books at the ready.

The phone was ringing later as Sherry and Chuck arrived home. It was Renée Earnest, saying, 'I've got someone here who wants to talk to you.' Justin came on the line and was still bugged, although he was as polite as ever. 'Mr Yerger,' he began. 'Don't you ever surprise me at a concert like that. How did you get there?'

'I bought tickets.'

'Don't you ever buy tickets again. You just let me know if you want to come.'

With that, Renée came back on the line to make sure Chuck understood. 'If you ever buy tickets again, I will take away your teaching licence,' she joked. Next to come on the line was Matt Morris, the former Mouseketeer turned songwriter, and now one of Justin's closest friends, and they chatted happily about old times.

One of the benefits of the tour was that it prolonged the life of the album. When Justin performed on the last UK date of his *Justified* world tour at Earls Court in January 2004, the album had been selling in huge quantities for fifteen months, spawning five hit singles. The concerts were rapturously received by the fans and grudgingly appreciated by the critics, who recognized Justin was riding the crest of a black wave in modern music. David Bennun, in the *Mail on Sunday*, said, 'He does the basics well with a touch of flair.' How he managed to hear anything above the sound of screaming girls is a mystery.

The tour in Europe was sponsored by McDonald's, a company keen for Justin to replace Ronald McDonald as the cool face of the burger franchise chain. It was as part of McDonald's 'I'm lovin' it' campaign that Justin appeared in commercials and sang a new theme tune. McDonald's announced, 'Our partnership will continue to evolve with dynamic surprises that will help connect McDonald's to the world of young adults through music, entertainment, fashion and sports.' Justin was certainly the man for those four branches of modern popular culture. One executive observed, without a trace of irony, 'He fits the McDonald's profile.' Justin's six-pack profile would not normally be one associated with munching his way through Big Macs every day. He does, however, like burgers, though nothing could compare to the cheeseburgers he used to enjoy at the Shelby Forest General Store. He sang their praises when he revisited his old haunts for a television special.

When he was in Memphis helping with the 'I'm lovin' it' promotion, he played basketball with children at the Ronald McDonald House and then went to the world-famous Peabody Hotel for a reception and to have his picture taken with some of the kids. Out of the corner of his eye, he spotted two familiar faces: his first headmistress, Mary Ann McNeil, and his basketball coach, Kim Lampkins. Mrs McNeil recalls, 'We would have been happy to stand to the side and watch Justin, but when he saw us, he said, "I know them!", and he grabbed us and said, "Come on in." I can't tell you how elated I was to see him and to know that he remembered us after all this time.'

Justin has to put the time in to honour his deal with McDonald's and make sure the company gets their money's worth. They reportedly were paying in excess of $5 million (£2.75 million) for the tie-in. That meant the audience at his concerts were shown the specially filmed commercial on a big screen before the man himself took to the stage. Justin cooed, 'I think it's a cool partnership' – a sentiment with which his bank manager would concur.

A privileged few were given a bonus after Justin had finished one Earls Court concert. He sped across London to the Coronet, a former cinema, to play a secret gig before an audience of 2,000. Tickets on the Internet were changing hands at up to $1,800 (£990). Justin used the extra performance as a vehicle for showcasing his musical talents, which remained hidden during his more formulaic main show. He can, for instance, play guitar on 'Like I Love You' or keyboards on 'Señorita' without having to dance

around with a microphone glued to his head. Justin generally has
plenty of energy left after a gig. On another night, after collecting
two Brit Awards in Earls Court he made an unannounced guest
appearance at a N.E.R.D. concert at the Brixton Academy. The
odd name, which stands for No One Ever Really Dies is the banner
under which the Neptunes perform. Justin was introduced as the
'little brother' of Pharrell Williams. The crowd understandably
went mad when Justin walked out and joined him to sing some of
N.E.R.D.'s hits, including 'Rock Star' and 'Lapdance'. 'The Justin
thing was really last minute,' said Pharrell afterwards. In such a
small world it is all about helping each other at the right time,
repaying a favour to a friend.

Justin was also able to give a boost to the hip-hop group Black
Eyed Peas, originally an LA-based alternative rap trio. When they
met at a local nightclub in LA, they immediately hit it off, to the
extent that when the Peas had a song called 'Where Is The Love',
they phoned Justin to see if he was interested. Peas' MC, Taboo,
explained, 'He called me back two days later with a hook for it.'
That hook turned an interesting rap record into the biggest UK
single of 2003. Once heard, the chorus of 'People killing, people
dying . . .' was impossible to get out of one's head. Justin's association with the Peas was a further move towards the West Coast for
Justin. The group were hardly mainstream, despite being
together for ten years. They cultivated an image that abandoned
the favourite hip-hop subjects of fast cars, fast women and jewellery
in favour of more serious political issues, especially in the wake of
9/11.

Despite their southern home-cookin' name, the Peas were born
and bred in LA. Will-i-am and apl.de.ap were well known around
the LA club scene since 1989, when they started rapping and dancing together and building up a stage act. They were joined in 1995
by Taboo, who had been part of Grassroots, a collective of rappers,
poets and actors, and they started performing at clubs and colleges
in LA. They sought to expand the audience's perceptions of hip
hop, refusing to cash in or overstate their tough upbringings in the
LA ghettos. Will told journalist Billy Johnson, Jr, 'Half of my
friends are dead, in jail, pregnant or on drugs.' This didn't sound

like Shelby Forest. Taboo, likewise, confirmed that he was a poor Mexican kid from East Los Angeles who had never had the money to attend a concert until he performed in one as a member of Black Eyed Peas. His ambition for a career in music did not blossom from success in southern pageants and *The Mickey Mouse Club* but from spending two summers in a job at Disneyland following the horses in the parade with a bucket and spade and clearing up the shit. 'I used to daydream, "One day I'm going to be in music and never have to do this again."'

Justin loves hip hop. He cited it as his favourite kind of music in the official 'N Sync book, an apparently odd choice for a boy band heart-throb. His and Black Eyed Peas' mutual regard for each other's music broke down the obvious social barriers. Justin has the intelligence to appreciate what the Black Eyed Peas were trying to achieve. Their alliance with him was to prove their big break, but they were anxious not to be too closely associated with the Timberlake bandwagon. Taboo explained, 'We don't change who we are. It's our record. That's why we didn't have Justin in the video. We want to stand on our own two feet.' Justin's familiar soulful high tenor was the ingredient that transformed a good song into a great one. The Black Eyed Peas grabbed their chance of commercial success by adding a fourth member, the sultry and beautiful Fergie (no relation to the Duchess of York). They accepted Justin's invitation to open the *Justified/Stripped* tour. By the time they released the album *Elephunk* and their second massive hit, 'Shut Up', on which Fergie was brought to the fore, they had successfully broken away from any dependence on the Timberlake name. Both will and apl do most of their own producing and it is easy to imagine them being involved in Justin's music in the future, especially as they, too, enjoy a close association with the Neptunes.

Evidence of the small clique in Justin's musical world came at the end of March 2004 at a concert at the Wiltern LG Theatre in Hollywood. The first half of the show featured the Black Eyes Peas, the second half, N.E.R.D. Midway through the Peas' encore of 'Where Is The Love', Justin casually strolled on stage for the chorus. The crowd went mad. It may be hip hop, it may be urban, but it's still Hollywood. Justin also came back for the second half to join Pharrell Williams on the chorus of 'Provider' and 'Things Are Getting Better'. Things, in fact, could not get any better.

Not everything on his world tour was such an unadulterated success. The SARS concert in Toronto was an unmitigated disaster. Mick Jagger had personally asked Justin to appear on the bill and to join him for a duet of the Stones' hit 'Miss You', which was entirely unsuitable for Justin's voice and style. But how do you turn down Mick Jagger? Justin was so excited at the prospect of joining the rock legend on stage that he let his heart rule his head. It proved to be the absolute low point of a fantastic 2003. Justin saw disaster coming: 'I woke up on that morning and said, "I think these people who are coming to the show are really going to hate me."' He was dead right.

'He gets the most nervous when he's singing in Memphis, because he's singing for his own folks.'

18

Hip-Hop Style

When he was thirteen, Justin was desperate to get his ear pierced like his friends. His stepfather Paul wanted him to earn the privilege, so he drew up a contract in which Justin agreed to write a song and perform it at a family gathering in return for being allowed to pierce his ear. Justin went to his room and wrote 'The Earring Song', a shameless rip-off of the Bobby McFerrin tune 'Don't Worry Be Happy'. He sang it for his parents on the beach during a holiday in Hawaii. As soon as they returned home to Shelby Forest, he went straight to the local mall for his first stud.

Justin Timberlake is almost anti-style. He has had to contend with a lifetime of bad-hair days, a wardrobe of dodgy matching suits and big hats. Somehow, he has emerged from years of shopping online at Ugly Duckling Inc. as a swan with a fabulous collection of sneakers. He has at least 500 pairs and has probably given away the same number to friends. It is only since he embraced hip-hop culture that he has cast off an image that was more *Hi-Di-Hi* host than coolest man in pop.

His style problems began at an early age because he inherited his mother's naturally curly locks. It did not help that she cut it for him. Rather unoriginally, he was nicknamed 'Curly' at E. E. Jeter, although he also had to bear the less polite 'Brillo Pad'. Justin told *Cosmo Girl*, 'I hated my hair. Everybody teased me about it. I was always trying to straighten the crap out of it. In second grade I took like paper scissors and cut all my hair all uneven. I was like, "I can't stand this – snip, snip, snip." That's the only time I really got a spanking.' He has contributed in other ways to his back catalogue of hair disasters. He once dyed his hair baby blue in honour of his favourite basketball team.

Who could forget the bleached blond tight curls of the teen 'N Sync heart-throb? Justin is proud of the fact that he had the short surfer-boy haircut before Eminem did, but acknowledged that it looked good on his pop rival but terrible on him: 'What was I thinking?' His hair became such a standing joke over the years that a spoof on *MadTV* depicted him and Britney entering his bedroom to reveal all his hair products, including straightening irons.

Justin first revealed his new curl-less look just after his twentieth birthday. He said he was sick of everybody going on about his hair all the time. Ironically, his new shaven look prompted everyone to talk about his hair even more. He immediately looked more grown up and was able to ditch the bleached blond colour as well. Not everyone was impressed, and the close-cropped look earned the accolade 'Celebrity with the Worst Hair' in a special poll conducted by the hair product company Wella.

The world of fashion, and being fashionable, is very fickle. The icons of 2003–4 could turn out to be yesterday's big mistake by next year. David Beckham always strives to be at the cutting edge of male fashion. Others, like Robbie Williams and Justin Timberlake, are all-round pin-up boys rather than trend-setters. All three share a love of one fashion trend that borders on obsession: they are devotees of body art, and pop in and out of tattoo parlours on a regular basis. Tattoos as a fashion accessory among young people are as common as pierced ears or shaved hair.

The word 'tattoo' originates from *ta-tau*, a Polynesian word meaning 'mark'. Captain Cook came across the body art in Tahiti in 1769 and noted it in his journal. Justin may not be aware that marking the skin was frowned upon in the Bible and banned in Christian countries. For two hundred years after Captain Cook's discovery, it was considered a vulgar form of self-abuse traditionally confined to sailors, who on dull days in far-flung ports would have a tribute to mum etched on a bicep or last night's girl forever inscribed on their knuckles. Justin has a tribute to his own mother tattooed on his back. It shows a cherubic angel holding a banner inscribed with his mother's initials. By the last count, he has had another six added to various parts of his anatomy.

At least he managed to eschew the temptation to pay tribute to Britney on his skin. The problem of trying to alter or erase a tattoo too hastily applied when love is blind is a common and expensive one in the celebrity world of rapid relationships. Pamela Anderson had to change 'Tommy', a tribute to her husband Tommy Lee, to 'Mommy' after they split. There would have been little Justin could have done with 'Britney' except to have it removed in a painful procedure. Patsy Kensit had to endure that agony after she and Liam Gallagher were divorced. It cost her $10,800 (£6,000) for the privilege of erasing 'Liam' from her ankle.

Justin has several ankle tattoos because that was the discreet place he and the rest of the 'N Sync group – except JC Chasez, who has a dread of needles – chose to celebrate their achievements. The first one was a flame tattoo on their left ankles to mark their first album going platinum in Canada in the spring of 1998. They had no way of knowing that this was going to be very small beer in the context of their overall record-breaking career and they would have to be more selective with the needle if they did not want to end up with every square inch of their bodies illustrated. They now have three tattoos to represent their three albums, having conveniently forgotten the *Home for Christmas* debacle – can a tattooist do a turkey? As well as the flame representing the first album, Justin has a marionette for *No Strings Attached* and red ropes to mark *Celebrity*.

Justin also has a large Robbie-style Celtic cross on his left shoulder, a Japanese symbol for music on his left ankle and a tribal band that he designed himself to incorporate an Aquarius symbol – his star sign – below his left knee. Justin is unusual because he never seems to show off his body art. The designs seem to be for his own individual satisfaction and not a 'look at me' statement to the world.

Lynn has never been that impressed by Justin's body art, urging him to stop inking his body because he will regret it when he gets older. Those pleas will probably fall on deaf ears when he gets married. Always prone to the big romantic gesture, he says he is saving a space for his wife's name – the marriage will hopefully last longer than Britney's first experience of wedlock. His pet name for Cameron Diaz is CD, so tattoo-watchers are on the lookout for those initials on Justin's body.

The awards and accolades for being eligible and beautiful have come to Justin in sackloads over the years, but at the end of 2002 he was given one of significance to his career and his longevity as a superstar. He was voted one of the Coolest Straight People of 2002 by the American gay and lesbian magazine *The Advocate*. He also appeared on the cover of the December issue. In an exclusive interview, he explained, 'If I was gay, that wouldn't be a big deal so why would I hide it?' He also admitted that he had once asked his mother how she would feel if he told her out of the blue that he was gay. Lynn had replied, 'I would be completely accepting.'

Giving the interview was very smart of Justin. He was accepting his status as a gay icon, and in the music business it is a well-known and accepted premise that a gay fanbase is an exceptionally loyal one. The quality of the artists who appear at G.A.Y. in London is testament to the importance record bosses place on promotion in the gay marketplace. Gay fans buy all the records and they see all the concerts. Madonna and Kylie both have the fanbase and it has helped keep them at the pinnacle of success for twenty years. Robbie Williams has it and has never denied a gay rumour, preferring to treat gossip and innuendo in a jokey fashion. He never takes offence: do that and it is career suicide. Jason Donovan's career was never the same after he sued a magazine for claiming he was gay.

Very few artists are genuine superstars and the majority of those who are in the modern era have a strong gay following. So why is Justin one of the lucky ones? Obviously, he is athletic and handsome, but on *Justified* he displayed the one ingredient that is essential to admission to the gay icon lounge – vulnerability. The tone of some of the tracks suggests he is a victim, mistreated by those he has loved. It displayed an emotional sensitivity and strength. Justin's claims that he has been cheated on by his first three girlfriends represents just the sort of 'tragic history' that attracts a gay audience. Writer Paul Watson explored this in his 1999 paper about gay icons in pop: 'Gay men embrace those who represent embodied conflicts similar to their own and whose expression explodes into a torrent of sensuality that is sublimated through their sound.' *Justified* is a very sensual record and, on some tracks, very wounded and hurt. Paul Watson had Kylie in mind when he wrote that her gay audience could 'share and reflect on the betrayal and indignation that they collectively experience'. Justin has a long way to go before he is in Kylie's league as a gay icon, but 'Cry Me A River' has enough betrayal and indignation to set him on the way.

Justin needs to keep a sense of humour, however. A particular T-shirt is very popular among gay men in Los Angeles. It carries the slogan 'I did Justin three times'.

One of the amusing side effects of being a celebrity is that as soon as you are famous and rich enough to buy anything your heart desires, everybody wants to give you free merchandise. Justin would probably never have to go shopping in a regular store again if he didn't want to. He is not a man who spends hours in front of the mirror changing outfits. A T-shirt, jeans, sneakers and perhaps a Pony jacket are the wardrobe favourites he reaches for at home. He tends not to wear shorts too often in public because he believes he has 'chicken legs'.

During his London gigs in December 2003, he persuaded Harrods to open especially for him and his entourage after he had finished his concert. He arrived at 11 p.m. and spent four hours there. It was good publicity both for the store and the singer. He bought the favourite Justin goods – electronic and computer equipment, jewellery and a Mercedes remote control car. Justin is not a great buyer of clothes, and sometimes lets his mother shop for him. Some of his worst style mistakes have been caused by his blindspot about what looks good. Veronica Finn's pictures of Justin wearing a shiny suit at a party in the Bahamas are matched only by him and Britney arriving at a do in matching denim outfits. She is in a backless strapless number, while he is dressed like John Wayne going to a wedding – blue denim from head to toe, including a cowboy hat. The whole ensemble is topped off by a pair of shades and a large silver medallion of a winged angel.

Justin does most of his shopping in the company of women, whether it's his mother or a current girlfriend. He shops all the time with Cameron Diaz and did with Britney too. He likes to try to find little things they might like. With his former girlfriends it was the same; he was always bringing them presents of clothes or shoes. In this respect he is very much a woman's man.

His look embraces hip-hop culture. He plays the right sport (basketball), wears the jackets and the sneakers, listens to cool urban music and makes some of it himself, loves his bling and has a hat for every occasion, even though he is not going bald. He once extravagantly spent $8,000 (£4,400) on a hip-hop cap encrusted with diamonds. The beauty of it was that it looked like any old cap, but you wouldn't want to leave it on the bus. Justin can be extravagant if the mood takes him. He leased a private jet to fly him round to gigs when he became tired of the tour bus.

Justin has the height and build to wear clothes well. He keeps in shape by dancing, playing ball and working out. His fitness regime includes 300 push-ups a day. He is gradually eating more healthily, as looking good becomes more important for his celebrity status. He may advertise McDonald's, but he is likely to eschew burgers in favour of sushi or fruit salads. He is not boring about food, however. When he had lunch with David Beckham in Manchester he ignored the chicken Caesar salad ordered by the England football captain preferring to stick with a club sandwich and French fries.

These days Justin seems to go principally for comfort with baggy sweats, large T-shirts and a variety of hats and caps. He has been called a walking advert for Gap. Rick Sky is critical: 'He only gets away with it because he is Justin Timberlake. If you saw him in the street, you wouldn't notice him.' It may be that he prefers not to be noticed. Teenagers are often trying to find an identity through the clothes they wear. Justin no longer needs to do that and so can wave goodbye forever to outrageous and gawdy clothing. If he wants to wear a tie, he can wear one. He's Justin Timberlake, so it doesn't matter.

'I don't really look at myself as sexy.'

19

California Dream

When he accepted the Grammy for his vocal on 'Cry Me A River, Justin said, 'I want to dedicate this to the most beautiful woman in the world!' While the star-studded audience waited for him to add the words 'Cameron Diaz', the cameras focused instead on the beaming face of his mother.

Justin bought his home in Los Angeles in August 2002. It was a snip at $8.3 million (over £4.5 million). He was earning fantastic money for a 21-year-old, but he had been paying his own way for ten years, since his mother started stashing away his talent contest earnings. His individual earnings from 'N Sync are reliably estimated at $25 million (nearly £14 million) and that was the figure before he started earning as a solo performer, as the face of McDonald's and as one of the most successful solo touring acts of the last two years. His current fortune is in the region of $50 million (£27.5 million), but that figure is not completely accurate. He is earning money very fast, especially as he now has songwriting credits on his records; providing he continues to be prudent with his cash, he will become one of the richest stars in show business.

After his break-up with Britney, Justin had nowhere to stay in Los Angeles. He was touring in the early part of the year and then was back east recording and sorting out his solo career in Orlando. Many of his friends had relocated from Florida to LA: his two post-Britney flings, Jenna Dewan and Alyssa Milano, were both based in the city, and almost all *The Mickey Mouse Club* cast had moved to the movie capital to pursue their careers. His best friend Trace was also keen to move to Hollywood, so this was the perfect time for Justin to settle permanently on the West Coast. He was not so stupid, however, as to give up his home in Florida, where the tax laws are much more amenable to high-earners. Britney had no desire to stay in her LA home after the split with Justin; she sold it to actress Brittany Murphy for a healthy profit of $1.5 million (£825,000) and bought a beachfront property in Malibu.

Justin's new Mediterranean-style house was in the Hollywood Hills and boasted stunning views, from downtown LA in the east all the way to the Pacific Ocean in the west. Five minutes down some twisting, winding roads lies Sunset Plaza, the name given to the 1,000-yard stretch of Sunset Boulevard that is dotted with trendy boutiques and restaurants where Justin likes to hang out, such as Le Dome, Chin Chin, Coffee Bean & Tea Leaf and A/x Armani. One of the big attractions of the property for Justin was that it may be a short drive in one of his nine cars or five motorcycles down to Sunset with its clubs and bars, but when he drives back through the gates of his home, it's a world away. One local resident explains, 'It's kind of like being in the heart of things but being a little bit hidden away and removed at the same time.' Justin's car of choice in LA is his relatively unassuming blue BMW 745i. He prefers to drive himself around town, usually dressed down in a baseball cap and hoodie.

The property is set in several acres with palm trees, jasmine bushes and an orange tree. The five-bedroom, eight-bathroom house and buildings are set around a cobble courtyard. All the movie star trimmings are here: the tennis court, personal gym, movie theatre, games room and swimming pool, as well as a guest house where 'Personal Assistant' and best friend Trace lives. Trace looks after the place if he is not keeping Justin company on his frequent tours. Justin is probably more at ease with Trace than with anyone else and that includes his mother and girlfriend: 'He's the person in my life that I can sit in a room with, not say anything, and it's cool.'

Lynn made sure a domestic service calls every week to clean the house from top to bottom. A pool guy also comes once a week, as does a three-man team to keep the gardens neat and tidy. This fabulous mansion is Justin's main home and the one he returns to when he is not on the road. He also has a million-dollar house on a golf club estate outside Orlando and property in the Memphis area. His California property is definitely a boy's home, still largely unfurnished, with large open spaces left free for playing ball or practising putting. Until he finished his *Justified* world tour at the beginning of 2004, Justin had scarcely spent enough time there to turn the house into a home.

Justin is not really a big deal in Los Angeles. He does not feel the need for a live-in bodyguard, although he is always well chaperoned on the road or at particular functions in LA. Bodyguards are a necessity as well as a status symbol for major stars. Celebrities are ten a penny walking down Rodeo Drive or cruising Sunset Boulevard. Ironically, nobody used to bother much with him back in Shelby Forest because he was plain ol' Justin. Now that he is a superstar, he lives in an area where superstars are largely ignored. Former UK pop columnist Gill Pringle, who has lived in LA for ten years, explains, 'It's decidedly un-hip to bother celebs in LA. Most people live and work in the industry here, so someone like Justin can just relax and have fun. People might notice who it is and nudge and stare but he is not going to get mobbed or anything. The biggest stars, like George Clooney and Leonardo DiCaprio – and Justin – go out all the time. They just make a point of not attracting too much attention to themselves. All the genuinely cool people just come and go without a big fuss. It's really only divas like J-Lo or Demi [Moore] who insist on lapping up all the publicity going.'

Famous neighbours, including Sandra Bullock, Courteney Cox Arquette and Kevin Costner, enjoy the same anonymity as Justin. His closest celebrity neighbour lives less than a mile away. She is notoriously secretive and private, while at the same time currently enjoying the status of Hollywood's biggest female star. Justin had no idea at the time how convenient it would be living so close to Cameron Diaz. The couple first 'sparked' at the Nickelodeon Kids' Choice Awards in LA in April 2003. Cameron is the first woman Justin has fallen in love with who is not a southern belle; she is a

California surfer girl through and through. She is blonde, a strong individual and a fan both of watching and playing sports. She is at least as rich as Justin, so she is no gold-digger. She is also the possessor of one of the widest mouths in Hollywood – literally the first thing Justin looks at in a woman. Cameron has a great, goofy mouth.

Cameron hails from Long Beach, about a 45-minute drive down the coast from Los Angeles but much quieter. An exotic mix of Cuban and Native American, she was always tall and slender and exuded charisma, especially on the dance floor, where she earned a reputation for being a 'white girl with soul' – a perfect complement for Mr JT. Like a typical teenage kid, she paid her way working as a waitress in a fast-food restaurant before starting college at Long Beach Poly, where she excelled at cheerleading and was one of the most popular girls in school, especially with the boys. Almost inevitably, she was spotted by a scout for the Elite Modelling Agency at a time when her glowing all-American good looks were very marketable. She was only sixteen and had to juggle her modelling assignments with going to school. One of her teachers observed, 'She was always beautiful with that smile of hers. She was so dynamic with the sort of personality that could turn the wind into a song.'

At the age of nineteen, when she was finishing school, she made the front cover of a magazine, *Seventeen*, for the first time. It would be the first of many covers. She also took the first of many career risks by going to Paris, the centre of the fashion world where, if successful, she could start to earn big money. By 1993 she was commanding a fee of $2,000 (£1,100) a day, travelling the world and earning the sobriquet 'supermodel', but Cameron had bigger plans. She wanted to be an actress. The movies are littered with models who have tried and failed to crack Hollywood: Cindy Crawford, Naomi Campbell and Christie Brinkley are just three who have had a brief flirtation with films. It's not easy being a star in one show business pond and moving to another, where looks and the way you slink down a catwalk count for very little. In Hollywood, everybody's beautiful. You have to bring something else to the table.

Cameron Diaz brought determination. She had the caught the eye of the casting director for Jim Carrey's film debut *The Mask*. She was one of several models who auditioned for the part of sexy singer Tina. The movie was a vehicle for Carrey's unique brand of comedy and no other role was going to gain undue significance – or so everyone assumed. The director, Chuck Russell, kept calling Cameron for more auditions because he recognized an indefinable quality in her personality that would appeal to both men and women. When he called her back for a final audition, she was in Paris, but she hopped straight on a plane, at her own expense, with no guarantee of the part at the end of it. She landed the role and lit up the screen when she made her movie debut with a memorable screen entrance in a dazzling red dress. She was paid only $50,000 (£27,500), but money was not the issue. Cameron was playing the long game, as she showed by her next move. Cameron was an overnight success, but instead of believing she was a star she went off and paid for acting lessons so that she could be better. It was just what Justin, the perfectionist, would have done.

Over the next four years Cameron appeared in a number of relatively minor films, such as *Feeling Minnesota* and *She's the One*, gradually earning enough to buy the house in the Hollywood Hills that has become a home from home for Justin. It's modest by the standards of his huge pile – she only paid $1.4 million (£770,000) – but Justin loves the rustic, homely feel to it, which perhaps reminds him of the old family home in Shelby Forest. Cameron's profile continued to rise when she appeared with Julia Roberts in *My Best Friend's Wedding*, before she hit the big-time with the gross Farrelly Brothers comedy *There's Something About Mary*. For the first time, she was making more than $1 million (£550,000) a movie. Her private life remained a closed book, although it later transpired that for five years she had been the companion of the video producer Carlos de la Torre.

Her co-star from *There's Something About Mary* was the raffish Matt Dillon; she had met him on the set of *Feeling Minnesota*. They began a relationship that quickly became an unpleasant introduction to the world of the paparazzi. She didn't much like the attention, especially when the spectre of Mariah Carey came into the equation. Dillon was rumoured to be seeing the singer, which quickly ended Cameron's relationship with him. She reportedly commented wittily that if you want to be tortured, listen to Mariah Carey loud. From that time on, Cameron has tried to safeguard her privacy. She was going out for several years with rugged actor Jared Leto, star of *Fight Club*, but the couple were rarely seen together in public. They were even secretly engaged for a couple of years. Her career, meanwhile, has gone from strength to strength. She was paid a six figure sum for her voice alone in *Shrek*. She was paid a reported $13 million (over £7 million) for her role as ditzy Nathalie in *Charlie's Angels*, even more for *The Sweetest Thing* and $20 million (£11 million) for the pretty dire Charlie's Angels sequel *Full Throttle*. Only Julia Roberts currently matches her earning power. Reports estimate that Cameron's earnings for 2004 will be $64 million (over £35 million).

Cameron is not squeaky clean. She suffered a reported bout of alcohol poisoning in Australia when she was eighteen. Any wild behaviour is now very much in the past, and she and Justin enjoy a healthy, sporty lifestyle. He has said, 'Drugs don't intrigue me.' Drugs are a big part of pop culture and Justin is unusual in the way he chooses to live his life. He has, however, always liked a drink. Reports that he is teetotal are wide of the mark. As a teenager, his then girlfriend Danielle Ditto recalls that they would enjoy drinking together. Occasionally, Justin is seen drinking in a bar or a club, but he is careful not to end up horizontal in the manner that used to afflict Robbie Williams. Justin is too mindful of his well-being and the physical demands of singing night after night on tour to jeopardize his career.

Cameron is a very independent, feisty woman who goes her own way in Hollywood, a trait that some might call eccentric. She chooses to drive around LA in an electric car. She washes her face in Evian water and is rumoured to be fixated on hygiene. Until she began her relationship with Justin, she was probably best known as the actress with the worst skin. Pictures of Cameron with spot eruptions have featured in the pages of many magazines, much to her embarrassment. She is a natural blonde (a first for Justin) and very fair, with sensitive skin that breaks out if you shout 'Boo' at it. She explained, 'I get inflamed spots at the smallest thing. If it's possible, I even touch door handles with tissues. On days like that I just stay away from the mirror.' Justin, from his teenage years, knows all about being called 'pizza face'.

Besides the obvious physical chemistry between Cameron and JT, as she calls him, they first got together because she is more into sports than any other female movie star. She loves all the sports that Justin loves, can match his ability in most of them and beat him in others. She is a fantastic driver and did her own driving in *Charlie's Angels*. She is so good that she is a regular in the Long Beach Celebrity Grand Prix. Justin did not manage to drag Cameron along to a basketball game on their first date. Instead, she took him bowling at Pinz at Studio City. Justin loves it and they have become regulars there, and even have their own private locker that says 'Cameron & Justin' – it must be serious if they share a sports locker. Part of the attraction is that they can enjoy a fun time there without being bothered. Like most celebrity couples, they value that commodity as much as anything else.

Practically every time they are seen out together they are doing something sporty: playing golf in Dallas or basketball in Fort Lauderdale, surfing in Hawaii where Cameron broke her nose, or snowboarding in Vale, Colorado. The director Bobby Farrelly observed, 'Her idea of a perfect date is playing thirty-six holes of golf and then going to a ball-game.' They are both very sociable and gregarious. They like to go out dancing. Justin also enjoys live music and chatting to his friends in his favourite bars and nightclubs, such as Avalon, Concorde, The Lounge and A.D., where he first danced with Cameron. Two of their best friends to hang out with are Drew Barrymore, who co-starred with Cameron in the two *Charlie's Angels* movies and her boyfriend Fabrizio Moretti, the drummer of The Strokes. They have seen Fabrizio's band play live and he and Justin have become good buddies. Justin also sees a lot of Pharrell Williams when he's in town, although Pharrell has been touring a lot in the past year. Pharrell is achieving a higher profile, and not just through production and as part of N.E.R.D. His solo disc *Frontin'*, featuring Jay-Z, reached number four in the UK charts in the summer of 2003. Justin also likes to hang out with

Joey Fatone's brother Steven, who totally approves of Cameron: 'Cameron is hot and hilarious. She can joke with the boys. Besides that, she's gorgeous. Who wouldn't want to date her?'

The media have made much of Cameron and Justin spending time with Demi Moore and Ashton Kutcher, suggesting the couples are two older women and their toy boys. Demi Moore is forty-one, more than fifteen years older than Ashton. Cameron has told friends that she feels embarrassed being lumped into that sort of bracket. One says, 'People have this false impression because when Justin and Cameron got together she was busy promoting *Charlie's Angels*, which Demi was in, so there were a couple of times Ashton and Demi were around. But they're not particularly good friends with either of them.'

Ashton Kutcher has a mischievous sense of humour. He devised a popular TV series called *Punk'd* in which he played practical jokes on celebrities, exposing the frauds with the catchphrase 'You've been punk'd.' The trick he played on Justin was classic. He employed actors to pretend to be bailiffs from the Internal Revenue Service, who started to repossess Justin's possessions while he looked on, upset and bewildered. Justin was on the verge of tears, trying to ring his mother to tell her what was going on. He realized it was a joke the moment he caught sight of Ashton and saw the funny side – sort of.

Although Cameron is eight years older than Justin, she does not have children, an ex-husband or some inevitable emotional baggage. Justin has always been old for his age, a product of being the youngest among older people, as he was in 'N Sync. Ashley Hoven, a former girlfriend of Chris Kirkpatrick, has kept in touch with Justin. She observes, 'I have always seen Justin as very mature for his age, so it doesn't surprise me at all that he's with someone older than him.' Another friend close to the couple says, 'Cameron and Justin share the same crazy sense of humour. They love to laugh and do simple things like dance, eat good food and hang out with friends. They both love to dance and go wild. If Justin is very mature for his age, then Cameron is very young and fun-loving for her age, so it doesn't surprise me that he's with someone older like her.'

Cameron and Justin fell for each other quickly, casting aside their usual caution in matters of the heart. And, unlike the Britney palaver, Justin was happy to let the world see that one of the most beautiful women in the world is his partner. In July 2003 Cameron was seen backstage at the *Justified/Stripped* concert in Orlando and a month later she was with Justin when he performed with the Black Eyed Peas in New York. He also took her to watch the first LA Lakers basketball match of the season. They are not seen out much but often enough for it to be obvious they are very much together. Cameron joined him for one special date: his return to Memphis for the concert at the New Daisy Theatre for NBC. This was an important moment in their relationship, when she met the folks in Shelby Forest. They threw a big party and everyone was introduced to Cameron, who was vivacious and charming. One of the guys who went to the party observes, 'They really just complement each other. Things that Cameron lacks, Justin has and vice versa, so they meshed really well.'

Cameron is old and smart enough to realize she has to win Lynn over or there is no future for her and Justin. She seems to be doing well at the moment. At the Grammys in February 2004, Lynn picked a pair of $104 (£57) Blue Dot jeans at one of the freebie suites and said to Justin, 'These will be perfect for Cameron.' She chooses clothes for her son, so why not for her son's girlfriend? The only time so far that there has been any friction was when Cameron and Justin were thinking of buying a property together in Malibu in September 2003. Cameron set her heart on a beach house there, but Justin dragged his heels, saying he needed to consult Lynn. His mother is his co-manager and very much involved in Justin's finances, so perhaps it was only natural, but Cameron was reported to be less than delighted.

Technically, Justin has not lived with anyone yet, but friends say that when he is in Los Angeles he spends all his time at Cameron's home. Justin hasn't lived in California long enough to have truly absorbed the lifestyle. He does much the same thing in LA as he would do in Orlando, New York or London. He is not into holistic treatment, does not drink soya milk or indulge in any 'faddy' behaviour. He does love sushi, however, and he and Cameron have been seen dining at practically every sushi bar in town, including Matsuhisa in Beverley Hills and Sushi Katsu in Studio City. He also owns a part share in a dim-sum restaurant called Chi, which is located in the Hyatt Hotel on Sunset Boulevard, so they eat there frequently. The restaurant is doing well, although it has yet to become the same sort of hot venue as Ashton Kutcher's Dolce.

Justin's LA lifestyle is a healthy one, but that's no change from his childhood in Shelby Forest, when he spent so much of his time outdoors. Cameron loves hiking in the Hollywood Hills, so Justin joins her for walks at Runyon Canyon or Fryman Canyon. Justin chooses not to keep any pets because of the amount of time he spends away from home. Cameron has a dog, although hers does not join them for walks – it is what Hollywood calls a handbag dog. Justin used to go out to the gym occasionally before he bought his house, but he generally considers them too posey. He prefers to stay in the comfort of his own gym room, get Trace over, crank up the music and bench press and push up in private. A friend observes, 'He's not fanatical about working out. He does it when he feels like it. He's always fit because of the time he spends danc-ing. He also has a basketball hoop at home that he uses a lot.'

When he and Cameron are not competing against one another at sport they love to do karaoke. Cameron knows all the words to Justin's songs and does a mean version of 'Rock Your Body'. They also like to shop in a serious way. Justin was spotted slipping out of Tiffany's on Wilshire Boulevard having spent $100,000 (£55,000) buying jewellery for Cameron. Together they favour the small, cool boutiques near their home or exclusive department stores in Beverley Hills like Barney's, Neiman Marcus and Saks Fifth Avenue. They have also been out to The Grove, a new open air-style mall in LA, where Justin particularly likes Abercrombie & Fitch, one of his favourite labels. He and Cameron like to wear matching clothes. They both love Diesel jeans – Cameron has such long legs that they could almost wear each other's. They have also been spotted wearing identical sand-coloured Ugg boots.

Justin and Cameron act like a couple in love. They are always touching, hugging and kissing. Justin is very demonstrative when he is in love. In so many ways, this is a perfect love affair for him, but every silver lining has a cloud and they have to face up to long periods when their work schedules keep them apart. Justin has so much energy that he cannot sit around for long. Cameron, say friends, was hoping he would settle down enough to spend 2004 at home, at least while she was filming her new movie *In Her Shoes* in LA. Justin finished the *Justified* world tour in January and then did the awards circuit, including the Brits and the Oscars, before he and Cameron were able to fit in some holiday time snowboarding. But, within a month, instead of resting his designer sneakers on the couch, he was off to make his film debut on location in Vancouver. Justin wants to stretch himself as an entertainer and though that means primarily in music, he loves being in front of the camera, acting and performing. He is very versatile, as his debut solo performance on *Saturday Night Live* proved. He dressed up in drag as blonde actress Jessica Simpson, did an impersonation of Ashton Kutcher and donned an omelette costume for a sketch. The overall effect was that here was a guy willing to try anything. He was also very funny.

Justin has always fancied himself as an actor but, until 2004, had no time to pursue that ambition seriously. He had been well received playing the part of a young Elton John in the video for 'This Train Don't Stop There Any More'. He had also been the guest star on a parade of the most popular shows on American TV: *Sabrina the Teenage Witch, Sesame Street, Clueless* and *Touched by an Angel*. In 2000 he had a part in a TV film called *Model Behavior*, which starred Canadian actor Jesse Nilsson. This ignited Justin's passion for acting, although his enthusiasm was temporarily damp- ened when Nilsson died suddenly last year from heart failure following a bad asthma attack.

For his feature film breakthrough, Justin landed a meaty role in a Kevin Spacey film, *Edison*. This is not a biopic of the inventor of the phonograph but a thriller that reunites Spacey with Morgan Freeman, with whom he starred in *Seven*. Spacey is similar to Justin in that he is a perfectionist who does not suffer fools gladly, so Justin would not have landed a part without an impressive screen test. He plays a news reporter called Joshua Pollock who discovers a den of corrupt cops. Unsure how to pursue his discovery, he befriends a jaded reporter (Spacey) and an investigator (Freeman) who works for a powerful district attorney. Spacey may be a hard taskmaster but he is also very funny, waspish and probably the finest vocal imitator in Hollywood – and that includes Robin Williams. He would appreciate Justin's sense of fun and his professionalism. Justin is taking acting very seriously. He was at the Los Angeles Supreme Court before he flew to Vancouver, researching public records with Associated Press reporter Bob Porterfield. When fans approached him for autographs, he apparently refused to sign, claiming that he was 'getting into character'.

Cameron and Justin have to deal with the classic celebrity issue of trust. Justin had been plagued by it during his previous relationships. He has to recognize that Cameron is very sociable with a wide circle of friends, including her ex, Jared Leto, while she has to accept that he is on set with very pretty actresses. On *Edison*, for instance, his love interest is the sexy Piper Perabo, who starred in *Cheaper by the Dozen* and *Coyote Ugly* and who, at twenty-six, is much younger than Cameron. One consolation for Cameron is Justin's reputation or, more precisely, his lack of a 'reputation'. A Hollywood insider observes, 'You never hear stories about Justin doing the whole rock star thing and sleeping with loads of girls. He's a one-woman kind of guy. You never hear any bad rumours about him.'

Justin's progress since the end of the 'N Sync *Celebrity* tour has been astounding. He has left the other members of the group coughing dust as he rides away. The other four have made a fortune, but Justin threatens to overshadow all their endeavours. JC Chasez's first solo album, *Schizophrenic,* was released in March 2004 but did not break the new ground *Justified* did. Ironically, JC supported Britney Spears on her spring UK tour. There were suggestions JC was not best pleased that Justin appeared to be getting all the momentum from Jive Records. Chris Kirkpatrick has been writing songs with the Dallas band Ohno and also working on material for his own solo project. He is still seen out and about in Orlando and likes to play golf whenever he can. Joey Fatone and Lance Bass are making progress as actors. Lance has made a Wes Craven horror movie called *Cursed,* while Joey has appeared on

Broadway in *Rent,* but those efforts are likely to look anaemic when *Edison* is released in the spring of 2005. Justin already has his second movie lined up – a spoof musical comedy called *Played,* in which rumour has it he will be playing basketball. If he wants to, Justin has the potential to go a long way in the movies. He is only twenty-three, so he may want to push both musical and acting careers along at the same time like a male J-Lo.

Professionalism – or a desire for perfection – is almost certainly one of the reasons why Justin Timberlake is going to have a long career. Nothing is too much trouble for him. In the music business, he has a reputation for being a genuinely nice guy who is not prone to any diva-like behaviour. A record company insider observes, 'If Justin gets a call asking him to re-record something in the studio, he gets on the next plane and does whatever's needed.'

Whatever happens with Cameron, Justin will always have the unswerving support and love of his mother Lynn. She has always maintained she is happy as long as he is having fun. She retains a presence even if he is spending his time chez Diaz. For his twenty-third birthday this year, she personally called up an LA gourmet delivery company, Cakes2Go, and arranged for a $250 cream and chocolate sponge birthday cake to be delivered to Cameron's home. With Love.

'This kid will be one of the greats.'

UK Discography

'N Sync singles

Release Date	Title
September 1997	*Tearin' Up My Heart*
November 1997	*I Want You Back*
February 1999	*I Want You Back* (reissue)
June 1999	*Tearin' Up My Heart* (reissue)
January 2000	*Music of My Heart* (with Gloria Estefan)
March 2000	*Bye Bye Bye*
July 2000	*I'll Never Stop*
September 2000	*It's Gonna Be Me*
December 2000	*This I Promise You*
July 2001	*Pop*
December 2001	*Gone*
April 2002	*Girlfriend*

'N Sync Albums

Release Date	Title (track listing in parentheses)
May 1997	*'N Sync* (Tearin' Up My Heart, I Just Wanna Be With You, Here We Go, For The Girl Who Has Everything, [God Must Have Spent] A Little More Time On You, You Got It, I Need Love, I Want You Back, Everything I Own, Thinking Of You [I Drive Myself Crazy], Crazy For You, Sailing, Giddy Up, U Drive Me Crazy)

September 2001 *Home for Christmas*
(Home for Christmas, Under My Tree, I
Never Knew The Meaning Of Christmas,
Merry Christmas Happy Holidays, The
Christmas Song [Chestnuts Roasting On An
Open Fire], I Guess It's Christmas Time, All I
Want Is You This Christmas, The First Noel, In
Love On Christmas, It's Christmas, O Holy
Night, Love's In Our Hearts On Christmas
Day, The Only Gift, Kiss Me At Midnight)

March 2000 *No Strings Attached*
(Bye Bye Bye, It's Gonna Be Me, Space
Cowboy [Yippie-Ye-Yay], Just Got Paid, It
Makes Me Ill, This I Promise You, No Strings
Attached, Digital Get Down, Bringin' Da
Noise, That's When I'll Stop Loving You, I'll
Be Good For You, If I'm Not The One, I
Thought She Knew)

October 2000 *No Strings Attached* [Special Edition]
(Bye Bye Bye, It's Gonna Be Me, Space
Cowboy [Yippie-Ye-Yay], Just Got Paid, It
Makes Me Ill, This I Promise You, No Strings
Attached, Digital Get Down, I'll Never Stop,
Bringin' Da Noise, That's When I'll Stop
Loving You, I'll Be Good For You, If I'm Not
The One, I Thought She Knew, Could It Be
You [Bonus track], This Is Where The Party's
At [Bonus Track])

July 2001 *Celebrity*
(Pop, Celebrity, The Game Is Over, Girlfriend,
The Two Of Us, Gone, Tell Me; Tell Me . . .
Baby, Up Against The Wall, See Right
Through You, Selfish, Just Don't Tell Me
That, Something Like You, That Girl [Will

222

Never Be Mine] [Bonus Track], Falling
[Bonus Track], Do Your Thing [Bonus track])

April 2002   *Celebrity* [Special Edition]
Disc: 1
(Pop, Celebrity, Game Is Over, Girlfriend,
Two Of Us, Gone, Tell Me; Tell Me . . . Baby,
Up Against The Wall, See Right Through You,
Selfish, Just Don't Tell Me That, Something
Like You, That girl [Will Never Be Mine],
Falling, Do Your Thing
Disc: 2
(Pop [Pablo La Rosa Funktified Mix], Pop
[Deep Dish Cha-Ching Remix], Pop
[Terminalhead Vocal Remix], Gone [Gone
Clubbing (I'll Be Back Later) Mix], Gone
[Spanish Version Radio Edit], Girlfriend
[Neptunes Remix Feat. Nelly] (Instrumental),
Pop [Enhanced], Gone [Enhanced],
Girlfriend [Enhanced])

Justin Timberlake Singles

Release Date   *Title (additional track in parentheses)*

October 2002   *Like I Love You*
(Like I Love You [Album Version],
Like I Love You [Instrumental]
Like I Love You [Extended Mix])

February 2003   *Cry Me A River*
(**CD1:** Cry Me A River [Album Version], Cry
Me A River [Dirty Vegas Vocal Mix], Cry Me A
River [Bill Hamel Vocal Mix]
CD2: Cry Me A River [Johnny Fiasco Mix],
Like I Love You [Basement Jaxx Vocal Mix],

	Like I Love You [Deep Dish Vocal Mix])
March 2003	*Work It* (Nelly feat. Justin Timberlake) (**CD1 (Enhanced):** Work It [Radio Edit], Put Your Hands Up, Air Force Ones, Air Force Ones [Video] **CD2:** Work It [DJ Swamp Remix], Work It [Nevins Universal Dub], Dilemma [G Force Full Vocal Mix])
May 2003	*Rock Your Body* (Rock Your Body [Album Version], Rock Your Body [Sander Kleinenberg Radio Mix], Rock Your Body [Paul Oakenfold Mix], Rock Your Body [Instrumental])
September 2003	*Señorita* (Señorita [Radio Edit Short Intro], Señorita [Eddie's Crossover Rhythm Mix], Señorita [Eddie's Extended Dance Mix], Señorita [Dr Octavo 2-Step Mix])

Justin Timberlake Albums

Release Date	*Title (track listings in parentheses)*
November 2002	*Justified* (Señorita, Like I Love You, [Oh No] What You Got, Take It From Here, Cry Me A River, Rock Your Body, Nothin' Else, Last Night, Still On My Brain, [And She Said] Take Me Now, Right For Me, Let's Take A Ride, Never Again, Worthy Of [Bonus Track])

Chronology

31 Jan 1981 Justin Randall Timberlake is born in the St Jude Hospital, Memphis, Tennessee.

1984 His parents, Lynn and Randy divorce. Lynn starts work in a bank in Millington where she meets Justin's future stepfather, Paul Harless. Justin grows up calling Paul 'Dad' and Randy 'Daddy'.

1989 Joins friends to perform as New Kids on the Block at a school concert. Takes singing lessons from Bob Westbrook in Memphis.

Aug 1992 Sweeps the board at the Universal Charm Pageant in Nashville. Collects prizes worth $16,000 for winning Best Model, Best Dressed, Best Sportswear, Most Handsome and Supreme Champion.

Dec 1992 Makes his debut on the TV talent show *Star Search* but loses in the first round to a 10-year-old girl called Anna Nardona. On the way home he auditions for the *Mickey Mouse Club*.

April 1993 Moves with Lynn to Orlando to join the cast of Disney's *Mickey Mouse Club*. He meets fellow Mousketeers Britney Spears, Christina Aguilera and JC Chasez.

Feb 1995 *Mickey Mouse Club* cancelled after Justin's second season in it. He finishes school year at E. E. Jeter in Shelby Forest and is voted Mr Jeter. His girlfriend Deanna Dooley is Miss Jeter.

Aug 1995 Moves back to Orlando to join new boy band. His mother Lynn names the band 'N Sync. They later sign with Lou Pearlman's Trans Continental company which brings in Johnny Wright as manager.

Oct 1995 Makes promotional video for 'N Sync at the Rock 'N' Roll Beach Club, Pleasure Island in Orlando.

Jan 1996 Gets a fifteenth birthday surprise when girlfriend Danielle Ditto pops out of the trunk of his mother's car at the 'N Sync House in Orlando.

Aug 1996 'N Sync sign record deal with RCA in Europe and travel to Germany for first concerts in Munich. They perform nearly fifty concerts there in the next twelve months.

Oct 1996 First 'N Sync single 'I Want You Back' released in Germany and enters the charts after one week.

May 1997 Justin's half sister Laura Katherine Timberlake is born but dies after one hour following complications. *'N Sync*, the album, is released in Germany.

July 1997 Justin is back home to have his tonsils removed in Memphis. Fortunately his voice is unaffected.

Sept 1997 Their first UK single 'Tearin' Up My Heart' is released but only reaches a disappointing number 40 in the charts.

Nov 1997 Justin performs in the UK for the first time when 'N Sync take the stage at the International Centre, Bournemouth. Second UK single 'I Want You Back' only makes it to Number 62 on the chart.

Jan 1998 Takes delivery of a bright red Mercedes Benz for his seventeenth birthday.

Mar 1998 The *'N Sync* album is released in the US.

Apr 1998 Gets a flame tattoo on his ankle to mark the success of the first album. It becomes a tradition for future albums. First MTV appearance performing 'I Want You Back'.

May 1998 The show that made 'N Sync – they perform at the Disney MGM studios in place of Backstreet Boys who had turned it down. The green room is the old school room where Justin and JC Chasez were taught during their *Mickey Mouse Club* days.

June 1998 Justin, with bleached blond hair, and girlfriend Veronica Finn join JC and Nikki DeLoach to celebrate a friend's wedding in the Bahamas.

Aug 1998 Justin's youngest half brother Steven is born. 'N Sync are joined by Petula Clark and Richard Branson for an open-air bus ride around Manhattan promoting the opening of his Virgin Megastore downtown.

Oct 1998 Opening act for Janet Jackson in Baltimore on her *Velvet Rope* Tour. 'N Sync perform *a capella* duet with Janet on Stevie Wonder's 'Overjoyed'.

Nov 1998 'N Sync know they have arrived when they appear on *The Tonight Show with Jay Leno*. Their second album, *Home for Christmas*, is released and joins *'N Sync* in the top 10 album chart. Britney Spears is the opening act in Orlando for their first headlining major tour, *Second II None*.

Jan 1999 Britney denies on TV that she and Justin are dating.

May 1999 Release of 'N Sync postage stamps in the Caribbean islands of St Vincent and the Grenadines.

Aug 1999 First annual 'N Sync Challenge for the Children

Basketball game in Atlanta, Georgia. The celebrity-studded event raises $50,000 for local children's hospitals.

Sept 1999 Justin and the band are pictured on boxes of Kellogg's Corn Pop cereal. Inside is one of four collector's cards. 'N Sync announce they are leaving Trans Continental and RCA/BMG to join Jive Records.

Oct 1999 Trans Continental and BMG file a $150 million lawsuit against the band. The Justin Timberlake Foundation to fund music education in schools is announced.

Nov 1999 'N Sync counter sues Lou Pearlman for $25 million. Justin denies in a newspaper interview and on TV that he is dating Britney.

Dec 1999 Million dollar lawsuit settled allowing 'N Sync to release their new album on Jive.

Mar 2000 Justin wins *People's* online poll of 'The Most Beautiful Person in the World'. Third 'N Sync album, *No Strings Attached*, becomes fastest seller in history with 2.4 million in its first week. Nearly one million tickets are sold in one day for upcoming tour, also a record.

Apr 2000 Justin is a guest at the White House as an honour for his work with the Justin Timberlake Foundation.

May 2000 Graduates in front of 20,000 fans at The Pyramid in Memphis. Tutors Chuck Yerger and Brenda Crenshaw surprise him with his diploma on stage. Britney tells *Rolling Stone* that she and Justin have kissed.

Aug 2000 'N Sync wins three awards at the MTV Video Music Awards.

Oct 2000 'N Sync are booed by boisterous baseball fans at game three of the World Series in Shea Stadium, New York, after they have performed the National Anthem.

Nov 2000 A pair of Justin's boots fetches $2200 at a charity Internet auction. 'Bye Bye Bye' placed 55 in *Rolling Stone*'s list of the 100 best pop songs of all time.

Dec 2000 Justin is named in a lawsuit filed by the mother of a 15-year-old fan who claims he harassed and verbally assaulted her after a concert in St Louis, Missouri – the case is later dropped. 'N Sync are number 1 on the *VH1/Money* magazine Rock Star index for the year having grossed $267 million in the US. 'This I Promise You' peaks at number 21 in the UK charts. Justin sends Britney twenty-six dozen red roses to her hotel suite as a birthday gift.

May 2001 'N Sync's *PopOdyssey* stadium tour of the US begins in Jacksonville, Florida.

July 2001 'N Sync's fourth album *Celebrity* becomes the second fastest selling album in history with nearly 1.9 million copies. Only *No Strings Attached* has sold faster. Justin and soul legend Al Green are featured on the front of the Millington Phone Directory as the leading local celebrities.

Oct 2001 Justin, complete with outlandish spectacles, plays the young Elton John for the British superstar's video of 'This Train Don't Stop There Any More'. It would subsequently win the Best Male Video at the 2002 MTV Video Awards.

Jan 2002 Joins movie stars Samuel L Jackson and Joe Pesci in the Bob Hope Classic, a pro-am golf tournament in Palm Springs. In successive rounds he is paired with Justin Leonard, Arnold Palmer and John Daly. Britney says in a newspaper interview and on British television that she and Justin will definitely marry in the future.

Mar 2002 Reports that Britney and Justin have split up are denied but prove to be true.

Apr 2002 The last 'N Sync concert, on the *Celebrity* tour, in Orlando. Justin finalizes his solo record deal with Jive and a week later begins recording *Justified* at The Neptunes' studio in Virginia Beach. 'Girlfriend' becomes 'N Sync's biggest UK hit reaching number 2 in the charts.

June 2002 Justin and his mother Lynn attend the world heavyweight boxing championship bout between Lennox Lewis and Mike Tyson at The Pyramid in Memphis.

Aug 2002 Buys an $8 million (£4.4 million) home in the Hollywood Hills complete with gym, swimming pool and a guest house where his best friend Trace Ayala now lives.

Nov 2002 First solo single 'Like I Love You' reaches number 2 in the UK charts. *Justified*, the album, is released. He breaks his foot while rehearsing for the *Justified* tour and returns to the family home in Shelby Forest to recuperate.

Jan 2003 Performs 'Cry Me A River' on *Top of the Pops* and then plays bass with The Flaming Lips while dressed as a dolphin.

Feb 2003 Justin's famous duet at the Brits Awards when he grabs Kylie Minogue's bum.

April 2003 Meets Cameron Diaz at the Nickelodeon Kids Awards in Los Angeles and fixes up a date to go bowling.

May 2003 The *Justified* tour opens at the Hallam FM Arena in Sheffield. Justin signs up with the TNT cable network as a special sports correspondent.

June 2003 *Justified* goes to the top of the UK album charts for the third time.

July 2003 Cameron is spotted backstage at the Orlando concert for the *Justified and Stripped* tour starring Justin and Christina Aguilera. Justin performs at the SARS benefit concert in Toronto and sings 'Miss You' with The Rolling Stones.

Nov 2003 Britney breaks down in tears when she is asked about splitting up with Justin on American TV.

Dec 2003 Dubbed the new 'King of Pop' by *Rolling Stone* magazine.

Jan 2004 Performs the last UK concerts of the *Justified* tour. Spends his twenty-third birthday with Cameron at home in LA where his mother sends him a chocolate cake.

Feb 2004 Performs a controversial duet with Janet Jackson at the Super Bowl. Justin tears off a leather cup to reveal Janet's right breast covered by a sun-shaped medallion. The pair later blame a 'wardrobe malfunction'. Wins two Grammy Awards for Best Male Pop Vocal Performance ('Cry Me A River') and for Best Pop Vocal Album (*Justified*).Wins two Brits for International Male Solo Artist and International Album (*Justified*).

Mar 2004 Starts work on *Edison,* his first major film, on location in Vancouver.

THE WELSH VETO

THE WALES ACT 1978 AND THE REFERENDUM

THE WELSH VETO

THE WALES ACT 1978 AND THE REFERENDUM

Edited by

DAVID FOULKES

J. BARRY JONES

R. A. WILFORD

CARDIFF
UNIVERSITY OF WALES PRESS
1983

British Library Cataloguing in Publication Data

The Welsh veto.
   1. Decentralization in government – Great Britain
   2. Wales – Politics and government
   I. Foulkes, David   II. Jones, J. Barry
   III. Wilford, R.A.
      328'.2   JW1152

ISBN 0-7083-0831-7

Typeset by Afal, Cardiff
Printed by CSP Printing of Cardiff

Contents

List of Tables

The Editors

David Foulkes   Reader in Law, UWIST, Cardiff.

J. Barry Jones   Lecturer in Politics, UWIST, Cardiff.

R.A. Wilford   Lecturer in Political Science, Queen's
                        University, Belfast.

Contributors

Denis Balsom   Director, Welsh Election Studies,
                        University College of Wales, Aberystwyth.

Geraint Talfan Davies   Assistant Controller for Programmes,
                        Harlech Television, Cardiff.

Mari James   Senior Research Officer, University of
                        Salford.

Harri Pritchard Jones   Author and Broadcaster

Peter Lindley   Senior Research Officer, Civil Service
                        College, London.

John Osmond   Journalist

Foreword

The devolution referendum of 1 March 1979 was a landmark in the history of the Welsh people. Indirectly, it was also a key episode in the political experience of the United Kingdom in the later twentieth century. For the first time ever, the Welsh electors had been offered, in however modest a form, a specific blueprint proposing some move towards self-government, some prospect of power being partially transferred from Whitehall to themselves. By a vast majority of about four to one, they rejected the possibility out of hand. The whole affair seemed to represent the end of an era. After the resurgence of national feeling in the 1960s, with the revival of Plaid Cymru, the activities of the Welsh language movement, new pressures for devolution within the major political parties, and the appointment of the Crowther/Kilbrandon commission, the wheel had come full circle. The fact that the Scots actually voted for devolution for their own nation on the same day – admittedly by the barest of majorities – merely underlined the hostility of the Welsh towards anything that resembled separatism, a mood as powerful in the 1970s as in the *Cymru Fydd* crisis eighty years before. The political culture that had moulded Welsh life since the early years of the century seemed to be fading away with barely a whimper.

Yet the devolution proposals for Wales put forward by the Callaghan government in 1976-9, and the campaign that led up to the referendum vote, are of wide interest and appeal, not only to Welsh people, but to all students of modern British politics generally. Many of the broader considerations that they raise are most ably discussed in this book, the work of academics, journalists and others concerned with the devolution issue over the past few years. The referendum campaign, for instance, must be projected against the background of the historical treatment of Wales as a political and administrative unit since the late nineteenth century. The actual passage of the bill and its legal and constitutional implications are highly instructive for students of British political processes. Some of the inherent problems of the referendum as a method for ascertaining the popular will are thrown into focus. The role of cultural and other lobbies and pressure groups, of the Welsh and English-language press, of the broadcasting media, and of a volatile and elusive public opinion also emerges in fascinating detail. In a variety of ways, the devolution campaign, for all its resoundingly negative outcome, provides a valuable case study of the idea of nationhood in microcosm, and of popular community involvement in government in modern Britain. The authors of this book deserve warm commendation for the wider political, cultural and social considerations that they have drawn out, in so impartial and open-minded a fashion, from the story of the devolution issue in Wales.

On the face of it, the devolution debate was a highly unsatisfactory affair. Indeed, as this book makes clear, it was hardly a debate at all, so overlaid did the question become with other issues, including the future of the Labour government itself during a bitter 'winter of discontent'. The drafting of a devolution scheme for Scotland and Wales at all owed much to short-term political factors, including the dependence of a minority government on Liberal and nationalist votes for its survival. The Welsh bill was a hurriedly-drafted and somewhat confusing document. Its system of 'horizontal devolution' on the West German model could have led to a legal and constitutional nightmare. But the debate, such as it was, was far from being a wasted exercise. Nor have its consequences disappeared from our consciousness since March 1979. Indeed, in some ways the alarming rise in mass unemployment and economic stagnation in Wales over the past three years has led to some new questions being asked about the quality of government, and its responsiveness to local Welsh opinion. There have been new developments such as the Welsh Select Committee, and an instructive episode like the forcing through of a Welsh-language Channel Four in the face of ministerial hostility. Meanwhile in Scotland, national feeling and enthusiasm for devolution remain powerful. Inevitably, the Scottish dimension will have some consequences for Wales as well, as so often in the past. More generally, British politics today remain in a state of remarkable flux, as is suggested in part by the rise of the Social Democrats, formally committed to decentralization and to a recasting of the regional and local governmental structure. How genuine this last commitment is in fact remains to be proven.

So the idea of Welsh devolution did not disappear from history in March 1979. Nor have its champions yielded the field to the apocalyptic exponents of mass popular insurrection. Those historic campaigns associated with men as diverse as Henry Richard and Thomas Gee, Tom Ellis and David Lloyd George, James Griffiths and S.O. Davies, Gwynfor Evans and Dai Francis may not yet have their course. The political administration of Wales, and its relationship to the other nations of the United Kingdom, will remain on the public agenda and within the public consciousness. The attempt to define the Welsh political personality will continue to fascinate and torment us in the future, as it did in the devolution referendum and the events that led up to it. In the light of this continuing, historic quest, all thinking men and women in Wales and beyond must welcome the appearance of this informative and illuminating book.

Oxford,   KENNETH O. MORGAN
May Day 1982

Preface

BY THE EDITORS

The referendum held in Wales on 1 March 1979, as to whether the *Wales Act 1978* should be brought into operation, was a remarkable and momentous event in Welsh political life. It seemed to us necessary and desirable to provide an account both of the referendum itself and of the circumstances surrounding it. This book therefore traces the emergence of Wales as an administrative and – to a lesser extent – as a political unit and explores the development of the political debate on the Welsh devolution issue particularly with reference to the period following the publication of the Kilbrandon Report in 1973. It is also concerned to examine the quintessential nature of the parliamentary debate and the passage of the *Wales Act*. It reviews the complex legal relationships that would have been created by the Act, between the Assembly on the one hand, and central and local government and other institutions of public administration on the other.

The central focus is the devolution referendum, a unique political exercise in Welsh history and one with profound implications for Welsh politics and the problematic issue of a Welsh identity. The book examines the composition of the contending issue-coalitions which emerged to fight the referendum and the issues that were raised during the campaign. The role and influence of the media during the course of the campaign are assessed and the shift in public opinion before and during the campaign is analysed on the basis of statistical data compiled from a variety of opinion research surveys. Finally, the results of the referendum are used in order to suggest possible changes in the structure of Welsh politics and to gauge the utility of the referendum as a decision making device.

Six of the nine contributors to the book, including the editors, are university teachers and researchers who have been concerned with the devolution issue for several years. One of the editors, J. Barry Jones, was Secretary of the Wales for the Assembly Campaign referred to in this book. The remaining three contributors who review the role played by the press and television during the referendum were actively engaged in those industries during the campaign. The views expressed are those of the individual contributors and are not to be attributed to the institution or organisations to which they may belong.

It should be noted that David Foulkes' contribution appeared in part and in a different form as 'Notes to the Wales Act' in *Current Law Statutes Annotated* (Sweet & Maxwell). Similarly, some of the sections contributed by J. Barry Jones and R. A. Wilford originally appeared as Research Paper 32 of the Centre for the Study of Public Policy (University of Strathclyde). Peter Lindley's contribution is Crown copyright and reproduced with the permission of the Controller of Her Majesty's Stationery Office.

The editors are very much aware of the assistance of several individuals and organisations who contributed to this book. We wish to express our appreciation to the contributors of the chapters for their co-operation in the revision of their original manuscripts, to the BBC and the ITN for agreeing to make available information from their news archives, and to the Department of Town Planning, UWIST, for drafting the map of the Welsh referendum results. Finally, our thanks are due to Mrs Margaret Aven and Mrs Sadia Matthews for undertaking the onerous task of typing several drafts of the manuscript.

CHAPTER 1

Wales: A Separate Administrative Unit

DAVID FOULKES, J. BARRY JONES, R.A. WILFORD

In strictly legal terms Wales, since the Tudors, has not existed but has been part of the legislative hybrid 'England and Wales'. Wales never acquired those autonomous institutions of statehood which Scotland enjoyed – an established church and separate legal, banking and educational systems – and retained despite the Act of Union of 1707. And yet the sense of Wales as a separate administrative and, periodically, a political entity has never been entirely extinguished.

Until the sixteenth century Wales was little more than a geographic expression, a westward facing promontory of the British Isles within which an anarchy of petty princedoms was perpetually at war, an inherently unstable situation exacerbated by the proximity of the Marcher-Lordships along the .Anglo-Welsh border. At the commencement of the fifteenth century the initial success of Owain Glyndŵr suggested that an effective central authority might be imposed upon Wales. The shadowy structure of a nation state began to emerge but the Glyndŵr regime lasted only a decade, hardly enough time for national institutions to be established. The sense of a separate Welsh entity was further obfuscated during this pre-Tudor period by the ambivalence in the Welsh attitude towards England which was coloured not simply by a desire for separation but for the restoration of the historic unity of Southern Britain. It was an attitude which Henry Tudor was to exploit prior to the Battle of Bosworth and which was recognised by contemporary observers, notably the Venetian Ambassador who reported to his government that 'the Welsh may now be said to have recovered their former independence for the most wise and fortunate Henry VII is a Welshman'.[1]

Despite the high expectations of his countrymen, Henry VII did little for Wales, preoccupied as he was with the larger and more pressing concerns of establishing the Tudor Dynasty. However, in deference to Welsh sensibilities he named his first son, Arthur, Prince of Wales and in 1501 carried into effect a scheme first mooted in

Edward IV's reign to establish a Council of Wales and the Marches. Arthur's untimely death frustrated the experiment whereby the Prince of Wales served as the Council's Chairman and the Council declined in significance until, in 1534, Rowland Lee was appointed and charged with the task of restoring law and order. An initial series of punitive measures was followed in 1536 by an Act of Union which ordained that Wales should be entirely incorporated within the realm of England, with all Welshmen given the same privileges, rights and laws as Englishmen. It was nothing less than a constitutional settlement in which the chaotic Marches completely disappeared, either incorporated into existing Welsh or English counties or merged to form the five new counties created by the Act. But fundamentally the Act reflected 'Henry VIII's ambition to fuse the English and Welsh people and bind them with indissoluble links of common aspirations'.[2] Although the Act of Union is highly significant in as much as it brought the whole of Wales within the realm of England and under the authority of Parliament, it was but the last stage in a process of assimilation that had been taking place for over two centuries and it took a further six years for the administrative machinery necessary for full incorporation with England to be set up. This was accomplished by the Act of Union of 1542: 'Broadly therefore it may be said that the Act of 1536 enunciates the general principle governing the Union and that of 1542 the details. Together they form the constitution under which Wales was henceforth to be governed'.[3] Under the Union the counties and boroughs henceforth sent representatives to Parliament. Welshmen were granted equality with Englishmen before the law: the severe disabilities previously applied to them were abolished. The English system of land tenure was introduced and *gavelkind*, where it still obtained in Wales was, over a period, displaced. The English system of local government was applied to Wales. The country was divided into twelve counties, grouped into four areas each with three counties. Sheriffs, coroners and other officers were appointed, and eight Justices of the Peace for each county: 'Local Administration was now placed in the hands of men drawn from local families and the energies of these families were now directed to the prevention of disorder rather than its perpetration as hitherto'.[4]

However, the system of government differed in some respects from that of England. Wales was given its own system of courts, the Courts of Great Session, largely independent of the courts at Westminster: in effect the system which had operated in North Wales for two and a half centuries was extended to the whole country. In these courts English law was administered – and in English, for the Act of Union required all official business to be in that tongue (out of a concern for administrative simplicity). Wales also had a separate organisation for revenue purposes, each group of three counties serving also as a fiscal unit with its own exchequer and system of audit. Finally, the Council of Wales and the Marches, formerly a prerogative court, was continued by the Act of Union as a permanent administrative body responsible to the Privy Council. 'Wales thus became a special administrative area'.[5] But the integrity of these Welsh institutions was not maintained. During the Civil War the Council fell into abeyance and, although it was revived in 1660, its authority was much restricted and the Glorious Revolution of 1688 finally brought it to an end. The other distinctive Welsh administrative institution, the Courts of Great Session, was significantly weakened by the Council's demise and in 1830, after a century of rivalry with the Westminster Courts, the Great Sessions were abolished in the face of the unanimous opposition of Welsh MPs and a considerable body of Welsh public opinion. With their abolition, the last vestiges of an identifiably Welsh system of government, erected by Henry VIII for the Welsh people, disappeared.

Consequently the emergence of Welsh political nationalism during the latter half of the nineteenth century occurred when Wales was devoid of distinctive legal and administrative institutions and disregarded as a separate political entity. Henry Richard speaking in the wake of the 1868 political evictions in Wales chided the House of Commons 'that no question relating to Wales had occupied the attention of Parliament in the memory of man'.[6] However, this situation was to change dramatically. The General Election of 1868 following the extension of the franchise in the previous year, marked the beginning of 50 years of 'Welsh political nationalism as a major force in British public life', in which the distinctive needs of Wales were brought 'into the general context of British politics after the obscurity and isolation of centuries.'[7]

The first administrative admission of Wales as a separate entity in the modern period was the Welsh Intermediate Education Act of 1889 which virtually created the modern system of Welsh secondary education. In 1896 an Inspectorate and Examining Body, the Central Welsh Board (CWB) was set up to administer the Act. However, there was by no means unanimous support in Wales for the Act. The Conservative *Western Mail* censured the government, claiming that the Act would enable 'bigoted and uneducated councillors to remove

3

clerical masters from [church] schools'. The paper went on to assert that the councillors 'want to cripple the influence of the church and pave the way for Welsh Home Rule.'[8] Thus, even at this early stage, the restructuring of Welsh administration could not be separated from political considerations, a tendency which became increasingly apparent during the course of the referendum debate. Subsequent to the 1889 Act there were regular demands for a Welsh National Council for Education but they fell on deaf ears until 1907 when the Liberal Government introduced a bill proposing a Council for Wales composed of representatives from Welsh local authorities which would regulate education policy throughout Wales. It generated a considerable volume of opposition which was largely concerned with the difficulty of ensuring fair representation on the national body for the rest of Wales as against the heavily populated South – another issue which is not infrequently raised today. The Bill was passed by the Commons but rejected by the Lords and by way of a consolation prize the Welsh Department of the Board of Education was set up in 1907; it was none the less a significant development creating the first regionally oriented department within a central government ministry. But too much should not be read into this; the Permanent Secretary had his office not in Cardiff but in London and the attempt to obtain a similar reform in the Ministry of Agriculture was rejected. However, the founding of the University of Wales in 1893 and the creation of the National Library and the National Museum in 1907 are further testimony to the growth of Welsh institutions.

The decade of 1910-20 represents a period during which a coherent and consistent policy of administrative devolution to Wales can be identified and when Wales came to be regarded as a 'special administrative area' for subsequent legislation. The passage of the National Insurance Act in 1911 followed by the establishment of the Welsh Health Insurance Commission in 1913 and the foundation of the Welsh Board of Health in 1919 all reflect this devolutionary trend. The same year also saw the creation of the Welsh Department of the Ministry of Agriculture responsible for a wide range of functions in Wales. Another issue to the forefront of political life in Wales during the first two decades of the twentieth century was the demand for the Disestablishment of the Church in Wales or, as it was seen, of the Church of England in Wales. As with any other issue affecting Wales, the Welsh interest in Parliament had to persuade a major British political party to its view – at this time this could of course only be the Liberal Party. Disestablishment was eventually provided for by the

4

Welsh Church Disestablishment Act 1914, but did not take place until 1920. The impetus generated by these initiatives was not maintained during the inter-war years largely because of the decline of Liberalism and preoccupation of all politicans with the Depression. However, Wales still made demands for special administrative treatment. In 1927 the Central Welsh Board, the Welsh Federation of LEAs and the University of Wales jointly called for a National Council for Education in Wales. The request was repeated in 1931 and 1935 but it was not associated with a significant political force and, despite the administrative attractions of the scheme, nothing was done.

The Second World War with the consequent dispersal of government departments and the appointment of Regional Commissioners (including one for Wales) renewed the process of administrative devolution. In 1940 the Welsh Board of Health acquired responsibility for a whole range of local government services in Wales. Two years later a Welsh Reconstruction Advisory Council was set up and recommended a 'new decentralised administrative pattern' to solve the post-war problems in Wales. In the immediate post-war years much was done in this direction; Wales was recognised as one of the Treasury 'standard regions' and a regular Conference of the Heads of Goverment Departments in Wales (of which there were 15 in 1945) was held which produced annual reports on government economic policies. Thus 'in the absence of a Department for Wales the Government evolved the necessary machinery to fill the gap, so that when the Welsh Office was created it did not have to work in a vacuum'.[9] Wales was created as an administrative unit by the National Health Service Act 1946 (the Welsh Regional Hospital Board) and the Gas Act 1948 (the Wales Gas Board – not at all convenient administratively); but not by the Electricity Act 1947 (South Wales Electricity Board and Merseyside & North Wales Electricity Board). On the education side some rationalisation took place with the setting up in 1948 of the Welsh Joint Education Committee which took over from the CWB and also acquired additional powers of recommending educational proposals to Welsh local authorities. In the same year an advisory Council for Wales and Monmouthshire was also established; a nominated body, whose function was to meet (in private) for the exchange of views and information, and to ensure that the Government was adequately informed on the impact of government action on the general life of the country. Thus by the end of the 1940s there was extensive administrative machinery in Wales but it was the result of a series of *ad hoc* decisions and the arrangements, which lacked both political direction and supervision, fell short of the demands voiced fifty years previously.

The desire to invest the Welsh identity with a political as well as an administrative dimension had been explicit in the aspirations of the *Cymru Fydd* (Young Wales) Movement in the closing decade of the nineteenth century. It was linked with the Home Rule campaign but whereas in Ireland it blazed dangerously, in Wales it flickered only uncertainly. A National Institutions (Wales) Bill was introduced to Parliament in 1891 which proposed – in addition to a Welsh Education Department and a National Council for Wales – a Secretary for Wales. The Bill failed to arouse either the interest or the approval of Parliament and similar legislative initiatives by private members were equally unsuccessful in 1908, 1921 and again in 1955. (see Chapter 2). In the 1930s the Welsh Parliamentary Party, consisting overwhelmingly of Labour and Liberal MPs, launched a series of initiatives to persuade successive governments to establish a Welsh Office and to give Wales a voice in the Cabinet; in effect to adopt the system that had applied to Scotland since the middle of the nineteenth century. But the requests were rejected, first by Chamberlain in 1938 and then by Churchill in 1943, on the grounds of cost, administrative disruption and the belief that Wales would not receive any practical advantage from the co-ordination of activities in a single department. Furthermore, Chamberlain, expressing an opinion that was to find echoes in the referendum debate, claimed that the analogy of Scotland could not be advanced because whereas Scotland had a different system of law and administration, Wales's close incorporation with England precluded the need for a separate minister. After the war, when Labour had the political power, the hostility of Morrison and Bevan prevented the creation of a separate Welsh Office. Bevan's concern – which also found expression in the referendum campaign – was that such a devolution of authority 'would divorce Welsh political activity from the mainstream of British politics'. [10]

Despite the Labour Party's close association with Wales it was a Conservative government which created in 1951 the office of Minister for Welsh Affairs, but it was a curious arrangement as the post, which existed until 1964, was always held in conjunction with another office — until 1957 by the Home Secretary, and from then until 1964 by the Minister of Housing and Local Government. In 1951 the Welsh Office of that Ministry had been created and in 1957 a Minister of State for Welsh Affairs was created as a junior officer in that Ministry. The

Permanent Secretary of the Welsh Department of Education whose office had until then been in London was also given an office in Cardiff; and the office of the civil servant in charge of the Welsh Department of the Ministry of Agriculture was upgraded.

In 1957 the Council of Wales produced a memorandum which set out the case for a Secretary of State for Wales and a Welsh Office. The Government remained unconvinced (its response included the appointment of the Minister of State referred to), but the report must have added weight to those in the Labour Party who had been arguing the case for some time. An undertaking to appoint a Secretary of State was given by the Labour Party in its manifesto for the 1959 general election and reaffirmed in the 1964 manifesto. Despite the long campaign and the undoubted sincerity of several leading Labour politicians, notably James Griffiths, at the time deputy leader of the Labour Party, the manner in which the Welsh Office was established and the functions of the new Welsh Secretary were announced, illustrates a lack of clear administrative thinking and suggests that the exercise was a political expedient to placate aggrieved Welsh interests. In the debate on the Queen's Speech on 3rd November 1964 Mr Grimond, the leader of the Liberal Party, commenting on the appointment of Mr James Griffiths to the new Office of Secretary of State, admitted himself perplexed as to the powers the new minister was to receive. Mr Griffiths was unable to enlighten him. It was the 19th November before the Prime Minister felt able to define the responsibilities of the Secretary of State for Wales. They were somewhat vague; the Secretary of State was to take over 'virtually all executive responsibilities of the Ministry of Housing and Local Government in Wales; to take over responsibility for the Welsh Roads Division of the Ministry of Transport and to co-operate with the First Secretary of the DEA in respect of regional economic planning in Wales'.[11] A former minister at the Welsh Office suggests a reason for the vague and tardy definition:

> Whitehall had made little or no preparation for the coming of the Welsh Office. The 'Charter' Secretary of State for Wales and his two ministers were immediately appointed, only to find themselves without functions to perform. Despite the fact that Labour's 1964 manifesto clearly envisaged executive responsibility for the Secretary of State covering housing, local government, health, education and agriculture, moves were afoot in Whitehall to confine his role to that of a watchdog, a

7

general oversight function over all government activities as they affect Wales. There were to be no executive functions. The Secretary of State's first major task was to demand and extract from Whitehall some real and effective powers.[12]

Initially the executive functions of the Secretary of State were those which had been administered by the Welsh Office of the Ministry of Housing and Local Government, mainly town and country planning, housing, water, sewage and other local government matters, together with economic planning and the responsibilities for roads in Wales formerly exercised by the Minister of Transport. The Secretary of State was also authorised to exercise 'over-sight within Wales of the execution of national policy by the Ministry of Agriculture. Fisheries and Food, the Department of Education and Science, the Ministry of Health, the Ministry of Transport, the Board of Trade and the Ministry of Labour'.[13] However, it would appear that the powers were extracted from Whitehall in a random fashion. If the Welsh Secretary was to play a significant part in the formulation of regional plans, why were the functions of the Board of Trade and Ministries of Power and Transport not taken over? Another curiosity of the establishment of the Welsh Office concerned the exclusion of education from the Secretary of State's responsibilities. This perplexed many people including Lord Crowther. Some years later, as the first Chairman of the Commission on the Constitution (on his death he was succeeded by Lord Kilbrandon), he enquired of the Permanent Under-Secretary at the Welsh Office:

> May I ask if there is any reason why it [education] was not transferred? One would suppose it is the oldest specific Welsh Department and it is a field in which there have been differences in policy and practice between Wales and England for longer than most. One would suppose it would be the very first function to be transferred. Is there some special reason why it was not?[14]

No complete or convincing answer stating the administrative reason for the exclusion was forthcoming. The lack of any clear administrative principle in the allocation of responsibilities to the Welsh Office is even more vividly illustrated in the case of the Secretary of State's 'oversight' powers. Mr. James Griffiths interviewed in November 1968 had a very clear view of these powers:

The Secretary of State is the master of the Welsh situation: [he]has oversight of other departments in Wales and gives instructions to the regional controllers of all seventeen government departments in Wales.[15]

Other observers have reached different conclusions which cast serious doubts on the 'oversight' power of the Welsh Secretary, inferring the possibility of a conflict of loyalties. Professor Cross, examining the new Office, reported that 'Welsh controllers do not necessarily inform the Welsh Office of every possible future development of departmental policy in Wales if the knowledge might prove embarrassing to their own department'.[16] The delay and the confusion surrounding the announcement of the Welsh Office's functions and the divergence of views regarding the 'oversight' role of the Welsh Secretary raise serious doubts as to the administrative principles behind the establishment of the Office which are reinforced by Crossman's opinion that it was 'a completely artificial new office for Jim Griffiths — all the result of a silly election pledge'.[17]

With the passage of years the Welsh Office has acquired additional functions the effect of which has been to make the office a more viable administrative department. In later stages the Welsh Office took over direct responsibility for the health service, forestry and agriculture, ancient monuments, tourism, child care and primary and secondary education in Wales and for financing the National Museum and National Library of Wales. In 1975 the Welsh Office acquired significant economic powers arising from Section 7 of the Industry Act with reference to the role and activities of the Welsh Development Agency. Taken together these functions have enabled the Welsh Office to present itself as a custodian of Welsh intersts and as an administrative expression of the Welsh identity.

The Welsh dimension has also been taken account of in Parliament. Under the House of Commons (Redistribution of Seats) Act 1949 Wales is guaranteed a minimum of 35 seats and presently has 36 although on the basis of her population should only have 31 seats. Since 1964 and the establishment of the Welsh Office, government action in Wales has been subjected to the same parliamentary scrutiny as all government departments. With regard to parliamentary questions Welsh Office questions are taken first every five weeks. In addition it has become the practice in each parliamentary session to have a 'Welsh Day' which usually consists of broad-ranging debate covering the whole area of government activity in Wales. The Welsh Grand

9

Committee, for which Welsh parliamentarians of all political persuasions had campaigned since 1886, was established on a sessional basis in 1960 and became a permanent standing committee in 1969. It consists of all 36 Welsh constituency MPs together with not more than 5 others. The committee meets about three times a session and has power only to 'consider such specified matters relating exclusively to Wales as may be referred to them' by agreement through the 'usual channels' and to 'report only that they have considered the said matter'. Votes are not taken: nor does it consider estimates or Bills. Furthermore its recommendations, if any are made, have no force. Thus it is no more than a forum for debate serving to air Welsh grievances and debate Welsh issues; in short, a 'talking shop' exhibiting all the vices and virtues of that type of institution.[18]

The Acts relating exclusively to Wales are very few in number. The Sunday Closing (Wales) Act 1881, referring to the closing of public houses, was the first Act to apply to Wales a legislative principle that did not apply to England. Even at that time it did escape notice that the principle of treating Wales as a national unit could be extended to matters other than liquor licensing. (The present statutory provisions are found in the Licensing Act 1964, as amended by the Local Government Act 1972, which give a local option exercised by referendum organised on a district council basis). One notable and exceptional piece of legislation relating to Wales alone was the Welsh Church Disestablishment Act (1914). Since the war, such particularistic legislation includes provision for the use of the Welsh language on election forms (Elections (Welsh Forms) Act 1964) and its use in official documents and the administration of justice (Welsh Language Act 1967). There has additionally been a series of Acts which enable Welsh local authorities to support financially various Welsh cultural institutions. However, such legislation remains extremely rare and for the overwhelming majority of cases England and Wales are treated as a single unit.

Although reform of local government in England and Wales was accomplished by the same Act of Parliament (Local Government Act 1972), the consultative procedures leading to the legislation were quite different for Wales. In fact, the structure of local government in Wales was under separate consideration from that in England from the end of the Second World War. Under the Local Government Act 1958, separate Commissions were created for England and Wales to make recommendations on the boundaries of counties and county boroughs. The Welsh Commission's draft proposals for, *inter alia,* a reduction to five counties met with hostility, and revised proposals, which were not more favoured, were rejected by the Government. In 1965 the first Secretary of State for Wales, James Griffiths, set up an Interdepartmental Working Party of senior officials of relevant departments to look at the problem again. The Working Party consulted informally a number of people experienced in local government in Wales as a result of which three broad lines of thought were noted:

(a) that the then existing structure should be retained but with fewer and stronger authorities;
(b) that that structure should be replaced by a single tier of all-purpose authorities;
(c) that some kind or regional or sub-regional authority should be formed.

Those who favoured a single tier system based on 16 authorities also, it seems, took the view that some functions could be exercised more effectively on all-Wales level and favoured an elected all-Wales council.

Thus from the mid-sixties proposals for reform of local government in Wales were entangled with proposals for devolution, a fact of some significance during the course of the referendum campaign. The government having considered the report of its Working Party opted for a two-tier system consisting of five counties, three county boroughs and 36 districts. The single tier proposal was rejected and with it proposals for a new all-Wales body.[19]However, the government acknowledged the need to improve the then existing machinery in Wales for advisory and promotional work. In 1965, a Welsh Economic Council had displaced the advisory Council for Wales and Monmouthshire. The Government now proposed, and in 1968 proceeded to the creation of, a more pretigious Welsh Council to provide a forum for the inter-change of information, to assist in the formulation of plans and to advise the Secretary of State on major land use matters, etc. In March 1970, following the report of the Redcliffe-Maud Commission on Local Government in England, another White Paper[20]produced by the Welsh Office proposed three unitary authorities for the area of the then counties of Glamorgan and Monmouthshire. The incoming Conservative Government of 1970 thought that it was wrong to treat that area differently from the rest of Wales, and proposed a two-tier system for the whole of Wales, with 7 (later increased to 8) county councils and 36 district councils. It was on this basis that the Welsh clauses, together with the Bill itself, were approved by parliament in the form of the Local Government Act of 1972. Subsequently, the

11

Local Government Act 1974 created a Commission for Local Administration in Wales (the local government ombudsman) separate from that in England.

The treatment of the reform of local government in Wales reveals the extent to which Government in the late 1960s and early 1970s was increasingly identifying Wales as a separate administrative unit. The Welsh Arts Council, a regional committee of the Arts Council of Great Britain since 1945, was established as a financially autonomous body in 1967. In 1968 the Countryside Commission appointed a Committee for Wales (after consultations with the Secretary of State) to which it delegated all its functions in Wales. The following year, 1969, the Development of Tourism Act created a Wales Tourist Board to promote the industry in the Principality, and in 1972 a Sports Council for Wales was created by Charter.

The Health Service in Wales, as a result of the 1973 reorganisation,[21] also differs from that in England in that in Wales there are no Regional Health Authorities, only Area Health Authorities which are responsible for certain functions additional to those vested in English AHAs. Furthermore there is in Wales a special health authority created by the Secretary of State, to provide various services on an all-Wales basis for the NHS in Wales, including design and construction of major capital works and computers. The Welsh Development Agency was set up in 1975 to promote Wales as a location of industrial development, to promote industrial efficiency and safeguard employment. The Community Land Act of 1975 enabled public authorities (in England and Scotland, local authorities) to acquire land for development. However, in Wales, an all-Wales body – the Land Authority for Wales – was established to exercise these functions. Significantly the Minister expressed the hope that the Authority was 'an interim measure in the context of future devolution'.[22]

It would not be appropriate to attempt to provide here an account of the significance of the Welsh language in Welsh politics and in the devolution discussions.[23] But it should be noted that the Welsh language has increasingly become recognised as a medium for the administration of government and justice in Wales. The linguistic restrictions imposed by the Act of 1536 were to some extent repealed by the Welsh Courts Act 1942. The Elections (Welsh Forms) Act 1964 authorised the use, in connection with elections in Wales, of translations of statutory forms into Welsh. The Committee on the Legal Status of the Welsh Language (Cmnd. 2785) recommended in 1964 that there should be a 'clear, positive, legislative declaration of general application, to the effect that any act, writing or thing done in Welsh in Wales or Monmouthshire should have the like legal force as if it had been done in English'. It was followed by the Welsh Language Act 1967 which authorised the use of Welsh in any legal proceedings in Wales by anyone who desires to use it, and provided for Welsh versions of statutory forms.

As has already been indicated, the lack of distinctive Welsh institutions from the sixteenth to the twentieth century functioned to erode social cohesion. During that period it was only the language that could claim to give meaning to a separate Welsh identity and this, in part, explains the pressure during this century to accord it full legal and administrative status. Consequently, the loss of language, which for many represents a sense of dispossession, is rendered all the more acute in Wales in comparison with, for example, Scotland which has a comprehensive range of national institutions. This loss is empirically verifiable. In 1901, 50 per cent of the population of 2 million claimed to be Welsh speaking; by 1971 the proportion had shrunk to under 21 per cent of the population of 2.7m (Table 1 – 1) The language is now largely concentrated in North and West Wales, areas which support the Welsh Nationalist Party, Plaid Cymru.

Table 1 – 1

Proportion of Enumerated Population (aged 3 and over) Speaking Welsh at Selected Censuses 1911-1971

Area	Percentage of persons speaking Welsh and not English				Percentage of persons speaking English and not Welsh			
	1911	1931	1951	1971	1911	1931	1951	1971
Wales	8·5	4·0	1·7	1·3	35·0	32·8	27·2	19·6
Anglesey	36·2	23·9	9·6	4·5	52·5	63·5	70·2	61·2
Breconshire	5·6	2·0	0·5	1·1	35·9	35·3	29·8	21·8
Caernarvonshire	35·6	21·4	8·9	4·3	50·0	57·8	62·8	57·8
Cardiganshire	34·2	20·0	7·4	3·7	55·4	67·1	72·1	63·9
Carmarthenshire	20·5	9·2	4·4	2·9	64·4	73·1	72·9	63·6
Denbighshire	10·1	5·4	2·3	1·8	46·6	45·1	36·2	26·3
Flintshire	3·4	1·0	0·3	0·8	38·8	30·7	20·8	13·8
Glamorgan	3·1	0·8	0·3	0·7	35·0	29·7	20·0	11·0
Merionethshire	36·7	22·1	9·2	7·8	53·6	64·0	66·2	65·7
Monmouthshire	0·4	0·1	0·1	0.1	9.2	5·9	3·4	2·0
Montgomeryshire	10·7	6·8	3·2	1·3	34·1	33·9	31·9	25.8
Pembrokeshire	7·7	4·0	1·6	1·0	24·7	26·6	25·3	19·7
Radnorshire	0·1	0·0	0·1	0·2	5·3	4·7	4·4	3·6

Source: Summary Tables, Wales, Census 1971 (H.M.S.O., 1975) p.132.

13

It is these areas that have experienced a not inconsiderable amount of rural depopulation between 1911 and 1971. (Table 1 – 2)

Table 1 – 2

Population at Selected Censuses 1911-1971

	Population (thousands)			
Area	1911	1931	1951	1971
Wales	2,421	2,593	2,599	2,731
Anglesey	51	49	51	60
Breconshire	59	58	57	53
Caernarvonshire	123	121	124	123
Cardiganshire	60	55	53	55
Carmarthenshire	160	179	172	163
Denbighshire	147	158	171	185
Flintshire	83	113	145	176
Glamorgan	1,122	1,229	1,203	1,259
Merionethshire	46	43	41	35
Monmouthshire	395	432	425	462
Montgomeryshire	53	48	46	43
Pembrokeshire	90	87	91	99
Radnorshire	23	21	20	18

Source: Summary Tables, Wales Census 1971 (H.M.S.O., 1975), p.2.

These figures suggest that the prospects for the language appear bleak. Welsh speakers become an aging population as the traditional influx of retired English-born into these areas proceeds.

Industrialisation was a key factor in fostering migration not only from rural areas of Wales into its developing urban areas, but also from England into Wales. The scale of this movement into the Welsh industrial enclaves is not even remotely approached in the equivalent areas of Scotland and Northern Ireland. (Table 1 – 3)

Table 1 – 3

Percentage of English-born Enumerated in the Peripheral Enclaves

Year	Wales	Scotland	Northern Ireland
1861	11	3	1
1871	9	3	1
1881	15	2	2
1891	19	3	2
1901	18	3	3
1911	22	4	3
1921	15	4	3
1931	15	3	3
1951	13	4	3
1961	12	5	3

Source: M. Hechter, *Internal Colonialism* (London: Routledge and Kegan Paul, 1975), p.188.

The high points of this movement coincided with the boom in the coal industry but it has continued and increased despite the decline of coal during the 1960s; the proportion of English-born residents in Wales at the time of the 1971 Census was 15 per cent. But all the traditional industries of Wales, slate quarrying and agriculture, as well as coal mining, have undergone substantial decline since 1921 in terms of job losses. The consistent decline in manpower in these industries has had a consequent weakening effect upon traditional industrial communities. (Table 1 – 4)

Table 1 – 4

Percentage of Welsh labour Force in Agriculture, Mining and Quarrying 1921-1975

	1921	1951	1961	1975
Agriculture	9.0	8.3	5.9	2.6
Mining and Quarrying	26.4	12.7	9.7	4.2

Source: Compiled from Census Data: 1921-1971.

The other traditional industry, iron and steel making, has also experienced marked job-losses particularly during the 1970s with the total closures at Ebbw Vale and East Moors, Cardiff, a trend continued after the referendum by the ending of steel making at Shotton and cutbacks at Llanwern and Port Talbot. Thus, the economy of Wales has undergone substantial change during this century. An index of this change is also provided by the growth of the tertiary or service sector in Wales which in 1975 accounted for more than half (52.7%) of the labour force.[24] The advent of the white collar workers, and the consequent *embourgeoisment* of Wales, has been in part assisted by successive governments who have sought to relocate administrative departments in Wales and develop Cardiff as the administrative capital, thereby fostering a further wave of English-born migrants into the Principality and cementing the bonds of integration and assimilation between the two nations. Cumulatively, these demographic shifts and socio-economic changes – with their inevitable deleterious effects upon Welsh language and culture – have served to complicate and render less certain a consensual perception of Wales as a separate and distinct entity.

Finally, discussion of institutions reflecting Wales as a separate entity is incomplete without reference to the non-governmental institutions that have been set up since the Second World War.[25] The major political parties now have recognisable Welsh identities. The Liberals set up North and South Wales Liberal Federations in 1886 and 1887 respectively and formally created the Welsh Liberal Party in 1897. The Labour Party created the South Wales Regional Council of Labour in 1937; ten years later it was merged with its North Wales counterpart to create the Welsh Regional Council of Labour which in 1975 was retitled 'Labour Party—Wales'. The Conservative Party has also had a 'Welsh area' within its organisational structure since 1930 and has held 'Welsh' Annual Conferences since 1972. In fact, all three parties, no doubt stimulated by the existence of Plaid Cymru, have assumed an increasingly Welsh profile. The creation of the Wales TUC in 1973, matched by the first annual conference of the Wales CBI in 1978, gave added weight to a general momentum creating a framework of Welsh institutions. However, the *ad hoc* institution building in Wales, whilst performing the manifest function of recognising the need for a distinctively Welsh administrative framework, also has promoted the assimilation of the Principality into the British body politic, part of the process of acculturation – popularly termed 'Anglicization'. The process, whether intended or

16

unintended, has acted to integrate the periphery into the dominant British political culture. We later discuss the effects of acculturation upon the referendum vote (chapter 11), but here it is pertinent to note that the unspoken, but underlying, question in the referendum was whether the Welsh identity achieved in the developed administrative and political institutions should be crowned by a national Assembly – or whether the continuing socio-economic and political integration of Wales with England had vitiated the assumed residual aspiration for a Welsh identity, thereby rendering the whole exercise of the referendum redundant.

NOTES

1. Quoted in D. Williams, *A History of Modern Wales*, 1950, p.20.
2. I. Jones, *Modern Welsh History*, 1934, p.22.
3. W. Rees, *The Union of England and Wales*, 1967, p.49.
4. D. Williams, *op. cit.*, p.44.
5. Rees, *op. cit.*, p.49.
6. K. O. Morgan, *Wales in British Politics: 1868-1922*, 3rd edn., 1980, p.2.
7. *ibid.*, p.297.
8. Quoted by Carter in *Welsh Studies in Public Law*, 1965, p.48.
9. *ibid.*, p.53.
10. Quoted in J. Griffiths, *Pages from Memory*, 1969, p.161.
11. H of C Debate Vol.702 col. 623. 19 November 1964.
12. E. Rowlands, 'The Politics of Regional Administration: The Establishment of the Welsh Office', *Public Administration*, Vol. 50, 1972, p.333.
13. See Welsh Office Written Evidence to the Commission on the Constitution (para 33-37) vol. 1, pp.91-111.
14. Minutes of Evidence I: Wales, *Commission on the Constitution*, 1970, p.12.
15. Quoted by P. Byrne, J. McCarthy, M. Tudor and J. W. Jones, 'The Welsh Office', unpublished research paper, UWIST, 1970, p.7.
16. J. A. Cross, 'The Regional Decentralisation of British Government Departments', *Public Administration*, Vol. 48, 1970, p.439.
17. R. Crossman, *Diaries of a Cabinet Minister*, Vol. I, 1975, p.117.
18. For a fuller discussion see Borthwick, Research Paper No. 5. *Commission on the Constitution*, 1973.
19. Local Government in Wales, Cmnd. 3340, 1967.

17

20. Local Government in Wales, Cmnd. 4310, 1970.

21. National Health Service Reorganisation Act 1973.

22. Standing Committee G, Col. 933: 12 June 1975.

23. For a discussion of this issue see, M. Stephens (ed.), *The Welsh Language Today,* 1973.

24. *Digest of Welsh Statistics No. 26,* 1980.

25. A full description of the development of Welsh institutions is given in A. Butt-Philip, *The Welsh Question,* 1975, Chs. 9-10.

CHAPTER 2

The Development of the Devolution Debate

J. BARRY JONES

The Labour government's proposals for devolution as contained in the Wales Act were prompted, in large measure, by the electoral threat posed by the nationalists, notably in Scotland. In that context it is possible to link the proposals to the nationalist advance made in by-elections during the late sixties and particularly to Gwynfor Evans' victory in Carmarthen in July 1966. But a debate concerning the appropriate form of Welsh devolution stretches back to the end of the nineteenth century albeit under the guise of the more evocative term, 'Home Rule'.

The initial push for Welsh home rule was almost entirely the product of the enthusiasm of one man, T.E. Ellis, the Liberal MP for Merioneth who, together with other London Welsh expatriates, founded the first branch of Cymru Fydd in 1887. Largely as a result of his promptings the society committed itself to a programme of federal home rule; 'to attain a national legislature for Wales with full control over all purely Welsh business and a Welsh Executive responsible to it and the Imperial Parliament, where Wales would still be represented'.[1] This aspiration for a particular form of home rule falling far short of independence, reflected the ambivalence with which Wales regarded the issue then and indeed subsequently. It is also to be found in the equivocal manner in which the first legislative attempts to secure a measure of home rule were made. During the parliamentary debate on the Local Government (County Councils) Bill in 1888 T.E. Ellis moved an amendment (subsequently withdrawn) to establish a Welsh National Council, on which would sit MPs and representatives from the new Welsh counties and which would have certain deliberative and administrative functions. A similar ploy was used by Lloyd George in 1895 during the passage of the Welsh Church Disestablishment Bill. His amendment, accepted by the government, would have vested the management of Welsh tithes in a Welsh National Council, an intriguing and somewhat ironic power of taxation but one which was destined to remain hypothetical because the government fell before it could be enacted.

The first of the Welsh Home Rule Bills had preceded Lloyd George's initiative by four years. In 1891 Alfred Thomas, MP, later to become Lord Pontypridd, introduced a National Institutions (Wales) Bill which, with minor modifications, was reintroduced in 1892. It involved the appointment of a Secretary of State, the establishment of a Welsh Education Department, further provisions for the reform of local government and the certain of a National Council for Wales. The roles which it was anticipated the Council would play were ill thought out and mutually contradictory; it was expected to act as a forum of the Welsh nation, a department of state, a legislature and a scrutinising committee of the Westminster government. These constitutional absurdities failed to commend themselves to the Commons which overwhelmingly rejected the bill. A similar fate awaited the Government of Wales Bill, introduced by E.T. John in March 1914, although it was based on much firmer constitutional ground and was heavily influenced by earlier Irish Home Rule bills. It envisaged a 95 member assembly with legislative and financial powers but it too was roundly defeated. Predictably, this was the last attempt before the first world war to achieve Welsh home rule. It also marked the close of the period during which Home Rule for Wales was viewed in a context of Ireland and spoken of in the rhetoric of nineteenth century nationalism.

The Home Rule debates in the post-war period were different both in form and in character from those that had gone before. In many respects they have a contemporary tone and are closer conceptually to the events of 1974-79 than to E.T. John's Bill of 1914. The most notable difference was in terminology; 'home rule' being dropped for 'devolution'. The debates recommenced in the immediate aftermath of the War. In 1918 a Llandrindod conference of Welsh notables approved a series of recommendations calling for a Welsh Parliament; known as the 'Llandrindod Resolutions' they were subsequently endorsed by 11 of the 17 Welsh counties and county boroughs. Shortly after, a Labour Conference in Cardiff approved a policy of Federal Home Rule for Wales. However by 1919, when the debate moved to Westminster, it was concerned with 'all round devolution' for Scotland, Wales and the English regions and the central issue was no longer 'nationalism' which was hardly mentioned, but the 'congestion of government'. A Speakers Conference set up in October 1919, reported in April 1920 but was deeply divided between those, led by the Scottish MP Murray Macdonald, who wanted limited but separate legislatures for Scotland, Wales and England and others led by the Speaker, who proposed Grand Councils for Scotland, Wales and England comprising the respective members of parliament for those three areas. The Speaker's plan which left the Westminster Parliament in full control of the purse, produced criticisms in Wales, as in Scotland, that such a form of local autonomy would be a fiasco. Dissatisfied Scottish and Welsh MPs looked to Murray Macdonald's alternative scheme and it was this which provided the basis for the Government of Scotland and Wales Bill in 1922. Its Welsh sections envisaged a bicameral legislature (Senate and Commons) with substantial powers of taxation, but the break-up of the Lloyd George coalition transformed the political situation and this, together with the deepening economic crisis, removed 'devolution' from the national agenda for the next thirty years.

During that period Plaid Cymru, which had been founded in 1925, made only a marginal contribution to political devolution. Although the party immediately sought to acquire dominion status for Wales equivalent to that enjoyed by Canada and Australia, it lacked a political instinct; a deficiency that persisted until the end of the Second World War. In its early days the party was socially conservative, possessed a strongly pacifist and moral tone and expressed its nationalism in a 'back to medievalism' approach. Furthermore, the Welsh language – the 'symbol of nationhood' – was its prime concern, and still in evidence as late as 1962 when Saunders Lewis, one of the party's founding fathers, asserted: 'the language is more important than self-government'.[2] As long as this hierarchy of values prevailed, the party's commitment to political devolution inevitably was qualified.

After its formation the party failed either to make a significant electoral advance or to fan the flames of home rule; it remained a fringe organisation, rather more cultural than political, only emerging temporarily onto the centre of the political stage in 1936 with the burning of the RAF bombing school in Pen-y-berth on the Llŷn peninsula. After the war Plaid Cymru adopted a more self-consciously political and parliamentary stance. In the early 1950s it lent its moral support, political organiser and party activists to the 'Parliament for Wales' campaign but with little success. Like the Scottish Covenant Movement, the Parliament for Wales campaign collected signatures

21

for a petition calling for a Welsh Parliament with legislative authority and financial powers. Eventually, 250,000, or 14 per cent, of the Welsh electorate signed and in 1955 S.O. Davies the Labour MP for Merthyr presented a Parliament for Wales Bill which was soundly defeated by 48 votes to 14. Only 6 Welsh MPs supported the movement and of these five were Labour whose involvement in the campaign earned them a severe rebuke from the party hierarchy. The campaign organisers in an assessment that was to be repeated in 1979 noted that either because of hostility or indifference, the Welsh MPs were 'the biggest obstacle of all'.[3]

But some of the responsibility must be shouldered by the campaign itself: its organization was defective; its executive committee was drawn almost exclusively from North Wales; and all its members were Welsh speakers, characteristics which set it apart from the majority of the population in Wales. Nevertheless, on balance, Plaid's involvement in the Campaign is presumed to have benefited the party, as demonstrated by its improved showing in the 1955 general election. But the campaign's defeat ensured that Welsh devolution occupied a low political priority until Plaid Cymru's remarkable victory in the Carmarthen by election in 1966 and the subsequent near successes in Rhondda West in 1967 and Caerphilly in 1968. However, the emergence of Welsh devolution was not solely attributable to the nationalists. In May 1966, some two months before the Carmarthen by-election, the Welsh Labour Party's Annual Conference endorsed a demand, voiced the previous year by its Executive, for an Elected Welsh Council below which would be a reorganised structure of 'most-purpose' authorities. Thus, it can be argued that the nationalist threat was responsible not so much for causing as for giving added keenness to Welsh Labour's growing enthusiasm for some form of devolution. Furthermore, the dominant position of the Labour Party in Wales in the 1966 General Election when 32 of the 26 Welsh seats were won by Labour ensured that most of the devolution debate now took place *within* the ranks of the Welsh Labour Party.

Initially that debate was conducted within the framework of local government reform (see Chapter 1) and there were many factors which suggested that a positive conclusion might be reached. The Welsh Secretary of State, Cledwyn Hughes, was an enthusiastic devolutionist who had supported the 'Parliament for Wales' campaign some fifteen years previously. Furthermore, Richard Crossman, Lord President of the Council, with special responsibilities for devolution, identified devolution as 'the great constitutional issue of the day' and wanted 'to go for a really ambitious plan for a Welsh Council or Parliament'.[4] But the Labour government could not consider Wales in isolation from Scotland where the nationalists were believed to pose a more serious electoral threat; any concession to Wales would have to be matched by one to Scotland and this, Willie Ross, the Scottish Secretary, steadfastly opposed. Consequently the Welsh opportunity was lost. The Government eventually opted for a minimal response and in October 1968 announced the setting up of a Royal Commission on the Constitution doubtless in the hope that the problem would either solve itself or go away.

The Royal Commission when formed invited interested organisations and individuals to give evidence and with some alacrity the Executive of the Labour Party in Wales set up a study group to help prepare its evidence. By April 1969 the group had produced a draft proposal of a quasi-federal nature, suggesting a Welsh Senate of 72 seats with certain legislative powers, particularly in domestic and welfare matters.[5] The proposals produced a storm of controversy in the parliamentary party. The then Welsh Secretary of State, George Thomas, who had replaced Cledwyn Hughes, was totally opposed not only to the federal proposals but any form of legislative devolution and, together with a substantial number of Welsh Labour MPs, was hostile even to a directly elected Welsh Assembly. In the face of such opposition the Welsh Executive progressively modified the proposed evidence; the quasi-federal features were extinguished as was any suggestion of legislative powers, instead greater emphasis was given to controlling and co-ordinating the nominated bodies in Wales. The evidence finally submitted by the Welsh Labour Party not only rejected separatism and federalism but also rejected a legislative Assembly because 'it would reduce the effectiveness of Welsh MPs and the influence of Wales in the UK, and would jeopardise the unity of the country as a whole'.[6] The evidence also documented the fundamental principles behind its demand for an elected Welsh Council, namely:

(i) The value of an all-Wales Authority as a top tier of Local Government.

(ii) The need to extend the principle and practice of democratic control over as many as possible of the several nominated committees and statutory boards operating in Wales.

(iii) To provide democratic machinery to allow for (Welsh) concentration on local problems.

(iv) To provide a structure of Government that will permit of devolution from the centre.

The heavy emphasis on the local government connection and the rather tentative suggestion that some Welsh Office powers might be transferred to the Assembly, illustrates the cautious strategy employed by the Welsh Labour Party. It also cloaks the considerable pressure exerted by the party leadership in attempting to ensure that the evidence presented by the party's Welsh organisation conformed to that presented by the more anti-devolutionist Labour Party in Scotland. By contrast the evidence presented by the Welsh Liberals boldly advocated a comprehensive federal structure, whilst Plaid Cymru proposed 'a Welsh state endowed with all the powers of a modern state'.[7] Several organisations and many individuals gave evidence to the Commission; of the major political parties in Wales, only the Conservatives declined to submit evidence.

In June 1970 while the Commission was still receiving evidence, the Conservatives won the General election. During the following four years of Conservative government, the devolution proposals became more firmly embedded into Welsh Labour's policy portfolio as the party sought to show that the devolution policy was not simply a response to nationalist threats. In 1972 Welsh Labour's original contention that an elected Welsh Council should be established within a local government context was reiterated. The party expressed concern that 'the Crowther Commission [had] not made approaches to the government to halt consideration of Local Government Re-Organisation until its report is available'.[8] During the course of 1973 the devolution debate began imperceptibly to move towards a policy of 'extending democracy', a far more acceptable ideological concept within the Labour Movement. The party also sought to broaden the issue beyond the boundaries of Wales arguing that regional problems would only be successfully solved 'if the wishes of the people in each part of Britain are directly heeded through democratically elected bodies and their support for the necessary policies mobilised'.[9] The new approach apparently won over the doubters and opponents of devolution in the Welsh Parliamentary Labour Group. George Thomas, now the shadow Secretary of State and one of the policy's sternest critics, threw his political weight behind devolution in November 1973. Speaking in Aberystwyth he assured his audience, 'We are firmly committed to an elected Assembly – which will give greater democratic control over bodies which influence the day to day life of our people'.[10]

A Tory Government, in particular a Tory Secretary of State at the Welsh Office, gave added respectability to Welsh Labour's devolution policy. The extension of Welsh Office powers in health and education were criticized by Labour because they were 'a concession to the devolution of centralized power to the executive and not to the Welsh people'.[11] Furthermore the fact that Peter Thomas, representing a London constituency, was appointed Welsh Secretary of State suggested to many Labour supporters that the Welsh Office could no longer be regarded as the absolute guarantor of Welsh interests and the case for an elected Welsh Council or Assembly was strengthened accordingly.

Part of the shift of opinion within the Labour Party was attributable to the Commission on the Constitution which published its Report in October 1973. The immediate response was hardly ecstatic. Alan Watkins, an expatriate Welshman, catalogued the ills which had beset the Commission in its four years of existence: death (of the original chairman Lord Crowther); resignations; retirements; a change of administration; disputes and a minority report. Given these discouragements, Watkins considered it remarkable that the report was to be published. He continued:

> The fact is all the more remarkable because of another discouragement which is that few major politicians are any longer much interested what Lord Kilbrandon (the new chairman) and his colleagues may or may not propose.[12]

The first reaction of the House of Commons confirmed this assessment, with much of the early cynicism stimulated by the fragmented nature of the report. Of the eleven Commissioners who signed the majority report:

(i) 8 recommended legislative devolution for Scotland and 6 recommended it for Wales:

(ii) 3 favoured a directly elected Welsh Advisory Council and 1 favoured a similar scheme for Scotland:

(iii) 2 recommended executive devolution for Scotland and Wales.

The two Commissioners responsible for the minority report advocated the extension of the principle of executive devolution from Scotland and Wales and its application to 5 designated English regions.[13] Despite the obvious differences there was a clear unanimity within the Commission that the constitutional *status quo* was unsatisfactory. It was this which encouraged the leadership in all political parties to give the Report what Mr. Heath, then Prime Minister, described as a 'proper consideration'.

In Wales the report was generally received with enthusiasm. It had the effect of legitimizing a policy which previously had been regarded as the preserve of a minority on the fringe of the political process. In this respect it assisted the emergence of an apparent consensus in the Welsh Labour Party. Nevertheless, the party was not unanimously behind the devolution proposals in either of the 1974 general elections. The materialist wing of the party still subscribed strongly to the idea of a unified working class movement with centralized institutions for social and economic planning. More significantly, the pro-devolution element in the Welsh Labour Group was diminished, through the electoral defeats of several key MPs in the 1970 and 1974 elections and the loss, through retirement, of Jim Griffiths, the most prestigious devolutionist within the Labour Party.

After the October 1974 general election there was increasing opposition to the idea of an elected Welsh Assembly from some Welsh Labour MPs. They questioned the wisdom of such a reform in the immediate aftermath of local government reorganization; they feared that the authority and status of the Welsh Secretary of State and the Welsh Office would be undermined by creating an alternative power centre; and they were also deeply suspicious of the role Welsh Assemblymen might play.[14] But they did not criticise the party's policy directly, calling not for rejection but a referendum.

In the case of devolution, there appeared much to commend a referendum; it was a constitutional issue and one on which the parties were imperfectly aligned. There was also the precedent of the EEC referendum. However the Labour government rejected the EEC parallel which, they argued, had been concerned with Britain's constitutional relationship with foreign countries, whereas devolution was entirely a domestic United Kingdom matter. Furthermore, anti-devolutionists were reminded that devolution was Labour Party policy approved by a 4 to 1 majority at the 1975 Annual Conference. Nevertheless, a ground-swell of opinion favouring a referendum emerged within Wales early in 1976 with 6 out of the 8 counties and 27 out of the 37 districts in support of its use.

Within the Welsh Labour group the devolution opponents found common cause with the demand for a referendum which had been launched by the Caerphilly constituency Labour Party in 1975. In a pamphlet distributed to all 36 Welsh constituency Labour parties the secretary of the Caerphilly party argued that the devolution proposals had 'failed to carry the movement', that they represented an 'irreversible constitutional change' and that a referendum was 'the

26

ultimate expression of a modern democracy'.[15] The pamphlet's arguments evoked a sympathetic response in several constituency parties and the Labour Party's Welsh Conference in May 1976 was characterised by a series of acrimonious debates which revealed an ominous gulf between the leadership and substantial sections of rank and file activists. In September, the Welsh Labour executive together with the Wales TUC felt it necessary to reply to the anti-devolution pro-referendum critics and produced their own pamphlet categorically rejecting the referendum demand, not only because devolution was a manifesto commitment but because a 'referendum would be a complete reversal of our whole system of government'. The pamphlet ended with a dire warning:

> Those who advocate a referendum must accept the full implications of this change and must be aware that any radical changes proposed by a Labour government would have to overcome this new hurdle before being carried out. In effect, Clause 4 of the Party Constitution would have to be re-written – 'To secure for the workers by hand or brain the full fruits of their industry etc. subject to referendum'.[16]

Throughout the remainder of 1976 a wide range of arguments against the use of referendums was deployed by Labour Party spokesmen both within the Government and the Welsh Executive; a referendum was essentially reactionary and would frustrate social and economic reforms (in this respect the Australian experience was frequently cited); it would disrupt and polarise the political debate; it would trivialise and obscure the issues; it was alien to the British system of government and it would undermine the supremacy of Parliament. The debate on whether or not a referendum should be held generated such political heat that the devolution issue itself was almost completely overshadowed. Those opposed to the referendum, who largely comprised the pro-devolutionists, were increasingly portrayed as anti-democratic, unwilling to permit the people to make their decision and fearful of the electorate's opinion. The pro-devolutionists consequently found themselves occupying an increasingly untenable position. By the end of 1976 the momentum for a referendum had built up to such a pitch that a general conviction emerged which presumed that progress towards devolution could only be assured if a referendum were conceded. It was this viewpoint which persuaded the *Western Mail*, a staunch supporter of Welsh devolution, to break ranks with other pro-devolutionists and assert that a referendum was 'the only thing that can possibly avert the worst of the obstructionism that the Bill is bound to face, and at the end save devolution'. (*Western Mail,* 1-12-76). Although subsequent events proved it to be a misguided analysis, it was one which the Government felt obliged to accept. On the second reading of the Scotland and Wales Bill the Government agreed that an advisory referendum should precede the implementation of the Act. But the concession was to no avail and the Government were defeated on the guillotine on February 22nd 1977 by 29 votes. However, the more serious and lasting defeat lay in conceding the referendum. It marked the end of the first phase of the devolution campaign which from any viewpoint was comprehensively won by the anti-devolutionists. It enabled dedicated opponents of the policy, like Neil Kinnock, to claim subsequently that the referendum had 'been wrung out of those whose enthusiasm for devolution was only exceeded by their determination not to allow the people of Wales to make a real decision through the ballot box on their future'.[17] This tactical defeat put the pro-Assembly campaigners at a serious disadvantage from which they never fully recovered.

The progress of the devolution legislation through Parliament effectively constituted the second phase of the preliminary campaign and extended from November 1976 to June 1978. (See Chapter 3). It took place against a unique parliamentary and political background; the worst economic crisis since the 1930s; the expediency of the 'Lib-Lab Pact'; a succession of damaging Government defeats on what had previously been considered 'resignation' issues; and a Government which, having lost its slim majority, was obliged to make a series of deals with both minor parties and individual MPs. It was not, therefore, the ideal launch-pad from which the Government might mount an effective and enthusiastic referendum campaign. Instead, as the weeks passed into months and the months into years the impression grew that the exercise, particularly the Welsh dimension, was a massive irrelevance.

The parliamentary phase represented another defeat for the devolutionists. The Government, increasingly embarrassed by the issue, operating with a tight parliamentary timetable and anxious to expedite the passage of the two Bills, was mute. Not so the anti-devolutionists. By comparison, they used the parliamentary arena to introduce and publicise arguments and issues which were subsequently to be deployed in the referendum campaign. The most vocal opponents, two Gwent MPs, Neil Kinnock (Bedwellty) and Leo Abse (Pontypool), ably voiced their opposition through the Welsh press.

28

Kinnock was opposed to any policy that might endanger the unity and coherence of the working class which he regarded as the only viable vehicle for social, economic and political change. But he also highlighted the numerous deficiencies in the Bill and in his most damning criticism claimed that, despite the creation of an additional extra tier of government, the vital decisions would remain with London government.[18] Leo Abse, in a more emotive contribution, suggested that a Welsh Assembly 'would increase bribery and corruption' and that Wales would be dominated from Cardiff by a Welsh-speaking bureaucratic elite.[19]

The very success of the anti-devolutionists in grabbing the headlines and injecting the virus of doubt into the public mind as to the desirability and efficacy of devolution prompted the pro-devolutionists to establish their 'pro-Assembly' coalition in an attempt to counter this propaganda. However far from creating an advantage, the time lapse between the launching of the coalition in January 1977 and the referendum in March 1979 was largely responsible for highlighting and eventually widening the divisions within the pro-Assembly camp. These divisions were the product of two factors:

(i) The initial role of the 'Wales for the Assembly Campaign' (WAC), as a ginger group designed to exert pressure on backbench Labour MPs and secure the passage of the Scotland and Wales Bill.

(ii) The subsequent decision by the Labour Pary/Wales TUC to run a referendum campaign quite distinct and separate from the all-party WAC coalition.

In respect of the first factor the attempt to exert pressure on Parliament required tactics and qualities quite different from those necessary to successfully mount a referendum campaign. Thus the full page advertisement placed in *Western Mail* and *Daily Post* in January 1977 was intended to impress upon MPs the broad range of influential opinion leaders in Wales who favoured devolution and were prepared to support the five-point declaration:

THAT an unanswerable case exists for a real extension of democracy and responsibility to the people of Wales within Britain;

THAT present arrangements for the accountability of the existing governmental administration in Wales are basically unsatisfactory;

29

THAT   as Parliament grapples with the increasing volume and complexity of European legislation it is unrealistic to expect it to devote more time to Welsh Affairs.

THAT   Welsh economic and social problems as well as the problem of accountability cannot be met through any reform of the procedures of one central Parliament;

THAT   the situation in Wales therefore demands the establishment of a DIRECTLY ELECTED WELSH ASSEMBLY ANSWERABLE TO THE PEOPLE OF WALES.[20]

Although one of the prime movers behind this declaration was Sir Alun Talfan Davies (a member of the Kilbrandon Commission), most of the activists comprised Labour Party members and trade unionists such as George Wright (Secretary Wales TUC) and Jack Brooks (Secretary-Agent in Mr. Callaghan's constituency). This party bias was both predictable and reasonable given that the object of the exercise was to ensure the successful passage of the Labour government's Scotland and Wales Bill. However, the defeat of the guillotine motion on February 22nd 1977 meant that even this limited objective was not secured. When it became apparent that a referendum would be held, the Labour Party and the TUC in Wales decided on a separate campaign with most of the Labour and TUC members withdrawing from the WAC coalition. Although it was sounder tactically for the Labour Party to appeal to its own supporters on what was a party manifesto commitment, the total effect was an erosion of WACs status to the point where it was in danger of being regarded as an intellectual fringe organisation. Subsequently, Plaid's decision not to campaign as a party but to operate through WAC accentuated the group's identific-ation with Plaid members and nationalist views. Consequently, in terms of its organizational base, its theoretical justification and its policy objectives, WAC was compromised before the referendum campaign had even begun.

From the outset the pro-Assembly coalition, particularly the all-party wing, eschewed a specific policy objective concentrating instead on the case for the general concept of devolution. There were several reasons why such an approach should be adopted. WAC had come into being in January 1977 to save the Welsh element in the Scotland and Wales Bill; it had to maintain and develop its attitude over a period of two years during which the first devolution bill was defeated and the second 'paired Bills' were progressively subjected to a wide range of damaging amendments (see Chapter 3). In these circumstances a specific and detailed commitment was impractical but it was also politically impossible. The Welsh nationalists were highly critical of the Bill because it lacked the legislative powers which had been granted to Scotland. Those Welsh Liberals in the devolution camp who subscribed to their party's federal policy were equally unhappy about the limited nature of the government's proposals, and the enthusiastic devolutionists from within the ranks of the Labour Party, while claiming 'this is the best devolution Bill available', were of the opinion that once the Assembly had been established, it would need to acquire those economic and legislative powers necessary for effective devolution. Consequently, the Wales Bill itself had few friends. If WAC were to have any kind of coherence and conviction it had to be based not upon the Bill but upon the broad values of devolution. Evidence of this approach became apparent in the early summer of 1978. In May, a 'Wales for the Assembly Campaign' leaflet entitled 'This is What Devolution is all about' failed to make one mention of the Wales Bill, criticising instead the over - centralised, bureaucratised British government system. Only in the last paragraph did the pamphlet describe the work of the proposed Assembly and then in the most general terms:

[The Assembly] will determine its own scale of priorities in tune with the needs and aspirations of Wales. It will decide what is more appropriate to the Welsh situation and more beneficial to Welsh people. It will provide a new focus and bring a powerful, beneficial and democratic impetus to Welsh life. This is what devolution is all about.[21]

The following month, on 24 June WAC held an All Wales Conference in Newtown which brought together politicians from the most diverse backgrounds: Michael Foot, John Morris (Labour Party), Archie Kirkwood (Wales TUC), Dafydd Elis Thomas (Plaid Cymru) and Geraint Howells (Liberal) made stirring speeches lacking in specifics but abounding in generalities about devolution and extending democracy. The conference gained much publicity and came on the heels of a poll published in May which showed public opinion evenly balanced on the devolution issue (40.8 per cent for and 40.8 per cent against). The indicators seemed favourable to the pro-devolution campaign.

However, by late autumn a subtle change had overtaken the Welsh political scene. The delay in holding the referendum predicted for September lost the pro-Assembly coalition considerable momentum;

the postponement of the General Election unsettled organisers and activists in both the Labour Party and Plaid; and the referendum came to be regarded as an additional and, for some, an unnecessary complication. The delay also witnessed the divergence of the Labour Party campaign, with its emphasis on democracy, from the all-party WAC which increasingly emphasised the Welsh dimension. Thus, whereas the Labour Party slogan was: 'VOTE YES: FOR DEMOCRACY, FOR WALES, FOR BRITAIN' the all-party organisation enjoined its supporters to 'VOTE YES FOR WALES ON MARCH 1st'. The national identity factor received a surprising emphasis from David Owen speaking at a WAC organisation meeting in Llandrindod on January 6th 1979. Referring to his Welsh origins Dr. Owen claimed that devolution:

> is not a mere mechanical legalistic or constitutional issue; it represents a great political cause lying at the core of democratic politics. It has its roots in the noble objective of self-government. In Wales it stems from the final military consequence of the overthrow of Prince Llewellyn the last in 1282.[22]

Although several of the WAC committee realised such nationalist sentiments would be counter-productive and attempted to underplay them, 'nationalism' became a serious liability for WAC and remained so for the duration of the campaign. By January the pro-Assembly coalition was already on the defensive attempting to refute the charges made by the anti-devolutionists: that the Assembly would mean more Government; that it was a sop to the nationalists; that it would result in a Welsh – speaking elite, and that it would cost too much. An opinion poll in September 1978 revealed a growing majority opposed to the government's proposals (37.8 per cent for and 47.7 per cent against) and shattered the belief that once the Devolution Bill had become an Act of Parliament and received the Royal Assent public opinion would consolidate in its support. Furthermore WACs strategy based upon a popular Labour Government and the personal prestige of Jim Callaghan was destroyed by a bitter winter of industrial discontent. The ace in the 'Yes' coalition's pack had been trumped, not by their opponents but by the industrial action of trade unions. Thus the pro-devolutionists entered the final stage of the campaign under attack, off balance and subjected to increasing pressure to answer the normative and instrumental critique presented by their opponents.

NOTES

1. Quoted in Edgar L. Chappell, *Wake Up Wales,* 1943 p.22.

2. Quoted in A. Butt Philip, *The Welsh Question,* p.90.

3. *ibid.,* p.258.

4. R.Crossman, *The Dairies of a Cabinet Minister,* Vol. 2, 1977, p.344.

5. For fuller details see J. Barry Jones and M.J. Keating, 'The British Labour Party as a Centralising Force', Centre for the Study of Public Policy Strathclyde, No. 32, 1978.

6. Evidence of the Labour Party in Wales to the Commission on the Constitution, Labour Party, 1969.

7. Minutes of Evidence I: Wales, *Commission on the Constitution* 1970, p.33.

8. Minutes of Executive, Labour Party Wales, 10 January 1972.

9. Reform of the Machinery of Government, Labour Party Wales, July 1973.

10. Press Release, Labour Party Wales, November 1973.

11. *op. cit.* Labour Party Wales, July 1973.

12. A. Watkins, 'Reactions to Kilbrandon', *New Statesman,* (26—10—73).

13. Summary of Conclusions, *Royal Commission of the Constitution* 1973. pp.484-487.

14. For a fuller review see, J. Barry Jones, 'The Welsh Labour Party and the Problem of Devolution', in R. Rose (ed.) *United Kingdom Politics 1977: Vol. 1, 1978.*

15. *Devolution and the Welsh Assembly: A Referendum,* Caerphilly C.L.P. 1975.

16. *Why Devolution – Some Questions Answered,* Labour Party Wales, Cardiff 1976.

17. N. Kinnock, 'The Real Decisions will stay in London', *South Wales Echo,* (18—12—77).

18. *ibid.*

19. Leo Abse, *Western Mail,* (25—10—76).

20. *Parliament must let Wales Decide,* Wales for the Assembly, January 1977, *Western Mail,* (13—1—77).

21. *This is what Devolution is All About,* WAC May 1978.

22. Dr. David Owen, Llandrindod Wells Rally, WAC 6 January 1979.

CHAPTER 3

The Parliamentary Passage of the Wales Act 1978

MARI JAMES, PETER D. LINDLEY

Introduction

The main events in the history of the passage of the Welsh devolution
legislation through the Houses of Parliament will be familiar to most
readers. The inclusion of the referendum clause, the guillotine on the
Scotland and Wales Bill, the emergence of the 'Lib-Lab Pact' from the
ensuing debacle, the redrafting of two separate Bills and the peculiar
alliances that emerged have now become part of the folk lore of Welsh
politics. It is not the intention of this chapter to go over the
chronological details of that period. The intention is rather to examine
how the Government, in maintaining a commitment to the legislation,
was obliged to change it in such a way as to lose the genuine support of
the devolutionists in the House of Commons. Such an analysis must
obviously be set against a background of the changing face of the Wales
Bill, and the many amendments carried during the course of its
passage. There is, therefore, a substantial appendix to this chapter
laying out the chronology of the Bill, detailing the amendments and
debates in both Houses of Parliament, which will serve as a reminder of
the Bill's stormy passage and, in particular, of the large number of
defeats suffered by the Government.

The events outside Parliament both during and after the passage of
the Bill are not directly of concern in this chapter. However, it would
be foolish in writing anything about Parliament to presume that events
in the outside world are totally unconnected with it. It is safe to assume,
for instance, that each speaker in every debate was aware of the coming
Referendum and therefore mindful of the probable effect which the
Parliamentary debates would have on the Referendum campaign.
This resulted in speeches of a 'Second Reading' character concerned
with the principle of devolution throughout the Committee Stage.

It could be argued that the case of Welsh devolution is a prime example of Parliament asserting itself and its opinions against those of the Executive. This is one conclusion that could be drawn from the juxtaposition of the Government's original proposals for establishing a Welsh Assembly with the many subsequent changes and modifications to those proposals and their ultimate defeat at the Referendum. But nothing in Parliament is ever quite as simple as it first appears. In order to more fully appreciate and understand the nature and characteristics of the Parliamentary passage of the Wales Bill this chapter will examine the various types of amendments moved in Committee and report Stages, primarily in the Commons; the types of alliances that emerged; the role of the Government's small or non-existent majority; the role of the 'Lib-Lab Pact'; the influence of the Scottish legislation; and last but not least, the significance of the internal disagreements in the Labour Party over this policy.

Amendments

Serious amendments were tabled by both pro and anti devolution sides, but in addition there were many other amendments which served, as intended, to discredit the Government's proposals and take up valuable debating time before the guillotine precluded further debate. The large number of amendments tabled was partly a result of widespread unease about the legislation on all sides of the House. There were many ready to defend the principle of the Bill but few (and probably none who were not on the Government payroll) who were willing or able to defend its details. Of the great mass of amendments tabled in both the Commons and the Lords at Committee and Report Stages, six main types can be distinguished according to their aim.

First there were amendments intended to increase the powers of the Assembly. These amendments included a Plaid Cymru amendment to Clause 10 in the Commons Committee Stage (see Chronology) to grant the Welsh Assembly legislative powers on a par with those being granted to the Scottish Assembly; amendments granting taxation powers to the Assembly, and others put by Liberals, Labour backbench devolutionists and even Conservative backbench devolutionists. This combination of MPs also found themselves together in the division lobby in support of this type of amendment.

Second, there were amendments which sought to reduce the powers of the Assembly. These were mainly the result of Conservative frontbench and Conservative backbench initiatives. Nearly every one of the amendments on which the Government were defeated in the Lords came into this category (see Chronology). Some of these amendments had already been unsuccessfully moved by the Conservative frontbench in the Commons; for instance, Nicholas Edwards (Pembroke), the Shadow Secretary of State for Wales, moved the reservation of the powers of the Welsh Development Agency and the Development Board for Rural Wales in the Commons but was defeated by a majority of eighteen at Report Stage. However, a similar amendment was inserted into the Bill in the Lords Committee Stage with a majority of five and the original clause was only finally restored to the Bill five days before it received the Royal Assent. Other amendments of this type were tabled on behalf of various interest groups concerned not to devolve particular functions such as forestry, betting and gaming, and the administration of the National Health Service in Wales.

Third there were 'wrecking' amendments which sought to make the legislation unworkable. These amendments are most effective when there is a timetable on a Bill since they take up scarce debating time and prevent debates on later clauses of the Bill. Predictably they were mainly tabled by anti-devolutionists ranging from the Opposition frontbench through the unofficial Conservative backbench 'Union Flag' group to the Labour backbenchers' anti-devolution group and individual back-benchers on both sides. Although the primary aims of the 'Union Flag' group were to oppose Scottish devolution and persuade the Conservative frontbench to drop its earlier pledge to set up a Scottish Assembly, one of its three secretaries, Ian Grist (Cardiff North), concentrated on opposing Welsh devolution. The group promoted a notable 'wrecking' amendment to the Scotland and Wales Bill moved by the Conservative frontbench. The amendment, which deleted all the Welsh provisions from the Bill, received substantial support, and, indeed, almost led to Welsh devolution falling at the first legislative hurdle.

During the Committee Stage of the Wales Bill, with the support of the Conservative frontbench, Plaid Cymru and the Liberals succeeded in securing the removal of the Commencement Clause. Without this Clause the Bill would have had to come into effect immediately after Royal Assent without a Referendum being held. This clearly embarrassed the Government with its reluctant backbenchers and again threatened its majority. However, following a Government concession on another issue – removal of the special provision for the Commons to override the Lords on a matter relating to Westminster oversight of the Assembly – the Conservative frontbench agreed to the restoration of the Commencement Clause at Report Stage.

Fourth there were amendments intended to make the implementation of the Act more difficult. These amendments were similar to 'wrecking' amendments but more specific. They nearly all related to the provision for a Referendum to be held before the Act could take effect. The reasoned amendment demanding that referendums be held in Scotland and Wales tabled by Leo Abse (Labour, Pontypool) at the Second Reading of the Scotland and Wales Bill was of this type. Other amendments in this category to the Scotland and Wales Bill concerned the wording of the Referendum question and whether the Referendum should be consultative or mandatory. Then, on the Wales Bill there were amendments on the timing of the Referendum and ground rules for its conduct (see Chronology). However, the Government backbench amendment imposing a 40 per cent threshold was easily the most significant amendment in this category.

The fifth and sixth categories of amendment took into consideration the world outside the debates at Westminster. *The fifth category comprised amendments that had the effect of providing ammunition for the coming referendum campaign.* These were anti-devolution in inclination and intended to expose weaknesses in the legislation. Amendments to the 'United Kingdom clause' were intended to show that the Bill posed a far greater threat to the unity of the United Kingdom than the Government claimed. Six hours were spent debating the clause on the first day of the Committee Stage in the Commons although the Government had agreed that it should be withdrawn from the Bill and it was known there would not be a vote. As well as getting the idea that the Wales Bill was the first step on the road to the secession of Wales from the United Kingdom established in the public mind, the obvious purpose of this exercise was to limit the time available for the following debate on the use of proportional representation for Assembly elections. Other recurring themes were the increase in bureaucracy and the corruption which the Assembly would apparently herald; Leo Abse and Iain Sproat (Conservative, Aberdeen South), were leading exponents of this view. Abse also introduced an amendment debarring the Assembly from making the ability to speak Welsh a condition of service for staff of the Assembly. This was designed to evoke an apprehension that a Welsh-speaking and thus unrepresentative elite might come to dominate the Assembly.

The sixth and final type of amendment we have identified linked issues in the devolution debate with wider campaigns. These included 'pet subjects' raised by individual MPs, for example Andrew Bennett's (Labour, Stockport North) amendment on a Register of Interests of Assembly members (see Chronology). The main amendment of this type, however, concerned the use of proportional representation for Assembly elections. This was not only part of a wider campaign for the use of proportional representation in all elections in Britain, but became the main plank of that campaign and, indeed, brought the issue more to the publics attention than any other part of the campaign had previously done. (The debates on the Wales Bill preceded those on the Bill on the form of European Assembly elections.)

Alliances

During the course of the debates it became obvious that there were as many cross-party alliances as there were ordinary intra-party alliances. The role of these cross-party alliances became especially important when it was obvious that not all the anti-devolutionist Labour MPs would be willing to compromise their principles and help the Government when it had no majority. It is useful to look at the voting alliances in the House of Commons in terms of those who were for and against the Government. In an examination of this subject Anthony King has divided the House of Commons into four main groupings; Government, Government backbenchers, Opposition frontbench and Opposition backbenchers. Opposition to the Government can come from any combination of the other three groupings. Some groupings, King argues, are more likely than others. One of the less likely groupings according to King, is a combination of Government backbenchers, Opposition frontbench and Opposition backbenchers,[1] although this was the typical coalition against the Wales Bill. King identified three important modes of opposition to Government in the British system: the Intra-Party Mode where Government backbenchers alone oppose the Government; the Opposition Mode where the Opposition frontbench and Opposition backbenchers combine to oppose the Government and the Non-Party or Private Members' Mode where Government backbenchers and Opposition backbenchers combine to oppose the Government.

For the purpose of our examination of the Welsh devolution legislation all three modes are of relevance. Government backbenchers and Opposition backbenchers hostile to the principle of devolution were united in their opposition to the advocacy of devolution by both frontbenches. Members of the 'Union Flag' group and Welsh Labour

38

antidevolution MPs supported each other in forthright and outspoken attacks on the Bill on the floor of the House, and established informal channels of liaison on tactics and strategy. However, whereas the Opposition frontbench had inherited a commitment to set up a Scottish Assembly, there was no such commitment to set up a Welsh Assembly. Consequently there was less difficulty about the Opposition frontbench combining with Opposition backbenchers in wholehearted opposition to the proposed Welsh Assembly than there was about their combining to oppose the Scottish Assembly. Thus the Conservative amendment to delete the Welsh provisions from the Scotland and Wales Bill was a frontbench amendment, whereas an identical amendment to delete the Scottish provisions was a 'Union Flag' amendment. On the Wales Bill then there was straight party conflict, with the Opposition frontbench and Opposition backbenchers combining to oppose the policy of the Government root and branch.

The Intra-Party Mode of King's is perhaps the most crucial to an understanding of what happened in the Parliamentary passage of Welsh Devolution. King says:

> What gives Government backbenchers influence? The answer lies in the needs that Government and Government backbenchers have of each other and in the bargaining resources that they possess *vis-a-vis* each other. On the one hand, Government backbenchers need from the Government policies they can approve of and that will help win the next election. The Government's resources *vis-a-vis* its own backbenchers include its own superior sources of expertise and information, which rests partly on the role accorded to government in Britain's political culture (the government is expected 'to govern') and partly on the fact that the Government's leaders are also the majority party's leaders. On the other hand, Ministers have need of Government backbenchers. They need their moral support. They need them not to cause rows and to make hostile speeches that will attract publicity. *They need, above all, their votes* (our emphasis). In each case Ministers' needs of backbenchers constitute backbenchers' resources vis-a-vis Ministers. Moral support can be denied, rows caused, hostile speeches made, votes (on occasion) withheld . . . From the Government's point of view, this relationship – the intra-party relationship – is by far the most important . . . As far as the Government is concerned, Government backbenchers are the most important Members in the House.[2]

This brings us full circle back to the problem that was at the very heart of the Parliamentary treatment of Welsh devolution, namely the Labour Party's internal disagreements. Despite its lack of an overall majority it is unlikely that the Government would have been defeated on such crucial votes as the 40 per cent threshold amendment if all its own backbenchers had supported it.

However, once it became clear that it was unable to prevent substantial defections on its own backbenches, the Government was increasingly forced to rely on the votes of the minor parties, some of whom were strongly in favour of devolution, in order to get the legislation through. Despite their dissatisfaction with many parts of the package, the Welsh Nationalists voted in favour of the two crucial guillotine motions and, indeed, gave general support to the Government until the Wales Act was on the Statute Book. This was precisely the course of action taken by Welsh Liberal Geraint Howells (Cardigan), who was one of only two Liberals to support the guillotine on the Scotland and Wales Bill, and who supported the Government in the lobbies throughout the passage of the Wales Bill. Thus, for our purpose, King's analysis of 'normal' British Parliamentary politics and the modes of opposition most common in the House of Commons, needs to be refined by the inclusion of minor party modes since these were a factor of major importance in the passage of the Wales Act. His analysis also provides evidence of the exceptional nature of the circumstances in which the Government found themselves.

The Role of the Government's Majority

For the entire course of the passage of the Wales Bill through Parliament the Government lacked an overall majority and relied on the support of minority parties, primarily the Liberals, to stay in power. The Labour Party had worked with a small or non-existent majority before. That in itself was not the main problem. Such a situation merely requires a little horse-trading and the careful selection of policies to be introduced. With the support of its own backbenchers in the lobbies and the kind of political will and determination it had shown on such socialist priority issues as steel nationalisation, the Government could have got Welsh devolution through intact. But devolution had never had the importance for the Labour Movement that steel nationalisation had. Historically it had been sacrificed in favour of more immediate and pressing priorities. The Kilbrandon Report and the unprecedented rise in support for Nationalist parties in the 1974 general election combined to put devolution firmly on the agenda of British Parliamentary politics, where it was destined again to be sacrificed, this time for the sake of Labour Party unity.

It is sometimes easier for a government to keep potentially dissident MPs in order when it only has a small majority than when its majority is substantial. This is because an MP who disagrees with a particular policy or issue is less likely to vote in accordance with his principles and against the Government when his vote might be all that stands between the Government's life and death, than when his vote is all that stands between a Government majority of, say, 35 and 33. It could therefore be argued that the best time for a government to get through a controversial policy which requires the bulk of legislative time in a session is when it has a small majority. This, however, is to view the Parliamentary scene from the Government's and the whip's viewpoint. The problem to which they address themselves is: 'given that we want to get this piece of legislation through what is the most likely and least risky way of doing it'? Viewed from the backbencher's viewpoint, however, the problem is altogether different. It is more one of: 'I have no position in this government and I will not be effective if I just toe the line all the time; moreover, I don't agree with what the Government is doing on this issue and as its majority is so small it will have to take notice if I threaten to vote against it'. If the backbencher finds himself one of a significant number of MPs of like-mind (significant here being any number more than half the Government's majority), he actually has a chance of changing the legislation in a formal way on the floor of the House and in the Division lobbies, rather than relying on informal talks and pressures on Ministers 'behind the Speaker's chair'. The latter case is extremely rare in practice in Parliament but it seems to have occurred on this particular occasion.

In order to ascertain how typical this situation and the Government's reaction to it was, it is illuminating to look at other instances of a Government attempting to get proposed legislation through in the face of opposition within its own ranks or with a small or non-existent Commons majority. An instance from the Labour side was the 'In Place of Strife' proposals in 1969. This must be considered a failure from the Government's point of view since it was forced to drop the legislation, although this was due to a combination of intra and extra-Parliamentary pressure rather than internal Parliamentary pressure resulting from a small majority. The Local Government, Planning and Land Act 1980 was an instance of Government backbench opposition on the Conservative side although on this occasion the legislation reached the Statute Book virtually unscathed and was a success story for the Government.

But the most suitable comparison is perhaps with the 1964-66 Labour Government which attempted to pass legislation nationalising the steel industry with a maximum majority of five. When Labour came to power in 1964 with a working majority of only five, their first Queen's Speech none-the-less contained an impressive list of substantial legislation including a Bill to establish the Highlands and Island Development Board; one to abolish prescription charges; one to restore rent control and, of course, the nationalisation of iron and steel production. The Queen's Speech was won by 5 votes only after some unwell members were brought in by ambulance and 13 Scottish MPs managed to defy a Glasgow fog. But the effort was made; the call went out and the troops obeyed. Harold Wilson recounts of those numerous tight votes when the Government was down to a majority of 3 during its first Finance Bill: 'During those all night sittings when I was allowed to go to bed . . . I frequently put the light out wondering whether we should still be a government when the day dawned'. But he adds: 'All was well as long as the Parliamentary Party was united'.[3]

In the case of steel nationalisation the Government was in danger of losing the most important plank in its legislative programme because two MPs disagreed with the policy. However they both finally supported the Government on the crucial vote. Commenting on reports of a Labour Party split, Harold Wilson acknowledged that the press 'were right to perceive that a revolt confined to no more than two Labour MPs could, on an issue involving confidence in the Government, bring us down'.[4] The main difference here between Wilson and steel nationalisation in 1966 and Callaghan and devolution in 1979 was that Callaghan did not formally make devolution into an issue involving confidence in the Government. Pro-devolution Ministers did not consider it a resignation issue when amendments which threatened the survival of the policy were incorporated in the Bill.

Again, Wilson's own comments on handling dissidents who appreciated the value of a small majority are of interest when contrasted with Callaghan's approach:

> This was, of course, one of the major difficulties of a majority as small as ours, and on occasions . . . we did not lack those who were at least tempted to take advantage of the Government's vulnerability. The first time this happened, I reacted sharply and said that once any group of people in the party decided to abuse

that position, and once the Government showed itself willing to submit to blackmail, then government as such would become impossible. I pointed out that within a party such as ours, there were many minorities . . . But if they were to exact (their) power, and I was stupid enough to give in to it, then the Parliamentary Labour Party would quickly become a rabble, and the Government would have to commit itself to a whole series of contradictory postures.[5]

This contrasts markedly with the tolerance shown towards some of those who 'took advantage of the government's vulnerability' over Welsh devolution. Notable here were Leo Abse and Neil Kinnock (Labour, Bedwellty), leaders of the anti-government campaign in South Wales where the mass of the Welsh voters live. After the General Election, with Labour in opposition, the Parliamentary leadership appointed Abse as Chairman of the Select Committee on Welsh Affairs and Kinnock as Shadow Secretary of State for Education.

When in 1965 the Government's majority was reduced still further Wilson was faced with the same dilemma that confronted Callaghan in March 1977: either to go to the country asking for a bigger majority to carry through the legislation in the way he wanted, or to come to an arrangement with the Liberals which would keep the Government in power and amend the legislation in ways agreeable to the Liberals. Wilson chose the former option, kept his policy intact, finally implemented it and in the process 'scuppered' the political realignment hoped for by the Liberals under Jo Grimond. Faced with opinion polls which ruled out going to the country for a fresh mandate, Callaghan chose the other option, left his policy vulnerable to further attack, was forced into further compromise, finally lost the policy and, in the process, contributed to the political realignment that the Liberals under David Steel had hoped for.

The Role of the Liberals

The establishment of a formal pact between the Labour Government and the thirteen Liberal MPs acted as a bridge between the debacle of the guillotine on the Scotland and Wales Bill and the reintroduction of two redrafted Bills; the Wales Bill and the Scotland Bill. In his account of the 'Lib-Lab Pact', David Steel, the Liberal Leader, recounts how the constitutional experiment of the Pact grew out of the Government's failure to get through its own constitutional experiment in decentralisation.

43

The Government was in a minority position and not all its own supporters would follow it into the lobbies on this issue. Without support from at least one other party no new devolution proposals were likely to get through. So the Callaghan Government, as it then was, conceded at last that consultations were inevitable . . . Our talks on devolution were virtually the forerunner of the 'Lib-Lab Pact' itself.[6]

There were over a dozen meetings between the Government and the Liberals to discuss details in redrafting the Scotland and Wales Bill. Only one of these meetings was exclusively concerned with the Welsh devolution proposals. Present at this meeting were, on the Government side, John Smith (Labour, Lanarkshire North), the Minister of State at the Privy Council Office responsible for devolution, John Smith's Private Secretary, Sir John Garlick, Head of the Constitution Unit, a special unit in the Cabinet Office which was responsible for the devolution legislation and one other civil servant ; on the Liberal side were Russell Johnston (Inverness), who was co-ordinating the Liberals' work on re-drafting the Bill, Geraint Howells (Cardigan) who was in charge of Welsh devolution for the party, Geraint Howells' research assistant and a researcher from the Liberal Whips' Office who attended all meetings as note-taker for the Liberals. No member of the Welsh Office was present, despite Liberal requests for Welsh Office representation and, indeed, there is no evidence that the Welsh Office was directly involved in the talks on redrafting the Welsh legislation. The business of the meeting was consideration of a Liberal document on the re-drafting of the Welsh part of the Scotland and Wales Bill. The Government were not as open to consideration of changes in the Welsh legislation as they appeared to be in respect of the Scottish legislation. This may have been because the Scottish legislation was perceived as being the mainstream policy. It may also have been partly due to the absence of any Welsh issues in David Steel's list of negotiating points for the Pact.

Of the four main issues raised in the Liberal document on Wales only two were finally accepted by the Government; the separation of the then single Bill into two and the inclusion of the power enabling the Assembly to review the structure of local government with a view to making recommendations for reform. These were both issues which attracted support within the Labour Party, both in Wales and in Parliament. There were some issues in the Liberal document on Scotland that were incorporated into the Government's new proposals on both countries: these included a narrowing in the scope of the override provisions and changes in the financing of the Assemblies. Thus although the Parliamentary Liberal Party (or at least the non Welsh part) had contributed to the guillotine defeat of the Scotland and Wales Bill, it could claim that the Pact had kept devolution alive and that without it there would probably have been a Conservative victory at a General Election and no devolution legislation would have been reintroduced. But the Liberals cannot claim to have improved the Welsh legislation to any significant degree.

'For Wales See Scotland'

The immortal entry in the *Encyclopaedia Britannica*, 'For Wales see England', could have been altered for the duration of the Wales Bill's Parliamentary passage to 'For Wales see Scotland'. Throughout the passage of the original Scotland and Wales Bill the debates on Welsh matters chronologically followed those on Scottish matters. More to the point, the policy on Welsh matters followed that on Scottish matters. The precedence given to Scotland had two obvious effects: first, the policy, as perceived by the Government, discussed by the Press and transmitted to the electorate, was a policy on Scottish devolution. Secondly, Welsh matters were given inadequate or non-existent coverage in Parliament and the Press (see Chs. 7 and 8).

The separation of the original Scotland and Wales Bill into two was seen as a means of rectifying the deficiency the second time around. It partly achieved this because it allowed for clearer consideration of the powers of the Welsh Assembly especially on specifically Welsh issues like the Welsh language and the democratisation of non-elected public bodies. But there the improvement stopped as the Wales Bill was timetabled to follow the Scotland Bill. Again the two ran in tandem with Scotland steering and Wales forced to follow behind – if it wanted to come on the ride at all! As a result, arguments brought forward in the Scottish debates were repeated in the Welsh debates. Examples of this in the passage of the Wales Bill included; the withdrawal of Clause 1 of the Bill dealing with the unity of the United Kingdom; the withdrawal of Clause 39 dealing with National Pay Policy after it had been defeated in the Scotland Bill the previous day; and the acceptance by the House of Lords of the Commons' rejection of proportional representation for Assembly elections at the 'Lords Consideration of Commons Reasons' Stage (see Chronology).

It is not within the remit of this chapter to argue the historical, cultural, social, economic and political reasons why Welsh devolution was an altogether different issue from Scottish devolution. Suffice it to say here that the details of the proposed Scottish Assembly intruded more into the Welsh debates than the merits of the Welsh case necessitated and thus became significant issues in the passage of the Wales Bill that were nothing directly to do with Wales. An ironic postscript to this part of the Welsh devolution story came after the referendums in Wales and Scotland on 1 March 1979. Orders in Council had to be put in Parliament to repeal the two Acts setting up the Assemblies. As had been the practice throughout, Scottish matters were dealt with first. So for a few days there was a law on the Statute Book to establish a form of Parliament in Wales but no such law for Scotland. The last laugh did not last long however and the Wales Act was also repealed.

Lack of Support from the Labour Party

The recurring theme in this examination has been the inability of the Government to rely on the support of all its own MPs. In trying to sustain a majority for its policy, the Government constantly came up against the problem of 'the revolving door' which came to be considered as one of the crucial features in the life and death of the devolution legislation. It was the problem confronting the Whips in trying to balance their books. The inclusion, or exclusion, of a clause, word or even comma in the Bill to win a few extra opposition votes frequently failed to produce a net gain in votes because more government supporters deserted due to the same clause, word or comma. The Government was also walking a tightrope, attempting to get enough votes from all parts of the House of Commons to get their measure through, while at the same time trying to maintain party unity both in the House and in the country as a whole. An example of the effect of this is to be found in David Steel's account of the Lib Lab Pact when he recounts a friendly conversation with John Smith about proportional representation in which the latter told him:

> there was no point in discussing the intellectual or political merits of the case; the Scottish Executive of the Labour Party would not have it, and that was that.[7]

Conclusion

In this chapter we have attempted to translate into the written word the flavour of the mixed emotions of the passage through Parliament of the Wales Act 1978. In so doing we have been able to touch on other issues of interest to the study of Parliament, the workings of Government and the politics of legislation. These issues have been, perhaps, more evident than those issues more closely related to Welsh devolution itself. But that is an accurate impression of Parliamentary procedures. When the norms and mores of the Palace of Westminster take over, whether the issue under discussion is steel nationalisation or Welsh devolution, the rules of the game are the same and it is the workings of Parliament that become the main issue.

The experience of the passage of the *Wales Act* was exceptional. The Government were faced with an unprecedented problem of trying to get through legislation which, it can be argued (see Chapter 2), it had been forced to introduce for reasons of political expediency; which was strongly opposed by a substantial number of its own backbenchers; but which nevertheless had become a symbol of its ability to survive. The problem of how to get the Welsh devolution legislation through was answered, in effect, by changing the question. Transferring the final decision to the electorate meant that the immediate aim was no longer the establishment of an Assembly in Wales but merely the passing of a Bill through Parliament. Thus, the Government no longer had to take final responsibility for the success or failure of Welsh devolution because its fate had been referred to the electorate to decide. Consequently, the Manifesto commitment, 'Labour will establish a directly elected Welsh Assembly'[8] was transformed to 'We shall provide the opportunity for the establishment of a Welsh Assembly if more than 40 per cent of the electorate so wish'. This was reflected in the response of John Morris (Secretary of State for Wales), to the resounding defeat of the Government's proposals in the referendum in Wales (see Chapter 6).

It became increasingly evident during the passage of the Wales Bill that the real fight was not to implement the policy in the legislation, that is to establish a Welsh Assembly, as would have been the usual practice. The real fight became to get the Bill through Parliament and on to the Statute Book. This is an important distinction which had crucial consequences for the Government's response to amendments which were hostile to the principle of devolution but which nevertheless favoured the passage of the Bill itself by attracting the votes of lukewarm supporters and even some opponents of devolution. The Referendum clause itself and the 40 per cent requirement in the Referendum were the prime examples, although the Government resisted the incorporation of the latter into the Wales Bill even though it had already been incorporated into the Scotland Bill. From the moment the Referendum clause was inserted, the Wales Bill became an enabling Bill dependent on the will of the electorate on a particular day. This deprived the anti-devolution camp in Parliament of those who, although opposed to the scheme themselves, were not willing to deny the electorate the option of supporting it. This position was epitomised by Neil Kinnock who spoke against the Bill throughout the debates in the House of Commons, abstained on the Second Reading, voted in favour of it thereafter and led one of the two campaigns against it at the Referendum, on the grounds that it was a scheme of partial devolution with adverse economic consequences for Wales, and not a comprehensive scheme for the United Kingdom as a whole.

Finally, if this incident in the history of the British Parliament is to be viewed as a means of implementing a policy of decentralisation of power to Wales one can perhaps agree with David Steel's view that 'the basic fault throughout was putting Labour Party considerations first and effective devolution second . . . The Labour Party proved to be the undoing of devolution and the handling of devolution proved to be the undoing of the Labour Government'.[9] If, on the other hand the Parliamentary passage of Welsh devolution is viewed as a Parliamentary incident then it provides a fascinating and revealing study of what becomes possible in British politics once some of the players ignore the accepted rules of the game. If this story were less unusual and more typical of the workings of Parliament then Britain would be ungovernable with the present political system. That it can happen at all suggests that some political reforms might be necessary: but that was where the story began.

NOTES

1. Anthony King, 'Modes of Executive – Legislative Relations: Great Britain, France and West Germany', *Legislative Studies Quarterly,* Vol. 1.1. February 1976, p.14.

2. *ibid.,* pp.15-16.

3. H. Wilson, *The Labour Government 1964-1970: A personal record,* London, 1971, p.99.

4. *ibid.,* p.100.

5. *ibid.,* p.102.

6. David Steel, *A House Divided,* 1980, p.93.

7. *ibid.,* p.101.

8. 'Wales Will Win With Labour', *Labour Manifesto,* Cardiff, October 1974.

9. David Steel, *op.cit.,* p.101.

48

CHRONOLOGY

Chronology of the Parliamentary Passage of the Wales Act 1978

This chronology seeks to outline the main events of the Parliamentary passage of the Wales Act. Its purpose is primarily factual rather than explanatory or analytical. Each day's business is arranged as follows: stage of Bill (e.g. Committee Stage. 5th Day), Clauses dealt with throughout the day, debates and divisions itemised with identification of clause, summary of issue of debate, mover of amendments, result of vote. Movers of amendments are identified as follows: Conservative – Official Opposition Front Bench; GBB – a Government backbencher; OBB – an opposition backbencher.

House of Commons

4 November 1977	First Reading
15 November	Second Reading Government majority of 31; 295-264.
16 November	Timetable Motion (Guillotine). Allowed 11 days for Committee, Report and Third Reading. Arranged to give maximum time to provisions unique to Wales Bill. Government majority of 27; 314-287.
1 March 1978	Committee stage. 1st Day. Clauses 1 to 9, Schedule 1. Clause 1 (Unity of the United Kingdom): withdrawn by Government. Six-hour debate on Clause 1. Clause 2 (Method of election to Assembly) Amendment tabled by all-party group providing for elections to Assembly by the Additional Member System of Proportional Representation. Free Vote. Amendment rejected by 263; 377-114. Clause 2 carried by Government majority of 40; 264-224. Schedule 1 and Clauses 3 to 9 agreed to without debate or division.

2 March	Committee Stage. 2nd Day.
	Clause 10. (Statutory functions of the Assembly).
	Plaid Cymru amendment to give Welsh Assembly same legislative powers as Scottish Assembly.
	Government majority of 94 against amendment, 104-10.
7 March	Committee Stage. 3rd Day.
	Schedules 2 and 3. Clauses 11 to 24.
	Minister of State, John Smith, moved series of detailed amendments to Schedule 2 (functions of the Assembly) reserving certain functions in relation to local government. Amendments agreed to. Plaid Cymru amendment to transfer responsibility for determining local government boundaries from Secretary of State to the Assembly. Withdrawn after debate.
	Schedule 2: Government majority of 29; 222-193.
	Schedule 3 (Concurrent powers). Agreed without division.
	Clause 11 (Cultural and recreational activities): Government majority of 32; 223-191.
	Clause 13 (Review of local government structure): Government majority of 7; 213-206. No debate.
	Clause 16 (Standing Orders): Conservative amendment giving the House of Commons power to approve Assembly standing orders debated, no division.
	Clause 17 (Pecuniary Interests) Andrew Bennett (GBB), moved amendment on Register of Assembly Members interests.
	Debate, no division.
	Clause 18 (Subject Committees), Conservative amendment making Clause enabling not compulsory.
	Government majority of 26; 203-177.
	Clause 18 carried. Government majority of 28; 201-173.
	Clauses 19 to 24: agreed without division.
8 March	Committee Stage. 4th Day.
	Clauses 25 to 35.
	Clause 25 (Staff): amendment preventing ability to speak Welsh being condition of employment by Assembly, moved by Leo Abse (GBB).

Negatived without division.
Clause 25 (Staff): Government majority of 27; 196-169.
Clauses 26 to 32. Agreed without division.
Clause 33 (Remuneration of Assembly members).
Government majority of 29; 194-165.
Clause 35 (Power of the Secretary of State)
Conservative amendment to broaden override power.
Government majority of 27; 169-132.

4 April	Committee Stage. 5th Day.

Clauses 35 to 42. Schedules 4 and 5.
Clause 35. Conservative amendment removing provision confining agreement to use override powers to Commons only, not Lords.
Government majority of 25; 170-145.
Clause 35 carried. Government majority of 22; 167-145.
Clauses 35 to 37. Schedules 4 and 5. Agreed without division.
Clause 38 (Industrial and Economic Guidelines).
Government majority of 16; 161-145.
Clause 39 (National Pay Policy).
Not moved by Government.
Clause 40 (Agency arrangements) and
Clause 41 (Provision of information). Agreed without division.
Clause 42 (Welsh Consolidated Fund and Loans Fund)
Conservative probing amendment. Clause 42 carried.
Government majority of 21; 142-121.

5 April   Committee Stage. 6th Day.
Clauses 43 to 60. Schedule 6.
Clause 43 (Payments out of Welsh Consolidated Fund).
Carried. Government majority of 35, 169-134.
Clauses 44 - 58. Schedule 6. (Remaining financial provisions).
Agreed without debate or division.
Clause 60 (Rate Support and Other Grants).
Government majority of 16; 128-112.

18 April   Committee Stage. 7th Day.
Debate on enabling amendment on 40% threshold in

referendum to be debated the following day.

Clauses 61 to 71. Schedules 7 – 9.

Clause 61 (Pow · to make new provisions as to certain bodies).

Conservative a ɩendment to delete power of Secretary of State to inc :ase powers under this clause without new legislatior..

Government majority of 19; 165-146.

Conservative amendment requiring affirmative resolution procedure accepted.

Clause 61 as amended, and schedule 7. Agreed without division.

Clause 62 (Assembly power to assume functions of certain bodies).

Carried. Government majority of 20; 150-130.

Clause 65 and Schedule 8 (Water).

Clause 65 carried. Government majority of 21; 150-129.

Schedule 8 agreed without division.

Clause 66 and Schedule 9 (Planning)

Clause 66 carried.

Government majority of 20; 148-128.

Schedule 9. Government amendment to restrict planning intervention to reserved matters concerning Wales agreed without debate.

Clauses 67 to 71. Agreed without division.

19 April   Committee Stage. 8th Day.

Clauses 72 to 84. Schedules 10 to 12.

Clause 72 (Determination of issues as to Assembly's powers).

Carried. Government majority of 230; 242-12.

Clause 73 (Confirmation by House of Commons of resolutions passed by it, but not by House of Lords).

Carried. Government majority of 33; 255-222.

Clause 74. Agreed without division.

Clause 75 (Orders).

Carried. Government majority of 220; 236-16.

Clauses 76 to 80. Schedule 10. Agreed without division.

Clause 81 (Interpretation).

Carried. Government majority of 211; 223-12.

Clause 82 (Commencement).
Liberal amendment ensuring commencement of main part of Bill on 1st January 1979.
Government majority against amendment of 225; 239-14.
Plaid Cymru amendment to provide for first Order after Commencement to be made within 120 days of Royal Assent.
Government majority against amendment of 204; 222-18.
Clause 82 defeated.
Majority against Government of 27; 259-232.
Clause 83 (Referendum).
Government moved 40% threshold amendment to allow a vote on it. (N.B. Government opposed amendment).
Amendment carried (government defeated) by majority of 72; 280-208.
Clause 83 as amended carried. Government majority of 239; 269-30.
Schedule 12 (Referendum). Clause 83 (Short Title). Agreed without division.

25 April

Committee Stage. 9th Day.
New Clauses.
New clause introduced by Government to allow minmum of three months between a General Election and Referendum.
Agreed without division.
New clause introduced by Conservative frontbench to allow for Speakers' Conference to consider appropriate number of post-Assembly Welsh MPs.
Government majority against clause of 23; 160-137.
New clause introduced by Conservative frontbench to allow for publication of daily proceedings of Assembly.
Not pressed to division.
New clause introduced by Plaid Cymru to allow for increase in powers of Assembly without further primary legislation.
Negatived without a division.

53

3 May	Report Stage.
	New Commencement Clause moved by Government. Government majority of 218; 235-17. (N.B. Opposition did not oppose amended clause).
	New clause (Employment Opportunities of Welsh Speakers) moved by Wyn Roberts (OBB) to prevent Assembly restricting employment opportunities due to ability or lack of ability to speak Welsh. Government majority against clause of 22; 243-221.
	New clause (Welsh Development Agency and Development Board for Rural Wales) moved by Conservative frontbench to remove these bodies from Assembly control. Government majority against clause of 18; 243-225.
	New clause (Audit of Welsh Comptroller and Auditor General) moved by Conservative frontbench to bring Assembly under the surcharge and disqualification provisions of 1972 Local Government Act. Government majority against clause of 24; 252-228.
9 May	Third Reading.
	Government majority of 28; 292-264.

House of Lords

23 May	Second Reading.
	Agreed without division.
6 June	Committee Stage. 1st Day.
	Conservative backbench amendment to allow elections to the Assembly to be by the Additional Member System of Proportional Representation. Amendment carried (government defeated) by majority of 85; 151-66.
	Conservative frontbench amendment allowing dates of Assembly elections to be approved by Resolution of both houses of Parliament. Amendment carried (government defeated) by majority of 7; 70-63.
	Conservative frontbench amendment allowing for disqualification of MPs as Assembly members.

Amendment carried (government defeated) by majority of 8; 37-29.
Conservative frontbench amendment disqualifying those ineligible to vote for the Assembly from being members of the Assembly.
Amendment carried (government defeated) by majority of 9; 37-28.

14 June   Committee Stage. 2nd Day.
Government backbench amendment to delete betting and gaming from list of devolved functions.
Amendment carried (government defeated) by majority of 15; 76-61.
Conservative frontbench amendment giving parents right of appeal to Secretary of State against closure or change of schools.
Amendment carried (government defeated) by majority of 7; 47-40.

15 June   Committee Stage. 3rd Day.
Government amendment introduced as first part of scheme for reserving pay and appointment standards of consultants and doctors, while at the same time devolving adequate powers to run the National Health Service in Wales. Amendment withdrawn for further consideration.
Conservative frontbench amendment not to devolve Welsh Development Agency, Devolopment Board for Rural Wales and Land Authority for Wales.
Amendment carried (government defeated) by majority of 5; 42-37.
Conservative backbench amendment not to devolve forestry and afforestation.
Amendment carried (government defeated) by majority of 10; 44-34.

21 June   Committee Stage. 4th Day.
Clause 13 (Review of local government structure) defeated by majority of 3; 82-79.
Conservative frontbench amendment ensuring that Executive Committee reflects balance of parties in Assembly.

Amendment carried (government defeated) by majority of 14; 57-43.

22 June   Committee Stage. 5th Day.
Conservative frontbench amendment altering procedure for removing Welsh Comptroller and Auditor General from office.
Amendment accepted by Government.
Clause 62 (Power to assume functions of certain bodies) defeated by majority of 17; 74-57.

23 June   Committee Stage. 6th Day.
Conservative frontbench amendment ensuring that Referendum held at least six weeks after laying of Referendum Order.
Amendment accepted by Government following incorporation of identical amendment into the Scotland Bill the previous week.
Conservative frontbench amendment making provision for Welsh language version of Referendum question.
Withdrawn for further consideration. Subsequently accepted by the government (see below).
Conservative backbench amendment entrenching appointment of 16 members of Welsh Water Authority by the local authorities in Wales.
Amendment carried (government defeated) by majority of 7; 39-32.
Conservative backbench amendment removing Secretary of State's power over certain aspects of the Health Service in Wales. The effect was to devolve those matters outright, the reverse of the intention.
Amendment carried (government defeated) by majority of 13; 39-26.

5 July   Report Stage. 1st Day.
Conservative frontbench amendment requiring Assembly to publish verbatim report of its proceedings.
Amendment carried (government defeated) by majority of 3; 80-77.
Conservative frontbench amendment to delete ''Chief Executive'' as title of Assembly leader.

Amendment carried (government defeated) by majority of 17; 61-44.

Independent Peer moved amendment deleting requirement for oral and written statements of the Assembly to be privileged.

Amendment carried (government defeated) by majority of 11; 58-47.

Conservative frontbench amendment transferring determination of salaries and allowances of Assembly members from Assembly to Secretary of State.

Amendment carried (government defeated) by majority of 22; 67-45.

Conservative frontbench amendment ensuring that Rate Support Grant allocation in Block Grant should be specified as such.

Amendment carried (government defeated) by majority of 26; 61-35.

6 July   Report Stage. 2nd Day.

Conservative backbench amendment enabling a water authority to appeal to Secretary of State in certain disputes with Assembly.

Amendment carried (government defeated) by majority of 29; 96-67.

Conservative frontbench amendment enabling Secretary of State to intervene in listed buildings procedures to protect the heritage of the United Kingdom.

Amendment carried (government defeated) by majority of 5; 87-83.

Conservative frontbench amendment allowing appeal to courts for redress of rights infringed by Assembly.

Amendment carried (government defeated) by majority of 8; 84-76.

Conservative frontbench amendment providing that Ministerial orders to amend existing legislation be subject to affirmative rather than negative resolution.

Amendment carried (government defeated) by majority of 14; 84-70.

Conservative frontbench amendment preventing Government spending money on referendum campaign.

Amendment carried (government defeated) by majority of 11; 71-60.
Conservative backbench amendment applying Public Bodies (Admission to Meetings) Act 1960 to the Assembly.
Amendment carried (government defeated) by majority of 11; 61-50.

13 July   Third Reading.
Conservative frontbench amendment tidying up amendment carried at Committee Stage giving right of appeal to Secretary of State in case of school closures.
Amendment carried (government defeated) by majority of 27; 101-74.
Conservative frontbench amendment requiring Referendum question to be bilingual.
Government accepted amendment.

House of Commons

18 July   Commons consideration of Lords Amendments.
Timetable motion.
Government to accept 83 out of total of 198 amendments made in the Lords.
Government majority of 31; 291-260.

19 July   Commons Consideration of Lords Amendments. 1st Day.
Lords amendment ensuring P.R. for Assembly elections.
Free Vote: Amendment rejected by majority of 227; 389-162.
Lords amendment to disqualify MPs from being members of Assembly. Government moved rejection.
Amendment accepted (government defeated) by majority of 33; 293-260.
Lords amendment deleting requirement for Assembly review of local government structure.
Amendment rejected by majority of 1; 278-277.
Lords amendment on publication of Assembly proceedings.
Government drafting amendment.

Amendment accepted without division.
Lords amendment to ensure party balance in executive committee.
Amendment rejected by majority of 24; 296-272.
Lords amendment deleting privileged status for Assembly statements.
Amendment rejected by majority of 34; 298-264.
Lords amendment allowing Secretary of State to determine salaries and allowances of Assembly members.
Amendment rejected by majority of 22; 296-274.
Lords amendment not to devolve W.D.A., D.B.R.W. and Land Authority for Wales.
Amendment rejected by majority of 5; 285-280.
Lords amendment specifying Rate Support Grant element in Block Grant.
Amendment rejected by minority of 17; 293-276.

20 July   Commons Consideration of Lords Amendments.
2nd Day.
Lords amendment deleting clause allowing Assembly to assume functions of certain public bodies.
Amendment rejected by majority of 28; 261-233.
Lords amendment giving right of appeal to courts against infringement of rights by Assembly.
Government gave assurance to include provisions in Order.
Amendment rejected by majority of 14; 286-272.
Lords amendment providing that Ministerial orders to amend existing legislation be subject to affirmative resolution.
Amendment rejected by majority of 20; 287-267.
Lords amendment deleting forestry from devolved powers.
Government recommended rejection.
Amendment accepted (government defeated) by majority of 33; 280-247.
Lords amendment enabling Secretary of State to intervene in listed building procedures to protect the heritage of the UK.
Amendment rejected by majority of 17; 272-255.

Lords amendment enabling Secretary of State to review Assembly decisions to close or change schools.
Amendment rejected by majority of 23; 172-149.
Lords amendment applying Public Bodies (Admission to Meetings) Act 1960 to Assembly.
Amendment rejected to majority of 23; 170-147.
Lords amendment to prevent Government using public money on Referendum campaign.
Amendment rejected by majority of 27; 164-137.

House of Lords

24 July   Lords Consideration of Commons Reasons for Rejecting Lords Amendments.
Lords agreed not to press any of their amendments with the exception of four.
Review of local government structure deletion replaced with amendment making Assembly's review of local government structure dependent on authorisation of Secretary of State after approval of Parliament.
Replacement amendment carried by majority of 32; 109-77. (government defeated).
Substitute amendment moved for reserving W.D.A. and D.B.R.W. (but not Land Authority for Wales) powers to Westminster. New amendment carried by majority of 11; 97-84.
Substitute amendment requiring Parliamentary approval of Assembly's assumption of functions of public bodies.
New amendment carried by majority of 23; 94-71.
Substitute amendment requiring Assembly to admit public to meetings.
New amendment carried by majority of 12; 79-67.

House of Commons

26 July   Commons Consideration of Returned Lords Amendments.
Government accepted, with drafting amendments,
Lords amendments on Parliamentary approval of Assembly assumption of functions of public bodies and

provision of public admission to Assembly meetings. Government recommended rejection of returned Lords amendment modifying Assembly's power to review structure of local government.
Amendment rejected by majority of 21; 292-271.
Government recommended rejection of returned Lords amendment reserving powers of W.D.A. and D.B.R.W.
Amendment rejected by majority of 20; 293-273.

House of Lords

27 July	Lords Consideration of Commons Reasons for Rejecting Lords Amendments. Conservatives agreed to drop objections to Assembly review of local government structure and devolving Welsh Development Agency and Development Board for Rural Wales.
31 July 1978	The Bill which has been debated for 29 days over a period of 9 months received the Royal Assent.
22 November 1978	A draft Referendum Order was laid before each House of Parliament, debated and approved without a division.
1 March 1979	The Referendum was held on 1st March 1979. The Act did not receive the required 40% minimum vote (see Chapter 10).
22 March 1979	The draft Order to Repeal the Wales Act was laid before each House of Parliament.
26 June 1979	It was debated and approved by 191 votes to 8 in the House of Commons.
5 July 1979	It was debated and approved in the House of Lords.
26 July 1979	The Order in Council for the repeal of the Wales Act was made and took effect immediately.

CHAPTER 4

An Analysis of the Wales Act 1978

DAVID FOULKES

Introduction

Before coming to the provisions of the Act, two matters must be
mentioned. First, some relevant constitutional principles. Governments are frequently able to give effect to their policies without having
to resort to Acts of Parliament. But if those policies involve a change in
the law – statute law or common law – or the creation of new
institutions which are themselves to exercise powers adversely
affecting third parties, an Act of Parliament will be necessary. The
Parliament of the United Kingdom can, by Act, legislate on any matter
whatsoever; it can repeal or amend an Act already passed, can create
new institutions (or abolish those already in existence), and grant them
powers. In particular, Acts of Parliament commonly give to Ministers
of the Crown wide powers of making rules and regulations (which
where they are of some generality may be referred to as delegated
legislation), issuing directions, determining appeals, making grants
etc. If an Act has granted powers to a body other than a minister, for
example a local authority, government can interfere with the decisions
taken by that body in exercise of those powers only insofar as it is itself
authorised by law to do so. Acts of Parliament being the highest form of
law known to our constitution, any act done or decision taken in the
exercise of a power granted by an Act which goes further than is
warranted by or is inconsistent with the Act is ultra vires, that is, is void
and of no effect. It is the role of the courts to say in litigation brought to
determine the issue, whether the act or decision is ultra vires. An Act of
Parliament can be repealed or amended only by a later Act, not by any
body subordinate to Parliament, unless the Act itself so provides.

The second matter to be mentioned concerns Scotland. As is noted
elsewhere the Scotland and Wales Bill had been introduced into
Parliament in November 1976 but was abandoned on the failure of the
guillotine motion in February 1977. Two separate Bills were then

prepared, one for Scotland, one for Wales. The two proceeded through Parliament together, the provisions of the Scotland Bill being dealt with first. The essays in this book are on the *Wales Act* and the referendum following it, and a detailed comparison with Scotland has not been attempted. A brief note on the *Scotland Act* is however to be found at the end of this chapter. It is enough to say here that the *Scotland Act* provided for an elected Assembly the principal character-istic of which was that it was to have legislative powers, unlike the Welsh Assembly whose powers were only administrative. The *Scotland Act* involved some fundamental and difficult constitutional issues: the *Wales Act* provided administrative machinery.

An Elected Assembly

Section 1(1) of the *Wales Act* provided, 'There shall be a Welsh Assembly'. It was to consist wholly of elected members, and the electoral arrangements were to have been these.[1] The Act provided that in due course Wales would be divided into *Assembly* constituencies, each returning *one* member. Any Assembly election held before that was done (and the first election would clearly have been so held, and possibly later ones) would have been on the basis of *Parliamentary* constituencies in Wales. Two Assembly members would be returned for each such constituency, except that three would be returned for those constituencies where the electorate was more than 125 per cent of the 'electoral quota'.

The division of Wales into Assembly constituencies would have been undertaken by the Boundary Commission for Wales. The link between Parliamentary and Assembly constituencies would have been retained as each Assembly constituency was to be wholly comprised within a Parliamentary constituency; there were to be two Assembly constituencies within each Parliamentary constituency but three within a Parliamentary constituency of which the electorate was more than 125 per cent of the electoral quota. These arrangements would have produced an Assembly of some eighty persons.

The right to vote at an Assembly election in an Assembly constituency was also based on the right to vote in Parliamentary elections.[2] A person wishing to vote in any particular Assembly constituency would have to have his name on that part of the Parlia-mentary register that related to that constituency, and would have to be entitled to vote at a Parliamentary election in the constituency comprising that Assembly constituency. Peers (who can vote at local

63

government but not Parliamentary elections) were to be able to vote in Assembly elections.

The date of the first Assembly election would have been fixed by the Secretary of State.[3] Subsequent elections would have been held on the third Thursday in March in the fourth year following that in which the previous election was held. The Assembly would thus have run for a four-year term. There was no provision for earlier dissolution even though political control of the Assembly might change during its term. These provisions parallel those in local government. It will be noted that the Assembly elections would have been for all seats – there was no provision for, for example, retirement by thirds. There were, of course, provisions in the Act for by-elections.

The 'first past the post' electoral system would have been used as in Parliamentary, local and European Assembly elections. A House of Lords amendment provided for a system of proportional representation but it was rejected by the Commons.

Who was eligible for membership of the Assembly?[4] The Act dealt with the question by setting out the grounds on which a person would be disqualified for membership. Many of those grounds were adopted from the law concerning disqualification for membership of the House of Commons, namely, the holding of certain judicial offices, employment in the civil service, membership of the armed forces or of any police force, or of the legislature of any country outside the Commonwealth, alienage, being under 21, a mental patient, a bankrupt etc. Peers as such were not to be disqualified, though Lords of Appeal in Ordinary were. Power was given in the Act to designate offices the holding of which would disqualify. The intention was to designate some offices which disqualify for membership of the House of Commons including membership of the boards of the nationalised industries. The House of Lords inserted a contentious disqualification into the Bill: membership of the House of Commons. It was agreed to by the Commons. The Lords also inserted a provision that would in effect, have disqualified for membership persons not resident in Wales. This was rejected by the Commons. There was no requirement that an Assembly member had to have a local connection with the constituency he represented.

Members were required to take the oath of allegiance.[5] They were to be excused jury service. Their salaries and allowances would have been determined by the Assembly itself. The House of Lords amended the Bill to provide for them to be fixed by the Secretary of State, but the Commons disagreed. (The Secretary of State's view was that members should be paid less than members of the Commons). The Assembly's standing orders were required to include provision for securing that members with pecuniary or other interests in any matter disclosed them before taking part in any proceedings dealing with that matter, and could include provision for preventing or restricting participation of such members in such proceedings or for excluding them from Assembly proceedings.

Conduct of business by the Assembly

A crucial point to an understanding of the Assembly and its operation is that the functions conferred were conferred on the Assembly as such and were to be exercised by it. In this respect the Assembly was to be likened to a local authority, and contrasted with central government arrangements where there is a vital distinction between Government and Parliament, between the executive and the legislature. The Assembly had executive powers only. (It was because it had such powers that it had to be created as a body corporate).[6]

To conduct its business the Assembly was required by section 17 of the Act to appoint 'subject committees' that is, committees 'with functions relating to all the areas of government with which the Assembly' was to be concerned. It was for the Assembly to decide how many such section 17 committees to appoint and how to group subjects together for that purpose, but between them they had to deal with all the Assembly's areas of government. The Assembly would also decide how many of its members to appoint to each committee. (There was no power to co-opt. but it seems that advisers (non-voting) could have been appointed). The Assembly had to name one of the members of each of these committees as its chairman and another as its leader: the leader would be known as the committee's executive member.

One of the committees appointed under section 17 was to be the Executive Committee. This was to consist of the leaders (executive members) of all the other committees appointed under section 17, together with no greater number of other members of the Assembly than one-third of the number of those leaders. The person named by the Assembly as the chairman of the Executive Committee was also to be its leader. Thus, consisting of the leaders, not chairman, of the other section 17 committees, the Executive Committee was given the central role in providing political leadership to the Assembly. It was also given certain specific functions in the realm of finance. In particular, paralleling arrangements in central government, payment of sums out of the Consolidated Fund and the Loans Fund could be made only on a recommendation of the Executive Committee.[8]

A party balance rule had to be applied to membership of section 17 committees. In the words of the Act,[9] the Assembly had to 'secure that the balance of parties in the Assembly is, so far as practicable, reflected in the membership of the committee'. This party balance rule did not however apply to the Executive Committee. A Lords amendment which provided that it should, was disagreed by the Commons. Assuming then that one party had overall control in the Assembly it would not have been able to take more than its arithmetic share of membership of section 17 committees; it would doubtless have taken the leadership of each committee; and it might have taken no more than its arithmetic share of chairmanships, the function of chairmanship being separated from that of political leadership. A majority of the Executive Committee would, of course, have consisted of members of the controlling party: indeed they could all have been, and it might well be thought that they should all have been, as the Executive Committee was to be as it were the 'Cabinet' whose chairman was also the leader: minority parties are not represented in the Cabinet.

There is no party balance requirement in local government. In drafting the Bill the government must have suspected that a party balance would not have been observed voluntarily by a party having overall control, or thought that it was necessary to allay public fears on that score.

In addition to section 17 committees, the Assembly was required to appoint two other committees, an Accounts Committee[10] and a Scrutiny Committee.[11] The former was intended to parallel the Public Accounts Committee of the House of Commons. The party balance rule applied, but it was not to have more than one member of the Executive Committee. As to the Scrutiny Committee, we shall see that powers exercisable by the Assembly include powers previously given to ministers to make orders, regulations etc. including the power to make statutory instruments. There is in Parliament a Scrutiny Committee the function of which is to examine certain general instruments made by Departments, and to report on them to Parliament. The Assembly Scrutiny Committee would have had much the same role as the Parliamentary Committee. The party balance rule applied to it, but no member of the Executive Committee could be appointed to it. This latter limitation, was, of course, required to ensure, as with the Accounts Committee that the Executive Committee did not dominate committees whose function it was to subject decisions to scrutiny and criticism.

The Assembly was empowered by section 17 to delegate any of its powers to a committee appointed under that section, and a committee with such powers could arrange for all or any of them to be exercised by a sub-committee or by its leader. The Act thus permitted extensive delegation to individual members of the Assembly – the committee leaders. Would the Assembly, for example, have delegated the determination of planning appeals to the leader of a planning committee? An opposition view was that it would be inconsistent with the transfer of powers from the Secretary of State to an *elected* body for that to be done. Another opposition view was that appointments by the Assembly to various public bodies *should* be delegated to one person to prevent the question of such appointments being bandied about in committee. The power to delegate decision making to committees was subject to some exceptions.

The Assembly had to elect a 'presiding officer' from among its members.[12] The Assembly could have decided on a suitable title.

The Assembly's standing orders (by which its procedure would be regulated) would have had to include provision as to the circumstances in which the public could be admitted to meetings of the Assembly and of its committees.[13] This was not in the Bill as drafted by government, which took the view that there was no need for such provision. Various attempts were made to amend the Bill to provide for public admission: the outcome was as stated.

Standing orders would also have had to include provision for the publication of a report of the proceedings of the full Assembly as soon as practicable after they took place. A Hansard-type verbatim report was not therefore required: nor a report of Assembly committees.

The Act provided that any written or oral statement made in Assembly proceedings, and any document published under its authority, should be absolutely privileged: no action in defamation would therefore lie in respect of such statements or documents.[14] Parliamentary privilege was, in that respect, therefore applied to the Assembly. The Opposition doubted whether it was right to confer absolute privilege; it was argued that qualified privilege would give adequate protection as with local authorities. The government view was that the status of the Assembly as a national Assembly, and the kinds of matters it would discuss, called for absolute privilege even though, unlike Parliament, it had no legislative functions.

Assembly Employees

The Act provided that the Assembly could appoint 'such officers and servants as it consider|ed| appropriate'.[15] It also provided that service as such official or servant was to be 'service in Her Majesty's Home Civil Service'.[16] This meant that there was to be no separate Welsh civil service, and that Assembly employees would be recruited strictly according to the standard procedures applying to the home civil service, including certification by the Civil Service Commissioners. Amendments to the Bill which sought to ensure that a person was not to be disqualified from being an Assembly employee by reason only of inability to speak Welsh were, after discussion, withdrawn, as were amendments which sought to ensure that the Assembly should not in considering appointments to its staff prefer a person solely by reason of being a civil servant over a person who was a local government official.

The permanent staff employed by the two Houses of Parliament are not civil servants: they are not employed by the executive, but by the legislature. By contrast all the staff of the Assembly would have been civil servants: the Assembly was an executive not a legislative body.

The Act did not provide for direct control by central government over the total number of Assembly employees. The government's view was that such control would have implied that the government could frustrate Assembly policies and would have been in its view an unwarranted interference in its affairs. (Central government control over the Assembly is referred to later).

The Assembly's functions

From the legal point of view the central problem in the establishment of the Assembly was what functions were to be given to it, how they were to be delineated with precision, and what was to be the relation between, on the one hand, any measures it might pass and decisions it might take and, on the other, Acts of Parliament and decisions of central government.

Section 9(1) of the *Wales Act* provided as follows:

> The Assembly shall exercise as regards Wales the functions given to Ministers of the Crown by or under the enactments specified in the first column of Schedule 2 of the Act, with the exception of functions specified in the second column . . .

There were in the Act, as is mentioned below, other provisions conferring functions on the Assembly, but this is the main power –

conferring provision, and it fixed the Assembly's constitutional position and function. It therefore requires a detailed comment.

(i) The Assembly was to have exercised certain functions given to *Ministers*. Therefore powers of making Acts of Parliament or measures of an equivalent status to Acts were not given to the Assembly. As stated above, Ministers are given wide and varied powers by Act of Parliament. Certain of these functions were, by the Act, to be transferred to the Assembly. In exercising them the Assembly would, in principle, be in law in the same position as Ministers who previously exercised them. The extent of a Minister's statutory powers is determined by the Act which conferred them. The Assembly's powers would likewise be so determined. Not having the power of making, repealing or amending Acts, the Assembly would have been confined to functions granted to it by Act. If it wished to do something that was beyond the powers conferred by this (or any other) section of this Act, (or of any later Act conferring powers on it) it would have had to obtain a change in the law by seeking the enactment of amending legislation.

(ii) *Only* functions exercised by Ministers were to be transferred. Functions exercised by bodies or persons other than Ministers, e.g. local authorities and nationalised industries, were not therefore transferred.

(iii) the functions to be transferred to the Assembly under this provision were those *precisely identified* in Schedule 2 to the Act by reference to the Acts by which they were given to Ministers. The transfer was not therefore by way of granting a general competence in specified areas.

(iv) Functions exercisable under various Acts listed under Schedule 2 were to be transferred; thus only functions under *statutes in existence* by the time the *Wales Act* was passsed were transferred. There was nothing in the Act authorising the transfer of functions under future legislation. Later Acts dealing with topics transferred by this Act to the Assembly would have had to make special provision for the Assembly.[17]

(v) The functions transferred were to be exercisable '*as regards Wales*'. By section 269 of the Local Government Act 1972 (as amended by the Interpretation Act 1978) Wales consists of the eight counties listed in Part I of Schedule 4 of the 1972 Act. The exercise of the functions 'as regards Wales' caused particular difficulties in devising relationships with the water industry. (This is referred to later).[18]

(vi) The Assembly would have been a Crown body. The Act does not expressly say this, but the functions conferred on it were Crown functions as they were previously exercised by Ministers, nothing in the Act caused them to cease to be Crown functions, and the Assembly's status as a Crown body was implicit in other provisions.

A more detailed examination of the method adopted for identifying and limiting the powers transferred to the Assembly is now necessary.

As section 9(1) states, the functions transferred were those contained in the statutory provisions listed in the first (left hand) column of Schedule 2. The Schedule was divided into 18 parts, each dealing with a devolved area of administration.[19] The first column listed 176 Acts or parts or groups of Acts. For example, education was to have been a devolved function. Thus in the first column of Schedule 2 will be found listed 'The Education Acts 1944 to 1976'. This means that all ministerial functions under those Acts were to have been exercised by the Assembly. Where an area of government was not to be devolved for example national taxation, social security, and sea fishing, then no statutes relating to those matters were listed in the Schedule. An area of administration was therefore excluded from devolution by omission from the Schedule.

However, the operation of a devolved function might involve or impinge on the exercise of a function which it was desired to keep in the hands of central government. In such a case the exercise of the function devolved by an entry in the first column of the Schedule was excluded by an entry in the second column of the Schedule. Education was a devolved area, but functions in respect of teachers' pay (but not teacher training) and the appointment of H.M. Inspectors were amongst those excluded by the entry in the second column of reference to the statutory provisions under which those functions are exercised. Functions under the National Health Service Act 1977 were transferred, but amongst excluded functions was that under s.23(4) of that Act which empowers the Secretary of State to modify the terms of the Vehicle (Excise) Act 1971: this was reserved as touching on the non-transferred topic of national taxation. In another area, pollution, wide powers under the Control of Pollution Act 1974 were to be transferred to the Assembly, including environmental noise and air pollution. However, ministerial functions relating to the control of pollution from motor vehicles, aircraft etc. were amongst those reserved to ministers as having implications for trade requirements and safety, and as international conventions might have been involved. Most functions under the Health and Safety at Work Act 1974 were reserved to ministers, including the safety of machinery at work. But that Act also deals with pollution of the atmosphere: as powers to deal with that matter were transferred under the Control of Pollution Act, functions which bear on it under the Health and Safety at Work Act were also transferred, including the power to prescribe premises, to make regulations and to provide for enforcement. But those powers were reserved so far as they applied to every other aspect of that Act.

A particularly complex case was the Mental Health Act 1959, which contains a wide variety of ministerial functions.[20]

It will be appreciated that various parts of what might be thought of as one administrative scheme may be authorised by different statutes. Take town planning. Appeals against the refusal by a local authority of planning permission lie by section 36 of the Town and Country Planning Act 1971 to the Secretary of State. That Act is listed in the first column of Schedule 2 to the *Wales Act*, so that appeal would have lain to the Assembly, which by section 36(4) of the 1971 Act would have had to afford to either party to the appeal an opportunity of appearing before a person appointed by the Assembly. What of the procedure at that appeal? That procedure is governed by the Town and Country Planning (Inquiry Procedure) Rules 1974. Those rules are made not under the Town and Country Planning Act 1971 but by the Lord Chancellor under section 11 of the Tribunals and Inquiries Act 1971. That Act is listed in Schedule 2 to the *Wales Act*, but only sections 5(1) and 12 thereof. The Assembly could not therefore have amended or repealed the Inquiry Procedure Rules. Enough has surely been said to indicate both the technique used to devolve powers to the Assembly, and the very considerable complexities involved. There would have been plenty to keep the lawyers busy.

What has been said so far indicates on which side of the line marking off the devolved from the reserved area various functions were to fall. There were some functions which could reasonably be argued to fall on either side. For example, agriculture was not to be devolved, but land use, rural development, the countryside and tourism were. Did forestry fall more conveniently into the devolved or reserved area? The government view was that on balance it was better for it to be dealt with along with the devolved matters, but the House of Lords deleted from the Bill that Part of Schedule 2 dealing with forestry, and the Commons did not seek to restore it. Again, while agriculture was not to be devolved, housing was. Should ministerial functions concerning

71

agricultural dwelling-house advisory committees be devolved or not? The government view, which was accepted, was that although there was an agricultural element in the work of the committees, the housing element was the more important: the relevant ministerial functions were therefore devolved.[21]

A comment on the technique of section 9

The technique was then to examine each relevant Act of Parliament, to 'unhook' from it those ministerial powers which it was desired to transfer to the Assembly and to convey them to the Assembly. The range of powers enjoyed by the Assembly depended therefore on the drafting of the Acts by which they were originally conferred on ministers. That drafting was not of course done with the needs of a devolved Assembly in mind but with the needs of government departmental administration throughout the Kingdom. If the powers enjoyed by the Assembly were found in practice to be coherent, logical, and suitable to a body with jurisdiction over a part only of the Kingdom, that would have been by chance rather than design. It seems very likely that amending legislation would soon be called for by the Assembly.

Another consequence of the technique used would have been this. Amongst the powers transferred to the Assembly was the power to make delegated, or secondary, legislation. The creation of primary and secondary legislation can be regarded as part of a single process of creating laws to regulate the matter in question. A Bill is drafted on the Department's instructions. Where resort to delegated legislation is thought by the Department to be necessary the regulations will be made by the Department itself in such a way as to achieve the aim of the legislative scheme it has itself evolved. In some cases the Department responsible for the Bill will have to study the matter in greater detail before the regulations can be made. Having made the regulations, the Department is well placed from its experience of their effect and the functioning of the scheme in question to decide whether amendment of the Act itself is necessary. It is a criticism of this scheme of devolution therefore that this unified responsibility for legislation and administration was to be divided between Whitehall and Cardiff.

Later legislation dealing with devolved topics would have had to make special provision for Wales. It does not follow that the same range of powers would in the future be granted to the Assembly as were granted by this Act.

Additional functions

As mentioned above, section 9(1) of the Act is the principal provision of the Act to confer powers on the Assembly and the one which determines the Assembly's constitutional status. Other provisions conferring further functions on the Assembly will now be considered.

The Assembly was, by section 10, empowered to do anything it thought appropriate to support museums, art galleries, libraries, the Welsh language, the arts, crafts, sport and other cultural and recreative activities. The word 'anything' had to be read in the context of the Assembly's general status: it would not have empowered the Assembly to take action for which legislation would have been necessary. The empowering of the Assembly to do the things listed in the section did not disable the government from continuing to act in those matters. By section 11 the Assembly could make arrangements for the provision in Wales of services for the war disabled; and could make grants towards the carrying on of public passenger transport undertakings in Wales.

The wording of section 12 may appear innocuous enough – 'The Assembly shall review the structure of local government in Wales and shall report its conclusions to the Secretary of State'. But that politically it was most contentious is suggested by the fact that it was discussed separately five times in the Parliamentary debates on the Bill (whereas some more important provisions were not discussed at all). The arguments are referred to elsewhere.[22] Legally it was not a significant section: the Assembly could have, and doubtless would have, discussed and arrived at a view on the structure of local government in Wales even without this section. The most the Assembly could have done was what the section required it to do – to review and report. Any change to the structure of local government would have required legislation.

Section 13 was a minor provision. By it the Assembly was required to exercise such functions given to Ministers by or under *local* Acts as the Secretary of State might specify. Local Acts do not frequently confer functions on Ministers, but by this section appropriate Ministerial functions arising under them could be devolved. (Only public general statutes were listed in Schedule 2).

Certain functions were given to the Assembly not by a transfer under section 9 or by a direct grant under the sections just referred to but by amendments made to other enactments. The amendments are to be found in Schedule 11 to the Act. To take a simple example. The

Banking and Financial Dealings Act 1971 specifies bank holidays and empowers Her Majesty by proclamation to change the days specified, and to appoint special days to be bank holidays. Schedule 11 amends that Act by substituting in relation to Wales an order of the Welsh Assembly for a proclamation.

A forbidden function

There was one function which the Assembly was expressly forbidden to undertake. Section 28 of the Act reads: 'The Assembly shall not in the exercise of its functions conduct relations with any country outside the United Kingdom'. International relations are conducted by sovereign states and international organisations.

Powers exercisable concurrently

Where ministerial powers were transferred to the Assembly, those powers could no longer be exercised by ministers. Further, ministers would have no control over the exercise of the powers transferred – unless, in each case, the Act so provided, and it did so provide in a number of ways.

First, section 9(2) provided that certain functions transferred under section 9(1) were nevertheless to continue to be exercisable by relevant ministers despite their exercise within Wales by the Assembly. They could thus be exercised concurrently. The ten relevant statutory provisions were listed in Schedule 3 to the Act. Section 9(2) was described as 'as device for coping with a few, relatively marginal powers which cannot be dealt with by the more usual mechanisms in the Bill'.[23] Two examples will illustrate the problem. Section 57 of the Transport Act 1968 contains a power to make grants for research into transport services. Some transport functions were devolved, others were not. Thus both government and Assembly needed to be able to exercise the power. Section 113 of the Town and Country Planning Act 1971 empowers the Secretary of State to acquire land compulsorily for the public service. This power is not devolved to the Assembly except 'in connection with the part of the public service with respect to which the powers of the Assembly are exercisable'[24]. The listing of this section in Schedule 3 meant that the whole of the power in the section was exercisable by the Secretary of State whether in respect of devolved or non-devolved functions.

There was also a concurrent power in ministers to make subordinate instruments where their making was required in order to fulfill any international obligation of the United Kingdom.[25]

The powers conferred by section 10, 11 and 12 were granted directly to the Assembly and not by way of transfer from ministers.[26] It follows that ministers could continue to exercise their own functions relating to such matters in Wales as elsewhere.

So much for powers exercisable concurrently. The controls exercisable by central government over Assembly functions require a separate section.

Central government control of the exercise of Assembly functions

Ministerial consent

Some powers transferred by section 9(1) of the Act were to be exercisable only with ministerial consent. These were listed in Schedule 4 to the Act. They related to 'excepted statutory undertakings' and 'reserved local matters', which are referred to below.

Reserved matters

We have seen that the effect of section 9(1) and Schedule 2 was that ministerial powers in certain areas were transferred to the Assembly, but that the exercise of those powers was withdrawn from the Assembly where they infringed areas reserved to ministers. In addition, ministers were given certain general powers of intervention in Assembly decisions: it is these we are now concerned with. The purpose of these powers was to enable ministers to protect areas which were not devolved against Assembly decisions. The Act therefore, in section 34(3), defined certain matters as 'reserved matters'[27]: a 'reserved matter' was one (a) which concerned Wales (whether or not it also concerned any other part of the United Kingdom) but (b) with respect to which the Assembly had no power to act. So for example highways and land use were not reserved matters, but defence and taxation were. The Act provided that if it appeared to the Secretary of State that any action proposed to be taken by the Assembly would or might affect a reserved matter, directly or indirectly, then he could direct that the proposed action should not be taken. In addition the Secretary of State could require action capable of being taken by the Assembly to be taken by it where failure to take it would or might affect a reserved matter. The Secretary of State could even revoke an 'instrument' (which would include regulations made by statutory instrument) made by the Assembly under any Act of Parliament, which affected a reserved matter.[28] These powers could be exercised only if the Secretary of State thought it 'desirable in the public interest' to use them. No indication is offered in the Act as to the meaning of 'public interest'. When asked for clarification the Lord Chancellor replied that it meant that the Secretary of State need not take action if he thought it would not be in the public interest to do so.[29] This hardly helps to isolate the meaning of public interest but doubtless a consideration the Secretary of State would have in mind would be that he would be overriding an elected body. In any event a measure of Parliamentary control over the exercise of these powers was provided for in the Act.

Planning

Town and country planning was a devolved and not therefore a reserved matter. Most ministerial functions concerning planning application and enforcement appeals, structure plans etc. were transferred to the Assembly. By the exercise of these powers a reserved matter, for example defence, might clearly be affected, and it might seem that the power to intervene to protect reserved matters, which has just been described, could be usefully used. However, the exercise by the Assembly of planning functions was subject to a different method of control by central government although the powers of intervention given to the Secretary of State would be exercisable in much the same circumstances as gave rise to the right to protect reserved matters. The effect of intervention (formally done by notice published in the London Gazette) was that no action or further action was to be taken in the matter by the Assembly, any action taken was to be of no effect except so far as the notice of intervention provided, and the Secretary of State was to have in relation to the matter all the functions that the Assembly would have had had there been no intervention.[30]

Water

A special power of intervention was also given to the Secretary of State in respect of the exercise of certain of its powers by the Assembly which might affect the national (i.e. England and Wales) policy for water. Where this power was available the general power of intervention to protect reserved matters was not available.[31] The provisions the Act made for the management of the water industry following the setting up of the Assembly are referred to below.[32]

Directions in NHS matters

The National Health Service was a devolved function so that, for example, as regards Wales it would have been the Assembly's and not the Secretary of State's duty to 'continue the promotion of a comprehensive health service', to provide hospital accommodation, medical services etc. However the government had decided that the remuneration of general practitioners (as of other public service employees) should be a reserved matter. Accordingly in the Bill as originally laid the relevant sections were listed in the second column of Schedule 2. During the passage of the Bill it came to be realised that that would not do, as the effect of listing the sections in question was to take from the Assembly the ability to make regulations on related matters which ought to be left within its competence. It was not possible to distinguish between those matters which should and those which should not be devolved simply by the Schedule 2 technique. That Schedule was therefore amended so as to devolve to the Assembly all the regulation-making powers in question, and an amendment was made in Schedule 11 to the National Health Service legislation so as to give the Secretary of State power to direct the Assembly about the exercise of those functions. Under this power the Secretary of State could have directed the Assembly as to what its regulations about remuneration could contain. A similar complication arose concerning NHS employees e.g. hospital doctors. (General practitioners are not NHS employees). In the Bill as presented the provisions of the NHS legislation dealing with the doctors' conditions of service were intended to be excluded from the Assembly's competence. But this exclusion also prevented the Assembly from making regulations about the appointment of *any* NHS staff, and that was not desired. The exclusions from the Assembly's competence were therefore excised from the second column of Schedule 2, and an amendment was made in Schedule 11 to give the Secretary of State the power of direction over the Assembly's regulations. A particularly delicate matter involved here was the composition of committees for the appointment of consultants. This is determined in ministerial regulations and under devolution would have been determined by the Assembly. The power of direction would have ensured that the Assembly could not go its own way in altering the structure or procedure of these committees – a matter of much concern to the medical profession.

Industrial and economic guidelines

By Schedule 2 to the Act 'development' was a devolved function. Thus, subject to some exceptions, ministerial powers in relation to the Welsh Development Agency, the Land Authority for Wales and the Development Board for Rural Wales were transferred to the

Assembly. Now the exercise of some at least of the functions of those bodies could infringe government economic or industrial policies. The Act therefore sought[33] to ensure that they could be kept in line with those policies by requiring the Secretary of State to prepare guidelines as to the exercise by the Assembly of its powers with respect to relevant functions of those bodies, including their functions relating to the disposal of land for industrial purposes. The exercise by the Assembly of its powers with respect to the last mentioned functions exercised by county and district councils and by a development corporation was also subject to Secretary of State guidelines.

The guidelines would be contained in or determined by an order which was to be subject to annulment in either House. They were not merely for the guidance of the Assembly, for it was required to exercise its powers 'so as to give effect to' them. If it did not, the government could act under its general powers of intervention in protection of reserved matters or could possibly have brought proceedings in the courts against the Assembly.

Provision of information

A minister might need to have information relating to the exercise of Assembly functions so as to enable him to carry out his functions. Any request for such information would have to be complied with by the Assembly.[34] For example, information about trends in the devolved area of secondary education could well be relevant to the provision of non-devolved University education. There was no provision requiring a minister to give the Assembly information it required in order to do its job.

International obligations

The government is required to do whatever is necessary to fulfill the international obligations of the United Kingdom whether arising from membership of the European Communities or otherwise. On the setting up of the Welsh Assembly as a body subordinate to Parliament it was therefore necessary for the Government to take powers to ensure that the Assembly fulfilled and did not act inconsistently with those obligations. So the Act gave the Secretary of State power to require or prohibit the Assembly from so acting, including the power to revoke an instrument made by it.[35] The requirement that the use of such powers could be undertaken only if it appeared to the Secretary of State desirable in the public interest to do so (which as we have seen applied

78

to intervention in reserved matters)[36] did not apply in this case: international obligations must be observed. Likewise there was no provision for Parliamentary approval.

Another tier?

One of the arguments against the Assembly was that it would be yet another tier of government, so that Wales would be administered by community councils (in most areas), district councils, county councils, the Assembly, the Secretary of State and the EEC organisations. The Secretary of State was most insistent throughout that there would not be another tier. For example, 'In a nutshell, what we are dealing with is the transfer of existing functions, not the creation of a new tier of government. Hon. Members who say that we are creating a new tier of government are living in cloud-cuckoo-land, because the tier already exists. It is there because some of the functions [of the Assembly] are those that I exercise and some of the functions are those exercised by the nominated bodies in Wales.'[37] However, the Secretary of State was given by the Act certain powers over the Assembly: he could in certain circumstances direct it to take or not to take certain action, could revoke its statutory instruments, intervene in planning matters, give it directions in certain NHS matters, etc. This looks like a hierarchy, and hence a tier. It might be replied that powers within a government are exercised hierarchically, and that a (sideways) transfer of some powers to the new Assembly did not create a new tier. In practice, of course, there would have been a vast difference between on the one hand the exercise of powers within a unitary government, and on the other between a minister and a national, elected, body. It is impossible to deny that a new form of administration, an extra part of government, had been created even if the idea of a new tier was anathema. What was undisputed was that by government calculations the Assembly would have meant some extra 1,150 civil servants (including twenty lawyers). This was certainly objected to, whether or not they constituted another tier. The part these arguments played in the referendum debate is discussed in Chapter 6.

The Assembly and nominated bodies

One of the arguments advanced in favour of the Assembly was the need to bring nominated bodies under closer democratic control. What did the Act provide?

Taking first the nationalised industries, the Act did not transfer any of their functions to the Assembly. And furthermore, they were

79

protected by the Act against action taken by the Assembly adverse to their interests. The undertakings in question were those referred to by the Act as 'excepted statutory undertakers' the definition of which included the statutory gas and electricity authorities, the Post Office, British Railways Board and the National Coal Board. Thus the exercise of a function transferred to the Assembly by an entry in the first column of Schedule 2 to the Act was withheld, by an entry in the second column, as against an 'excepted statutory undertaker'; the exercise by the Assembly of certain powers in relation to those undertakers required ministerial consent; and ministerial consent was required by the Assembly when they objected to the compulsory acquisition of their land.[39] These undertakers had to be protected in the carrying out of their statutory functions.

Secondly, the Act permitted the functions of certain nominated bodies to be transferred to the Assembly.[40] The provisions were these. Where a minister had statutory powers to appoint members of a statutory body, and all those powers were by the Act transferred to the Assembly then all or any of the functions of that body could be transferred to the Assembly by ministerial order (not by the Assembly itself). Thus if any ministerial power of appointment was withheld from the Assembly, the functions in question were not transferable – this was the case with the Welsh Water Authority. But if appointment to a body was made by some one other than a minister as well as by a minister, then if the totality of the minister's power was transferred, the functions were transferable – this was the case with the Area Health Authorities. Some other bodies whose functions could have been transferred were the Development Board for Rural Wales, the Historic Buildings Council for Wales, the Welsh Development Agency, the Land Authority for Wales.

Thirdly the bodies referred to in the last sentence operated wholly within Wales. There also had to be considered a group of bodies which exercised throughout England and Wales (and in some cases the United Kingdom) functions which were relevant to functions devolved to the Assembly. The principle of transferring ministerial powers in devolved areas to the Assembly could not be applied without some modification in the case of bodies whose functions were exercised over a wider area than Wales. The Act therefore gave ministers power to confer on the Assembly functions in relation to the bodies in question, and also to divide the responsibilities of those bodies so that they would be responsible to the Assembly for what they did in Wales, and to the government for what they did elsewhere.[41] The bodies in question included the Housing Corporation, the Dental Estimates Board, the Public Health Laboratory Service Board and the Advisory Council on Child Care.

Fourthly, we consider the water authorities. The Water Act 1973 created nine Regional Water Authorities and the Welsh Water Authority (hereafter the Welsh Authority). The areas within which the authorities exercise their functions are defined by reference to the previously existing areas of river authorities, and these were determined by river drainage areas. The boundaries of these are not coincident with political boundaries. A part of Wales is within the area of the Severn-Trent Authority and parts of England are within the area of the Welsh Authority.

Water was a devolved area of administration, and most ministerial functions in that area were transferred to the Assembly. The Assembly could, of course, exercise its functions only 'as regards Wales' but as parts of the area of the Welsh Authority are in England, and part of the Severn-Trent Authority is in Wales, the Act provided that certain ministerial powers so far as they were exercisable in relation to the Welsh Authority were deemed to be exercisable as regards Wales (even though they in fact affected part of England), and so far as they were exercisable in relation to the Severn-Trent Authority were deemed not to be exercisable as regards Wales (even though they in fact affected part of Wales).[42] The former were thus to be exercisable by the Assembly, the latter by central government. The powers in question related to the constitution, etc., of the two water authorites, their financial duties, and charges; and to appointments to regional land drainage committees, etc.

The Assembly was empowered to give directions to the Severn-Trent Authority in respect of the exercise of its functions in Wales, as well as to the Welsh Authority.

By the Water Act 1973, it is the duty of ministers to promote jointly a national policy for water in England and Wales. As Wales is an important source of water for England, decisions there could affect a policy for England and Wales. The overall effectiveness of a national water policy was therefore sought to be safeguarded by an amendment to that Act[43] which required the Assembly to promote a water policy for Wales in harmony with the national policy for England and Wales.

The Secretary of State's power to intervene in the exercise by the Assembly of certain of its powers in this area has been referred to. It was the view of the Severn-Trent Authority that those procedures were inadequate to protect national policy. Strenuous efforts were made in

81

the Lords by the water interests to extend ministerial control over the exercise by the Assembly of its water functions. An amendment which provided that either of the two water authorities could apply to the Secretary of State to use his intervention powers was agreed to on a division and agreed to by the Commons.[44]

Fifthly, the Act dealt with the Countryside Commission. The Countryside Act 1968 created the Countryside Commission with functions for England and Wales, and provided for the appointment of a Committee for Wales. The Wales Act dissolved that Committee and created a Countryside Commission for Wales.[45] The relationship between the Assembly and that Commission was to have been as follows. The Assembly would have determined the number of members, appointed them, and appointed one of them to be Chairman; it would have determined and paid their remuneration, and determined the number of staff; its approval to the appointment of the Commission's Secretary was required; it could have given the Commission directions of a general character; and it could have taken over its functions under the provision previously referred to.[46]

Finally, the Assembly was empowered[47] to make arrangements with the British Tourist Authority for that Authority to undertake activities outside the United Kingdom for the purpose of encouraging people to visit Wales. In addition the Act authorised the Wales Tourist Board to undertake such activities.

The Assembly's finances

The Block grant

The Assembly had no taxing powers. None was given it by the Act and therefore it had none, as although powers not expressed may sometimes be implied, that is never the case with a taxing power. Where then was it to get its money from? From the Secretary of State – the U.K. government – in the form of a block grant. The key section (S.44) was this:

> The Secretary of State shall from time to time make out of moneys provided by Parliament payments into the Welsh Consolidated Fund of such sums as he may determine by order made with the consent of the Treasury.

This was a crucial feature of the Assembly. It would have been a body which spent money which it was not responsible for raising. Such an arrangement does not encourage responsible behaviour. And if the Assembly were to be criticised for failing to spend enough on a particular service, it might reply that the fault lay not with it but with the 'English' government for not providing it with enough money.

The devolved services would therefore have been financed on an expenditure basis: the expenditure requirements of the devolved services would have been measured and the devolved administration furnished with the income needed to meet them. The alternative, rejected, method of finance was the revenue basis: the Assembly would have been given certain sources of revenue and been obliged to finance the devolved services out of the income those sources provided. The Government's reasons for adopting the expenditure basis were explained in the 1977 White Paper, *Devolution: Financing the Devolved Services* (Cmnd. 6890). Basically they were that traditionally the allocation of public expenditure between different areas of Great Britain has not been determined by the amount of revenue raised in them but by their needs; and that the economic unity of the United Kingdom requires the continued pooling of all United Kingdom resources (including for example revenue from off-shore oil) and the consideration of expenditure needs of the United Kingdom as a whole. In the Government's view the adoption of the expenditure basis did not rule out altogether giving the Assembly power to levy limited additional taxation to finance extra expenditures which they might think especially important. However, its proposal to give them power to levy a surcharge on local rates for that purpose was dropped, and no other way of revenue-raising was found possible.

How was the block grant to be calculated? The Act is silent on that vital matter. The government had explained however, that a reason for deciding on the block grant expenditure-based financing of the Assembly was the desirability of ensuring that Wales's needs would continue to be met. How then were those needs to be assessed? The government acknowledged that the assessment of needs and hence the calculation of the block grant, should be made as objective and as generally acceptable as it was possible to make it, but insisted that the decision must be a matter of political judgment. The remarkable proposal of the Commission on the Constitution for expenditure to be allocated by an independent (i.e. politically unaccountable) Exchequer Board, was rightly rejected. But the Government thought that the provision of a basis of information about needs and standards of public services could be assisted by the creation of an independent advisory and research board. The creation of such a body would be discussed with the Assembly (there is therefore nothing in the Act about it) (Cmnd. 6890, para. 72).

The Government acknowledged that the annual discussion of levels of devolved expenditure might well lead to detailed central government involvement in the work of the Assembly, and might make it difficult for the Assembly to determine its own plans on a satisfactory basis. The Government therefore also proposed for discussion with the Assembly a formula-based system. The total of devolved public expenditure in Wales would be related to comparable expenditure elsewhere in the country on the basis of relative needs. This would be expressed as a percentage of comparable expenditure in the country as a whole. This percentage would be maintained over a period (which might be four years – the term of the Assembly), but changes in the level of comparable expenditure outside Wales would automatically lead to corresponding increases or decreases in devolved expenditure. There is nothing of this in the Act: in the Government's view to deal with the matter on a statutory basis would lead at best to 'extremely cumbersome provisions of a doubtful validity and effectiveness' (Cmnd. 6890, para.77). Was it rather the case that the government had not sufficiently thought through its ideas to put them in the Bill, or, in any event, that it preferred the flexibility of administrative decision to the formality of an Act of Parliament?

The block grant having been agreed between the Assembly and the Secretary of State, with Treasury approval, the Assembly could then allocate the block grant amongst the devolved services in accordance with its own priorities, for example, more for education than would have been the case without devolution, and therefore less for housing or health. Thus though the grant would be calculated on the basis of comparable needs in various services, the Assembly would not be required to allocate expenditure in accordance with that view of needs. (The same applies, of course, to the use of rate support grant by local authorities).

Although the block grant would be the only effective source of finance for the Assembly, it would not be the only source of finance for devolved services. Part of the Assembly's block grant would be expended on them as at present is part of central government's expenditure. In addition local authorities raise money by way of rates and borrowing to help pay for these as for other devolved services. In determining the amount of the block grant it would be necessary to take account of this and other sources of finance for devolved services. The Government would therefore have had to determine two sets of figures: the amount of the block fund, and the limit on capital expenditure on devolved services by local authorities and public corporations which is

84

financed from borrowing and require authorisation by the Assembly. Both figures would have required parliamentary approval.[49] As for rates, a contribution from rates would be assumed. The Government would have had to decide whether by comparison with rate income in England this was fair, for a lower rate would mean the need for a higher block grant to provide services to the desired level.

The Welsh Funds

The scheme of the Act was to reflect on a smaller scale the United Kingdom arrangement of a Consolidated Fund and a National Loans Fund.

Thus the Act provided that there was to be a Welsh Consolidated Fund, and payments of the block grant were to be made into it by the Secretary of State. No payment was to be made out the Fund except in accordance with credits granted by the Welsh Controller and Auditor General (an office created by the Act – see below). The Welsh C & AG would grant credits on the Fund at the request of the Executive Committee of the Assembly but was not to grant credit for payment of any sum unless that sum (a) had been charged on the Fund by or under any Act of Parliament – see for example s.50 (5); or (b) was part of the sums appropriated for any purpose by an order of the Assembly (s.41(2)). For what purpose would sums be appropriated? By s.42(1)) sums forming part of the Fund could be appropriated only for a purpose (i) for which the Assembly could exercise its powers; or (ii) for which they were payable out of that Fund under the Act or any other Act. The need for (ii) was that the purpose of payment could be one for which the Assembly did not exercise its powers, but which was nevertheless one for which sums could by statute by payable out of (but not charged on-(a) above) the Fund – see for example s.49(8).

No sum issued out of the Fund on credits under para. (a) or (b) above was to be applied for any purpose other than that for which it was charged or appropriated (s.41(2)).

The Act also provided (s.40(1)) that there was to be a Welsh Loans Fund. Payments into this were to be made from time to time by the Secretary of State of such sums as he with Treasury consent determined (s.45(1)). The Treasury would issue to the Secretary of State such sums out of the National Loans Fund as were required to enable the Secretary of State to make payments to the Welsh Loans Fund.

Payments into the Welsh Loans Fund were deemed to be advances made to the Assembly, and were to be payable at such times and with interest at such rates as the Treasury determined. Any sums received by the Secretary of State by way of repayment or interest were to be paid into the National Loans Fund (s.45(3)).

The maximum amount outstanding in respect of the principal of sums advanced to the Assembly under these provisions was fixed by the Act at £250 million but this could be increased by ministerial order with the approval of the House of Commons (s.45(4),(5),(6)).

As with the Welsh Consolidated Fund, no payment was to be made out of the Loans Fund except in accordance with credits granted on the Fund by the Welsh C & AG. He was to grant credits at the request of the Executive Committee, but was not to grant any such credit for the payment of any sum unless (a) the Assembly had power to lend that sum, (and such sum was not to be applied for any purpose other than the lending of money by the Assembly); or (b) the sum was required for certain other specified purposes (s.43(2)).

A Treasury Minister explained the need for the Loans Fund in this way:[50] these are certain public bodies which borrow with the Secretary of State's consent from the National Loans Fund. The functions of the Secretary of State over the bodies in question were transferred by the Act to the Assembly. It was not appropriate for those bodies to borrow directly from the National Fund. Thus since control over their borrowing was to be exercised by the Assembly, the Assembly itself would borrow from the Welsh Loans Fund (which is fed from the National Fund). (The bodies in question are listed in s.48(3) of the Act). By s.48 (1) the Assembly was to try to ensure that the amount of capital expenditure financed by borrowing by those bodies and by local authorities did not exceed such amount as was fixed by ministerial order, which required Parliamentary approval (s.48(3)).

We refer now to Short-term Borrowing. By s.46 the Assembly could borrow temporarily (which in Treasury terms means less than 12 months) in sterling by way of overdraft or otherwise, such sums as might appear to the Assembly to be required to meet a shortfall in either Consolidated or Loans Fund or in order to maintain a working balance in either Fund. The amount outstanding was not to exceed £35 million, but this figure could be increased by ministerial order (subs. (5),(6)). The Treasury could guarantee the repayment of sums borrowed (s.47).

The Act provided (s.40(2)) for transfer between the Funds. The Executive Committee of the Assembly could cause sums to be transferred from one to the other of the Funds. The requirement (referred to above), that no payment was to be made out of either Fund

86

except in accordance with credits granted by the Welsh C & AG, did not apply to transfer between the Funds (s.41(1), 43(1)). This was because the Welsh C & AGs consent was necessary for payment *out* of the Funds, and transfer between the Funds is not payment out of them to a third party.

What was the reason for authorising this transfer between the funds? It was to enable the Assembly to deal with the situation where one fund was in surplus, the other in deficit. In such a case the fund in deficit could get an overdraft from the bank (see above). If it did that, interest would, of course, be payable. The transfer to the surplus of one fund to reduce the deficit of the other was therefore simply to avoid interest charges.

In the course of the debate a Treasury Minister said that money paid into one fund but transferred to another could be used only for the purpose of the first fund. He later acknowledged (in a letter to the chief Opposition Spokesman on devolution)[51] that this was incorrect, that 'money can be paid out of either fund, no matter what its source, upon a decision by the Assembly to do so and subject only to a certificate from the Welsh C & AG; a certificate which would be forthcoming if the Assembly were acting within its powers in making its spending decision'. However he gave an assurance that the section permitting transfer (s.40(2)) would not permit evasion of the limitations laid down in the Act on the use of the Assembly Funds. Thus payments by the Secretary of State into the Welsh Consolidated Fund could not exceed the block fund (the total of which was to be agreed by the House), and the size of that fund would not be affected by a decision to transfer sums from the Consolidated to the Loans Fund. Secondly, payments from the National to the Welsh Loans Fund were subject to the limits specified in s.45(4) and (5), and would have to remain within the s.45 (4) limit whether employed for lending or transferred to the Consolidated Fund. Thus there was control over the two funds taken together, with the freedom to the Assembly within that control to spend the money allocated to it. The Minister added, 'An additional safeguard in both cases is that payments into the Welsh Consolidated and Loans Fund are subject to the discretion of the Secretary of State who would have the power to reduce or delay the payment if some situation arose for which the arrangements in the Bill had not adequately provided'.

Various Acts of Parliament charge sums on the Consolidated Fund, or require or authorise the payment of sums into or out of the Fund or out of moneys provided by Parliament. By s.55 of the Wales Act 1978 such Acts were to have effect so far as they related to the exercise of functions by the Welsh Assembly as if they provided for the sum to be charged on or paid into or out of the Welsh Consolidated Fund.

Likewise, where the power to advance money under certain enactments was exercisable by the Assembly, the Welsh Loans Fund was substituted for the National Loans Fund, the rate of interest was specified, and provision was made for the auditing of the relevant accounts by the Welsh C & AG. Provision was also made for the repayment into the Welsh Loans Fund of advances previously made under those enactments by the Secretary of State, and for subsequent adjustments.

For each financial year (that is, each year ending with March 31) the Assembly had to prepare appropriation accounts of sums paid and received by it; and the Executive Committee had to prepare an account of payments into and out of the Welsh Consolidated Fund and an account of payments into and out of the Welsh Loans Fund. The Assembly had to publish those accounts and the reports made on them by the Welsh C & AG and by its Accounts Committee.[52]

The Welsh C & AG

Mention has been made of the office of Welsh Controller and Auditor General. The *Wales Act* created this new office and naturally based it and its functions on the United Kingdom office of the same name.[53] In the debates on the Bill some members queried the need for a separate office of Welsh C & AG. Would it not be preferable, they asked, for the existing office of C & AG to do the work? As the Assembly was not a taxing body, but was to spend money provided by Parliament, why should not the Assembly's spending be audited by the same officer who audits other expenditure approved by Parliament? Was sufficient expertise available for the two bodies? How would the two career structures be related? The Government's view was that the new institution of the Assembly required its own internal audit office; that the Welsh C & AG would not necessarily work in the same way as the present office, but would perhaps look to what was done in other countries; that the C & AG had been consulted on the proposals in the Bill; that the career structures would be for discussion.

The Opposition moved in both the Commons and the Lords a new clause which would have applied s.161 of the Local Government Act 1972 to the Assembly: that is to say, it would have given the Welsh C & AG the powers of the district auditor and subjected Assembly members to possible surcharge and disqualification. The government view was that as the Assembly is to act on behalf of the Crown, central rather than local government arrangements provided the more apt analogy. The clause was rejected in the Commons and withdrawn in the Lords.

The Assembly and Local Authorities

The relationship between the Assembly and local authorities in Wales was one of the important issues in the devolution debate. Three matters are relevant here. One of them, the discussion about section 12 of the Act, has already been referred to. The other two are the rate support grant, and reserved local matters.

The Rate Support Grant

The Assembly's functions with regard to the payment of rate support grant can be understood only by reference to the Local Government Act 1974. By s.1(1) of that Act the Secretary of State (for the Environment) is to make rate support grants to local authorities in England and Wales. By s.58 of the Wales Act such grants would have been made to local authorities in Wales by the Assembly out of the Welsh Consolidated Fund, that is, out of the block grant, and not by the Secretary of State.

Section 1 of the 1974 Act goes on to specify how the Secretary of State is to fix the estimated aggregate amount of the rate support grant for any year, provides for consultation with local interests, and the matters he must take into account. Section 2 requires the Secretary of State to divide the aggregate amount of rate support grant into various elements, state to which class of authority payments in respect of the various elements are to be made etc. By the *Wales Act* the Wales Assembly was substituted in those matters for the Secretary of State.

Section 3 of the 1974 Act requires the estimated amounts of rate support grant to be fixed and prescribed by a rate support grant order made by the Secretary of State with the consent of the Treasury and after consulting local authority interests. Under the *Wales Act* the order would be made by the Welsh Assembly after consultation, but Treasury consent was not required.

Section 4 powers referring to the variation of rate support grant orders and the section 5 power of reducing grants in case of default would be exercisable by the Assembly.

Sections 6, 7, 8 and 9 of the 1974 Act provide for the payment of certain additional grants by the Secretary of State. These would be payable by the Assembly except those specified in s.8(2) of the Act, viz.

grants paid in respect of university and teacher training grants. These would remain payable by local authorities and reimbursable by the Secretary of State.

Thus the general position as far as Welsh local authorities was concerned was that the Assembly was substituted for the Secretary of State. They would look to and negotiate with the Assembly for the payment of their rate support grant as in the past they looked to central government. The Assembly would, of course, pay the grant out of the block grant of which it would in fact form a considerable proportion – about 50 per cent. Thus the amount payable by the Assembly to local authorities by way of rate support grant would form a major element in the Assembly's claim to the Secretary of State for the block grant. When the amount of the block fund was being worked out, assumptions would be made as to the needs of RSG (or any other major expenditure by the Assembly) 'but such assumptions would cease to have any validity once the total amount was fixed . . . Whatever assumptions it may be necessary to make when the block fund is settled, the amount of the statutory rate support grant settlement must be left to the discretion of the Assembly'.[54] In other words it would not be obligatory for the Assembly, when it received the block grant, to pay out of it by way of rate support grant the amount that was negotiated for that purpose as part of the block grant. Theoretically, the Assembly could use some of the rate support grant element for some other lawful purpose leaving it to local authorities to meet their financial needs by putting up the rates. This emerged as a significant issue in later stages of the referendum campaign, as referred to in Chapter 6.

Reserved local matters

'Reserved local matters', were 'reserved' in that local authorities remained responsible for them to ministers not to the Assembly. The twenty-seven matters in question (they are listed in Schedule 5) included the police, small holdings, protection of birds, building regulations, diseases of animals, civil defence and mandatory grants for students. These were withdrawn from the Assembly in a number of ways. First, where a function affecting them was listed in the first column of Schedule 2, there was an entry in the second column excepting 'reserved local matters'. For example, the ministerial power under the Local Government Act 1972 to confirm bye-laws was transferred, but not the exercise of that power as it affected reserved local matters. Second, local authority interests in land held for the purpose of any of those matters were safeguarded against compulsory purchase. Third, when determining the amount available to local authorities by way of the rate support grant the Assembly had to have regard to such considerations affecting reserved local matters as the Secretary of State might indicate. In other words the level of expenditure on these matters would for rate support grant purposes in effect be determined by the Secretary of State.

The Assembly and the Courts

There is no doubt that the Assembly could have been sued in the courts. The citizen would have the same recourse against the Assembly as he has against government departments whether at common law (for breach of contract or in tort for example) or by virtue of a statutory provision. As an example of the latter, a decision of the Secretary of State on an appeal made to him against the decision of a local authority on a planning application is challengeable in the courts by a procedure, within the time limits, and on the grounds laid down by statute. Under the *Wales Act* the Assembly would have determined such appeals in place of the Secretary of State, and its decisions would have been challengeable in the courts in the same way.

In addition to proceedings brought by individuals and bodies affected by acts of the Assembly, the Act provided in section 70 that the Attorney-General could bring proceedings against it for a declaration (that is, a statement of the law on the matter in question) as to whether the Assembly had failed to discharge a duty, had done or was proposing to do anything beyond its powers, or whether a statutory function fell to be discharged by it.

As a Crown body the Assembly would have enjoyed the privileges and immunities enjoyed by the Crown in litigation, for example, an injunction could not have been obtained against it.

The Assembly could itself have brought legal proceedings and thus enforced obligations owed to it by an individual or private or a public body. In addition the Act provided that the Assembly could bring proceedings for the promotion or protection of the public interest.[55]

The Ombudsman

There already exist the Parliamentary, Health, and Local Government Ombudsmen who investigate complaints made against government departments, health authorities and local authorities respectively. The Scotland and Wales Bill had proposed the appointment of a Welsh Assembly Commissioner, but this idea was abandoned in the *Wales Act*, presumably for the reason that there was no need to add to the number of Ombudsmen. The Act therefore provided in section 68 for the Parliamentary Ombudsman to be empowered to investigate complaints of maladministration by the Assembly.

The Referendum

The Act received the Royal Assent on 31 July, 1978. By s.79 it was not to come into operation until such day as the Secretary of State by order appointed and different days could be appointed for different provisions of the Act. (Such a provision is common: it is necessary where a new administrative scheme is to be established). The first such order was not to be made unless a draft had been laid before and approved by Parliament. However, before a draft of the first order was laid a referendum had to be held. (Attempts to have the referendum held at an earlier stage, e.g. after Second Reading, failed.) The date of the referendum was to be fixed by the Government but might have been limited by s.81. This provided that if there was a general election before the referendum, the referendum was not to be held earlier than three months after the election. But if an Order in Council had been made fixing a date for the referendum earlier than the expiry of the three months, the Order in Council was not to take effect, that is, the referendum would not be held on that date but another date for the referendum could be fixed. This section was added to the Bill on a government motion during the committee stage. A similar clause had been added to the Scotland Bill by the Commons (against the Government's advice), and the Government accepted that it was desirable that the two Bills should contain the same provision. The thinking behind the section was that the two questions 'which party is to form the Government?' and 'shall there be devolved administrations in Scotland and Wales?' should be kept separate. Some feared that the referendum might even be held on the same day as a general election. (At the time these matters were being discussed – summer 1978 – it seemed likely that a general election would be held in the autumn of that year). The Government stated a number of times that it was their intention that the referendums in Scotland and Wales would be held on the same day but recommended against a legislative provision to that effect in case of some totally unforeseeable circumstances arising. (The known result of one referendum could affect the outcome of the other). The Conservative opposition stated that though opposed to the Bill they would, as a Government, hold and give effect to the result of the referendums.

Those entitled to vote in the referendum were those entitled to vote as electors at a parliamentary election in any constituency in Wales, and peers entitled to vote at a local election in Wales. (Electors in England were thus excluded). Electoral law requires that to be entitled to vote one's name must be on the electoral register, and one must not be disqualified for voting by reason, for example, of age.

The form of the ballot paper to be used in the referendum was set out in the Appendix to Sched. 12 to the Act. If a majority of the answers to the question posed in the referendum was 'no'; or if a majority of the answers was 'yes' but nevertheless fewer than 40 per cent of those entitled to vote said 'yes' (or rather if it appeared to the Secretary of State that either of those situations existed), the Secretary of State had to lay before Parliament the draft of an Order for the repeal of the Act – which Parliament might or might not approve. The referendum was in that sense consultative. If the necessary number said 'yes', the draft of the first order bringing the Act into force would then be laid for approval. Here again parliamentary approval was necessary.

The 40 per cent requirement was, of course, an amendment to the Bill moved by a private member; it was agreed to by the Commons by a majority of 72. It read as follows:

> If it appears to the Secretary of State that less than 40 per cent of the persons entitled to vote in the referendum have voted 'Yes' in reply to the question posed in the Appendix to Schedule 12 to this Act or that a majority of the answers given in the referendum have been 'No' he shall lay before Parliament the draft of an Order in Council for the repeal of this Act.

The 40 per cent was of those 'entitled to vote'. Those 'entitled to vote' is not the total number of entries in the register for the Welsh Parliamentary constituencies, as from that total number one would have to make some deductions. There would be those who though entered (in error) on the register, were disqualified for voting by reason for example, of being under age, or foreign. There would be those who had died since the compilation of the register. And there would be those whose names were on more than one register, for example, students whose home was in Wales and were at the University of Wales. Calculations more or less accurate, could, of course be and were made. In any case, as things turned out, no such fine-tuning was necessary. (In the EEC referendum, the totals of the electoral lists were reduced by 2% to take account of the factors mentioned here). The government rejected the idea of bringing the electoral register specially up to date to ensure that the dead would be excluded as far as possible. It also rejected the proposal to seek powers to allow next-of-kin of dead voters 'to vote as they think the dead person would have wished' – probably the most absurd idea thrown up in the devolution debates.[56]

The Opposition moved at the Report Stage in the Lords an amendment to the Bill which sought to prevent the Government doing anything which involved the use of public funds to secure a result one way or the other in the referendum. The Government stated that they did not intend to provide public funds for campaigning organisations, and had no plans themselves to issue any leaflet, etc., explaining the provisions of the devolution legislation. However, devolution being government policy, the normal facilities available to ministers in furthering government policy should be available. The Opposition amendment would have forbidden this. It was agreed to by the Lords but disagreed by the Commons and is not in the Act. A similar provision had been inserted in the Scotland Bill with the same result.

The Repeal of the Act

Following the referendum, an Order in Council was made on 26 July 1979.[57] The operative part read:

'The Wales Act 1978 is hereby repealed'.

Verdict

The verdict offered here on the *Wales Act* 1978 is that it was a legal minefield, unstable, and rich with possibilities of litigation. It was doubtless not drafted with the intention of promoting confusion and conflict, but it could materially have contributed to their realisation.

A note on the original clause 1 of the Bill

Clause 1 of the Bill as laid read:

The following provisions of this Act make changes in the government of Wales as part of the United Kingdom. They do not affect the unity of the United Kingdom or the supreme authority of Parliament to make laws for the United Kingdom or any part of it.

The same clause (mutatis mutandis) appeared as clause 1 of the Scotland and Wales Bill and, of the Scotland Bill and indeed comprised the whole of Part 1 of each Bill.

The government's view was that the Wales Bill and others just referred to not only maintained but strengthened the unity of the Kingdom by meeting demands for change. Clause 1 of the Scotland Bill had in fact been deleted by the Commons at the Committee stage and when the Wales Bill later went into Committee the government announced that it was 'not seeking to retain' clause 1. The Opposition suggested that this withdrawal was a recognition that the Bill did indeed affect the unity of the Kingdom. The Government said that the Bill was consistent with that unity, that as the Committee on the Scotland Bill had disagreed with it, 'it might assist the Committee and speed up the debate if the Government made their position clear at the outset'. (H.C. Debs. Vol.945. Col.591). Other views were that the clause accurately stated the position, but was surplusage; and that it broke a basic rule of drafting, that when introducing an Act one does not make expressions of opinion. (The government might have got itself in less difficulty if it had made use of a preamble).

There was a six hour debate on the withdrawn clause, with the result that one hour was left for a debate on the method of voting for Assembly members, and that there was no discussion at all of seven clauses or of Schedule 1.

A note on the Scotland Act 1978

This Act devolved legislative powers to a directly-elected Assembly, and executive powers to a Scottish Executive. Legislative measures passed by the Assembly and approved by the Queen in Council would be known as Scottish Assembly Acts. On a matter within the legislative competence of the Assembly an Act could amend or repeal provisions made by Act of Parliament. A matter was within its competence if it related to a 'devolved matter' as listed in the Act, but the power to impose, alter or abolish any tax was specifically excluded.

Parliament retained legislative competence over all matters affecting Scotland, whether or not it was within the legislative competence of the Assembly, and whether or not the Assembly had legislated on those matters.

The Assembly had a fixed life of four years, but by a two-thirds majority the Assembly could require its own dissolution.

The Executive would consist of the First Secretary and other Scottish Secretaries. These, together with their assistants, would be appointed from amongst members of the Assembly. Presumably the relationship between the Executive and the Assembly would have broadly been that between Government and Parliament at Westminster, the First

95

Secretary being (like the Prime Minister) the leader of the party able to command a majority in the Assembly. Executive powers were not to be conferred on the Executive as such (any more than they are conferred on the Government as such), but on the Secretaries. The powers of the Secretaries would be those which would otherwise be exercised by a Minister of the Crown, were exercisable as regards Scotland, and related to devolved matters. Thus Assembly legislation would be administered by Scottish Secretaries, as would legislation of the United Kingdom Parliament which dealt with matters falling within the legislative competence of the Assembly. The devolved services would be financed by a system of block grants from central government.

The Secretary of State was given many supervisory powers over both Assembly and Executive. In particular if he thought that a Bill passed by the Assembly was not within its competence he was to refer it to the Judicial Committee of the Privy Council for its decision. If he thought a Bill was not compatible with the United Kingdom's obligations within the European Communities or other international obligations, he was to refrain from submitting the Bill for the approval of the Queen in Council.

A note on the House of Lords and the Wales Act 1978

The Wales Bill as laid before the House of Commons in November 1977 contained 82 clauses and 12 schedules. The Bill was considered by that House for about 98 hours over twelve days. During that time only 13 of those clauses and two schedules were debated. The Lord Chancellor commented that the time had been used 'extravagantly and not well'.[58] The Commons was operating under a guillotine motion when there is particular need to use the time available efficiently and economically.

In the House of Lords some 64 hours were spent on the Bill. Almost every clause was discussed. There were thirty-five divisions. Four of these were on government motions. Of these four, three were 'clause stand part' motions, the fourth a re-wording of a clause. The government won the last mentioned and one of the 'clause stand part' motions. The two 'clause stand part' motions lost were much more significant, the clauses in question being what become sections 12 and 60 of the Act. They are referred to below. In addition to the two motions just mentioned won by the government, the government also won on an opposition motion concerning grants to the arts. Thus the government won three of the thirty-five divisions.

According to the printed lists of amendments 469 amendments were put down to the Bill, 128 of which were put down by the Government. This was not, of course, the number moved. Some of the 469 were not moved, and some amendments were moved which were not in the printed lists but were last minute manuscript amendments. As is common, many of those moved were not intended to be voted on, only to elicit information.

We are clearly indebted to the Lords for ensuring a more detailed examination of the Bill than the Commons was able to provide. But, of course, the Lords did not only examine it, they altered it, to the extent of 198 amendments; 115 of these amendments were moved by one of the five ministers dealing with the Bill in the Lords.

What were the reasons for the 115 government amendments? Some can be grouped together as being purely technical or terminological. Thus eight substituted 'Welsh Water Authority' for 'Welsh National Water Development Authority' to accord with the change made to the Authority's name while the Bill was before the Lords. Nine, referring to reports to be made to the Assembly, changed the phrase 'laid before the Assembly' to 'sent to and published by the Assembly'. Eleven were made to take account of Bills which were enacted whilst the Wales Bill was before the House.

Other amendments can be grouped together as being necessary to correct various errors in the Bill. Some involved a recognition by the draftsmen that they had inadvertently devolved functions which should not have been. Thus Attorney-General and Treasury functions, and ministerial functions concerning excepted statutory undertakers, navigation authorities and office development permits were, by amendment, saved from devolution. Four other amendments excluded from devolution provisions which would have given the Assembly power to expand the seaward boundaries of Acts.

Five highly technical amendments were made to the rate support grant provisions of the Bill (to some of which the opposition had drawn attention).

Four amendments were made to remedy defective provisions which had also been in the Scotland Bill and which had been corrected in that Bill on its earlier passage through the Lords when attention had been drawn to them by the Opposition.

Three amendments were moved as a consequence of other successful opposition amendments, in order to make the Bill a coherent Bill to send back to the Commons. A few were moved to meet opposition criticism, including the clauses relating to the disclosure of pecuniary interests and to the composition of subject committees.[59] An amendment on the latter topic was one of the few government amendments not agreed to.

Five amendments were made at the Report stage because it was realised that discussion at the Committee stage had shown the need for clarification.

Only one amendment was made for the purposes of implementing an undertaking given by the Government in the Commons following an opposition amendment put down there, and withdrawn in the light of that undertaking.[60]

Let us now look at the 83 non-government amendments made to the Bill in the Lords. Perhaps the most politically significant provided for proportional representation in Assembly elections. (This involved a total of 18 amendments). This proposal had been thrown out in the Commons as it had in the debates on the Scotland and Wales Bill and the Scotland Bill. Another amendment made by the Lords excluded what became section 60 of the Act, concerning the assumption by the Assembly of the powers of certain nominated bodies. The Commons reinstated the clause, though it was subject to a number of last minute amendments there. The need to bring nominated bodies under democratic control (by providing for nomination to be by the Assembly rather than by ministers, and for possible assumption by the Assembly of their functions) was one of the major arguments relied on by the government for its Bill. The Lords also excluded the clause that became section 12 of the Act. This required the Assembly to review the structure of local government in Wales and report thereon to the Secretary of State. This clause was dealt with no less than six times. The Commons, on a division, agreed to it. The Lords deleted it. The Commons reinstated it. The Lords deleted it. The Commons reinstated it. The Lords did not insist on the deletion but amended the clause.[61] The Commons rejected the amendment. The Lords gave way. This might seem an excessive expenditure of time on what might appear to be a minor issue. The section only required the Assembly to do what it could in any case have done without the section. However, as shown elsewhere in this book, the relation of an Assembly to local government structure and functions was a contentious issue.

Other opposition amendments would have empowered the Secretary of State, rather than the Assembly itself, to determine the salaries of Assemblymen, and would have extended the party-balance rule, which applied to subject committees, to the Executive Committee. Other amendments rejected by the Commons concerned the degree of privilege to be given to Assembly proceedings, and the restriction of Assembly membership to those living in Wales.

The Commons did not however dispute the exclusion of forestry from devolved functions nor amendments affecting water authorities. Nor did the Commons dispute an amendment which provided that a member of the Commons could not be a member of the Assembly. There is no such disqualification in the *Scotland Act*.

The function of the House of Lords in relation to Bills is usually said to be that of 'revising' them. The 115 government amendments made no major change to the Bill. The summary given above shows that they were on points of detail. The draftsmen were necessarily involved in a continuous examination of the Bill during its passage through Parliament (apart from having to consider the effect on the Bill of Opposition amendments). The time needed to get the Bill through the Lords gave the draftsmen more time to get the details of the Bill right.

Important changes were made to the Bill by the non-government amendments. These were not mere revision if by that is meant a correction of detail not affecting an issue of substance. The politically most significant were, as shown above, rejected by the Commons.

NOTES

1. S.1 and Schedule 1.
2. S.3.
3. S.2.
4. S.5,6,7 and 8.
5. For material in this paragraph, see S.30, 32, 33, 16.
6. S.1(4).
7. S.18.
8. S.19 The Assembly's financial arrangements are dealt with later.
9. S.22.
10. S.53.
11. S.21.
12. S.15.
13. S.15(5).
14. S.23.
15. S.24.
16. S.65(1).
17. Some Acts passed after this Act but before the referendum was held made special provision for the Assembly, see e.g. Vaccine Damage Payments Act 1979, S.11.
18. See p. 81.

19. The 18 Parts were, local government, local matters, education, landlord and tenant and housing, fire services, health and social services, pollution, land use and development, water and land drainage, freshwater fisheries, countryside, ancient monuments and historic buildings, tourism, transport, highways, road traffic, registration services, general.

20. The principles on which the government acted in deciding which functions should be devolved and which left with ministers are explained at H.L. Debs. vol.394, cols.1023 – 1027.

21. H.L. Debs. vol.394, col.1022.

22. See p. 127.

23. H.L. Debs. vol.394, col.1010.

24. Schedule 2, Part VIII.

25. S.29.

26. For these sections, see p. 73 above.

27. These are not to be confused with reserved *local* matters, dealt with at p.90.

28. S.35(1).

29. H.L. Debs. vol.393. col. 1335.

30. S.34 and Schedule 9.

31. S.63 and Schedule 8.

32. See p. 81.

33. S.37.

34. S.39.

35. S.34(2) and S.35(2).

36. See p. 75 above.

37. H.C. Debs. vol. 935 col.796.

38. S.78(1).

39. S.36.

40. S.60.

41. S.59.

42. S.63.

43. Schedule 11 to the Wales Act.

44. Schedule 8, Part II, para. 8.

45. S.62.

46. p. 80 above.

47. S.61.

48. Royal Commission on the Constitution 1969-73, Cmnd. 5460.

49. S.44(2) and S.48(4).

50. H.C. Debs. Vol. 947, col.317.

51. I am grateful to Mr. Francis Pym, MP, for giving me a copy of the letter.

52. S.52 and 54.

53. S.49.

54. H.L. Debs. Vol.394, col.1144.

55. S.55 Cp. Local Government Act 1972 S.222.

56. H.C. Debs. Vol.945, col.215 written answer.

57. S.I. 1979 No. 933.

58. H.L. Debs. Vol.392, col.946.

59. Secs. 16 and 17 of the Act respectively.

60. Cp. Griffith, *Parliamentary Scrutiny of Government Bills,* p.231.

61. A Law Lord, Lord Edmund-Davies, voted with the government (but did not speak) on the motion. No other Law Lord participated in proceedings on the Bill.

Appendix

EXTRACTS FROM THE WALES ACT 1978

This Appendix contains ten of the eighty-two sections of the Act, Part VII of Schedule 2 (so as to illustrate the technique used for conferring powers on the Assembly), and the whole of Schedule 12 which dealt with the Referendum.

SECTIONS

9.—(1) The Assembly shall exercise as regards Wales the functions given to Ministers of the Crown by or under the enactments specified in the first column of Schedule 2 to this Act, with the exception of the functions specified in the second column.

(2) Any function given to a Minister of the Crown by or under an enactment listed in Schedule 3 to this Act shall continue to be exercisable by him as regards Wales notwithstanding that it is exercisable by the Assembly by virtue of subsection (1) above.

10. The Assembly may do anything it considers appropriate to support museums, art galleries, libraries, the Welsh language, the arts, crafts, sport and other cultural and recreative activities.

11. The Assembly may—
- (a) make arrangements for the provision in Wales of services for the war disabled, and
- (b) make grants towards the carrying on of public passenger transport undertakings in Wales.

12. The Assembly shall review the structure of local government in Wales and shall report its conclusions to the Secretary of State.

26. Where it considers it expedient for the promotion or protection of the public interest, the Assembly may institute in its own name, or appear in, any civil proceedings relating to matters with respect to which the powers of the Assembly are exercisable.

27. Subject to the provisions of this Act, the Assembly may do anything (whether or not involving the acquisition or disposal of property) which is calculated to facilitate, or is conclusive or incidental to, the discharge of its functions.

28. The Assembly shall not in the exercise of its functions conduct relations with any country outside the United Kingdom.

79.—(1) The preceding provisions of this Act shall not come into operation until such day as the Secretary of State may by order appoint.

(2) Different days may be appointed under this section for different provisions of this Act and for different purposes of the same provision.

(3) An order under this section may contain such transitional and supplementary provisions as appear to the Secretary of State to be necessary or expedient, including provision for expenses to be defrayed out of moneys provided by Parliament.

(4) The first order under this section shall not be made unless a draft of it has been laid before and approved by resolution of each House of Parliament.

80.—(1) Before a draft of the first order to be made under section 79 above is laid before Parliament a referendum shall be held in accordance with Schedule 12 to this Act on the question whether effect is to be given to the provisions of this Act.

(2) If it appears to the Secretary of State that less than 40 per cent of the persons entitled to vote in the referendum have voted 'Yes' in reply to the question posed in the Appendix to Schedule 12 to this Act or that a majority of the answers given in the referendum have been 'No' he shall lay before Parliament the draft of an Order in Council for the repeal of this Act.

(3) If a draft laid before Parliament under this section is approved by resolution of each House, Her Majesty in Council may make an Order in the terms of the draft.

81. If a proclamation summoning a new Parliament is made before a referendum is held in pursuance of section 80 above, the referendum shall not be held earlier than three months after the date of the poll at the election of members of the new Parliament; and if an earlier date has been appointed by Order in Council under paragraph 1 of Schedule 12 to this Act, the Order shall not take effect, but without prejudice to the making of a new Order under that paragraph.

SCHEDULE 2

PART VII

POLLUTION

Enactment	*Excluded functions*
The Alkali, etc. Works Regulation Act 1906 (c.14).	
The Public Health Act 1936 (c.49).	The functions under sections 53 and 61 to 71.
	The powers of consent under the proviso to section 143(3).
	The powers under sections 291 and 340.
	The power under section 341 except so far as exercisable in relation to land vested in or held for the purposes of the Assembly.
The Public Health (Drainage of Trade Premises) Act 1937 (c.40).	
The Radioactive Substances Act 1948 (c.37).	The functions under sections 2 and 5(2) and, so far as exercisable in relation to those functions, the functions under sections 7 and 9.
	The functions under section 5(1) (*b*) in relation to sites and premises mentioned in section 2(1) and (2) of the Radioactive Substances Act 1960.
The Rivers (Prevention of Pollution) Acts 1951 to 1961.	The powers under section 6 of the Rivers (Prevention of Pollution) Act 1951 (c.64).
	The powers under section 9(6) of the Rivers (Prevention of Pollution) Act 1961 (c.50).

The Clean Air Act 1956 (c.52)	The functions under section 22 so far as exercisable otherwise than in relation to land vested in or held for the purposes of the Assembly.
	The functions under section 23.
The Radioactive Substances Act 1960 (c.34).	The functions under sections 6(1), 8 to 12 and 15 so far as exercisable in relation to premises mentioned in section 8(1) or radioactive waste on or from such premises.
	The functions under section 18(6).
The Clean Air Act 1968 (c.62).	
The Deposit of Poisonous Waste Act 1972 (c.21).	
The Health and Safety at Work, etc. Act 1974 (c.37) sections 1(1)(d), 3(3), 5, 11, 12, 14, 15, 16, 18(2), 20(3), 27(1), 44, 45, 50 and 80.	The functions under those sections so far as exercisable in relation to matters other than the control of emissions into the atmosphere of noxious or offensive substances.
	The functions under those sections so far as exercisable in relation to the control of emissions from vehicles, aircraft or hovercraft.
	The power to prescribe vehicles, vessels, aircraft or hovercraft for the purposes of section 1(1)(d).
The Control of Pollution Act 1974 (c.40).	The functions under sections 21(2) and (5), 30(5) and 31(9).
	The power under section 39(2) to issue a certificate.
	The power to prescribe parts of the territorial sea for the purposes of the definition of 'controlled waters' in section 56(1).
	The functions under section 56(4).

105

	The powers under section 70 to make regulations as to appeals to magistrates' courts.
	The functions under sections 73(2)(a), 75 and 76.
	The functions under section 80 except so far as exercisable in relation to premises used for the purposes of the Assembly and to its officers and servants.
	The functions under sections 91(1), 92(5), 93(1), 96, 104, 108 and 109 except so far as exercisable in relation to matters with respect to which the powers of the Assembly are exercisable.
	The powers under section 100 to 103.
The Refuse Disposal (Amenity) Act 1978 (c.3).	The power under section 13 so far as exercisable in relation to section 4(2).

SCHEDULE 12

REFERENDUM

1. The referendum shall be held on such day, not less than six weeks after the making of the Order, as Her Majesty may by Order in Council appoint.

2. Those entitled to vote in the referendum shall be—

 (a) the persons who, at the date of the referendum, would be entitled to vote as electors at a parliamentary election in any constituency in Wales; and

 (b) peers who at that date would be entitled to vote as electors at a local government election in any electoral area in Wales.

3. The question to be asked in the referendum and the front of the ballot paper to be used for that purpose shall be in the form set out in the Appendix to this Schedule.

106

4. Subject to the following provisions of this Schedule, Her Majesty may by Order in Council make provision as to the conduct of the referendum and apply in relation to it, with such modifications or exceptions as may be specified in the Order, any provision of the Representation of the People Acts, any provision of the enactments relating to returning officers and any provision made under any enactment.

5. An Order in Council under this Schedule shall not charge any sum on the Consolidated Fund but may provide for the expenses of the returning officers to be defrayed as administrative expenses of the Secretary of State.

6. The functions which, in relation to a parliamentary election, are conferred on returning officers by any provision applied by an Order in Council under this Schedule shall in relation to the referendum be discharged by the persons who under section 41 of the Local Government Act 1972 are, or may discharge the functions of, returning officers at elections of councillors of districts.

7. The Secretary of State shall appoint a Chief Counting Officer, who shall appoint a counting officer for each county in Wales. and each counting officer shall conduct the counting of votes cast in the area for which he is appointed in accordance with any directions given to him by the Chief Counting Officer.

8. The counting officer for each area shall certify the number of ballot papers counted by him and the number of respective answers given by valid votes; and the Chief Counting Officer shall certify the total of the ballot papers and the respective answers for the whole of Wales.

9. The council of each county in Wales shall place the services of its officers at the disposal of the counting officer for the county; and if the council or the counting officer for a county so requests, the council of any district in the county shall place the services of its officers at the disposal of the counting officer for the county.

10. Section 2(1) of the Welsh Language Act 1967 (power to prescribe Welsh version) shall apply in relation to an Order in Council under this Schedule as if the Order were an enactment within the meaning of that Act.

11. No court shall entertain any proceedings for questioning the numbers, as certified by the Chief Counting Officer or any counting officer, of any ballot papers counted or answers given in the referendum.

12. No recommendation shall be made to Her Majesty in Council to make an Order under this Schedule until a draft of the Order has been laid before Parliament and approved by resolution of each House of Parliament.

APPENDIX

FORM OF BALLOT PAPER

Parliament has decided to consult the electorate in Wales on the question whether the Wales Act 1978 should be put into effect.

Mae'r Senedd wedi penderfynu ymgynghori ag etholwyr Cymru ynglyn â ddylid gweithredu Deddf Cymru 1978.

DO YOU WANT THE PROVISIONS OF THE WALES ACT 1978 TO BE PUT INTO EFFECT?

A YDYCH AM I DDARPARIAETHAU DEDDF CYMRU 1978 GAEL EU GWEITHREDU?

Put a cross (X) in the appropriate box

Rhowch groes (X) yn y blwch cymwys

YES YDWYF	
NO NAC YDWYF	

CHAPTER 5

The Character of the Lobbies:
Some Theoretical Considerations

R. A. WILFORD

One means of seeking to understand the nature of the devolution campaign in Wales is to identify the political support which the competing lobbies represented. The pro-Assembly lobby included the following institutions: the Executive of the Welsh Labour Party; the bulk of Welsh Labour MPs; Plaid Cymru; the Welsh Liberal Party; Wales TUC; and the Conservative Party. This institutional diversity was reflected at the individual level whereby the lobby recruited under its collective umbrella a variety of Welsh personalities with no publicly acknowledged partisan preferences in order to broaden the lobby's appeal. Among these were the rugby players Gareth Edwards and Barry John, the entertainers Max Boyce, Nerys Hughes and Harry Secombe and the distinguished opera singer Sir Geraint Evans. A related tactic was to link the pro-devolution cause with Rugby Football, probably the only institution uniting all Wales, North and South, English and Welsh speaking alike. On the occasion of the Welsh Rugby XVs home international against Ireland in early February 1979, the pro-devolutionists distributed leaflets which referred to: 'The Other Big Match: Wales v Rest' due to take place on March 1st – St. David's Day – and listed those Welsh celebrities who supported the devolution proposals. The 'Rest' were represented as a somewhat motley crew: 'Mrs. Thatcher and hard-line Tories; Leo Abse's group of MPs; and the National Front'. The 'guilt by association' imputed to the 'Rest' in the leaflet exposed an inherent contradiction in the strategy of the 'Wales for the Assembly' campaign: although officially an umbrella, non partisan lobby, its supporters found it virtually impossible to avoid the temptation to score party-political points over its opponents. The decision to include Michael Foot, then Deputy Leader of the Labour Party and MP for Ebbw Vale and George

Wright, Secretary of the Wales TUC, as patrons of the campaign further compromised the non-partisan image that it sought to present. Grouped under the anti-Assembly umbrella were: the Conservative Party in Wales; seven of the eight County Councils; the National Federation of the Self-Employed; NALGO; the Country Landowners Association; and the gadflies of the Welsh Labour Party, the so-called 'Gang of Six' MPs – Leo Abse, Donald Anderson, Ifor Davies, Fred Evans, Ioan Evans and Neil Kinnock.

Thus it is apparent that the two umbrella campaigns were broadly based in both institutional and individual terms. Such heterogeneity raises an obvious question: why were such disparate political interests able to achieve a working consensus under their respective umbrellas? The seemingly obvious answer would be their respective attitudes towards the *Wales Act* 1978. However, this simplistic response is not a wholly sufficient explanation – at the least it is insufficient as an explanation of the character and subsequent conduct of the pro-Assembly coalition. For example, Plaid Cymru regarded the provisions of the Act with real ambivalence. One faction perceived the Act as totally inadequate as it did little, if anything, to weaken the power of Parliament at Westminster over the future of Wales. The other larger faction, whilst critical of the provisions of the Act, adopted a pragmatic position, regarding it as a step in the right direction, a means of achieving in the long run the end of an independent and sovereign Welsh state. On the other hand, the mainstream of the Welsh Labour Party regarded the *Wales Act* as an end in itself: it represented an attempt to grant to Wales a measure, albeit limited, of political autonomy and manifested an aspiration to extend participatory democracy within the United Kingdom. This aspiration was also shared by the Welsh Liberals who have consistently favoured a policy of decentralising decision-making power within the U.K. Thus there were real differences in motivation and purposiveness evident within the pro-Assembly lobby, differences that were to have a marked effect upon the nature of its formal campaign. We will deal below with the three-week campaign; however it is still necessary to suggest possible explanations for the emergent character of the two lobbies.

It must of course, be recognised that, when the Wales and Scotland Bills were being drafted and subsequently presented to Parliament, the Labour Government did not anticipate that the proposed legislation would be presented to the Welsh and Scottish electorates in the form of a referendum. The Parliamentary opponents of the two Bills forced the referendums in both Wales and Scotland and compounded their

110

opposition by imposing the '40 per cent hurdle' on the electorate. In effect, this entailed that the Labour Party in Wales and those other institutions in the pro-Assembly lobby were impelled to adopt a missionary role, that is they had to 'sell' the Act to the Welsh electorate. During the period following the passage of the Bills through Parliament, from July 1978 to the beginning of the formal referendum campaign on 8th February 1979, the Labour Party in Wales sought to mobilise support into a pro-Assembly lobby. During this seven month period the pro-Assembly lobby did emerge, claiming to represent the undirected aspirations of the Welsh for some tangible form of political autonomy. That is, the lobby sought to make manifest what was perceived by them as a latent demand for a set of political institutions which would give substance to an undirected search for Welsh identity in other than narrowly linguistic and cultural terms. Whilst the Labour Government had proposed the legislation to accommodate this 'we – feeling' it had assumed did exist in Wales – and also to contain the growth of support for Plaid Cymru – it found itself having to test this assumption by engaging in missionary campaign politics.

While there was evidence of ambivalence towards the *Wales Act* among those who were pro-devolutionists – notably within Plaid Cymru – the Government and more particularly, the Labour Party in Wales sought to encourage the emergence of an all-party coalition which would lead the Assembly campaign in Wales. However, given the ambivalence towards the Act, a formula had to be devised whereby the politically disparate elements could coalesce under a pro-Assembly umbrella and give some semblance of unity and organisation to the assumed undirected movement. Indeed, to the extent that the pro-Assembly lobby was advocating a range of political and economic changes for Wales, it could be construed that its several constituent parts represented that species of collective behaviour designated a social movement. Gusfield, for example, has argued that social movements are 'socially shared demands for change in some aspects of the social order' which take the form of 'an explicit, conscious critique of the established *status quo* – either in whole or in part'.[1] On this basis, it might appear credible to designate the pro-Assembly groups as severally constituting a social movement. Given the partial, indeed somewhat tentative, support lent by Plaid Cymru to the proposed Assembly, this would appear to be an even more reasonable ascription. However, 'classical' social movements are normally possessed of an elaborate and consistent ideology which justifies the goal of seeking comprehensive and fundamental social change – a goal that was

111

certainly not shared by the Labour Party in respect of the Assembly proposals.

Despite the social dimension of the Labour Party in Wales and the support (admittedly bridled) of Plaid Cymru, the emergent pro-Assembly campaign contained merely the trappings, not the substance of a social movement. This is evident for a number of reasons. First, the proposals contained in the *Wales Act* were presented to, if not imposed upon, the Welsh electorate – they did not emerge as the result of the articulated demands of a broadly-based, organised and directed social movement. Rather, as it turned out, the Government misperceived the existence of a largely undirected and uncoordinated 'we-feeling' in Wales, a misperception for which the Labour Party in Wales must shoulder a large measure of responsibility. Secondly, the Government was by virtue of intra-Party opposition, constrained to engage in a campaign in order to test its assumption that there existed in Wales at least a latent demand for political devolution. Thus, the organization which emerged on the pro-Assembly side was essentially *ad hoc,* expedient and somewhat tentative* – in essence a pragmatic issue-coalition. Such expediency and pragmatism also characterised the anti-Assembly lobby, composed as it was of equally diverse political elements, so that it too can best be described as a loose-knit issue-coalition, formed exclusively to defeat the *Wales Act.*

Given the ambivalence evident within the pro-Assembly issue-coalition, its component organizations had to achieve a *modus operandi* that would enable them to offer a coherent united front during the course of the formal campaign. They thus sought to assume the mantle of a social movement in as much as the latter typically resort to abstract principles in order to justify their aims – 'liberty' and 'equality' are ideas which tend to be common to major social movements. In this respect it can be argued that the nascent pro-Assembly coalition did bear a superficial resemblance to a social movement since its pre-

---

* Its tentativeness was largely occasioned by two factors: ambivalence about the terms of the Act, notably on the part of Plaid Cymru and the fact that when the pro-Assembly issue-coalition first placed advertisements in the Welsh press canvassing for support, they took the form of full-page spreads containing the names of over 1000 'opinion leaders' and personalities urging a 'Yes' vote. (see Chapter 2). This tactic rebounded however. The opponents of the Assembly proposals characterised the signatures to the appeal as representative of the *crachach,* the Welsh and predominantly Welsh speaking elite. This charge of elitism, whilst a populist tactic, was difficult to refute and introduced a class dimension into the campaign which effectively constrained the pro-Assembly coalition from issuing similar advertisements.

campaign literature stressed that a vote in favour of the *Wales Act* was a vote for the extension of democracy. This claim was common to all the organizations ranged under the pro-Assembly umbrella, for whilst an all party issue-coalition did emerge – the 'Wales for the Assembly Campaign' (WAC) – the Labour Party in Wales, the Wales TUC and the Cooperative Party maintained a separate identity both before and during the formal campaign. (see Chapter 6).

If we now focus our attention on the pre-campaign literature produced by the opposed issue-coalitions we can identify the terms upon which they sought to debate the *Wales Act.*

The pro-Assembly coalition attempted to capture the middle ground and set the terms of the debate by identifying themselves as exponents of the extension of democracy. For example, the major campaign poster produced by the Labour Party, Wales TUC, and Cooperative Party read as follows: 'Say "Yes" for Democracy: If You Want A More Democratic Wales Vote "Yes" on March 1st'. Similarly, WAC issued posters and leaflets which rehearsed the same theme:

> On March 1st the Government is asking you to give the go-ahead to the Welsh Assembly and so bring more democracy to Wales . . . On March 1st you can ensure a stronger democratic Wales within the U.K. and Europe by voting "Yes" for Wales.

On the eve of the formal campaign WAC published its major campaign document, the 'Referendum Manifesto', which prefaced a similar appeal by stressing the coalition's non partisan basis of support:

> The campaign involves those who regard the issue of establishing a Welsh Assembly as of supreme importance, which transcends the cynical conflicts and petty bickering that disfigures much of the political scene . . . Although there are numerous differences within our ranks as to the extent and pace of the policy of devolution, we are united in the recognition that the *Wales Act* represents an historic step in the process of democratic decentralization.[2]

This statement was instructive in that it demonstrated the pro-Assembly coalition's heterogeneity and clearly indicated that the catalyst uniting the politically distinct elements within the coalition was the extension of democracy implicit in the terms of the *Wales Act.* It was this *expressive* appeal to the abstract concept of democracy which provided the central appeal of the coalition's pre-campaign literature and which can be characterized as what Smelser has termed a *value-*

orientation.[3] Smelser sought to distinguish between forms of organised collective behaviour in terms of the beliefs which the organisations represented and drew an analytical distinction between what he, after Parsons and Shils,[4] described as value oriented and norm oriented movements. Whilst we have discounted the idea that the opposed lobbies represented broadly-based social movements, rather describing them as loose-knit issue-coalitions, the distinction between value-oriented and norm-oriented beliefs is a useful heuristic device. The former represents a belief system which seeks to regenerate social values whilst the latter merely involve the attempt to reconstitute, protect, modify or create social norms. Whilst this distinction is analytically useful, it does involve a conceptual problem in as much as one group's value may be another group's norm. However, we have sought to characterise the pro-Assembly issue-coalition as heterogeneous and multi-dimensional: whilst Plaid Cymru was ambivalent about the Act, the Labour Party regarded it as an end in itself. Plaid Cymru, though believing the *Wales Act* did not go far enough, regarded it as providing the means, viz the Assembly, for stimulating the growth of nationalist sentiment culminating in the emergence of a popular separatist movement. The Labour Party, however, regarded the provisions implicit in the Act as capable of satisfying the assumed latent demand for a measure of political devolution by creating an institutional structure that was enabled to modify the normative framework of Welsh society. Thus, the pro-Assembly coalition encompassed both value-oriented and norm-oriented beliefs, those who sought to effect wholesale social change and those who merely sought to achieve limited social change. However, the *ad hoc* pro-Assembly coalition chose to couch its campaign primarily in value-oriented terms *viz* by identifying itself as expressing the aspiration towards achieving a political value – the extension of democracy in Wales.

Thus:

> Fundamentally, our involvement in the campaign arises from our belief in democracy . . . decision-making must be democratised and made more accountable to the Welsh Electorate. This is what the Welsh Assembly is all about.[5]

Recourse to the abstract principle of democracy was probably the only ground upon which the pro-Assembly coalition could present a united and coherent campaign, largely because of the widespread ambivalence and confusion about the terms of the *Wales Act* itself.

114

Whilst this value-orientation represented its primary appeal, the pro-Assembly coalition also sought to indicate the instrumental benefits that would accrue to Wales following the establishment of the Assembly. At this secondary level, the coalition exhibited a *normative orientation* in its pre-campaign literature by identifying the kinds of reforms that the Assembly would be enabled to effect as a means of improving the material conditions of Welsh society. Thus, the Assembly would 'provide better job opportunities'; 'expose waste and inefficiency'; 'improve housing and health care'; 'secure better educational facilities'; and 'improve transport'.

While these projected benefits represented an important element in the pro-Assembly coalition's pre-campaign literature, they were subsidiary to its basic appeal – that the Assembly would provide an effective means of extending participatory democracy within Wales and at the same time reverse the trend towards bureaucratisation: 'The Assembly represents the first halt to the tide of bureaucratic centralization that has swept across the British political society during the last fifty years'.[6]

However, the equally, if not more, diverse issue-coalition represented by the 'No-Assembly Campaign' (NAC), which emerged on the eve of the campaign was to have a crucial effect upon the terms of the debate. Whilst the pro-Assembly coalition sought to couch its campaign largely in terms of an abstract, though positive value-orientation (the extension of democracy) and largely neglected the detailed provisions of the *Wales Act,* its opponent, NAC, marshalled its critique on two fronts. First, as a counter to the positive value-orientation of the pro-Assembly coalition, NAC offered its negative value-orientation – the creation of the Welsh Assembly would lead to the growth of a separatist nationalist movement. In the Welsh context this projection became known as the 'slippery slope' argument. The *Campaign Guide* produced by NAC on the eve of the campaign made this issue wholly explicit: 'The prime reason for our opposition is that the Assembly endangers the unity of the United Kingdom'.[7] The 'Labour No Assembly Campaign' (Labour NAC) reiterated this attitude, arguing that the proposals would 'shatter British unity':

> The proposals are for a system of Home Rule in Wales and Scotland – two new 'semi-states' within one State. That is disunity not diversity; it is fracture not flexibility.[8]

It was this argument that primarily served to unite the heterogeneous elements under the umbrella of NAC and which enabled it to achieve a working relationship with those individuals organised into the Labour NAC. Secondly, and unlike its opponents, the emergent anti-Assembly coalition focused much of its attention upon the detailed provisions of the *Wales Act* itself as a means of identifying populist issues which were considered capable of mobilizing broad if not mass support. To no little extent this entailed that the anti-Assembly coalition engaged in what can best be described as scare-mongering, i.e. they specified, and perhaps magnified, the social, political and economic costs that they argued would befall Wales if the Assembly were to be established. In this respect, the pre-campaign literature manifested a normative orientation in as much as it sought to document the negative instrumental effects that would accrue from the acceptance of the *Wales Act* by the Welsh electorate. For example, the Labour NAC argued that the proposals would:

> impoverish Wales by imposing new costs on the Welsh people; will weaken Wales by jeopardizing the flow of public funds from other parts of the United Kingdom; introduce an extra layer of Government; endanger the strength of Parliamentary representation; and threaten the future of community-based local government.[9]

NAC reiterated these instrumental reasons for rejecting the Act in its *Campaign Guide*. Thus, Welsh MPs 'would be reduced to the status of "parliamentary pygmies"; unable to ask Parliamentary questions about the whole range of matters which will become the province of the Assembly'; the Civil Service in Wales would be required 'to serve two political masters, the Assembly and Government which could lead to ineffective Government'; the Assembly would 'threaten the financial base of local government' and thus 'strike at the heart of its independence . . . if the Assembly held back on the Rate Support Grant local authorities would have to increase rates or cut the services which they provide for the public'. Further, the direct costs of establishing and running the Assembly would, they estimated, amount to some £270m. by the end of the century – 'money which could be better used on improving the infra-structure of Wales'. Additionally, the 'No-Assembly' campaign also cited the indirect costs that would result from the establishment of the Assembly and raised the spectre of its seeking to secure tax-raising powers. Moreover, the Assembly would increase the size of Welsh bureaucracy and create 'a sixth layer of government which would confuse the public on where political responsibility lies on specific issues'.[10]

116

Thus, the terms upon which the anti-Assembly issue-coalition sought to conduct their campaign were essentially two-fold. First, they adopted a negative-value orientation in as much as they argued that the *Wales Act* represented a real threat to the unity of the United Kingdom. Second, they tried to catalogue the negative, normative and instrumental effects that would arise from an acceptance of the Assembly proposals. Their opponents, hampered by the ambivalence (within their own ranks) towards the terms of the Act, sought to capture the centre-ground of the campaign by focussing on the abstract concept of the extension of democracy represented by the proposals. If the pro-Assembly coalition were to achieve its aspirational objective of projecting itself as a reflection of the assumed movement for devolution then it had to adopt a missionary role as a means of successfully conveying its central positive value orientation. The next chapter focuses upon the formal three-week campaign in order to assess the extent to which each issue-coalition succeeded in holding its chosen centre-ground, how far the respective campaigns had to accommodate themselves to the arguments of their opponents, and what effect the divisions of labour within each issue-coalition (i.e. respectively WAC and the Labour Party – Wales TUC campaign and NAC and Labour NAC) had upon their respective campaign strategies.

NOTES

1. J. R. Gusfield, 'The Study of Social Movements', *International Encyclopedia of the Social Sciences.* Vol. 13-14, pp.445-450.

2. *Referendum Manifesto.* Wales for the Assembly Campaign. 7 February 1979.

3. N. M. Smelser, *Theory of Collective Behaviour.* 1962.

4. T. Parsons & E. Shils, *Towards a General Theory of Action.* 1951.

5. *Referendum Manifesto. op. cit.*

6. *ibid.*

7. *Campaign Guide.* No Assembly Campaign, 7 February 1979. p.8.

8. *Declaration.* Labour No Assembly Campaign. n.d.

9. *ibid.*

10. *Campaign Guide. op. cit.* pp.8-16.

CHAPTER 6

The Referendum Campaign: 8 February – 1 March 1979

J. BARRY JONES, R.A. WILFORD

The Devolution referendums in Wales and Scotland were not heralded by a government publication detailing the contending arguments, similar to that which had preceded the Common Market referendum. John Morris, the Welsh Secretary of State, made it clear that sufficient agreement could not be reached within the two issue coalitions: 'we found it impossible to draw up a form of words acceptable to all parties in the campaign. There would be major controversy and nobody would be satisfied'. *(The Guardian,* 8 – 2 – 79). This was true of the pro-Assembly campaign characterised as it was by differing and conflicting aspirations but less accurate in the case of the anti-Assembly coalition. The umbrella 'No Assembly Campaign' was separate both ideologically and organisationally from the 'Labour No Assembly Campaign' marshalled under the aegis of the 'Gang of Six' Labour backbenchers. But far from being a weakness, the organisational distinctiveness of the two campaigns proved to be a tactical and functional advantage.

The Preliminaries

During the first week of the campaign both NAC and Labour NAC published their respective *Campaign Guides* which although united in their opposition to the government's devolution proposals revealed a significant difference in emphasis. Both subscribed to the 'slippery-slope' political metaphor, implying that devolution would inevitably lead to complete separation. The NAC, dominated by the Conservative Party focussed its attack at this level. Thus: 'The prime reasons for our opposition to the Act is that it endangers the unity of the United Kingdom'.[1] Such a view was entirely predictable given the Conservative Party's traditional commitment to Unionism. Labour

NAC placed its emphasis more on the negative instrumental effects which, it argued, would follow from an acceptance of the *Wales Act*. 'The economic cost of devolution is the most important single factor to be taken into account when the Welsh people cast their votes on March 1st'.[2] The strategy of the two anti-devolution campaigns was thus advanced by what was in effect a functional division of labour between the two camps. A realisation that their respective campaigns complemented each other also contributed to the fact that for most of the campaign they were tactically in unison.

In sharp contrast the pro-devolutionists' precipitate decision to argue the instrumental aspects of devolution substantially contributed to the differing emphases of WAC and Labour Party – Wales TUC campaigns. The differences were latent in the campaign leaflets of the two organisations. Whereas the WAC document presumed economic powers for the Welsh Assembly sufficient for it to tackle unemployment, the Labour Party broad-sheet was far more modest. The contrast was heightened when John Morris argued that the Assembly would 'relieve [the Welsh Office] of responsibility for social matters, including health, education and housing and leave [it] free to focus attention on the Welsh economy' (*Western Mail*, 7-2-79), enabling it to become a high powered industrial and economic department. Subsequently, he returned to this theme and rejected the view that the Assembly would control the Welsh economy which 'was indivisible from England' (*South Wales Echo*, 20-2-79). This was quite different from the case presented by WAC that the Assembly would provide the 'Welsh Development Agency with the democratic muscle it needs to plan the Welsh economy and promote economic growth'.[3] The inconsistency of two approaches noted by both the anti-devolutionists and the media, seriously eroded the credibility of the pro-Assembly coalition in the crucial area of the economics of devolution.* Thus from the beginning of the campaign the initiative lay with the anti-devolutionists.

Further, it soon became clear that the centre-ground of the pro-devolutionists, the 'extension of democracy' value-orientation, had been undermined by the 'slippery-slope' argument of their opponents in so far as the threat of separation implicit in an acceptance of the

*Donald Walters, the Welsh Conservative chairman, seized on the point. 'The Yes men were claiming economic powers for the Assembly which it would not possess'. He concluded: 'This is either deliberately mis-leading or already the beginning of pressure to enlarge its powers if it is actually set up.' (*Western Mail*, 21-2-79).

Wales Act had been firmly implanted in the minds of the electorate prior to the nominal start to the campaign on 8 February. This aspect of the anti-devolution campaign tended to be implicit – it provided the context within which the No-Assembly issue-coalition could develop a wide ranging critique of the normative consequences of devolution. During the three weeks of the campaign, the organised opponents of devolution orchestrated their appeal by effectively issuing a series of challenges to their opponents. Thus, not only were they providing the initiatives, they were also to a large extent dictating the style and tempo of the debate and as a result pushing their opponents off-balance and into a defensive posture. Nowhere was this more apparent than in the *Speaker's Notes*[4] prepared by the Labour Party which were as much concerned with explaining the devolution policy to party activists as providing them with propaganda to persuade the general public. Only three pages of the eleven page document dealt with the proposals and their benefits for Wales. The remainder was concerned with describing and explaining the commitment and answering the difficult questions already raised in the Parliamentary context by Labour backbenchers. The pro-devolutionists were in this intrinsically weak position for two reasons. First, there was deep-seated ambivalence about the *Wales Act* itself, characterised by Plaid Cymru's view that it did not go far enough; secondly, this ambivalence to a considerable but predictable degree hampered the performance of the missionary role which the pro-devolutionists were constrained to adopt. The anti-devolutionists in centering their attack on the *Wales Act* itself and particularly upon the projected negative instrumental effects which they argued it would have upon the social, economic and political infrastructure of Wales, were thus able to exploit the intrinsic weaknesses of their opponents.

The Debate on Costs

The anti-devolutionists also employed to good effect the argument that Wales would suffer financially as a result of devolution. The NAC, for example, argued that regional jealousies within the UK would be excited if the Assembly were to be established, and that the current *status quo,* whereby Wales received, on a *per capita* basis, £167 more of public expenditure than the rest of the UK would be upset:

> With the creation of the Scottish and Welsh Assemblies the whole issue would take on a different aspect: the demand for resources would be framed in nationalistic and sectional terms, and the debate over resource allocation, now held in Cabinet, would be

exposed to the rigours of competitive clamouring from all the regions of Britain. Rather than partnership, competition would become the theme.[5]

As the Labour NAC put it, 'Wales would stick out like a sore thumb'. Whereas the proponents of devolution sought to project the view that Wales would benefit financially by devolution their adversaries argued that there was more likely to be a cut in Wales's share of the national cake.

A key issue in this context related to the negotiations over the block grant to Wales and its subsequent allocation. If devolution were to be realised Parliament would control the revenue of the Assembly through its determination of the size of the annual block grant to the Assembly – a Parliament in which Wales would be 'a sitting target' claimed the Labour NAC, for 'representatives of parties broadly unsympathetic to Wales's needs'.[6] Further, the Labour NAC pointed out that apart from the statement in the *Wales Act* that 'the Assembly will have the fullest possible freedom to decide how the money from the block grant should be spent', there was no precise formula or definition of how the Assembly should or would allocate money within Wales. This issue could lead not only to conflict between Wales and the rest of the UK but also to conflict within Wales. Both Labour NAC and NAC sought to argue that the rate support grant – an important element in the block grant – would not only be negotiated through the Assembly, thus undermining the role of local government in Wales, but further that the Assembly would be responsible for allocation of the RSG. As the NAC put it:

> there is no compulsion on the Assembly to consult with local authorities or in fact to distribute one penny of the money from the block grant notionally earmarked for rate support purposes.[7]

Thus the No issue-coalition was effectively raising two separate, although related, fears. First that the role of the local authorities in negotiating the RSG would be diminished by the Assembly; and second, that since there was no compulsion upon it to distribute the RSG the local authorities would have either to increase rates to make up the deficit or alternatively to cut those services they provide to the public. This latter scenario was, of course, straightforward scaremongering; if such an event were to happen it would be tantamount to an act of political suicide by the Assembly men. However, the NAC *Campaign Guide* persisted with this bleak prognosis:

if the Assembly were to hold back completely on RSG, rates in Wales would have to rise . . . if all Government grants were 'consumed' by the Assembly then rates would have to be more than three times higher than their present level to recoup the loss.[8]

In anticipation of this cost argument the WAC manifesto launched at a press conference in Cardiff on the 7th February asserted that positive benefits would flow from devolution. It would mean:

(i) better job opportunities through democratic control of the Welsh Development Agency and the supervision of an economic plan for Wales

(ii) better housing through the Assembly's power to win more cash from central government

(iii) better health services through the Assembly's ability to decide what hospitals are wanted and where

(iv) better education through the Assembly's power to cut class sizes.[9]

However, under pressure from local newsmen, the Chairman was unable to quote figures showing how these improvements would be funded. His arguments were he said, 'based on honest estimates. I cannot prove it, but I believe there is every reason in truth to believe that is the case'. (*South Wales Echo*, 8-2-79). The following day the WAC Manifesto had made such little impact that the group felt obliged to issue a press release accusing the anti-Assembly politicians of resorting to 'misleading statements' and on several occasions 'blatant untruths'. The two most damaging which were contained in a leaflet published by Labour NAC claimed that the Assembly would take powers from local councils and that the number of Welsh MPs would be cut. With some justice the WAC press release described both as false and expressed the hope that while 'public opinion may have swallowed some of the untruths – we believe that during the course of the three-week campaign these falsehoods will be exposed and shot to pieces'.[10]

The evidence suggests that this desire to 'expose the falsehoods' and confront the anti-Assembly coalition distracted the pro-Assembly campaign from its only effective cohesive value, the objective of devolution. Although WAC began by pressing the merits of extending democracy; the need to establish proper control over the nominated bodies throughout Wales; the inadequate consideration given to Welsh affairs at Westminster and the urgent necessity of democratising bureaucracy in Wales and making the Welsh Office more accountable,[11] there were clear indications at an early stage that it was preoccupied with the detailed, operational and instrumental aspects of devolution. Thus devolution was presented as a means to, although never a guarantee of, better education, hospitals and roads as well as more jobs and houses. 'The cost of all this', according to the Labour Party-Wales TUC *Broadsheet* was a 'staggering ½ penny per person per week'. The same cost-benefit analysis was undertaken by WAC which while favourably comparing the costs of the Assembly with the upkeep of military bands and the House of Commons car park, concluded that, on an individual level 'the Assembly will cost less than a packet of cigarettes a year'.[12] The statement had a certain journalistic flair and made some impact on the campaign, but the total effect was to trivialise the devolution case and contribute to focusing the debate on discernible and measurable costs and benefits, precisely the chosen battleground of the No-Assembly campaigners.

However, the Labour NAC document, *Facts to beat Fantasies,* which appeared on 15 February promptly kicked the ball of direct/indirect costs back into the pro-devolutionists court by demanding that they demonstrate that the Assembly would be worth £20 million (the estimate of current prices of establishing and running the Assembly during the first full year). The Labour NAC argued that the figures produced by their opponents amounted to 'cheap and meaningless propaganda':

> when democracy is not going to be advanced and the money spent is desperately needed elsewhere, we can think of much better things to spend £20m on in Wales.[13]

This was a powerful argument. Issuing from the 'rebel' Labour camp it was practically irrefutable by Labour party supporters within the pro-devolution issue-coalition who could only tacitly acquiesce in the view that the Welsh infrastructure would otherwise benefit from the infusion of funds designed to establish and run the Assembly. The Labour NAC and the umbrella NAC pressed this argument to their advantage during the campaign by pointing out that the money could, for example, be better spent on housing, hospitals and the social services.

However the pro-Assembly campaign was not fought totally on the defensive. Mid-way through the campaign two issues were raised which, although part of the mistaken strategy of fighting on the operational role of the Assembly, were tactically successful. On 20

123

February WAC published a report[14] by a Gwent Labour Party councillor which showed that housing expenditure in Wales in 1977-78 was £69 a head compared to £85 a head in England. The report claimed that only an Assembly with the authority of an elected body would have any hope of winning a fair share for Welsh housing. On the same day John Morris at a Cardiff press conference described the advantages of the block grant which was to fund the Welsh Assembly. Whereas, at present it was not possible to transfer money left underspent (it just went back to Treasury coffers), with a Welsh Assembly the unspent cash would remain in Wales. Mr. Morris mused, 'I wonder how many hospitals and schools could be built with money that is underspent by government departments'. (*South Wales Echo*, 21-2-79). Later that day at a meeting of Labour anti-devolutionists, Lord Heycock described these allegations as a 'complete misrepresentation' arguing that it was as a result of Welsh Office instructions, not local government policy that the 'stop gaps in spending' occurred:

> in 1976 the Government told my authority, West Glamorgan County Council, that unless it cut its budget by £1.5m there would be a reduction in its rate support grant. (*South Wales Echo*, 21-9-79).

Despite this rejoinder, both housing and the block grant were potent issues but they were never fully exploited because of political inhibitions. They implied serious flaws in the existing system of Welsh administration, run by the Welsh Office, which was a Labour Party creation, and a Labour Secretary of State. Too vigorous a denunciation of the *status quo* would clearly embarrass the Labour government and John Morris, who was spear-heading the pro-Assembly campaign. It further revealed the problems and difficulties encountered as a result of the pro-devolutionist's inability to sustain a missionary value-oriented campaign.

Within the context of the 'extra-tier' argument, another aspect of the pro-Assembly campaign turned to the advantage of their opponents, concerned the number of Civil Servants who would staff the Assembly. The pro-devolutionists claimed that the creation of the Assembly would entail the recruitment of 1150 civil servants – in effect creating over 1000 jobs which were badly needed in Wales. However, the anti-devolutionists pointed not only to the Government's estimate as providing concrete evidence of an increased bureaucracy but further cited the open-ended clause in the *Wales Act* which stated that 'the Assembly may appoint such officers and servants as it considers appropriate' – thus encouraging scepticism about the numbers of bureaucrats (a term, incidentally, used as a perjorative by both pro and anti-devolutionists) who would actually be employed.

The Spatial and Linguistic Divide

There was little evidence of partisanship on the side of the anti-Assembly issue-coalition during the campaign; although there was perhaps one exception which was expressed by Wyn Roberts, Conservative MP for Conway. In a newspaper interview he stated: 'The Assembly would establish a more complex and cumbersome machinery of government . . . tailor-made for the Labour Party caucus in South Wales' (*Western Mail*, 14-2-79). This statement was not merely overtly partisan but also betokened another theme that was implicit throughout the campaign, viz. the 'North-South' divide. Simply stated, the argument ran thus: the electorate in North Wales were convinced that an Assembly would be dominated by ranting socialists from the valleys and industrial centres of South Wales. A blunt expression of this view came from Mrs. Gwen Mostyn Lewis, Chairman of the 'Clwyd "No" Campaign':

> People in South Wales are very charming, but as a crowd they are loud and coarse. We do not want to be governed by Cardiff. The Assembly will be permanently dominated by Labour. It will be a dictatorship. (*Western Mail*, 23-3-79).

The prevalence of this attitude, particularly in the rural areas of Mid and North Wales (areas which in the subsequent General Election witnessed the emergence of the Conservative Party as the party with majority support), could only serve to strengthen the support for the 'No' campaigners. On the other side of the divide, in South Wales, there were other, perhaps latent, suspicions afoot which served to assist the anti-Assembly campaign, suspicions which centred on the 'language question'. Traditional Labour voters, mostly Anglophone, suspected that the Assembly would come to be dominated by a Welsh speaking caucus, the *crachach*, a linguistic elite. This fear was also traded on by the anti-devolutionists capitalising on a perceived politico-linguistic gulf between North and South Wales. This Janus-like quality of the 'No' campaign revealed an element of sheer opportunism and crude pragmatism which could, perhaps, best be described as the 'politics of fear'. It was a tactic characterised by the pronouncements of Leo Abse, Labour MP for Pontypool, a politician noted for his baroque rhetoric:

The English speaking majority would be condemned to be strangers in their own land. The Nationalists, by insisting on Welsh being spoken in the Assembly, will ensure the creation of a Welsh speaking bureaucratic elite who will attempt to impose a false homogeneity upon Wales. There is no magic superiority of one language over the others though Nazi and German academics practiced that dangerous doctrine. (*South Wales Echo,* 21-2-79).

Anti-devolutionists like Abse were not simply arguing that the Assembly itself would become dominated by a Welsh-speaking elite; they were also seeking to evoke the fear among English-speaking Welshmen that if the proposals were accepted not only would linguisitic criteria increasingly come to be applied in the employment market, but also that bilingual education would become the norm.

The related emotive issues of the Welsh language and the North-South divide were thus being pressed to advantage by the anti-Assembly campaigners. The all-party WAC, besides seeking to assuage any aroused fears and apprehensions, argued that, for example, the political 'clout' of North Wales would be enhanced by a devolved Assembly – whereas under the *status quo* North Wales had 9 seats in the 635 seat House of Commons it would have 20 of the 79 seats in the Assembly. (*Western Mail,* 23-2-79). As a counter to possible linguistic prejudice in the mainly Anglophone areas of Wales the pro-Assembly campaign also sought to capitalize on territorial differences and local loyalties. For example, the Pembrokeshire committee of the campaign argued its cause on the basis that the Assembly would mean the 'abolition of Dyfed' and the 'restoration of the local authority of Pembrokeshire'. In South Glamorgan the local campaign committee produced a pamphlet which claimed that the Assembly would revive Cardiff's dockland and make Cardiff 'a real capital'. However, by this stage the linguistic and spatial divide appeared to have widened. Two opinion polls were published which suggested that the language question was a major factor in accelerating the support for the opponents of the Assembly (See Chapter 10). So prominent was it as an issue that the then Prime Minister, James Callaghan, in his single campaign speech at Swansea, felt constrained to answer what he described as 'wholly unjustified scaremongering' by the anti-Assembly campaign:

They paint a picture of a Welsh Assembly totally dominated by Welsh speakers actively practising discrimination against non-

Welsh speakers. I believe the Assembly by its very composition will put a stop to any such tendency – it is inconceivable that a body representing all parts of Wales should, or could discriminate against the vast majority of the electorate of Wales. (*The Guardian*, 21-2-79).

The fact that Callaghan considered it necessary to refer to the issue was an overt recognition by the proponents of the Assembly that the linguistic and spatial nexus had been raised from its subliminal status to a position of prominence by the activities of those opposed to the proposals.

The Local Government Issue

The Labour Party had decided at a very early stage that the Conservative reform of Welsh local government was so unpopular that to associate devolution with a further reform would substantially increase the chances of victory in the referendum. It was with this consideration that the local government review provision was written into the *Wales Act* and the issue was well to the forefront for the duration of the campaign. However, it was not the unqualified bonus the pro-Assembly coalition had anticipated. On 10th January NALGO's decision to spend £5000 in support of the No campaign was denounced by WAC as 'protection money to sustain the vested interests of high level bureaucrats – [who] fear being brought to democratic account by the Welsh Assembly'.[15] Later in the month the well known hostility of the largely Labour Gwent County Council and the Conservative controlled South Glamorgan Council, was confirmed by their decision to raise money from the rates to fight devolution in their respective counties. The Welsh Secretary of State warned them of the dangers of stretching section 137 of the Local Government Act 1972 to cover expenditure on a political issue[16] (*Western Mail*, 29-1-79) while the WAC weighed in with a furious denunciation.

The Referendum is now becoming a battle of the People versus the Bureaucrats, with the Bureaucrats predictably doing all in their power to cling on to the *status quo*. The 'No' side's funds are now to be swollen with ratepayers' money by certain County Councillors who place their own petty and personal vested interests above the substantial benefits that the people of Wales can receive from the elected Welsh Assembly – So County Councillors in Gwent and South Glamorgan join the high level bureaucrats in NALGO in dipping their hands into other people's pockets to finance their campaign against the government's proposals. While the 'No' campaign depends on public officers and bureaucrats donating other people's money the 'Yes' campaign relies entirely upon voluntary contributions from the people of Wales.[17]

Potentially, local government was an issue which could have been successfully utilized. It was entirely consistent with the framework of general democratic values which was the greatest source of strength for the 'Yes' campaign. Most of the pro-devolutionists from all political parties recognised the advantage inherent in the local government issue and exploited it as strongly as possible. Ted Rowlands, the Foreign Office minister, speaking in Merthyr on the 8th February promised that 'fundamental and vital changes in the structure of local government will follow the establishment of the Welsh Assembly' (*South Wales Echo,* 9-2-79). Later that month, Emlyn Hooson MP (Liberal Montgomery), speaking in Denbigh in North Wales suggested that the Assembly would provide the means of cutting wasteful public expenditure, a point which had been developed the previous day by George Wright when he accused West Glamorgan County Council of 'the politics of extravagance' over their decision to spend £16 million on a new county headquarters. (*South Wales Echo,* 21-2-79). The following day John Morris promised that 'the days of the present system of local government in Wales [would be] numbered if there was a Welsh Assembly on March 1st'. (*South Wales Echo,* 23-2-79). However, in an aside which suggested Mr. Morris was concerned that local government criticism should not go too far, he gave assurance that town hall employees, of whom there are almost 100,000 in Wales, need not fear for their jobs. This was not only a recognition that the local government sector accounted for a substantial number of electors; it also revealed the Labour Party's growing unease that the local government issue might backfire.

The anti-devolutionists had argued from the start that the Assembly would interfere in fields operated by local government. This argument proceeded from the clause in the *Wales Act* which placed a duty on the Assembly to review the structure of local government in Wales with a view to placing recommendations for change before Parliament. Given that the Welsh Labour Party, who would undoubtedly have provided the majority of Assembly members, had devised a policy intended to replace the existing 8 counties and 37 districts with a single tier of 25 unitary authorities, it was to be expected that the existing authorities would be reluctant to endorse such a plan. Furthermore, NAC and

Labour NAC argued that the restructuring of local government in Wales would be costly, disruptive and lead to centralisation. Commenting on the Labour Party's policy for creating 25 unitary authorities Nicholas Edwards predicted:

> The transfer of power away from the people will not be democratic if we see the abolition of the existing councils and their replacement by unitary authorities. These will be too small to deal with some of the larger responsibilities which will be taken from them to Cardiff, while the most local functions, such as housing, would be administered even further from the people than at present. (*Western Mail* 21-2-79).

Both NAC and Labour NAC isolated the argument that an Assembly would entail dimunition of decision-making power by local government and continued to press this issue throughout the campaign. The Labour NAC devoted much of its attention to this question arguing that an Assembly 'would either do the job that local government does now at greater cost or would take powers from local authorities without reducing their costs – it is a very expensive way of doing nothing to help Wales out of its economic, political and cultural problems'.[18] Proof that the anti-Assembly groups had persuaded Welsh local authorities that their interests were in danger, was demonstrated in February when Dyfed County Council reversed its pro-devolution stance by 31 votes to 23 and ten days later the Labour leaders of Mid Glamorgan County Council urged their electors to vote against the devolution proposals on the ground that the Assembly would not bring decision-making closer to the people. Councillor Philip Squire, the Labour leader of the Council stated the argument thus:

> the evidence to-date suggests that the Assembly will create administrative chaos . . . in our view devolution should be about reducing interference by central government bureaucrats and strengthening government at a local level. (*South Wales Echo,* 23-2-79).

In a few short sentences Councillor Squire had effectively summed up the major normative arguments against the Assembly – it would lead to centralisation, bureaucratisation, administrative chaos and would undermine the autonomy of local authorities. Coming from the leader of the largest Labour controlled Welsh local authority in the latter stages of the campaign, the statement carried considerable weight and dealt an effective body-blow to the pro-devolutionist cause. The effect of Mid Glamorgan's decision on the referendum cannot, of course, be accurately gauged. However, the fact that it was made just two days after the then Prime Ministers' speech at Swansea urging the people to 'take power: have the vision and the courage to vote ''yes''' suggests that its timing was strategic, intended to provide something of a counterbalance to Callaghan's avuncular advice. Consequently, just 6 days prior to the referendum almost all the local notables of Welsh public life (and all the counties save Gwynedd) were on record as opposing devolution, which increasingly assumed the guise of a distasteful political medicine being forced on the Welsh people and their local representatives by an insensitive government.

In view of these developments it would appear that local opinion leaders had accepted the view expressed in the Labour NAC document *Facts to beat the Fantasies,* namely:

> Proximity to the people is no guarantee of democracy. Crucial decisions about spending in Welsh localities will be *centralised* in the hands of the Welsh Assembly and its bureaucracy. Far from bringing decisions nearer home, the Welsh Assembly would take those decisions and the money that goes with them further away . . .[19]

The 'Slippery-Slope'

During the final week the Tories in the NAC tended to focus on the separatist theme. Nicholas Edwards, for example, in a speech at Conway on 21st February referred to this issue whilst at the same time indicating the potential conflict likely to arise between an Assembly and Parliament:

> How is the British Government going to control the economy of Britain in the future faced by a rebellious Assembly in Wales that challenges its efforts to act in the interests of the British people? It is appalling that on top of all the other problems that face the Government in managing the economy and controlling inflation, we are to see an Assembly claiming all the authority of nationhood, standing up and challenging its rights to do so. (*Western Mail*, 22-2-79).

Certain of the members of the Labour NAC also reasserted the separatist aspect of the proposals, although in a more strictly ideological sense. That is, the prospect of separatism which they perceived to be implicit in the Assembly proposals was, they argued,

130

against the interests of the working class and would serve to divide the Labour movement in Britain. Neil Kinnock, MP for Bedwellty, was prominent in arguing this, maintaining that the Assembly debate represented a distraction from the main objectives of the British Labour movement since it would tend to excite regional loyalties that would only serve to weaken the unity of the working class.

This analysis, however accurate, was not given pride of place in the Labour 'No' camp. Like their counterparts in the Tory dominated NAC, they tended to devote most of their energies towards a normative critique of the provisions of the *Wales Act*; costs, the trend towards centralisation and bureaucratisation were as much the populist hallmark of the Labour 'No' campaigners as of their Tory allies.

Counter-Attack

The build up of depressing evidence from successive opinion polls had a profound impact on the tone and tactics of the pro-Assembly coalition in the later stages of the campaign. Each poll seemed to invalidate points raised and arguments used by the pro-devolutionists and encouraged experimentation with new issues in an attempt to halt the continuing drift of public opinion. The coalition's reaction took two forms. One was employed by the Prime Minister in his Swansea speech when he called on the Welsh people to have 'the vision and courage' to vote 'Yes'. The following night John Smith MP, Minister with special responsibility for devolution speaking in the Rhondda, expressed a similar hope that 'the people of Wales [would] have the self confidence to vote for the democratic opportunity which the Assembly presents' (*South Wales Echo*, 23-2-79) and speeches made by Tony Benn MP in Cwmbran and Merlyn Rees MP in Pontardawe returned to the same theme on February 27th. (*South Wales Echo*, 28-2-79). The second reaction involved the pro-Assembly campaigners abandoning their positive, idealistic approach and moving on to the offensive against their opponents, both Labour and Conservative.

The 'Gang of Six'

WAC Campaigners turned their attacks on the 'gang of six' group of Labour NAC MPs. Much was made of the fact that four of them had severed their Welsh connections and lived in or around London but they were also condemned for 'playing the Tory game' in using reactionary and anti-socialist arguments to undermine the devolution policy.[20] But the rebels were quite unrepentant. On the same day that

Callaghan was speaking in Swansea they held a meeting in Cardiff where they rehearsed the familiar themes that had emerged during the two-week debate. Fred Evans, the outgoing MP for Caerphilly, in one of his last public speeches before retirement emphasised the point that had it not been for the action of the six there would not have been a referendum to allow the people of Wales to express their view; the Assembly would have been imposed on the Welsh. This was irrefutable and helps explain why the most bitter recriminations against the six Labour rebels came from within the ranks of the Labour Party itself. On 20th February the Labour Party-Wales TUC campaign issued a statement giving details of personal commitments to devolution contained in each of the six MPs October 1974 election addresses (*Western Mail*, 21-2-79). In much of the same vein Michael Foot, with a long history of rebellion against the party establishment, merely indicated that he was in favour of Leo Abse and Neil Kinnock carrying out the election pledges they had made in 1974. (*South Wales Echo*, 27-2-79). But George Wright had no such inhibitions. He accused the six anti-devolution MPs of disloyalty to the Labour Movement and continued:

> By their behaviour they are not only reneging on their own commitments and that of their manifesto but they are dividing the Labour Movement in Wales, indulging in personal attacks on fellow party members, and acting in such a way that they could bring down the Labour government. (*Western Mail*, 21-2-79).

Although his intervention was intended to emphasise the need for solidarity and unity in the Welsh Labour Movement, it merely revealed the degree to which the movement was divided. His comments provoked a flood of letters to the local press most of which were variations on the same theme; that as a full time officer of the TGWU he was ill-fitted to accuse anybody of disloyalty to the Labour Government when his union had breached the government's anti-inflation policy and seriously weakened the party's election chances.

The Anti-Tory Card

The Welsh Labour Party, ill at ease with the missionary role, now turned its attack on the Conservaties, a well tried and successful ploy in Welsh politics. The anti-Tory card had always been regarded as a referendum winner. As early as the WAC Newtown meeting in June 1978 Dai Francis a leading Welsh Communist and a past president of the South Wales miners, had predicted that the referendum campaign would be polarised along the lines of 'Wales against the Tories'.[21] The local government issue was also implicitly anti-Tory, and as early as the 5th February Michael Foot speaking in Brynmawr expressed the view that 'our opponents are mostly just plain Tories — and they are wrong as usual'. (*South Wales Echo*, 6-2-79). But the logic of the argument that a 'No' vote was equivalent to a vote for the Tories meant that such a vote could also endanger a Labour government. George Wright speaking at the press conference launching Labour Party-Wales TUC campaign on the 13th February had been the first to assert that a 'No' vote could bring the government down. (*Western Mail*, 14-2-79). It was a dangerous tactic because it presumed a high loyalty factor on the part of Welsh Labour voters and ran the additional risk that the electorate might use the referendum to vote against the Labour Government at a time of considerable unpopularity. Furthermore, it compromised WACs policy of promoting all-party support for the Government's proposals. For these reasons little was made of the tactic until the last week by which time it was obvious that the 'Yes' campaign was failing to get its message across. In these circumstances it appeared both tactically sound and ideologically congenial to discard the value-oriented approach and make the old fashioned appeal to party loyalty which had served Labour in Wales so well in the past. On the 26th February John Morris insinuated that the referendum could not be separated from the Government fate; 'its future is at stake'. He claimed the Tories were using the referendum to bring down the Government and Merlyn Rees echoed the same theme the following day. (*Western Mail*, 27 and 28-2-79).

In the final days of the campaign two leaflets were rushed out by the Labour Party-Wales TUC campaign in an attempt to stampede the electorate. Although some devolution arguments were re-iterated the basic appeal was unambiguously partisan.
One read:

> Support Labour – defeat the Tories
> Vote Yes on March 1st

The other urged the electorate:

> Vote Yes: to maintain the Labour Government. Don't let the Tories win a victory in Wales. A vote against the Assembly will weaken the Labour Government at Westminster, and could force an early General Election.
> Vote for the Government on March 1st
> Vote Labour.

133

This completed the reversion to electoral adversary politics and almost completely extinguished the positive value-orientation of the early stages of the campaign. Whether this was because the message was basically flawed or because the Labour Party was constitutionally incapable of sustaining a missionary role, is difficult to judge. What is clear, however, is that the Labour Party was never able effectively to counter their opponents' three pronged critique on cost, bureaucratisation and separatism (which was inseparably linked with the language question). Their studious concentration on these three issues was vindicated with the publication of a *Western Mail/HTV* opinion poll on devolution on 24th February, just five days before the referendum, which not only revealed that support for the Assembly had declined during the campaign (from 33 per cent on 1st February to 22 per cent on 24th February) but that the three major issues consistently argued by the anti-devolutionists as reasons for voting 'No' were cited as the most influential arguments by those intending to vote against the proposals: 61 per cent stated that the Assembly would cost too much; 43 per cent stated that it would create another level of bureaucracy; 40 per cent agreed that the Assembly would be used by the Nationalists to break up the United Kingdom.

The Finale

Encouraged by the results of this poll, the opponents of devolution continued to press home their advantage during the final three days of the campaign, restating the arguments of cost, the extra tier of Government and bureaucracy, which were played upon against the backcloth of a separatist threat. Although other issues had emerged during the campaign — the language question, the related North-South divide, the anomalous position of Welsh MPs if an Assembly were created — the 'No' campaigners, by focussing the attack on the *Wales Act* itself, had largely engaged in pragmatic tactics. The 'No' issue-coalition was assisted by unfortunate gaffes committed in the last few days by pro-Assembly campaigners. Lord Crowther-Hunt speaking at the Labour Party Rally in Cardiff considered the Act to be so badly drafted (he described it 'a dog's breakfast') that 'it must amount to sabotage by the drafters in London' (*Western Mail*, 28-2-79) but he still recommended the Welsh electorate to vote in its support. The following night at an eve of poll meeting Denzil Davies, a junior minister at the Treasury, alluded to the Welsh Assembly as an extension of democracy and then, in a burst of unnerving honesty, conceded that 'democracy is not necessarily the most efficient form of

134

Government'. (*Western Mail*, 1-3-79). However these indiscretions came so late in the campaign as to have no tangible effect on the final result.

The initiative had passed from the 'Yes' campaign at an early stage; the decision *not* to persevere with promoting the aspirational objectives of devolution but to adopt a more limited pragmatic and normative approach had trivialised what should have been the resolution of a great constitutional issue and played into the hands of the Assembly's opponents whose Act-centred tactic was directed towards exciting a conservative reaction, in effect an implicit endorsement of the *status quo*. While there had been some evidence of the utilisation of devices from the 'dirty tricks' department — notably Abse's arousal of fear about the language division and his later speech implying that the Assembly would create an opportunity for corrupt practices — by and large the ' No' campaign had aimed their appeal at an instrumental level. Not only were they able to capture the centre-ground of the debate by projecting the 'slippery-slope' scenario, but they consistently forced their opponents onto the defensive about costs, bureaucratisation and centralisation of decision-making within Wales. Their normative critique of the legislative proposals seemed amply justified by the overwhelming 'No' vote recorded at the referendum on 1 March.

The Results
The count did not take place until the day following the referendum. There were in consequence no midnight vigils anxiously awaiting the results, not were such ever likely as the final opinion polls had removed whatever doubts that might have persisted concerning the outcome. The initial count to determine the percentage turnout took place on Friday morning at the district level. Those districts whose boundaries coincided with Parliamentary constituencies produced intriguing indicators of the influence of local MPs. For example, the Plaid Cymru seat in North Wales equivalent to the district of Meirionydd registered a turnout of 70.6 per cent and provided convincing evidence of the influence of an enthusiastic local MP and an efficient party machine in stimulating public interest and involvement. However, this is the most 'Welsh' of the 37 districts in Wales and contrasted sharply with the more anglicised districts along the English border and in the industrial South East; for example in Alyn and Deeside and Wrexham Maelor, two district Councils in North East Wales immediately adjacent to the Merseyside connurbation the turnout was 46 per cent and 45 per cent

respectively while in the industrial South the figure for Blaenau Gwent was 56 per cent and that for Newport 53.2 per cent.

Gwynedd was the first county to declare shortly after 1.00 p.m. and its result realised the worst fears of the 'Yes' campaigners who had hoped and expected the county to register the largest pro-devolution majority. However, 71,157 votes were cast against the proposals as compared with only 37,363 for; a 2:1 majority against. In the course of the afternoon the enormity of the public's rejection of the proposed Assembly became increasingly apparent as the larger, industrial and more Anglicised counties declared their results. Gwent, the heart of the Labour 'No' Assembly campaign and a county in which Neil Kinnock and Leo Abse have their constituencies, produced the final result. A mere 6.7 per cent of the county's electorate voted 'Yes' and the proposition for an Assembly was rejected by an overwhelming 8:1 majority.

The pro-Assembly coalition was clearly taken aback by the scale and magnitude of the defeat. The Labour government's Welsh Secretary of State, John Morris who had fought a committed and sometimes lonely battle, acknowledged 'this is defeat loud and clear', but then in an apparent attempt to distance the government from the disaster added that 'as a government we carried out our obligations'.* His remarks carried the implication that the government's prime obligation had been to the referendum rather than to devolution. However, he conceded that 'the devolution issue would not go away' an opinion re-inforced by the Secretary of the Welsh Labour Party, Emrys Jones when he insisted; 'the policy of the Welsh Assembly remains central to the whole existence and purpose of the Labour Party'. A similar determination not to be deflected by the referendum result was expressed by Gwynfor Evans (Plaid Cymru). 'The circumstances of the referendum' he asserted, were 'so heavily loaded against the 'Yes' vote, it cannot be said that Wales has rejected the idea of a Welsh Assembly'.

The 'No' camp was naturally gleeful but their statements were all characterised by an implied admission that the referendum's overwhelming majority did not represent the final word on the devolution issue. Kinnock, in a carefully worded response to the result, claimed 'we killed this particular form of devolution stone dead'. In a similar admission of political homicide Nicholas Edwards, shortly to

*All the reactions to the results are from the *Western Mail* (3-3-79).

136

become the Conservative Welsh Secretary of State, declared:

We have killed the *Wales Act*. But we will go on thinking about improvements to the machinery of government, particularly in Parliament. We should have a parliamentary select committee for Welsh affairs.

Confirmation that the Conservative Party in Wales was not simply wedded to the *status quo* came from its Chairman, Donald Walters, who expressed the opinion that 'because these Labour proposals have been rejected it does not mean that devolution is a dead duck'.

Press reaction was somewhat muted because of the proximity of the weekend. However, *The Guardian* (3-3-79) considered the referendum results in its Saturday editorial but other than noting that Callaghan's policies for Scotland and Wales had been humbled 'because his own party had repudiated them' the paper completely disregarded the Welsh situation, an eloquent if silent testimony to its belief that Welsh devolution was no longer worthy of note. The *Daily Telegraph* (3-3-79) reached a similar conclusion that Welsh devolution was finished:

The Wales Bill to which (Mr Callaghan) and his colleagues have pinned their prestige and their considerable influence, in his own political fief suffered rejection virtually without precedent in its finality.

However, in a perceptive qualification to its initial judgement that 'devolution is dead', the *Telegraph* continued:

Of course it does not mean that the nationalists have been exorcised — Nationalism in Scotland and Wales is essentially a heart-cry against the excessive power of the modern state. If that power is not sharply and swiftly diminished then the fortunes of SNP and Plaid Cymru will soon revive and next time there may be no stopping short of the full disintegration of the United Kingdom.

Two of the most widely read Welsh papers, the morning *Western Mail* and the evening *South Wales Echo* although both part of the Thomson group had adopted opposite positions on devolution. (See Chapter 7). Where the *Mail* was a commited and enthusiastic devolutionist the *Echo* had been bitterly opposed. However, despite their differing attitudes the considered editorials of the two papers published on Monday the 5th revealed a surprising similarity. The *South Wales Echo* (5-3-79) expressed the view:

137

There is no doubt now, in Wales at least, that the Devolution Bill is dead. But devolution in some other form isn't. For the sake of everybody lets get it right next time, whenever that may be. We don't want power devolved on a nationalist basis. It must go to the regions and they must be identified clearly, with their needs and affinities taken into account. The need now is for some constructive thinking on how best to decentralise government power.

In contrast the *Western Mail* (5-3-79) expressed disappointment at the result. However, in common with its stable mate and all the Welsh party leaders it remained unconvinced that the devolution question had been finally settled:

We have to accept that *this* concept of a Welsh Assembly is now dead and buried. However devolution will not die with this particular *Wales Act*. The rejection of the Assembly does not mean that the *status quo* has been fully endorsed.

Table 6-1

The Results

	VOTES			%	
Counties	*Yes*	*No*	*Turnout*	*Yes*	*No*
Clwyd	31,384	114,119	51.1	11.0	40.1
Gwynedd	37,363	71,157	63.4	21.8	41.6
Dyfed	44,849	114,947	64.6	18.1	46.5
Powys	9,843	43,502	66.0	12.2	53.8
W. Glam	29,663	128,834	57.5	10.8	46.7
Mid Glam	46,747	184,196	58.5	11.8	46.7
S. Glam	21,830	144,186	58.7	7.7	51.0
Gwent	21,309	155,389	55.3	6.7	48.7
Wales	243,048	956,330	58.3	11.8	46.5

YES Vote as Percentage of Electorate

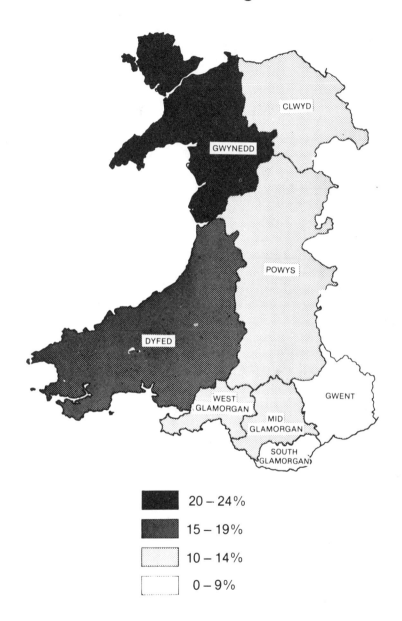

CLWYD

GWYNEDD

POWYS

DYFED

WEST GLAMORGAN

GWENT

MID GLAMORGAN

SOUTH GLAMORGAN

20 – 24%

15 – 19%

10 – 14%

0 – 9%

NOTES

1. *Campaign Guide,* op.cit p.8.
2. *Facts to beat Fantasies,* Labour N.A.C. 15 Feb 1979 p.10.
3. *The Assembly – A Bargain for Wales,* W.A.C. Study Paper January 1979 and *Speakers Notes* (1st edition) W.A.C. January 1979.
4. *Speakers Notes,* Labour Party Wales, January 1979.
5. *Campaign Guide,* op.cit p.9.
6. *Facts to Beat Fantasies,* op.cit p.29.
7. *Campaign Guide,* op.cit p.13.
8. *ibid* p.14.
9. *Referendum Manifesto* op.cit.
10. *Nail the Untruths,* W.A.C. Press Release February 8 1979.
11. *Speakers Notes,* (W.A.C.) op.cit.
12. *The Assembly, a Bargain for Wales,* op.cit.
13. *Facts to Beat Fantasies,* op.cit. p.21.
14. *The Welsh Assembly and Housing: Bringing home the Benefits,* W.A.C. Study Paper February 1979.
15. 'Yes Campaign Slams NALGO', W.A.C. Press Release 10 January 1979.
16. This section permits a local authority to incur expenditure not exceeding the product of a 2p rate which in its opinion is in the interest of its area or of its inhabitants.
17. 'People versus the Bureaucrats', W.A.C. Press Release 26 January 1979.
18. *Facts to Beat Fantasies,* op.cit. p.20.
19. *ibid.* pp.7-8.
20. 'Yes, It's – Leo Abse's Lying Circus', *Y Faner Goch,* 15 February 1979.
21. It was also the theme of his article 'It's Wales Against the Tories' *Miner,* February/March 1979.

Appendix

CAMPAIGN DOCUMENTS OF THE FOUR MAIN ORGANISATIONS

WALES FOR THE ASSEMBLY CAMPAIGN

Vote Yes on March 1st

On March 1 the Government is asking you to give the go-ahead to the Welsh Assembly and so bring more democracy to Wales.

The Assembly plans have now been debated in Parliament since 1974. In July 1978 the Wales Act setting up the Assembly became law and was approved by the Queen.

All that remains is for the Welsh people to give the green light to this major advance in the life of Wales. On March 1 you can ensure a stronger democratic Wales within the United Kingdom and Europe by voting YES for Wales.

Yes for Wales

What the Welsh Assembly will do for you
It will give Wales a stronger voice

The Welsh Assembly has been approved by the Government and Parliament because it will improve the Government of Wales within the United Kingdom. Parliament will still make our laws and Wales will still keep its quota of 36 MPs in Westminster.

The Secretary of State for Wales will remain a full member of the Cabinet. His voice will be strengthened by the Assembly.

The Assembly will make sure that the voice of Wales will be heard loud and clear in the European Community, where more and more vital decisions are taken.

It will control the bureaucrats

An elected Welsh Assembly is necessary now because more and more decisions over our lives are taken by civil servants in the Welsh Office.

More government policies in health, education, roads, agriculture — accounting for £1,000 million of public spending in Wales — have been shifted from London to Cardiff during the last fifteen years. These decisions are supposed to be supervised by the Secretary of State for Wales. But in practice this growing burden is too much for one person. A whole chunk of government lacks adequate supervision. This existing layer of government will be transferred to the Welsh Assembly.

The Assembly will take over appointments to nearly 100 public bodies including the Welsh Development Agency, the Tourist Board and Health Authorities. Hundreds of government orders affecting our every day lives which at present go through the House of Commons without discussion will now be properly decided by the Welsh Assembly.

It will tackle unemployment

Wales urgently needs more jobs. But we can no longer expect new jobs to be diverted from London and the Midlands. They have unemployment problems of their own.

That is why the Government has set up the Welsh Development Agency and the Development Board for Rural Wales.

Wales now needs an Assembly to make these policies work. The Welsh Assembly will —

Give the Welsh Development Agency the muscle it needs to plan economic growth.

Stand up for Wales in the UK and EEC in attracting new jobs.

Create the new atmosphere of confidence Welsh industry needs.

North East England MPs think our Assembly will give Wales a headstart in the fight for jobs. They are right. With jobs so scarce, only a fool would not seize this golden opportunity. Without our own Assembly, Wales would lose influence and jobs to other parts of the UK — particularly Scotland.

After March 1 Scotland will get its own Assembly — and we shall have to help pay for it.

For our children's sake, we cannot afford to let this opportunity slip by.

Our Assembly will have 80 members elected throughout Wales.

They will meet in Cardiff's magnificent Coal Exchange — helping to breathe new life into the traditional heart of our capital city.

The Assembly will be responsible for housing, education, health, roads, water and the environment.

Its first task will be to sort out local government and cut out waste.

The Assembly will bring effective control over the £1,000 million of Welsh Office public spending presently not subject to proper democratic control.

The Arguments answered

MORE GOVERNMENT? *No.* What the Assembly means is democratic control for the first time over the increasing number of nominated bodies that are already running Wales — the Welsh Office and nearly 100 nominated bodies.

A SOP TO THE NATIONALISTS? *No.* The Assembly has been approved by the Royal Commission on the Constitution, Parliament and the Labour Government. It is supported by all political parties in Wales (except the Tories) as well as by Wales TUC, the trades unions, and the main religious denominations.

COST TOO MUCH? *No.* The Assembly will cost less to set up than the new House of Commons underground carpark! The Assembly's running costs are modest and amount to less than ½p per person per week. A bargain for Wales!

A WELSH-SPEAKING ELITE? *Rubbish.* The Assembly will be elected by the people of Wales, and 80 per cent do not speak Welsh.

142

A few of those in Favour

The Government, The Labour Party, Wales TUC, The Liberal Party, Plaid Cymru, National Union of Mineworkers, Transport and General Workers' Union, the Main Religious Denominations, Welsh Farmers Union.

Those Against

Tory Party, Country Landowners, Leo Abse's group of MPs, National Front.

Whose side are YOU on?

Vote YES on March 1st.

LABOUR PARTY WALES TUC CAMPAIGN

WHAT A WELSH ASSEMBLY WOULD MEAN

*Wales is run by a vast bureaucracy. The Welsh Assembly would make it responsible to you the voter. If you vote YES.

*The Welsh Assembly will help you decide policies for our hospitals, roads, schools and homes. If you vote YES.

*Nominated bodies throughout Wales spend £millions of our money. The Welsh Assembly will control them. If you vote YES.

*The Welsh Development Agency was set up to provide more jobs in Wales. The Welsh Assembly will give it more power. If you vote YES.

*Local Government is in a mess as a result of the Tories. The Welsh Assembly will sort it out. If you vote YES.

*The future of the Welsh language will be decided not by a group of extremists but by Assembly members representing ALL the people of Wales. If you vote YES.

Government in Westminster simply cannot devote enough time to Welsh Affairs. A Welsh Assembly will make certain that all the important issues are always debated in the open and decided by your elected representatives.
If you vote, Vote Yes.

143

Vote Yes for Democracy for Wales – for Britain

If you want a more democratic Wales vote **Yes** on March 1st.

The Welsh Assembly – Making our Government Work Better

The Labour party has always been the leader in making the running of our country more democratic.

In 1948 the principle of one man one vote was finally established – by a Labour Government. But much remains to be done.

Much remains to be done!

The undemocratic House of Lords needs to be abolished.

The undemocratic appointment of public officials and magistrates needs to be reformed.

We must establish industrial democracy so that workers have a greater say in the future of their industry.

The bureaucratic mess the Tories made of local Government needs to be put right.

It is most important that we democratise the regional level of bureaucracy that has developed in Britain. In Wales this means setting up a Welsh Assembly. Government in Westminster at the moment is simply overworked. How often have you heard of late night sittings at the House of Commons? What this means is that insufficient time is often spent on Welsh affairs that are of critical importance.

A Welsh Assembly will make certain that all these critical issues are always thoroughly debated.

A Welsh Assembly will put right the mess the Tories made of Local Government.

The Welsh Assembly will make sure that nominated bodies such as the Welsh Water Authority, Health Authorities, Arts Council and Tourist Board will be responsible to the people of Wales and members appointed by our representatives in the Welsh Assembly.

The cost of all this

The running cost of the Welsh Assembly will be a staggering ½ p per person PER WEEK. An amazingly low price to pay for safeguarding and modernising our democracy.

The Welsh Assembly makes a great deal of sense to the Labour and

Trade Union Movement.

If this makes sense to you Vote Yes for Wales on March 1st.

Anti-Assembly Myths

A great deal of nonsense has already been talked about the Welsh Assembly – predictably most of this nonsense has come from the Tory Party. These are some of the myths you may have heard.

Myth 1 A Welsh Assembly will be just another layer of bureaucratic Government. False!

The bureaucracy already exists. The Assembly will control it. There are in Wales some 70 nominated bodies with over 2,500 members and responsible for spending almost £500 million per year. In addition Welsh Office civil servants deal with almost £1,000 million of public expenditure a year. A staggering total of £540 per every man, woman and child. This is the bureaucracy that needs to be controlled and made fully responsible to the people of Wales.

Myth 2 The Welsh Assembly is a sop to the Nationalists. False!

The Labour Party started on the policy of devolution in 1959 when it decided to establish the Welsh Office. This it did immediately after it became the Government in 1974. The policy to create an elected Welsh Council was approved in May 1966 before the Nationalists made any serious impact.

Myth 3 Welsh-speaking Welshmen will get the best jobs. False!

80% of the population of Wales do not speak Welsh. It is their voice that will return 80% of Assembly Members. So the interests of both Welsh and English-speaking Welshmen will always be safely protected.

Myth 4 A Welsh Assembly will take over the powers of Local Government. False!

There is a great deal wrong with Local Government in Wales. The Tories were responsible for this and it needs to be put right. The Welsh Assembly will play a vital part in sorting out how that should be done. But Local Government responsibilities will remain with Local Government.

Vote YES for democracy for Wales for Britain.

145

ALL PARTY NO ASSEMBLY CAMPAIGN

Keep Wales united with Britain

VOTE
NO
TO THE WELSH ASSEMBLY

Polling Day Thursday 1st March
Why you should VOTE NO

1. By voting 'NO' you will be stopping the start of the slide down the slippery slope to the break-up of the United Kingdom ... Your Country!

2. Full Independence is Plaid Cymru's main aim ... Your Country!

3. At present Government expenditure is over £167 per head higher in Wales than in England – do you want to lose this advantage ... Your Money!

4. The Assembly would cost £6½ million to set up ... Your Money!

5. The Assembly would cost £12½ million, and possibly more, to run ... Your Money!

6. The Assemblymen would be able to fix their own salaries, pensions and gratuities ... Your Money!

7. The Assemblymen would be able to appoint as many officers as they like ... Your Money!

8. The Assemblymen would need at least another 1,150 Civil Servants ... Your Money!

9. The Assembly would mean yet another tier of Government – more money ... Your Money!

10. Welsh M.P.s will no longer have the power to decide on matters of education, housing and health ... Your Interests!

Keep Britain united by voting 'NO' on Thursday 1st March.

146

LABOUR NO ASSEMBLY CAMPAIGN
DECLARATION

If they are ever put into effect the Assembly proposals –

will divide Wales from the remainder of the United Kingdom in many crucial areas of finance, government and political representation.

will impoverish Wales by imposing new costs on the Welsh people

will weaken Wales by jeopardising the flow of public funds from other parts of the United Kingdom

will introduce an extra level of government without effectively adding to democratic control of decisions

will endanger the strength of Parliamentary representation in the House of Commons

will threaten the future of community-based local government at district and county level

There has been no widespread demand from the people of Wales for constitutional changes of the kind that would result from these proposals. The only beneficiaries would be Nationalists, who seek the break up of the United Kingdom and who see an opportunity of achieving that end through what they have called 'the first step' of Devolution and from the platform of the Cardiff Assembly.

Wales has a strong and urgent need for more jobs, increased health provision, improved education and social services, and better housing and leisure facilities. But these Assembly proposals will not help us to meet these needs in any way. On the contrary, the very act of setting up the Assembly risks the money, the power and the support which we rightfully claim from central Government and our fellow citizens in the United Kingdom.

Because we recognise the costs and risks which would result form the Assembly proposals, and feel that the people of Wales cannot bear them, we shall be working for the NO vote in the Referendum on March 1st.

We urge people throughout Wales who value full membership of the United Kingdom and want to safeguard the future of themselves and their children against the financial, political, social and cultural burdens of the Assembly proposals, to join with us in using the opportunity of the Referendum to defeat those plans by VOTING NO and by JOINING THE LABOUR NO ASSEMBLY CAMPAIGN.

147

LABOUR PARTY ■ WALES TUC ■ CO-OP PARTY

THE WELSH ASSEMBLY
-MAKING OUR GOVERNMENT WORK BETTER

Labour party has always been the leader in making the running of our country more democratic.

'48 the principle of one man one vote was finally established - by a Labour Government. But much remains to be done.

Much remains to be done!

The undemocratic House of Lords needs to be abolished.

■The undemocratic appointment of public officials and magistrates needs to be reformed.

■We must establish industrial democracy so that workers have a greater say in the future of their industry.

■The bureaucratic mess the Tories made of local Government needs to be put right.

It is most important that we democratise the regional level of bureaucracy that has developed in Britain. In Wales this means setting up a Welsh Assembly. Government in Westminster at the moment is simply overworked. How often have you heard of late night sittings at the House of Commons? What this means is that insufficient time is often spent on Welsh affairs that are of critical importance.

A Welsh Assembly will make certain that all these critical issues are always thoroughly debated.

A Welsh Assembly will put right the mess the Tories made of Local Government.

The Welsh Assembly will make sure that nominated bodies such as the Welsh Water Authority, Health Authorities, Arts Council and Tourist Board will be responsible to the people of Wales and members appointed by our representatives in the Welsh Assembly.

ANTI-ASSEMBLY MYTHS

A great deal of nonsense has already been talked about the Welsh Assembly - predictably most of this nonsense has come from the Tory Party. These are some of the myths you may have heard.

Myth 1 A Welsh Assembly will be just another layer of bureaucratic Government. **False!**

The bureaucracy already exists. The Assembly will control it. There are in Wales some 70 nominated bodies with over 2,500 members and responsible for spending about £500 million per year. In addition Welsh Office civil servants deal with almost £1,000 million of public expenditure a year. A staggering total of £540 per every man, woman and child. Thus a bureaucracy that needs to be controlled and made fully responsible to the people.

Myth 2 The Welsh Assembly is a sop to the Nationalists. **False!**

The Labour Party started on the policy of devolution in 1959 when it decided to establish the Welsh Office. Thus it did immediately after it became the Government in 1964. The policy to create an elected Welsh Council was approved in May 1966 before the Nationalists made any serious impact.

Myth 3 English-speaking Welshmen will get the best jobs. **False!**

% of the population of Wales do not speak Welsh. It is their case that will return 80% of Assembly Members. So the interests of both Welsh and English-speaking Welshmen will be safely protected.

Myth 4 A Welsh Assembly will take over the powers of Local Government. **False!**

A great deal wrong with Local Government in Wales and were responsible for that and it needs to be put right. The Welsh Assembly will play a vital part in sorting out what should be done. But Local Government will remain with Local Government!

The cost of all this

The running cost of the Welsh Assembly will be a staggering $\frac{1}{2}$p per person PER WEEK. An amazingly low price to pay for safeguarding and modernising our democracy.

The Welsh Assembly makes a great deal of sense to the Labour and Trade Union Movement.

If this makes sense to you Vote Yes for Wales on March 1st.

VOTE YES
FOR DEMOCRACY FOR WALES FOR BRITAIN

WHICH SIDE ARE YOU ON?

FOR
A WELSH ASSEMBLY

LABOUR
The Labour Government
The Labour Party
The Trades Union Congress
The Wales TUC
The Cooperative Party

AGAINST
A WELSH ASSEMBLY

TORY
The Conservative Party
The Confederation of British Industry
The Country Landowners' Association
The Tory Controlled Association of County Councils
The National Front

SUPPORT LABOUR-DEFEAT THE TORIES
VOTE YES MARCH 1st

THE WELSH LIBERAL PARTY
says YES on March 1st

EMLYN HOOSON M.P.

GERAINT HOWELLS M.P.

DAVID STEEL M.P.

DAVID LLOYD GEORGE

Nat...
More...
NOT TRUE...
70 nomin...
now runn...
More cent... ...of power?
NOT TRUE. All the Assembly's powers will be decentralised from London

A Welsh speaking elite?
NONSENSE. The Assembly will be elected by the people of Wales. 80 per cent of whom don't speak Welsh. How can the majority be told what to do by a 20 per cent minority?

Separation?
RUBBISH. The powers of the Welsh Assembly are set out clearly in the Wales Act and the Assembly can't go further. Parliament decides our laws and Wales keeps its full quota of M.P.s in Westminster and its Secretary of State in the Cabinet

HELP THE "YES" CAMPAIGN
Just drop a line /SEND A DONATION to:
Raymond Edwards, 90 Neville St., Cardiff

| YES | X |
| NO | |

Je it cynulliad ar Fawrth 1af gyda'r...

THEY ALL SAY YES!

VOTE YES ON ST. DAVID'S DAY

BACK WALES ON ST. DAVID'S DAY
●VOTE YES because the Assembly will be good for Wales
●VOTE YES because the Assembly can tackle unemployment
●VOTE YES because with the Assembly, Wales will gain a greater share of resources within the U.K. to tackle our social problems
It will mean more bargaining power for Wales where it counts - in London and Brussels. That means more jobs, better health and education services
The cost? It's spread over the whole U.K. and is less than $\frac{1}{2}$p a week'

In the Referendum, if you stay at home and do not cast your vote, you will be treated as a "NO" vote. So please come out and vote "YES" for Wales on St. David's Day.

VOTE YES ON ST. DAVID'S DAY

Former P.M. EDWARD HEATH	World Opera Star SIR GERAINT EVANS		TV Liver Bird NERYS HUGHES	Rugby Star GARETH EDWARDS
Liberal Leader DAVID STEEL	Welsh Secretary JOHN MORRIS		Celebrated Comedian HARRY SECOMBE	Ex-international BARRY JOHN
Authoress ELAINE MORGAN	Prime Minister JAMES CALLAGHAN		Singing star TOM JONES	Welsh Ballad Star MAX BOYCE

Yes for Wales March 1st

VOTE YES
SAVE MONEY
■ THE ASSEMBLY WILL SAVE MILLIONS OF POUNDS A YEAR - AND ITS RUNNING COST IS A TINY
$\frac{1}{2}$p
per person per week

With the elected Welsh Assembly we will reform the councils. Instead of local government. This will cut out waste and duplication. Last year Wales lost £35 million that could have been spent on our housing, our health and our roads. Wales gets a better deal from central government. Although we've got 100,000 until homes in Wales we received per head less than the UK average for housing last year.

Published by the Wales for the Assembly campaign, 90 Neville St., Cardiff

YES [X] For Cardiff

OUR DUE
The Assembly will cost less than
10p per person per week to run.

Cardiff has made a massive contribution to
the economy of the U.K. and the
Assembly is no more than a just reward —
it will greatly revitalise the heart
of Cardiff's depressed dockland.

OUR SAY
The electors will choose the Assembly members,
so the Assembly will be answerable to the people.

OUR NEEDS
Matters now rejected by the Welsh Office or
ignored by Westminster would be freely
discussed in the Assembly. Problems of special
or local interest, such as Leasehold, would be
properly debated and Westminster advised of
any reforms felt necessary.

ON MARCH 1st
VOTE Yes for Wales

LABOUR PARTY ▪ WALES TUC ▪ CO-OP PARTY

WHAT A WELSH ASSEMBLY WOULD MEAN

▪ Wales is run by a vast bureaucracy. The Welsh Assembly would make it responsible to you the voter. **If you vote YES**

▪ The Welsh Assembly will help you decide policies for our hospitals, roads, schools and homes. **If you vote YES**

▪ Nominated bodies throughout Wales spend £ millions of our money. The Welsh Assembly will control them. **If you vote YES**

▪ The Welsh Development Agency was set up to provide more jobs in Wales. The Welsh Assembly will give it more power. **If you vote YES**

▪ Local Government is in a mess as a result of the Tories. The Welsh Assembly will sort it out. **If you vote YES**

▪ The future of the Welsh language will be decided not by a group of extremists but by Assembly members representing all the people of Wales. **If you vote YES**

Government in Westminster simply cannot devote enough time to Welsh affairs. A Welsh Assembly will make certain that all the important issues are always debated in the open and decided by your elected representatives. If you vote **YES**

VOTE YES FOR DEMOCRACY FOR WALES FOR BRITAIN

you want a more democratic Wales Vote Yes on March 1st.

VOTE Yes ON March 1st

On March 1 the Government is asking you to give the go-ahead to the Welsh Assembly and so bring more democracy to Wales.

The Assembly plans have now been debated in Parliament since 1974. In July 1978 the WALES ACT setting up the Assembly became law and was approved by the Queen.

All that remains is for the Welsh people to give the green light to this major advance in the life of Wales. On March 1 you can ensure a stronger democratic Wales within the United Kingdom and Europe by voting YES for Wales.

Yes for Wales

IF HE'S AGAINST IT, IT MUST BE GOOD FOR US!

SUPPORT LABOUR VOTE YES ON MARCH 1st

PUBLISHED BY THE LABOUR PARTY WALES TUC 1 CATHEDRAL ROAD CARDIFF

Keep Wales united with Britain

VOTE

NO

TO THE
WELSH ASSEMBLY
TODAY

Vote	YES YDWYF	
	NO NAC YDWYF	X

Vote ... *like this.*

Published for the No Assembly Campaign by A. J. Mackay, 9 Cowbridge Road East, Cardiff

DON'T JUST STAY HOME AND SAY 'NO' — GET OUT AND VOTE "NO" TODAY!

"NO TO THE ASSEMBLY CAMPAIGN" HON. SEC. 91 UZMASTON ROAD, HAVERFORDWEST

7. I'r Cenedlaetholwyr, cam cyntaf yw'r Cynulliad tuag at annibyniaeth a chwalu'r Deyrnas Unedig—cam cyntaf tuag at arwahanrwydd diffrwyth, marweidd-dra diwydiannol a dirywiad economaidd. Gwthiwyd y Cynulliad arnom gan y cenedlaetholwyr a'u cyfeillion. Gallwch roi NA pendant iddyn nhw yn y bwth pleidleisio ar Fawrth 1af.

Bu gan Ogledd Iwerddon Gynulliad ers 1921. A ydych am weld HYNNY'N digwydd yma?

PWYSIG YW PLEIDLEISIO NA AR DDYDD GWYL DEWI.

Rhowch NA i Genedlaetholdeb.

Rhowch NA i'r Cynulliad.

Published by Morfina Chalmers, Brynawelon, Beulah, Newcastle Emlyn and printed by E. L. Jones & Son, Cardigan

Saith rheswm dros ddweud NA i'r Cynulliad Cymreig

VOTE NO TO THE ASSEMBLY

151

CHAPTER 7

The Referendum and the English Language Press

JOHN OSMOND

It is difficult to discuss the English language Press in Wales and its role in the referendum campaign because in an important sense Wales does not possess such a Press. Unlike Scotland – and this is a crucial contrast when considering the devolution argument in both countries – Wales does not have an integrated newspaper network. The closest title to a national newspaper of Wales – indeed it describes itself as such – is the *Western Mail,* but this does not have a significant circulation north of a line drawn eastwards from Aberystwyth. In North Wales the Welsh edition of the *Liverpool Daily Post* predominates. The largest circulation daily paper within Wales is the *South Wales Echo* but its sale is largely restricted to Cardiff and the valleys of South-East Wales. The other three Welsh-based English language daily news-papers are the *South Wales Evening Post* based in Swansea, the *South Wales Argus* based in Newport and the *Evening Leader* at Wrexham. By their nature these three papers are local and in many senses perform the role of a traditional weekly paper, except that they appear daily.

There is a highly developed network of some 65 English language weekly newspapers in Wales, and these can be described as the only truly indigenous Welsh Press. But their value in any discussion of the role of the Press during the referendum is limited by two factors: they are, by their very nature, exclusively local, and generally pay only small attention to political matters. Their main function, so far as the referendum campaign went, was to act as a vehicle for readers' letters on the issue and for a barrage of advertisements by the pro- and anti-Assembly camps.

This leaves, in terms of their frequency of appearance and sales at least, the most influential group of newspapers in Wales: the London Press. Their combined circulation in Wales of slightly more than

700,000 compares with the combined circulation of Welsh-based daily newspapers of 421,000 (See Table 7-1).

Table 7-1

Circulation of Daily Newspapers Appearing in Wales (Estimates)[1]

WELSH PAPERS

Morning

Western Mail (Cardiff)	94,000
Daily Post (Welsh Edition: Liverpool)	50,000

Evening

South Wales Argus (Newport)	53,000
South Wales Evening Post (Swansea)	69,000
South Wales Echo (Cardiff)	120,000
Wrexham Leader (Mon to Fri)	35,000
	421,000

LONDON PAPERS

The Sun	239,000
Daily Mirror	230,000
Daily Express	92,000
Daily Mail	73,000
The Guardian Daily Telegraph Financial Times The Times* Morning Star	70,000
	704,000

*The Times was not printed during the referendum campaign.

An examination of these figures reveals the clear dominance of the *Sun* and the *Daily Mirror*. Yet their coverage of Welsh politics is at the best of times peripheral and this proved to be the case during the referendum campaign. The penetration of English-based newspapers into Wales and their general lack of attention to Welsh issues (with the

154

honourable exceptions of *The Times, Financial Times,* and *Guardian* whose combined circulation in Wales is in any event negligible) is crucial to an understanding of Welsh political attitudes. It means that the mass of the Welsh people — certainly those classed in C and D bracket of the newspaper audience — are by and large left in ignorance of Welsh political issues and the arguments that surround them. With a complex question such as devolution, and indeed with any question that implies change, ignorance militates in favour of the status quo.

In as much as the mass of the people received comprehensive information about the issues entailed in the devolution referendum it was through television (see chapter 9). But television in Wales is strongly influenced by newspapers; the way that television deals with the news, issues and personalities is more often than not a consequence of the way those same items have been dealt with by newspapers. So in an important sense the influence of newspapers is both direct and indirect *via* television. In Wales there is no doubt that the *Western Mail* plays a leading role in this respect. The *Western Mail,* in fact, was the only newspaper in Wales that systematically covered, and indeed, promoted the devolution debate in the years that led up to the referendum. To be fair it was the only newspaper in Wales either equipped or predisposed to do so. For the *Western Mail,* the devolution debate that culminated in the 1979 referendum began in the late 1950s with the campaign for a Welsh Office and Secretary of State for Wales. Once that was established, in 1964, a commitment by the newspaper to some form of democratic extension to the decentralised administration was a natural development.

The paper was also much influenced by the political events of the 1960s in Wales, specifically by the emergence of Plaid Cymru as a political force. It was in 1968 that an important change occurred in the *Western Mail's* news coverage. Until that time the *Western Mail* was a highly 'editionalised' newspaper with an extensive network of district reporters and freelance contacts feeding into as many as sixteen separate editions of the paper per issue. Although this method of organisation ensured a comprehensive local coverage for every part of the paper's circulation area, it prevented any development of an all-Wales news coverage and an all-Wales editorial outlook. In 1968 it was decided to carry at least one page of news that would be used in all editions of the paper. This page, known as the 'Main Welsh page' rapidly became the central focus of the paper with stories having an all-Wales interest and relevance gravitating towards it. To begin with, such·stories were not readily found on a daily basis and so had to be sought after. In a very real sense news for this new page had to be created. As part of the development the *Western Mail* also created a new senior journalistic post with the uneasy title of 'Welsh Affairs Correspondent'. The brief that went with this position was wide: the job entailed seeking out political, local government and economic news which could be said to have an all-Wales relevance. In particular the job was to entail covering any institutions which, however distant from politics and economics, were concerned with Wales as a whole; but events soon overtook the newspaper's initiative in this area and shaped the role in a way that was only dimly perceived at the start.

The establishment of the Royal Commission on the Constitution in 1969 meant that the Welsh Affairs correspondent was soon busily engaged in charting its progress. The Commission's report in late 1973, the electoral successes of the Welsh and Scottish Nationalists in the 1974 general elections and the subsequent government White Papers and Devolution Bills ensured that the correspondent's job rapidly developed into a straightforward political one, so much so that perhaps a more accurate title would have been 'Devolution' rather than 'Welsh Affairs' correspondent[2].

This background to the referendum debate meant that the *Western Mail* had an important advantage over all other newspapers in awareness, knowledge and, more fundamentally, interest in devolution. But though an advantage overall, the position also entailed dangers for the newspaper and a great deal of heart-searching. Throughout this period the paper continually had to justify to itself the coverage it devoted to the issue. Devolution, in the eyes of probably a large majority in Wales, is synonymous with nationalism in one form or another. Yet the *Western Mail* is far from nationalist editorially. Rather, its allegiance is at the other end of the political spectrum in the Conservative camp. Thus, it found itself beset by contradictions throughout the course of the devolution debate. From the start its editorial commitment to devolution was intellectual rather than emotional. In contrast, for example to *The Scotsman's* attitude to Scottish devolution and, for that matter, to nationalism itself, the editorial line of the *Western Mail* was always equivocal. Most saliently this shakiness of conviction was demonstrated during the debates over whether a referendum should be held. In gut terms the referendum debate was about the devolution issue; significantly in early 1978 the *Western Mail* succumbed to pressure and advocated the referendum road.

156

The Role of the Press in the Debate

By 1978 cut and thrust politics had overtaken the academic 'devolution debate' and had transformed it into the 'referendum debate'. The two proved to be very different. The terms of the former were dictated by pro-devolutionists; the terms of the latter by the anti-devolutionists. The Welsh Press, including the *Western Mail*, followed the change in terminology with equanimity. In the case of the *Western Mail* there was almost an air of relief that it was now able to put two sides and so demonstrate 'fairness and impartiality'.

The point is well illustrated by the way the referendum campaign opened in early January 1979. The first weekend after Christmas, the Wales for the Assembly Campaign organised a rally at which the guest speaker was the Foreign Secretary, Dr David Owen. He made a remarkable speech, almost nationalist in tone, and relating Welsh consciousness to the pressure for decentralisation in Britain. But with superb timing, the Welsh anti-Assembly forces engineered the release of the damning, and apparently objective, academic report on Welsh devolution by the National Federation of Self-Employed which stole the headlines completely. It captured the front pages of the *Western Mail* and *South Wales Echo* on the Monday morning and relegated the Foreign Secretary's speech to an inside story. The *Echo* headlined the report across the top of its front page: 'If you haven't decided on the Wales Bill — see page 4'; and inside it carried the headlines 'Devolution — "A Disaster for Wales"'. The *Western Mail's* front page story stated, as though it were fact, the report's conclusion that a Welsh Assembly would cause: large-scale unemployment; increasing number of bankruptcies; confusion in decision-making; delays in legislation and discouragement to investment. In mitigation it should be noted that the *Western Mail's* uncritical treatment of this report was partly due to a journalists' strike amongst the provincial Press that was underway at the time. As a result there was no attempt to glean any reaction, critical or otherwise, to the report on the day of its publication. Intense critical reaction came in following days, but by that time it was too late: the report had achieved the purpose intended.

The treatment of these two stories set the tone for the whole coverage of the referendum campaign. The initiative was in the hands of the anti-Assembly forces, partly because the Press generally favoured them but equally importantly, because their message was simple, short and eye-catching. A threat of disaster is always more newsworthy than a vague promise of reform and the lurid threat of disaster that characterised many of the anti-Assembly campaign's pronouncements also went some way in compensating for the general lack of personality clashes in the campaign. Put bluntly, the newspapers were off-balance in covering the referendum. They were accustomed to a diet of elections where people, as opposed to issues, were at the centre of the political struggle. By contrast, at the centre of the referendum was a rather anonymous Assembly.

This last consideration helps explain the general lack of coverage that the referendum campaign attracted from most of the newspapers, right up to polling day itself. Part of the explanation, too, was that the electorate, and consequently the newspapers, had a lot of other things on their mind. The appalling conditions of January and February 1979 successfully competed for coverage and picture space. Hard on the heels of the timeless topicality of weather was another eminently newsworthy item — Britain threatened to become strike-bound. The haulage drivers' dispute and industrial action by the public service workers generated such news items as: black-bagged rubbish piling up in snow-filled streets; hospitals threatened by closure; and graves being left undug. In one other important respect the atmosphere of the moment influenced the debate — the disputes, stoppages, perhaps even the weather contributed to the government's decline in popularity. All this the newspapers unconsciously but faithfully absorbed and reflected both in their news judgement and presentation.

The *Liverpool Daily Post* woke up to the campaign somewhat abruptly in January. It failed to carry the David Owen story on the Monday two days after his speech at Llandrindod. Instead, following protests from the pro-devolution camp, the story — which was re-written from a hand-out — found its way into the paper's news columns on the Tuesday. The speech had, in fact, been previewed by the *Post* in a story a few days before it was made, illustrating perhaps the problems of a paper with such entirely separate editions. Gradually through January a handful of stories about speeches made 'For' and 'Against' the Assembly crept into the paper. On 22 January its commentator, Charles Quant, was even moved to remark that the campaigns on both sides were 'hotting up'. But he queried: 'Do Mr and Mrs Jones of Wales really rate the Wales (for or against the) Assembly as an issue to bear comparison with strikes, pickets and pay?' A little later in the campaign, on 7 February, he followed this up with the view that 'The over-whelming majority are still the don't knows, bewildered, bamboozled, battered by the politicians and propagandists'.

They certainly were not being battered in the columns of the *Daily Post*. Until well into February the main exposure devolution received

158

was in the letters page where a number of issues were raised and hotly argued. For example, on 23 January Tom Hooson, at that time prospective Conservative candidate for Brecon and Radnor, declaimed:

> The Big Welsh Lie is that a Cardiff talking shop will bring democracy closer to us. It will do the opposite: power will move from local people to an Assembly of strangers . . . If you want to drive on safe winter roads in Brecon and Radnor you should vote No in the referendum.

The most crucial day in the referendum campaign so far as coverage by the Welsh English-language Press was concerned was 10 February. Until then, although the coverage was patchy in many of the papers, they all managed to generate an impression that a real fight was underway: that there were two sides of roughly equal weight measuring up to one another. Until that date for instance, the Wales for the Assembly campaign (WAC) had secured extensive Press coverage with its series of Referendum Study papers examining issues of cost, bureaucracy, the 'separatist scare' and the economic benefits an Assembly might be expected to bring. The *Swansea Evening Post* on 4 February prominently displayed a story based on a WAC study paper with the headline 'Assembly to Strengthen UK Unity — Elystan Morgan'. But on 10 February all the English language daily papers led on their front pages with the first BBC Wales opinion poll predicting 45.8 per cent 'Against' the Assembly, 33 per cent 'For', with 21.2 per cent 'Don't Knows'. The *Liverpool Daily Post* headline exclaimed: 'Poll Shock on Assembly' — the first time that year that the devolution issue had appeared as its leading headline story. 'A shock report released last night revealed support for the Assembly has surprisingly dwindled' opened the story beneath. The impact of opinion polls on political behaviour is a well-worn question. But in the devolution referendum there is no doubt that they played a crucial role, not least because of the prominence given them by the Press. So far as the newspapers were concerned, the publication of the 10 February poll marked the beginning of the campaign. It was at this stage that the heavy feature side of the papers was mobilised into action. For some weeks the *Liverpool Daily Post* had been labelling stories 'The Great Welsh Debate', and from Monday 12 February through 19 February it carried a series of half page features written by Welsh politicians presenting both sides of the argument. The *Post's* choice of protagonists on the 'Anti' side were Wyn Roberts (Conservative MP

Conwy), Sir Anthony Meyer (Conservative MP West Flint) and Neil Kinnock (Labour MP Bedwellty): on the 'Pro' side were Tom Ellis (Labour MP Wrexham), Emlyn Hooson (then Liberal MP for Montgomery) and Dafydd Williams (General Secretary of Plaid Cymru). These articles were interesting mainly because of the personal, if sometimes tangential views of the authors. For example, Hooson concluded: 'If we are going to have a United States of Europe, then we must have Welsh Devolution, for the former will only be tolerable if we also have the latter'; while Sir Anthony Meyer provided a hostage to fortune he doubtless would prefer to forget:

> I do not believe that once the present scheme for an elected Assembly in Cardiff has been cleared away there would be any difficulty in drawing up a scheme agreeable to the Conservative, Liberal and Labour parties; and one which would give Plaid Cymru as much as most of them in their innermost hearts, really want.

In the latter part of the campaign all the Welsh daily papers attempted to a greater or lesser extent to provide some 'in-depth' treatment of the issues. On Saturday 24 February the *Swansea Evening Post* carried long, adjacent articles by the Secretary of State, John Morris, arguing the case for the Assembly, and his Shadow, Nicholas Edwards, the case against. On 21 February the *Newport Argus* carried an informative page on 'How Wales Will vote' with short factual statements on: what the Assembly would do; the 40 per cent hurdle; costs of the Assembly; unity of the United Kingdom; nominated bodies; and the possible impact on local government structure. The same issue of the paper also carried a leader, the only one the paper wrote on devolution in the campaign. It was a sane examination of the question but avoided any commitment. Devolution, it argued, already existed — at the Welsh Office. What was at issue was whether it should be taken a stage further:

> Should the people of Wales directly elect representatives who will apportion some of the cake at present being sliced at the Welsh Office? And should those elected representatives control the functions of some of the authorities in Wales at present only nominated — like area health authorities, the tourist board and the sports council?

> What you must decide is whether this increased democracy will mean better government for Wales. Or will it add another costly

tier of bureaucracy?

It is almost an impossible question to answer, and one that will only be resolved with the benefit of hindsight.

In the last week of the campaign, on 27 February, the *Argus* asked Gwent MPs to record their views on the subject and gave them a whole page to do so. Only Jeffrey Thomas, then Labour MP for Abertillery, declined because as the *Argus* disarmingly explained in its headline about the feature 'he is Parliamentary Private Secretary to the Secretary of State for Wales'. Mr Leo Abse, Labour MP for Pontypool, surpassed himself. His piece opened:

> Are the English speaking Welshmen and Welshwomen of Newport, Pontypool and Gwent to become second-class citizens in their own land?
>
> Is Newport to be governed from Cardiff by a huge Welsh speaking Civil Service?
>
> These are the forbidden questions the 'Yes' campaigners do not wish to ask on March 1st. Yet the answers to these queries are clear, not conjectural.

It is beyond question that the 'collective' editorial line of the English language Press was overwhelmingly opposed to the Assembly. Only the *Western Mail* held out in favour, and then falteringly. A survey among its readers would probably have found a majority in favour of the Assembly and many were dismayed by the paper's behaviour on polling day. In the final week of the campaign the paper carried leading articles each day putting a variety of arguments in favour of devolution. It also attacked the character of the 'No' campaign:

> Throughout they have gone for the gut, rather than the intellectual reaction. Three topics in particular they have brought to the fore — the language, the dangers of separatism and the cost. All three have been dangled before the electorate like some death's head of doom, wreathed around with warnings of cataclysm and disaster.

But despite such stirring phrases in its leader column the *Mail* had no qualms about placing prominently on its front page on polling day a large advertisement, apparently sponsored by the 'Haverfordwest "No" Committee', declaring 'Don't just stay home and say No, GET OUT and VOTE NO'. Inside was a full-page advertisement put in by the 'Central "No" Committee' in Cardiff urging voters to: 'Keep

161

Wales united with Britain — VOTE NO'. Despite such aberrations the *Western Mail's* coverage was, on the whole the fairest and most comprehensive of all the English language Press in Wales. Its main feature was a series of ten half page investigations in the middle two weeks of February entitled 'Devolution Countdown'. These put the 'For' and 'Against' arguments on whether the Assembly would result in 'a bigger or smaller voice for Wales'; on bureaucracy versus democracy; on whether an Assembly would result in economic benefit for Wales; on the cost; on separatism; on the Welsh language; on the impact on local government and, most interestingly, on the debate within the Labour Party in Wales. Yet, in leaning over backwards to be fair and balanced in its coverage, many in the pro-devolution camp felt the newspaper had fallen over. Certainly, the 'No' side were happy enough with the *Western Mail's* coverage — they made a special point of congratulating the newspaper on its objectivity (see Table 7-2).

Elsewhere there was less editorial fastidiousness. Late on in the campaign the *Liverpool Daily Post,* as if despairing of injecting any straightforward personality clashes into the campaign, sent one of its feature writers, John Williams, to a selection of North Wales communities to discover their mood. In Abergele he found, as the paper's headline writer put it, 'a tidal wave of indifference'. Other writers testing the mood in Wales also found it extremely difficult, apparently, to find anyone in favour of the Assembly. A *vox pop* piece in the *Newport Argus* failed to find anyone in the whole of Gwent who intended to vote 'Yes'. The *Liverpool Post* left its editorial comment on the subject until 1 March itself, but then it was unequivocal in its condemnation. 'Wales', its leader thundered:

> . . . deserves better than this half-baked folly . . . a pretentious little super council, housed in a Cardiff backwater, trifling endlessly with minor governmental issues and failing to achieve anything of primary importance.

But no paper matched the *South Wales Echo* in its sustained campaign of vindictive fury against the Assembly proposals. On one day, 7 February, it slipped and presented a totally uncharacteristic fair-minded appraisal of the arguments on a page headed 'Your Dossier on Devolution'. For the rest of the time its editorial comment and news columns were united in their complete hostility. For instance, headlines regularly referred pejoratively to the 'Yes Men'. On 14 February its leader column listed the names of 60 of Wales' leading authors which the Wales for the Assembly campaign had published as

162

supporting devolution. The *Echo* commented: 'There now! You are impressed by those names, and each one is so well known to you!' In its opposition the *Echo* appeared to be motivated entirely by fears of separatism. Its leader on 13 February stated:

> The vote on March 1st is about separatism in the long term and we, like many others, indeed the majority in Wales know that a 'Yes' majority will start the ball rolling; the extremists will be on their way.

On 22 February the paper added: 'A majority of the people of Wales will vote 'No' in a week's time because they are afraid of being hived off from the rest of the country. They are right to be afraid'.

The evidence suggests that the majority of the English language Press primarily perceived the devolution proposals as representing more and more costly government at a time when that was the very last thing they wanted. The emphasis placed by the *Echo* on irrational fears of separation can only be traced to a xenophobic South East Wales fixation, coupled with a gut rejection of that identity being merged with any all-Wales view. Rather than accept any affinity with localities or people north of Merthyr and west of Bridgend the *Echo* preferred, if necessary, to link up with Bristol and pretend to some kind of Severnside identity. In turn this was a straightforward rejection of anything remotely smacking of nationalism — that is, Welsh nationalism; British nationalism as portrayed in the devolution campaign by figures like Enoch Powell and Neil Kinnock was permissible. This syndrome was well illustrated by the *Echo* when on 23 February, it promoted the predictable decision of the Labour-dominated Mid Glamorgan county council to oppose the Assembly. This won banner front page headlines and an enthusiastic response from the *Echo's* leader writer: 'The Mid Glamorgan decision is a break-through. It means that almost the whole of South East Wales is speaking with one voice'. The leader quoted, with great approval, the leader of Mid-Glamorgan, Philip Squire, 'Our real strength in Wales lies in the fact that we are a nation of strong and individualistic communities'.

The most cursory examination of the Welsh-based English language daily newspapers during the six weeks leading up to the referendum reveals clearly that they were dominated by the simple, straight gut arguments of the 'No' campaigners. For instance, a front-page analysis of the *Western Mail* and *South Wales Echo* for February 1979 (see Table 7.2) produces three overwhelming impressions: first, the general lack of coverage of the devolution issues; secondly, the generally hostile character of what coverage there was (on only one occasion could a front-page story in either paper during February be described as favouring devolution); and, finally, the extent to which the front pages were dominated by strikes in the public services and the appalling weather. The 'No' side had the advantage of simple, easily communicable arguments. In contrast, the case for the Assembly was much more complex and sophisticated and by definition much harder to communicate. The issues had never been sufficiently aired by the popular Press and this last reality was partly a result of a general attitude within the Press itself: that the devolution question was irrelevant to people's main interests and, moreover, extremely boring. But primarily it resulted from the lack of an integrated Welsh newspaper network capable of giving the issue comprehensive coverage.

NOTES

1. I am indebted for much of the information in this table to a similar compilation in J. Barry Jones and R.A. Wilford: 'The Welsh Veto: The Politics of the Devolution Campaign in Wales' (*Centre for the Study of Public Policy*, University of Strathclyde, 1979).

2. The author was Welsh Affairs Correspondent of the *Western Mail* between 1972 and 1980.

Table 7-2
Western Mail/South Wales Echo Front Page Analysis for February 1979

Date	Newspaper	Lead Story	Second Story	Referendum Story	Attitude to Devolution Referendum	Column Inches given to Referendum Coverage*
Thurs. 1st	Western Mail	Hospital Closure Threat	School-children Pay	Labour Club Protests at use of funds	Anti	8
	Echo	Strikes hit Cardiff	Floods threaten Cardiff	—	—	—
Fri. 2nd	Western Mail	Casualty Units escape closure threat	Grave-diggers strike	South Glamorgan spends £3000 on No Vote	Anti	9
	Echo	Merthyr hospital fails to diagnose injuries	Cardiff rubbish mounts up	—	—	—
Sat. 3rd	Western Mail	Rugby fans create rubbish problem	Closure threat to hospitals	—	—	—
	Echo	Rubbish — plea to rugby fans	Hospital to deal with emergencies only	—	—	—
Mon. 5th	Western Mail	Litter hits Cardiff	Man found dead on Snowdon	—	—	—
	Echo	Clean-up SOS launched	Callaghan seeks deal with Unions	—	—	—
Tues. 6th	Western Mail	Steel plants face shutdown	Some hospital staff return to work	—	—	—
	Echo	Council strikes spread	School boy in boots row	Assembly will cost £20m a year	Anti	6

Date	Newspaper	Lead Story	Second Story	Referendum Story	Attitude to Devolution Referendum	Column Inches given to Referendum Coverage*
Wed. 7th	Western Mail	Dustbin strike spreads	Johnny Owen wins sports award	—	—	—
	Echo	B.L. hit by strike	Hospital officials deliver meals	—	—	—
	Western Mail	N.U.P.E. strike aims at Cardiff S.E.	Cardiff clean-up operation foiled	—	—	—
	Echo	S. Glam. schools face strike	Lending rate up to 14%	—	—	—
Fri. 9th	Western Mail	Leyland strike ballot	Ambulance men call off strike	—	—	—
	Echo	Schools to stay shut	Hospital waiting lists at Merthyr	—	—	—
Sat. 10th	Western Mail	45% to vote No in Assembly poll	Hospital rubbish story	*as lead	Anti	31
	Echo	Thatcher hints at strike ban	Only ⅓ to stay Yes in Assembly poll	*as second	Anti	18
Mon. 12th	Western Mail	Iran Revolution	Snow hits Wales	—	—	—
	Echo	Snow hits Wales	Caretakers defy school strike call	—	—	—
Tues. 13th	Western Mail	Missiles down Rhodesian aircraft	Road gritting banned	—	—	—
	Echo	Shah kidnapped — report	Anti-Assembly group ejected from meeting	S. Glam council say No	Neutral/Anti	32

Date	Paper	Headline 1	Headline 2	Note	Stance	Days
Wed. 14th	Western Mail	Gwent schools to close	Cardiff murder hunt	Bookmakers say odds Against	Anti	1½
	Echo	Iranians siege U.S. Embassy	Church leaders deny claim they back Assembly	—	Anti	24
Thurs. 15th	Western Mail	TUC/Government deal on pay offer	Snow returns	—	—	—
	Echo	Callaghan to carry on	Paris match venue switch?	Assembly non-runner say bookies	Anti	4
Fri. 16th	Western Mail	9% Pay deal could end crisis	Paris rugby fans grounded	Govt. reduces 40% yes vote target to 38%	Neutral	7½
	Echo	Shah's men executed	Ex-manager sues Cardiff City	—	—	—
Sat. 17th	Western Mail	High speed Tain catches fire	Rugby fans reach Paris	—	—	—
	Echo	Train blaze vandals	Iran airlift	—	—	—
Mon. 19th	Western Mail	U.S.S.R. tells China: hands off Vietnam	Rugby fan stabbed	—	—	—
	Echo	Chinese call invasion halt	Rugby fan killer identified	—	—	—
Tues. 20th	Western Mail	Vietnam says Chinese attack repulsed	Rugby fan stab story	—	—	—
	Echo	Cardiff 9% rate rise	City rubbish moved	Assembly would not control economy	Anti	12
Wed. 21st	Western Mail	Civil servants to strike	J.P.R. to sue the Sun	815,000 must vote yes in Wales to clear 40 per cent "hurdle"	Neutral	9
	Echo	Rubbish clean-up deadlock	Cardiff lecturer row	Heycock slams underspending claims	Anti	15

Date	Newspaper	Lead Story	Second Story	Referendum Story	Attitude to Devolution Referendum	Column Inches given to Referendum Coverage*
Thurs. 22nd	Western Mail	Vote Yes says Callaghan	Dirty jobs strike to end	*As lead	Pro	26
	Echo	Services manning crisis	ACAS to strike	—	—	—
Fri. 23rd	Western Mail	N.U.P.E. chiefs say No to 9% deal	Vietnam crisis	—	—	—
	Echo	Mid Glam. calls for No Vote	Civil Servants strike	*As lead	Anti	20
Sat. 24th	Western Mail	Poll predicts rout for Yes vote	IRA bombs	*As lead	Anti	36
	Echo	Poll predicts massive D-Day No	Somerset IRA bomb blast	*As lead	Anti	37
Mon. 26th	Western Mail	China and Vietnam	Soldiers shot in Belfast	Callaghan says he may be forced to call election	Neutral	6
	Echo	Cardiff docks fraud	Rubbish hazards	Assembly No vote may force election	Neutral	21
Tues. 27th	Western Mail	Ambulance men ignore 999 calls	World War II bombs found at Bridgend	Scots Yes – No gap narrows	Neutral	9
	Echo	Ambulance men in S. Wales to ignore stoppage	Assembly expenses attack: vicious suggestion	Government's future at stake – Morris	Anti	22
Wed. 28th	Western Mail	Welsh firms in fraud inquiry	Another Poll predicts big No vote	*As Second	Anti	20
	Echo	Why there should be a No vote – Editorial	Curb on late night drinking at Barry	*As lead	Anti	44

*There is a total of 126 column inches on the front page of the *Western Mail* and 200 column inches on the front page of the *South Wales Echo*

CHAPTER 8

The Referendum and the
Welsh Language Press

HARRI PRITCHARD JONES

The extent and nature of the Welsh language Press. There are, broadly, two
secular national weekly papers. *Y Faner* is a serious journal offering
commentary on and discussion of social, political, religious and artistic
issues, both within Wales and beyond, and stems from papers founded
by the mid-nineteenth century Liberal radicals, Thomas Gee and
Gwilym Hiraethog. *Y Cymro* is a popular paper, with many more
features and items of a light nature, together with local and national —
but rarely international — news, and coverage of sport and popular
entertainment, as well as of political, industrial and social matters.
Both papers reflect that broad consensus that was thought to exist in
Wales, especially Welsh-speaking Wales, comprising a mixture of
socialism, radicalism and nationalism with a strong element of
pacifism. Both have a natural involvement with the language. (It is
hardly surprising, therefore, that the two papers supported the
devolution campaign).

The two secular magazines surveyed are *Barn,* and *Y Genhinen* (now
defunct), both non-denominational and non-political, but which cover
social issues and comment on political matters of considerable
significance.

There are various local papers too, either completely Welsh or
bilingual to some degree or other. The principal ones are those of the
Herald Group in Caernarfon, under the managing-editorship of John
Eilian (J.T. Jones), a leading Welsh Conservative and a past
prospective Tory MP for Anglesey. The two Welsh language papers in
the group, *Yr Herald Gymraeg* and *Herald Môn,* like their English
counterparts, were predictably against the proposed Assembly, and
indeed, gave little space to the pro-devolutionists.

On the other hand, a network of recently founded Welsh language
local papers (35 in all) which serve small communities or districts, and

which normally appear on a monthly basis were almost without exception pro-devolution.

Before describing the tone and content of the referendum campaign as seen by Welsh speakers it is necessary to note the basic differences in the background and assumptions of the two linguistic groups. These refer also to the coverage on radio and television, which was extensive and — unlike the English language media — balanced, even as to intonation and implication as well as in what was made explicit. There were no innuendoes which might serve to make such a vital subject either a great bore, or a passionate crusade.

The major difference between the linguistic communities is in the matter of cultural background. Welsh speakers would hardly ask Gwyn Williams's admittedly rhetorical question, 'where was Wales?' As a minority linguistic community our knowledge of Welsh history and geography and of national institutions, poor and patchy as it too often is, in general is much greater than that of non-Welsh speakers. And I am not referring to knowledge about any particular part or portion of Wales or the Welsh. This greater awareness about what belongs uniquely to us, as Welsh people, extends to a greater awareness in general of other peripheral areas aspiring to nationhood, such as Brittany, the Basque country, Catalonia, and even to the fact that the Manx parliament was a thousand years old in 1979.

There is a different usage of words which is greater and more profound than simply the use of Welsh, as opposed to English words. In general, politicians and commentators — apart from conscious nationalists — when speaking English would use the word 'country' to denote England, the UK — or, even that conglomerate 'England and Wales'. On the other hand, when speaking Welsh, those same people would mean Wales when using the Welsh word for country, *gwlad.*

There is also an expectation regarding nationhood commoner amongst Welsh speakers which presumes that one day there will be some sort of parliament in Wales. It is compounded of various and varying elements including some knowledge of the Arthurian legends, the history of conquest and subjugation, and an awareness of the national revival in the last century and beginning of this which, through various movements within the Liberal and Labour parties, was responsible for creating so many institutions. Some of its movements also espoused a form of Home Rule, under Lloyd George and Tom Ellis or Keir Hardie and Mabon.

It is little wonder then, that almost each and every Welsh speaking

Table 8-1

Welsh Language Weekly Press: January-June 1979

Title	Publisher(s)	Circulation figure	Area	Political attitude
Y Cymro	North Wales Newspapers Ltd., Oswestry	7,800	Whole country	Independent socialist nationalist
Y Faner	Gwasg y Sir, Bala	1,800	Whole country	Radical, broadly nationalist
Herald Môn	Herald Newspapers	3,200	Anglesey	Pro-Conservative and Unionist
Yr Herald Gymraeg	Caernarfon	3,800	Former Caernarfonshire	Pro-Conservative and Unionist
Y Cyfnod	Gwasg y Sir, Bala	3,200	East Meirionydd	Independent
Y Dydd	Gwasg y Dydd, Dolgellau	1,800	West Meirionydd	Independent
Y Llan	Church in Wales, Penarth	600	Whole country	Independent
Y Goleuad	Presbyterian Church of Wales, Caernarfon	3,200	Whole country	Independent
Y Tyst	Welsh Congregational Union	3,500	Whole country	Independent
Seren Cymru	Baptist Union of Wales	1,600	Whole country	Independent

(The study of all these papers and journals is basically restricted to the period January 1st to mid-March although some publications gave continuous attention to the issue until mid-April.)

literary figure supported the Assembly campaign, together with a large proportion of their Anglo-Welsh counterparts. I believe that Welsh speakers in general were more aware of the issues involved in the devolution debate, and more deeply personally affected by the result one way or another.

The progress of the two devolution bills had been widely reported, against a constant tradition of discussing Home Rule or devolution in Welsh for over a century. The measures were widely expected to succeed though one voice warned:

> non-Welsh speakers would be swayed by arguments advanced by Abse and Kinnock. Their psychology is subtle, and so many of our non-Welsh speaking compatriots will swallow outright their Goebbelsian lies about the Welsh speaking minority being able to hold power in a Welsh Assembly, and that our standard of living would be lower in Wales than in England. *

This was said by the editor of *Y Genhinen* in the Spring issue for 1978, and he went on:

> The only answer is for the Labour Party to attack such arguments and put the facts before the people . . . They must venture to declare that Wales deserves and desires an Assembly of its own because it is, after all, a nation. That was what happened when the Council of Labour demanded a Secretary of State in 1959, and James Griffiths said his appointment (to the Secretaryship) was a 'recognition of the nationality of Wales'.

Generally though, the only real caveat about devolution was tied up with Saunders Lewis's warning (in the famous radio lecture in 1962) that achieving some sort of home rule before the language had been extensively restored and rehabilitated over most of Wales might well be inimical to that process. This is the reason why *Cymdeithas yr Iaith* (the language society) was indifferent, if not hostile, to the Assembly campaign, and deaf to appeals by nationalist leaders, both publicly and in private, for a moratorium on direct action — notably in the campaign for a Welsh television channel — until after the referendum. In fact, two of the society's leaders were in Swansea prison during the whole period, for conspiring to damage television masts and transmitters.

---

*Extracts quoted have been translated from Welsh.

The *raison d'être* of the movement for what Michael Foot called 'a real measure of home rule,' was patently obvious to most Welsh speakers. It was to be a recognition or expression of nationhood. There were arguments heard over the years against such a development, on the grounds of cost, Welsh national proverty, an increase in bureaucracy, because it might, somehow, lead to an Ulster situation here, and before and immediately after the last war, by south Welsh Labour MPs who argued that 'the brotherhood of man was more important than the survival of small nations'. But then these MPs did not speak Welsh, and were rarely heard, whilst the more eloquent and abler Labour members for the north did speak Welsh and had supported the Campaign for a Parliament for Wales in the 1950s. (They were Lady Megan Lloyd George, T.W. Jones, Goronwy Roberts, Cledwyn Hughes, and Tudor Watkins, joined by the lone southerner S.O. Davies. Only Cledwyn Hughes played a full part in the 1979 campaign).

It was notable, then, that when the actual pro-devolution campaign was launched, at Llandrindod, though it was given full coverage — all over the front page of *Y Cymro,* for instance — the arguments and the whole premise of the debate seemed incongruous, strange and almost irrelevant. Apart from David Owen's reference in a speech at Swansea to the historical background extending back to the conquering of the last Llywelyn, we were asked to see the issue which had previously been one of nationhood, as essentially of 'administrative efficiency', 'control of a bureaucratic tier and of nominated bodies;' 'as a backdoor way of reforming local government;' 'as an aid to an overworked Westminster parliament'. And reports of the lack of recognition of the place of the Welsh language, and use of it, in the meeting at Llandrindod, and the campaign literature distributed there, were reported with quiet disappointment in *Y Cymro,* side by side with the usual reports of the continuing activities on the language front. Letters in the same vein appeared in subsequent issues, though there was a great effort not to rock the boat. This desire did not extend to the hard-hitting editorial of the language society's magazine *Tafod y Ddraig,* in February, which attacked the notion of postponing activity on behalf of the language until Wales had an Assembly. There was no time for this it argued, and the language was more important than the Assembly. Indeed there was no provision in the Bill for the use of Welsh in the proposed Assembly, so that the use of the language might easily have become an issue between any assembly and local and central government, and indeed between the assembly men themselves.

173

It was also noted by correspondents and columnists in both *Y Faner* and *Y Cymro* that far from being a modest 'consensus proposal for national advance', emerging from all the submissions to the Crowther, then Kilbrandon, Commission on the Constitution, George Wright (Secretary, Wales TUC), had aggressively asserted that this measure was going to 'stop separatism and preserve the unity of the kingdom . . . The vast majority of Welsh people are not Welsh nationalists but international nationalists *(sic)* or British nationalists' (*Y Cymro*, 30 January).

The umbrella devolution campaign's chairman, Elystan Morgan, on the other hand (in *Y Cymro* and on radio and television), had welcomed 'the healing of old political wounds and the willingness to co-operate across party boundaries to further the wellbeing of Wales'. But George Wright and various Labour party spokesmen were soon reported to be unwilling to share any platform with a member of Plaid Cymru. A columnist in *Y Cymro* (6 February), 'Rhoslyn', looked forward to continuing co-operation after the referendum, adding that for any group, such as *Cymdeithas yr Iaith,* to indulge in direct action before the referendum was 'only to be seen as a form of linguistic, cultural and national hara-kiri'. In the same column, in the 16 January issue of the paper, 'Rhoslyn' had warned of the danger to even a broadly based campaign from the large numbers 'who had second homes here'.

The Herald group of newspapers was also motivated by cultural and linguistic considerations but reached opposite conclusions from the vast majority of the Welsh language Press. Here, for instance, is the editorial leader for both the Herald Welsh language papers for 23 January 1979:

> As the Preacher (in Ecclesiastes) says, there is a time for everything, and the Herald's view from the start has been that this is an inappropriate time to legislate on a matter such as this, when we have only recently had a re-organisation of local government, which we have hardly had time to get used to. We feel that there are powerful arguments against the idea of disrupting our councils fundamentally again like this.
>
> North and South do not make easy bed-fellows. All the weight is in the South, and there would be the danger with an 'Assembly' in the South for the whole of Wales, of the North being just chaff in the scales. And since it is the North which is the bastion of what remains of the Welsh language, the language would be under a

174

disadvantage. We feel that the wise thing for us to say, in the vote, is 'No, thank you'.

Throughout the campaign, the Welsh language Press (apart from the Herald group) were in favour of an Assembly, though there was a fair coverage of the anti-devolution campaigns. Most editorials and regular columns during the period of the campaign exhorted people to work for a 'Yes' vote. What was absent was any nationalistic or patriotic rallying cry — as reportedly raised by Clive Rowlands when he used to send his team out to represent Wales! The voice of Plaid Cymru, and it seems of basic patriotism, was muted if not stilled. It was heard on a couple of occasions on the media, from Denzil Davies (Labour MP, Llanelli) and Geraint Howells (Liberal MP, Cardigan) and reported in a couple of campaign speeches.

But the historical background *was* described. The main political commentator of *Y Faner,* Emyr Daniel, recalled (5 January) that 'the important dates in English history were probably 55 BC and 1066 AD. Perhaps in Wales they might by 1282, 1536 and 1979'. He went on to describe the Midlothian campaign of 1879, when Gladstone, relinquishing a seat in England, fought one in Scotland, vanquishing not only his opposing candidate, but also Disraeli and his government. It was suggested that Mr Callaghan would have to campaign vigorously for an Assembly (if a referendum was held prior to a general election), in order to sustain the momentum which could win him the subsequent general election. But it was noted, also, that some felt 'he might well distance himself from the Welsh campaign, feeling it to be a lost cause'. It that were the case, suggested Daniel, the vote in Wales might go against devoluton. In that same (5 January) issue, Emyr Humphreys, the novelist, in his regular personal column, saw the forthcoming debate as 'being really in the mind. . . It was a question of national self-confidence. . . an expression of our long-standing serf-like attitude. Were we to be happy with our lot as a dependent province, living off the backs of the bounteous English?' Such a note was rare, as I have said. Leo Abse was then quoted as warning about the inherently corrupt nature of Welsh-based politicians, whilst as Humphreys stated, 'England is shaken by one political scandal after another'.

The following week Gwilym Prys Davies (at that time political adviser to John Morris at the Welsh Office), provided an 'official' article on behalf of the pro-Assembly movement in the same paper. In it he tried to allay fears that the devolution measure was a 'hotch-potch', which did not satisfy any basic aspiration. He argued that it achieved a genuine consensus between those views and proposals (proffered) to the Kilbrandon Commission by 'all those who wanted to promote the welfare of Wales'.

The editor warned, in the same issue, that this apparent consensus could only be sustained 'if the higher position of those who espouse national freedom was sustained and articulated as well. . .' Pragmatic considerations demanded that all who favoured any degree of national advancement work for the devolution campaign, and she praised the speech to this effect by Emrys Roberts at the previous Plaid Cymru conference, which had swayed the party towards supporting the campaign. Concluding, she raised the language issue, saying how little stress there had been on it during the campaign. A week later the first real attack on the Assembly campaign from a supporter of devolution was printed in *Y Faner*. Hywel Teifi Edwards, a university lecturer and occasional columnist, and Plaid Cymru county councillor in Dyfed, launched into an attack on the inaugural meeting at Llandrindod. He saw it as *deja vu,* a re-run of the old *Cymru Fydd* (Young Wales) movement in the Liberal party, in the hey-day of that party and of Llandrindod, almost a century ago. He castigated George Wright for:

> referring to the 'people of Wales' rather than 'the Welsh people,' and for urging people to 'win an historic victory for Wales' without letting Wales or 'Welshmen' be part of the discussion in any way. All was to be debated in terms such as 'good industrial relations'. It is difficult to swallow water from Mr Wright's pump. It is impossible for many of us to forget that there would be no devolution campaign of any sort without the consciousness and struggle of those people over the centuries who have sustained some sort of Welsh nationhood.

Henceforth, there was a general closing of ranks, together with more formal expositions and counter-expositions of the arguments (heard also in English), but the exhortations to support the Assembly continued in the editorials. An interesting article by Emyr Daniel in *Y Faner* on 9 February, referred to an article in the *South Wales Echo* a few nights previously. The *Echo* editor had referred to the Secretary of State, John Morris, in a derogatory fashion, as being 'a *Cardi*'. *

---

* a pejorative term for a miserly person, derived from the name of the old county of Cardigan.

adding, 'perhaps we are seeing once again the deep division between South Walians and the rest on this issue'. Emyr Daniel recalled Lloyd George's vain attempts to persuade the 'richer counties of Glamorgan and Monmouth' to join the rest of the country to espouse Home Rule, and of the subsequent demise of the *Cymru Fydd* movement. It seemed likely that 'the devolution campaign's main task was to win over the people of those same counties'.

By mid-February there was a realisation that things were not going too well for the Assembly campaign. The front page of *Y Cymro* carried a banner headline 'More People in Two Minds', over a report of the BBC commissioned poll showing an increase in the 'Don't know's' from 14.5 per cent in September 1978 to 21.2 per cent mainly at the expense of the number intending to vote 'Yes'. 'Rhoslyn', in the same 13 February issue offered the faint hope that:

> even if the vote in Wales went against the Assembly, given a near 40% favourable vote in Scotland, the government might still set up assemblies in both countries, in order to spike the guns of a Tory government which might be then expected to succeed it, after the general election.

A week later, *Y Cymro* carried an impassioned plea by veteran Plaid Cymru campaigner, author Islwyn Ffowc Elis, to all patriots to close ranks and pull out all the stops on behalf of a 'Yes' vote. He appealed to *Cymdeithas yr Iaith* activists to desist from any impending direct action, citing the alleged adverse effect on Plaid Cymru's subsequent electoral performance of the protests during investiture year. This plea was in reply to a letter the previous week by the vice-chairman of the language society, Angharad Tomos, saying that to put devolution above the language was to get one's priorities all wrong. 'There was a trap in the devolution movement for nationalism', she claimed. A week after Islwyn Ffowc Elis's appeal, he got two replies. One was another letter from Angharad Tomos, re-stating her position rather sarcastically, though adding that she intended voting 'Yes'. The other was contained in a report on the front page of *Y Cymro,* telling of the arrest in Sussex of six language society activists for damage to a television transmitter. 'Rhoslyn', in the same issue, lamented the lack of 'grass-root organisational support for the Assembly campaign from Labour party members, which had, instead, to rely on Plaid Cymru members, even to distribute Labour/TUC pro-Assembly literature'. In spite of that, however, he looked forward to continued Labour party, Wales TUC and Plaid Cymru co-operation after the referendum, even to the extent of electoral pacts: especially, he thought, in those constituencies held by Tory members who worked so hard against the Assembly, in Conwy and West Denbigh, 'where such pacts might unseat Wyn Roberts and Geraint Morgan'. Rather naively, and paradoxically, he added that 'one of the greatest gains of the campaign had been that the electoral machinery of the Labour Party and the Trade Unions in Wales have identified themselves, quite definitely, with the demand for some sort of parliament in Cardiff'. The same issue carried a small advert by the Labour Party/Wales TUC campaign — in English!

In its last issue before St David's day — D-day indeed — *Y Faner* carried a piece by their correspondent Dylan Iorwerth on the situation in Scotland. This was the only detailed survey in Welsh of the Scottish campaign, which saw the pro-Assembly movement as likely to succeed, although unlikely to reach the 40 per cent requirement. He noted that there were:

> more Tories working for a 'Yes' vote there, but that Labour party workers were conspicuous by their absence. One of the main differences between the campaign in the two countries is the absence of a Plaid Cymru one in Wales. An SNP member told me 'We would never have paid the price Plaid Cymru have had to pay in order to get the Labour Party to take part in the umbrella organisation — with all that talk about not weakening the unity of the kingdom'.

Rather incongruously, it was to Gwynfor Evans that the Welsh language media turned for a pre-emptive explanation of the impending disastrous failure of the pro-Assembly campaign. It seemed, as the editorial of *Y Faner* for referendum day had it, that people, especially nationalists, were rueing the lack of a nationalistic or patriotic core to the pro-Assembly campaign. The editor alluded to the concurrent tour of a play by Saunders Lewis based on the biblical *Esther* and quoted lines about 'Wives and mothers who put their language and the beauty of Jerusalem before their daily bread. . . Putting bread first secures willing slaves'. The editor, sensing the coming failure, praised a new book by the historian, Professor Glanmor Williams, which was being published on St David's Day, *Religion, Language and Nationality in Wales*. The author was quoted as saying on radio that there was 'a crying need for the ordinary intelligent layman to realise what strands had gone into the wave of Welsh nationality over the centuries'. The editor asked again why it was necessary to keep people like Gwynfor Evans off the pro-Assembly platforms, and ended with

178

another quote from *Esther,* when Mordecai taunts his niece, wife of the King of Iran, 'If you remain silent, and hide your lineage, Israel will find her salvation elsewhere'.

When the actual result came, the most memorable quote was by veteran Welsh language journalist John Roberts Williams, a former editor of *Y Cymro.* On radio, he declared 'We (the Welsh nation) got on to the world stage for a brief moment. And what did we do? We filled our pants!'

Y Cymro for 6 March again devoted nearly its entire front page to the issue, under the headline, 'Continuing the Battle.' There was a glossing over of the extent of the failure, with an emphasis on the fact that 'already the Executive of the Labour party in Wales has met to discuss the next steps.' Emrys Jones was quoted as saying 'there are many things to be cleared up,' but John Morris bemoaned the fact that 'Wales had lost an opportunity. We have fought hard and lost, and the sooner we realise that the better.' The article saw the possibility of recriminations within the Labour Party, especially in areas such as the Rhymney Valley, Ceredigion, Meirionydd and Anglesey, which might weaken party moral just when an election was imminent. Phylip Rosser, Treasurer of the Wales for the Assembly Campaign, who became a national figure for Welsh speakers through the campaign, was quoted as being very critical of his party (Labour), for not campaigning with sufficient resolve. He accused party members of siding with the Tories. He thought it hardly possible to heal the wounds and 'looked forward to the party splitting on the issue. If the referendum had succeeded, we could have looked forward to the development of a Welsh socialist party.' Dafydd Wigley was then quoted:

> Henceforth the Labour party will be the party of Abse and Kinnock and many 'moderate' Labourites will turn to Plaid Cymru — as happened after the failure of the Parliament for Wales Petition in the fifties and S.O. Davies's parliamentary bill.

He added a scathing attack on the Prime Minister for:

> not making a Prime Ministerial broadcast on behalf of the Assembly, and for creating a political vacuum. Something has to fill that void, and it may well be something much more unyielding than Plaid Cymru. The events of this last week have lent a strong hand to those who argue for unconstitutional action.

179

The truth is that democracy has received as hard a beating as has Wales during this last month.

The editorial of the same paper had this to say:

The way in which Wales refused her Assembly so definitely on St David's Day is as much a condemnation of the concept of holding referendums as of the government's measure. It is not our disappointment at the result which leads us to say this, but the evidence that the public's confusion over the issue increased rather than decreased as the campaign proceeded. To the mass of our populace, readers of the *Sun* and *Mirror*, to talk about democratising a bureaucratic tier of government was as strange as if we were to talk Hindustani to them. Politicians should lead people on such complicated matters. . . It was the rebellion of six Labour Members of Parliament that secured the referendum, and it is within that party that one will find the main explanation for the result.

The blame having been laid, what was the next step? The meagre hope was that Scotland, after all, would be granted an Assembly — 'surely that would awaken Wales from her deep sleep'.

Y Genhinen, in its first issue after the poll, saw the result as part of a disenchantment, drawing us back 'from the world of our romantic dreams into the sad situation that actually exists. . . Even a majority of Welsh speakers do not want their nation to be one that can stand up with self-respect amidst other nations'. They then alluded to an article in the same issue about the great numbers who have moved into Welsh-speaking Wales, diluting the native element markedly. *Barn* (mid-March), in its editorial, made the point that, though the result was a victory for those who wished to exploit old divisions, based on geography, party loyalties and language, the result was also a protest against:

the whole way we are governed at present. The slogan 'We have too much government already', was an expression of distaste and surfeit at all government. . . Words like 'democracy' and 'open government' have become jokes because the actual language used has been debased and polluted by politicians and political journalists for many years. The result was the fruit of the cynicism which has been created, partly, by those who represent us.

180

This echoed the contribution of one of the main pro-Assembly umbrella's campaign officials in *Barn* for February. However, an alternative interpretation of the result was given in the leader columns of the *Herald Papers* on 6 March.

> We can consider the Referendum, with its sweeping result, as marking the end of an era; the end of an old one, and the beginning of a new one when the real ancient traditions of Wales will start to flower again, having been under cobwebs for a century.
>
> The Referendum was a simple and plain vote about Welsh nationalism, and the clear voice of the country was heard to say 'No'. The 'No' was so loud and strong that it conveyed annoyance if not anger. The voice of the people must be accepted, and a lesson drawn. . .
>
> The very word 'nation' is misleading, if not a mockery. If you look closely, you will see that there is no such thing as an English nation, nor a Welsh nation nor a Scottish one. But there are English peoples, Welsh peoples, and Scottish peoples who, together, make up the kingdom. This high tree took centuries to grow.
>
> When we cease to make a political issue of Welshness, we will see precious Welsh traditions waiting to be repossessed, and amongst them the ancient language of the whole of Britain — traditions that have been sinking since they were associated with politics during recent times, but which have not been drowned. Let them be breathed upon, and they shall live.

Further issues of *Y Cymro* tended to forget the issue, but the feeling in editorials in *Y Faner* was a fear of unconstitutional actions arising from frustrations produced by the failure of the Assembly campaign. Emyr Daniel, in the same paper,thought the main loser in the whole debacle would be the Labour party, but added that it was possible that a Tory government might, with its fear of nationalism abated, be more generous towards Welsh national cultural institutions and movements. But for Hywel Teifi Edwards, again in the same issue, the result was the realisation of his worst fears about the campaign and about us as a nation. He quoted a poem by Gwenallt which bewailed that Ireland's passion had not been given us. 'What normal Welsh person', he exclaimed:

181

would not curse at the victory of the alliance of denigrators for whom Wales and Welshness does not exist — only to the extent that they can become fodder for their malice, frustrations and revengefulness? What normal Welsh person would not curse as he saw 'sincere socialists' cohorting with Tories in order to eternalise the British centralist system which has long become obviously effete? Let us not cheat ourselves. The campaign by the negativists was essentially a campaign against the unity of Wales, and there is rejoicing today in the Philistine camp in Kingston-upon-Thames.

He ended with a quote from a lecture *Motives for Progression,* delivered in Llanidloes in the 1860s,

We have been long conquered or compromised for our good, we wish to set up no petty mountain sovereignty like Greece; no monster meeting 'for Repeal', no war with the Saxons. Though the original proprietors of the soil, we have no quarrel with our reforming and noble invaders, we take a pride in remembering that Cambrian blood flows in the veins of our beloved Queen, and that the heir to the throne is emphatically 'the Prince of Wales'.

The following week there was no mention of the whole issue, but on 6 and 13 April, John Davies, a history lecturer, produced a detailed analysis for *Y Faner* of the results county by county, in the two countries involved. The main relevant conclusion was the correlation he found with the Plaid Cymru vote, and that Cardiff and Gwent were noticeably more anti-devolution than the rest of the south-east.

Let the last word go to the movement which was least involved in the actual campaign for the Assembly, but yet in many ways centrally involved in the whole issue, *Cymdeithas yr Iaith.* Many of those questioned on radio and television after the result of the referendum, and who had voted 'No', said they did it 'to get at' those language activists. Here is part of the editorial of *Tafod y Ddraig* in mid-March:

The referendum result shows what difficult, un-yielding work faces any Welsh person who worries about the future of his country and language. It has shown clearly that this last decade has not resulted in any loosening of the British knot in Wales. It has silenced the argument of those few people who said the only way to change the order of things was by penetrating the system and working within it. That is what Elystan Morgan did, by

182

joining the Labour party, but he has failed. During the referendum campaign the government has been prostituting the cause of Welsh freedom. Now is the time for us to declare again clearly what we wish for our nation. Let us no longer lie with this one, but stick loyally to the fundamental principles which ought to be the foundation for every nationalist.

The language society's call remained for direct, unconstitutional, but non-violent action. But some observers predicted a violent backlash to the failure of the devolution movement. It is salutary to note that the violence which has occurred, it seems, has emanated from the non Welsh speaking sector of the population. Has this, one wonders, anything to do with the greater depth and length of the debate in the Welsh language press about nationality, devolution and the failure of the campaign in 1979? Perhaps, also, the greater awareness of the historical background enabled Welsh speakers to see the 1979 campaign in some sort of perspective.

CHAPTER 9

The Role of Broadcasting in the Referendum

GERAINT TALFAN DAVIES

At one of those official luncheons that tend to fill a junior minister's diary, a Welsh Office minister was due to speak. He had scraped in at a by-election during the nationalist hey-day of the late 1960s. He had a reputation as one of the more rumbustious 'nat-bashers'. But when he rose to speak, to describe the Welsh interest in his chosen subject, to describe the work of the Welsh Office in fighting for that interest, he sounded more than a shade nationalistic to his Cardiff suburban audience. The very terms of his job had dictated the tone as well as the content of this speech. Many journalists in Wales are in a not dissimilar position. It is their job, their duty even, to seek out any Welsh dimension in current affairs, to explain the local relevance of larger seemingly more distant events. Small wonder then that some thought that journalists themselves had a vested interest in the devolution issue. For here was a *bona fide* Welsh issue: not an extra artificial dimension to a British issue, but a distinctively Welsh (and Scottish) issue that would have significant repercussions for the rest of Britain. It was a heady time.

Pressmen, unconstrained by royal charters or statutory requirements of balance and impartiality, were in demand from the TV and radio producers. At the BBC, its Welsh specialists were in demand from the corporation's London-based services. Wales may not have been at the centre of the stage, but neither was it confined to the wings. Newspapers and magazines ran supplements on Wales, and political pieces were added to the age-old staple diet of coal and steel and communications. Pressmen and broadcasters regularly disgorged their information, names, addresses and telephone numbers for the flying foreign correspondents of the day — from *Newsweek* and *Pravda, Le Monde* or the *Los Angeles Times*. Some of us lectured, some chaired seminars, some wrote books (books that even London publishers were eager for). Horizons were suddenly wider. Federalism in Germany, America or Australia seemed relevant, and London embassies were keen to press the point — and pay the fares. For better, for worse, for richer for poorer, on 1 March, 1979 the phone stopped ringing.

Other prospects had vanished too. As early as 7 December 1976 a meeting was held at the Welsh Office under the chairmanship of its Director of Information to discuss the media's requirements for reporting facilities at the Welsh Assembly which was to have been housed at the old Coal Exchange in Cardiff's dockland. BBC, HTV, Swansea Sound, the *Western Mail, South Wales Echo, Liverpool Daily Post,* Press Association, London newspapers and news agencies were represented. It was stressed that the Property Services Agency needed information urgently so that work on adapting the building could begin. Although the PSA had provisionally allocated 25 seats in the public gallery for the Press, there was general dissatisfaction at the supporting facilities offered and a 'media working group' was formed. It was clear from the discussions of this group that broadcasting organisations and the main newspapers anticipated appointing full-time staff to cover the Assembly's proceedings. The assembly would have had a Press corps of up to twenty. The building was to be wired for simultaneous translation and for sound broadcasting of the Assembly and its committees, while the main chamber was to be wired and lit to allow for the possibility of televising its proceedings. It was these last factors that had led many journalists to believe that whatever the merits or demerits of the whole devolution package at least Government would be more open. The media working group had not really begun to discuss this aspect of the Press's involvement when the Scotland and Wales Bill was defeated in February 1977. No further formal discussions were held.

In Scotland, however, the process had begun earlier. An 'Association of Political Correspondents in Scotland' had been formed, and in October 1976 had submitted to the Scottish Office and all political parties a 'Memorandum on the reporting and information arrangements of a Scottish Assembly and Executive'. Under the influence of Neal Ascherson, a radical journalist who had moved from *The Observer* to *The Scotsman,* this memorandum dealt not only with the physical facilities needed in the Scottish Assembly building but with the whole question of information policy. It condemned the idea of a Westminster-style lobby system, demanding instead general access to information for all journalists. It urged the abandonment of the letter and ethos of the Official Secrets Act, and expressed the hope 'that the traditional corset of anonymity (around civil servants) will continue to be loosened'. In particular it asked the political parties to state whether they would be prepared to legislate for more liberal information practices if they were to gain political control in the Scottish Assembly. There is no doubt that, despite the absence of any plans for legislative devolution to Wales, a similar debate would have occurred here.

In that pre-referendum climate it was not possible to deny that a small band of journalists had a vested interest in shouting *vive la difference*. But did we 'talk it up'? Did we create a climate? Did we ever stop to ask whether the scene we described was a mirage? Those who would answer 'Yes' to the first two questions flatter the media and those who labour within it.

Rarely do newspapers or programmes create or dictate events, or generate movements. The emergence of the devolution issue was not an exception to this general rule. The Welsh Office had been in existence for six years before the *Western Mail* appointed a Welsh Affairs Correspondent, and before BBC Wales appointed a political correspondent. If anything, press and broadcasting were not overly quick to respond to events, let alone in the depth and with the intelligence that some thought events demanded.

The machinery of Government was changing: the Welsh Office was expanding; the *Digest of Welsh Statistics* — the statistician's version of the journalist's 'Welsh angle'—grew fatter year by year; regional policy took on increasing importance and bigger budgets. Political parties pushed and shoved towards new Welsh policies. The annual meeting of the Wales Area Council of the Conservative Party suddenly became a big blue butterfly called the Annual Conference of the Conservative Party in Wales. Journalists followed. They also reinforced these changes. Often, only because they chose to cover them, but also because the very act of inquiring whether an event has a larger significance can invest the event with that significance. It was not a question of committed journalism, though many journalists were committed. The unconvinced were little less obsessed with the issue than the convinced. Political journalists tend to take their cue from politicians and parties, especially when it runs parallel to the apparent direction of events. The trap into which too many of us fell, was in believing that the trend of events was more important and powerful than the trend of public opinion. It was an understandable habit developed before the era of plebiscitary politics.

As the devolution issue took on a more precise form, as legislation and decisions approached, it was inevitable that all the media would be carefully watched. Broadcasters would be more carefully watched than most, because of the presumed power of their medium and their inescapable requirement to maintain balance. Sensitivity about political bias in Welsh broadcasting has a long history and is related in the main to the fact that both programme organisations are bilingual in character. In the fifties and sixties the Labour Party openly criticised the BBC for alleged political bias, while in 1980 it was perhaps significant that one of the first requests by the new Select Committee on Welsh Affairs to the broadcasting organisations was for a list of all mentions of political parties or their members or representatives, and of appearances by MPs, councillors or party officials in all Welsh language programmes for a period of six months.

Sensitivity to the media's handling of the referendum was likely to be particularly acute for a number of reasons:

(i) the referendum (unlike a general election) was restricted to Wales and Scotland. Broadcasting organisations in Wales would now be in the front line;

(ii) the paucity of campaign funds both in pro and anti camps would mean that both sides would be heavily reliant upon media coverage;

(iii) the Government decided not to intervene in the referendum in the same way as it had in the EEC referendum in 1975. There was to be no Government campaign literature nor even a dispassionate statement of what it was proposing;

(iv) there were to be no party political broadcasts.

On 22 November 1978, the House of Commons debated the draft orders required to set up the referendums. Much of the two separate Scottish and Welsh debates were taken up by concerns over media coverage. As usual, Tam Dalyell MP put things more bluntly than most. He was worried that the broadcasting authorities and their staffs had an interest in the creation of Assemblies because these would provide 'extra jobs and avenues to promotion'. In particular, he was disturbed that the BBC's Controller in Scotland, Alaistair Hetherington (formerly editor of *The Guardian*), was a known staunch devolutionist. Tam Dalyell suggested he be given leave on full pay during January and February 1979, lest his influence should 'permeate his organisation'.

In the Welsh debate Michael Roberts MP and Leo Abse MP

187

expressed similar concerns, claiming that devolution was an issue 'on which we would not be prepared to rely completely on professional integrity in the same way as we would be prepared to rely upon it in the media's general approach to current affairs' (Michael Roberts). On this occasion it was Leo Abse who took the 'softer' line claiming that the BBC must be particularly circumspect, 'especially in view of the appointment of very good officers in charge of the news, but who have very committed views'. Equally, he was concerned at my own move from the pro-devolution *Western Mail* to be Head of News and Current Affairs at HTV and delivered a predictable shot across the bows. Michael Roberts had demanded the creation of machinery to ensure impartiality, but this amounted to little more than a demand that the broadcasting organisations should consult with the various groupings about the ground rules for the media's handling of the campaign. In the intensely partisan atmosphere of the Commons, sensible arguments were stretched or reduced to absurdity. The Government refused to concede that allowing party political broadcasts would result in unfairness, despite the parties being split (officially) three to one in favour of devolution. Leo Abse spoilt a good argument in favour of sticking to a balance between pro and anti, by going one stage further and suggesting that because the 'No' lobby was in the lead in a current BBC Wales opinion poll that lobby should get proportionately more airtime.

The question of party political broadcasts turned out to be the main point of issue in the debate. Harry Ewing, MP, then Parliamentary Secretary at the Scottish Office, had argued in favour of allowing party political broadcasts. Alec Jones MP, a minister in the Welsh Office, took the same line. It was Leon Brittan MP, the member for Cleveland and Whitby, who warned the Welsh Secretary of State, John Morris MP, that there might be legal considerations, and that a decision to allow party political broadcasts might by challenged in the courts. It was a warning that Government and the broadcasting authorities were unwise to ignore.

The initial view of the BBC and IBA was that, in the absence of formal umbrella organisations which existed in the European referendum campaign of 1975, there were only two choices:

(i) to allow each party to express a view about the referendum issues in a party political broadcast taken from its normal allocation;

(ii) to make it impossible for the parties to discuss in party political broadcasts a matter of great importance in Scotland and Wales.

In the absence of clearly identified umbrella groups with whom some other alternative might have been negotiated, the IBA was inclined to the first of these alternatives. The broadcasting authorities had received requests for radio and television party political broadcasts and on 8 February Mr Hardiman Scott, Chief Assistant to the BBC's Director General, wrote to the secretary of the All-Party Broadcasting Committee to say that despite the clustering of the party political broadcasts (normally unacceptable outside general election periods), the broadcasters would accept bookings for party political broadcasts in the order in which the applications were made. This proposal would have given the Conservatives the last word on Wednesday, 28 February; the Labour broadcast would have appeared on Tuesday, 27 February; Plaid Cymru's on Monday, 26 February; and that of the Liberals, on Friday, 23 February. (The same arrangements would have applied to radio party political broadcasts.) Ironically, the only party that had not, at that date, requested a party political broadcast was the Scottish National Party. It need not have worried.

In February, the 'Scottish Labour Vote No Campaign' sought an injunction from the Court of Session against the Independent Broadcasting Authority to prevent the broadcasting by it of the proposed party political broadcasts. The Authority is under a statutory duty 'to ensure that the programmes broadcast by (it) in each area maintain . . . a proper balance . . . in their subject matter . . .' Of the proposed broadcasts, three were designed to persuade the voters to say 'Yes', one, 'No'. The Authority argued that the contents of party political broadcasts were not in the same category as the content of programmes provided by the programme companies. The court ruled against the Authority. The referendum was a 'subject-matter' and the programmes about it had to maintain a proper balance.* The BBC which was not a party to the action, also withdrew the proposed broadcasts.

In the event, despite the worries of anti-devolution groupings, it was the pro-devolution camp that ended up making the most protests about coverage. Both Plaid Cymru and the Wales for the Assembly

* *Wilson* v. *Independent Broadcasting Authority* (1979) SLT. 281.
In its Annual Report for 1978-79 the IBA said, 'Two months afterwards, in connection with the General Election, the Court placed a different interpretation on Section 2(2), confining it to balance of programme categories in a non-political sense, a decision which corresponded with the traditional understanding of the intent of the Section'. The court had, however, in *Wilson's* case expressly contrasted a referendum with a general election campaign.

Campaign (WAC), complained about the absence of educative programmes in HTVs plans, a complaint that was due more to a misunderstanding than anything else. They also complained that HTV Wales' programmes were not to be transmitted on English transmitters whose signals could be received in Wales — HTV West and Westward in the south, Granada in the north and ATV in mid Wales. The BBC's analogous situation attracted a similar complaint from WAC. It suggested that Welsh devolution programmes should be transmitted by English transmitters like Mendip, Holme Moss and Sutton Coldfield. Plaid Cymru made the same point, stressing that the 40 per cent threshold meant that the result of the referendum depended more than ever upon all people having reasonable access to the facts at issue. However, the point was conceded neither by the IBA nor the BBC. Both organizations considered that the course of action advocated by WAC would ignore the interests of the much larger number of people in England served by these border transmitters.

All this reflected the fact that it proved more difficult to establish prior ground rules than in the 1975 referendum on Europe. Although in the end the IBA simply re-issued, in slightly amended form, its guidelines for the 1975 poll, the conflicting claims of Conservative 'No' and Labour 'No' campaigns, not to mention the partially controlled differences between the Wales for the Assembly Campaign, the Labour Party/Wales TUC 'Yes' Campaign, and Plaid Cymru, made the guidelines difficult to implement, at least in theory. In the November 1978 debate Leo Abse had taunted John Morris for appearing on platforms with Plaid Cymru and Liberal members. He had 'offended and wounded deeply' by so doing. The Labour Vote No Campaign, he said, would have their separate voice. 'The BBC and IBA cannot expect that they can mould the Labour Vote No Campaign and compel us to appear with those who may have come to the same conclusion but for wholly different reasons'. Even Mr Abse could not counter the magnetic attractions of the television camera. In HTV's final studio debate, 36 hours before polling, the 'No' case was proposed by Nicholas Edwards and seconded by Leo Abse. All in all, the contrived balance in BBC and HTV programmes proved acceptable, although Mr Geraint Morgan, the Conservative MP for Denbigh, almost upset the apple-cart in one Welsh language programme by suddenly declaring that he did not speak for the Tory Vote No Campaign, but only for himself.

For the broadcasters, however, these were the least difficult issues. As with the first European elections that were to take place later in 1979 it was clear that the Press and media had a considerable job of education to do. Opinion polls had shown that the public was ignorant and confused about the proposals and their provenance. (See chapter 10). Even by the opening of the campaign in February 1979 only 36 per cent in a BBC poll understood that devolution was Government policy. In HTV's February 1979 poll, although 92 per cent expressed a firm intention to vote in the referendum, 21 per cent of that 92 per cent still did not know which way they would vote. Indeed precise knowledge of the proposals was rare in both Wales and Scotland — a fact that was hardly surprising in view of the complex nature of the proposals for both countries. Furthermore, constitutional proposals have rarely been a major issue in modern British politics, largely because there is no written, codified constitution and as a consequence no constitutional court.

In the pro-devolution camp there was a belief that during the period 1976-78 the natural pre-occupation of all newsmen with the running battle at Westminster — the knife-edge divisions, the guillotine votes, the concession of a referendum, the 40 per cent clause and so on — diverted us from the more valuable job of explaining the devolution proposals. There is some substance in the allegation in relation to television in Wales, perhaps less so in Scotland. Two factors may explain the difference. First, the party political situation and the state of public opinion in Scotland differed significantly from the Welsh situation. (Indeed, London based media saw the Scottish story as more important or, as one ITV executive put it me, 'sexier' than the Welsh story. And they were right.) As a result producers in Scotland in both BBC and ITV felt able to devote proportionately greater attention to the issue than producers in Wales. Second, Scottish broadcasters hemmed in, like Welsh broadcasters, by schedules that are dominated by network considerations, did not have to share their limited airtime between coverage of the same issues in two languages. However, producers in all organisations in Wales and Scotland devoted the bulk of special programming to coverage of the developing debate rather than planned exposition. Yet there was logic in attempting to undertake explanatory tasks through the medium of existing programmes which had established audiences that were almost always far larger than the size of audience that a specially billed programme on the subject might have attracted.

Thus, BBC Wales, which had set up a devolution unit to service radio and television requirements for the campaign, ran an explanatory series of five pieces in its nightly news magazine *Wales*

Today. These involved cartoons and graphics. Its Welsh language counterpart, *Heddiw,* condensed its analysis to two 30-minute programmes just prior to the start of the campaign period. HTV Wales used its shorter news programmes, *Y Dydd* and *Report Wales,* to broadcast potted explanations of different aspects of the proposals over ten days during the last fortnight of the campaign. These short pieces were conceived as a reinforcement to a longer analysis attempted through two film documentaries in Welsh and two in English, the first of both pairs dealing with the historical background and the second with the details of the *Wales Act.* It was radio where the regional organisation enjoys, unlike television, complete freedom on its wave-length that broadcasters were able to produce a daily stream of informative programming. Throughout the campaign period the BBC Wales political correspondent Patrick Hannan, managed to create, through journalistic analysis, the regular questioning of an independent academic expert, and a series of 'phone-ins', a stream of programming that certainly promised to achieve considerable cumulative impact.

Whether it actually achieved such an impact is a different matter. People rate the influence of radio and television highly, yet neither radio nor television in Wales managed to create a measurable and observable impact. Programmes produced no incidents that changed the course of the campaign. It would have been surprising if Welsh broadcasters had created such an impact, for broadcasting in Wales is an integral part of British broadcasting. In the case of the Welsh and Scottish referendums only part of the vaunted panoply of British broadcasting was brought into play. In a general election, the election efffectively takes over large parts of the TV and radio schedule. There is less chance of escape.

In Wales this factor was more crucial than in Scotland. Scottish television is, in transmission terms, self-contained (apart from an insignificant overlap with the English based Border TV region in the ITV system). By contrast, Wales presents its long eastern flank to a whole range of English transmitters to which a significant proportion of Welsh viewers turn. Later research by HTV suggests that about 35 per cent of the population get their TV pictures from transmitters outside Wales. This part of the population would therefore have been wholly reliant upon London-based programmes for coverage of the referendum campaign. These were remarkably few in number.

BBC's early evening magazine *Nationwide* devoted four days (two for Scotland, two for Wales) to devolution. These programmes included discussion but are chiefly remembered for some satirical songs which incensed the 'No' campaigners in Scotland. Apart from that, BBC network output was confined (outside news programmes) to one issue of BBC 2's *Money Programme* which canvassed the views of businessmen, and to a one and a half hour, eve of poll debate from the Oxford Union. This was also broadcast on BBC 2 which in Wales, as in Britain, is a minority channel with at that time, an average audience penetration in Wales of less than 10 per cent. ITV's network contribution was even more scanty, confined to a controversial analysis by London Weekend's *Weekend World,* broadcast on the Sunday morning before polling. In this a scenario was outlined which suggested that a 'Yes' vote in Scotland could lead inexorably to independence. This was followed by a studio discussion with Michael Foot and Enoch Powell, evidently on the assumption that this was a subject which affected British interests. The assumption may have been correct, but the quantity of network output on the issue did not reflect a widespread acceptance of the assumption by all metropolitan broadcasters. Both these programmes illustrated the problem of dealing with parallel campaigns in Scotland and Wales. The *Weekend World* programme was devoted exclusively to Scotland, while BBC 2's Oxford Union debate encompassed both. Again, in London-based news programmes more time was devoted to Scotland. It is an open question how far perception of the devolution issue in Wales was affected by extraneous Scottish arguments. It is a question that arises as much in relation to newspaper coverage as to broadcasting. (See Chapter 7)

All in all there is no reason to suppose that television or radio was decisive in the campaign in the way that television may have been in the Kennedy/Nixon presidential campaign. If television did not alter public perception of the issues, broadcasters may ask whether that is proof of our impartiality or of our failure. Although in its own terms most of the broadcast output from BBC and HTV was relatively successful, broadcasters should ask whether it is sufficient in any campaign period simply to provide a platform. Rather, should we not adopt more rigorous techniques than studio debate and discussion in order to subject political argument to forensic analysis, despite the greater risk of accusations of bias or journalistic arrogance?

Radio Coverage

BBC RADIO WALES

1. An educational and explanatory series of short duration by Harry Calvert and Patrick Hannan in the A.M. programme. (February 5 to February 27).

2. Campaign reports in *A.M. News, News at One* and *Dateline* (from Monday, February 19).

3. Three Special *Straight on the Line* 'phone-ins' (Sunday, February 11, 18 and 25).

4. A daily 'phone-in' – chaired by Patrick Hannan, (between February 19 and February 27) transmitted 9.03 every morning.

5. A series of seven *About Politics* programmes examining some of the arguments for and against the Devolution proposals.

BBC RADIO CYMRU

1. An educational explanatory series of reports in *Helo Bobol* from February 5 prepared by Emyr Daniel, Deian Hopcyn and John Davies.

2. Five outside broadcast radio programmes transmitted at 1.03 every day between February 19-23.

3. Two 'phone-in' programmes at 1.03 on February 26/27.

BBC RADIO NETWORK

Devolution discussed in the following programmes:

World Tonight; File on Four (3 programmes); *Analysis* (1 programme); *One Man One Voice* (3 programmes); *Referendum Call* 'phone-ins'; A two-hour *Debate* linking London, Cardiff and Edinburgh; *In Britain Now.*

Television Coverage

BBC TV

English Language

A series of 5 educational films presented by Patrick Hannan in *Wales Today* (News programme) for 2 weeks from January 21.

BBC Wales, 8 February, Transmission 9.25 p.m. (50 mins).	Studio debate chaired by David Dimbleby and Patrick Hannan.
BBC Wales, 16 February, Transmission 10.15 p.m. (50 mins).	Outside broadcast in Caernarfon, chaired by Vincent Kane.
BBC Wales, 23 February, Transmission 10.15 p.m. (50 mins).	Studio debate chaired by Vincent Kane.
BBC 1, 19-23 February, Transmission 6.20 p.m. (30 mins).	Nationwide on Devolution. Presented jointly from Cardiff and Edinburgh.
BBC 2, 28 February, Transmission 9.35 p.m. (100 mins).	Oxford Union Debate on Devolution.
BBC 2, 28 February, Transmission 8.15 p.m. (50 mins).	*Money Programme* Financial implications of Scottish devolution with some reference to Wales.

194

Welsh Language

BBC Wales, 31 January,
Transmission 6.50 p.m. (30 mins).
Heddiw educational and explanatory
programme presented by Emyr Daniel.

BBC Wales, 7 February,
Transmission 6.50 p.m. (30 mins).
Heddiw educational and explanatory
programme presented by Emyr Daniel.

BBC Wales, 27 February,
Transmission 9.25 p.m. (50 mins).
Outside broadcast debate in Swansea
chaired by Alun Evans.

Regular campaign reports from 20 February to 27 February on *Heddiw* (news programme) transmission 6.50 p.m.

ITV

English Language

Explanatory packages about the *Wales Act* and the conflicting arguments in *Report Wales* (6.15 p.m.) from February 14.

HTV Wales, 9 February,
Transmission 11.05 p.m. (30 mins).
Part one of an English film documentary
The Welsh Assembly. Presented by John
Morgan.

HTV Wales, 16 February,
Transmission 9.00 p.m. (50 mins).
Second part of an English film
documentary *The Welsh Assembly*.
presented by John Morgan.

HTV Wales, 23 February,
Transmission 11.05 p.m. (50 mins).
'Phone-in' programme – studio
discussion chaired by Geraint Talfan
Davies.

London Weekend Television 25 February
Transmission 12 noon (56 mins).
Weekend World presented by Brian Walden

HTV Wales, 27 February,
Transmission 9.00 p.m. (50 mins).
Studio debate chaired by Geraint
Talfan Davies.

Welsh Language

Explanatory packages about the *Wales Act* and the conflicting arguments in *Y Dydd* (6.00 p.m.) from February 14.

5 February,
Transmission 8.30 p.m. (30 mins).
First part of a film documentary
presented by Tweli Griffiths.

12 February,
Transmission 8.00 p.m. (50 mins).
Second part of a film documentary
presented by Tweli Griffiths.

19 February,
Transmission 10.35 p.m. (50 mins).
'Phone-in' programme and studio
discussion chaired by Gwilym Owen.

26 February,
Transmission 8.00 p.m. (50 mins).
Studio discussion.
chaired by Gwilym Owen.

195

Table 9 – 1

Coverage of Referendum Campaign on BBC and ITN
Main Evening News Programmes

Date	BBC 9 o'clock News Scotland Mins. secs.	Wales mins. secs.	ITN News at Ten Scotland mins. secs.	Wales mins. secs.	Combined mins. secs.
8-2-79	—	—	—	—	5:12
9-2-79	—	—	—	—	3:41
11-2-79	0:28	—	—	—	—
12-2-79	1:32	—	0:30	—	—
13-2-79	—	—	3:12	—	—
14-2-79	—	—	—	2:44	—
15-2-79	0:45	2:57	2:18	—	—
16-2-79	3:21	—	3:17	—	—
17-2-79	—	—	—	2:31	0.48
18-2-79	0.29	—	—	—	—
19-2-79	2:52	1:42	—	2:22	—
20-2-79	1:11	3:01	—	—	0:52
21-2-79	2:42	1:05	—	—	2:29
22-2-79	1:21	—	—	—	—
23-2-79	2:02	0:24	—	2:08 .	0:58
24-2-79	—	—	—	—	—
25-2-79	—	—	—	—	—
26-2-79	5:04	—	—	—	5:00
27-2-79	0:36	1:40	2:40	—	—
28-2-79	2:28	1:20	—	—	0:58
1-3-79	0:56	0:25	9:00	2:00	—
2-3-79	4:33	4:24	—	—	22:06
TOTAL	**30:20**	**16:58**	**20:57**	**14:12**	**59:35**

CHAPTER 10

Public Opinion and Welsh Devolution

DENIS BALSOM

Reacting to the freshly declared referendum result, John Morris, the Labour Secretary of State for Wales, declared 'when you see an elephant on your doorstep, you know it is there'.[1] The Welsh electorate's rejection of the devolution proposals was of truly elephantine proportions, and as such unidimensional victories are relatively uncommon in Western democracies, an additional question is posed: how did such a vastly unpopular measure successfully complete Parliamentary procedures and come to be posed at the referendum? The anti-devolutionists, the victors in the referendum campaign, suggested that somehow an 'Establishment' plot had been perpetrated upon the Welsh people, who, in their wisdom, saw through the devious scheme and rejected it forthwith. A more dispassionate view however, shows that the proposals for constitutional reform were not made wholly in the face of public opinion. The provisions of the *Wales Act 1978* may be seen either as the culmination of a long period of political evolution, dating, according to choice, from the time of Henry Tudor, Lloyd George and Cymru Fydd (see Chaps 1 & 2), or as a contemporary phenomenon associated with the growth of Plaid Cymru since the Carmarthen by-election of 1966. This chapter adopts the second view. It examines the role and movement of public opinion on the issue of devolution over the period from Gwynfor Evans' sensational by-election victory until the referendum held upon St David's Day 1979: a period that will surely come to be seen as a distinct historical episode in the sweep of Welsh political development.

Public opinion is an elusive concept — constantly courted by politicians; much is justified in its name or sacrificed in its favour. In the absence of genuine popular democracy, the channels for the expression of public opinion are varied and diffuse. In institutional form, the conduits offered by interest groups and political parties are obviously important. A less formalised, but potentially far broader, vehicle for opinion which has emerged in the second half of the twentieth century is the scientifically based opinion survey. Such opinion polls are now commonplace and extensive coverage of their findings ensures not only transference of information to levels of decision making but also the broader dissemination of such opinions. In assessing public opinion on a specific issue such as devolution to Wales, data may be drawn from a number of sources: the declared policy programmes of political parties, evidence of support for those parties (see Table 10-1), the degree of pressure exerted by specific interest groups and in, what is the central concern of this chapter, the responses to well-founded sample surveys.

Table 10-1

Welsh Electoral Opinion

1966 – 1979

General Elections:	Turn Out	Lab %	Con %	Lib %	PC %	Other %
1966	79.0	60.6	27.9	6.3	4.3	0.9
1970	77.4	51.6	27.7	6.8	11.5	2.4
1974F	80.0	46.8	25.9	16.0	10.7	0.6
1974O	76.6	49.5	23.9	15.5	10.8	0.3
1979	79.4	46.9	32.2	10.6	8.1	2.3
By-Elections:						
1966 Carmarthen	74.9	33.1	7.1	20.8	39.0	—
1967 Rhondda West	82.2	49.0	4.3	—	39.9	6.8
1968 Caerphilly	75.9	45.6	10.4	3.6	40.4	—
1972 Merthyr Tydfil	79.5	48.5	7.4	2.4	37.0	4.7

Source: Denis Balsom and Martin Burch, *A Political and Electoral Handbook for Wales,* (Farnborough, 1980).

In examining the survey material available it is convenient to discriminate between three distinct time periods; firstly, up to the publication of the government's proposals in the 1975 White Paper, secondly, the 1975-78 period whilst Parliament considered the details of the devolution bills, and finally, the campaign period from late 1978 until referendum polling day. In each of these phases public opinion can be seen in a different role. In the early period expressions and

198

assessments of the public mind were an important input to the policy process on a subject that had yet to establish itself universally. During the parliamentary period, with devolution now central to domestic politics, public opinion affected treatment of the issue by ministers and MPs, and coverage of these debates and discussions helped, in turn, to shape public opinion. During the referendum period, with the legislative details finalised, the various campaigning groups came into open confrontation and public opinion was largely influenced by the campaign. It may also be assumed that during this lengthy political gestation, the public's general level of information concerning devolution and its implications steadily rose.

Prologue: 1966-1975

The first opinion polls in Wales to explore the attitudes related to devolution followed the surge of interest generated by the nationalist parties' successes at Carmarthen and Hamilton. An Opinion Research Centre poll in April 1968 found 54 per cent of their sample in favour of more power to make government decisions being given to authorities in Wales. A further 25 per cent were reported as being in favour of Wales having its own government separate from England. In September 1968 a Gallup poll recorded 51 per cent against the idea of a separate Parliament with the remainder supporting varying degrees of institutional reform. A further ORC poll discovered 59 per cent agreeing that it would be a good idea to have a Welsh Assembly or Welsh Parliament for dealing with Welsh affairs.[2] The Government's response to such attitudes and to continued nationalist successes at by-elections was to establish a Royal Commission on the Constitution.

In Wales, the political pressure engendered by the increased Plaid Cymru presence and fear, on the behalf of the major political parties, of an even greater nationalist presence kept the issue of reform and devolution alive. In particular, the series of by-elections in Labour constituencies ensured the close attention of the Government in formulating a response. The longer term pattern of Plaid Cymru fortunes at general elections is less impressive (see Table 10-1) but over time, Wales benefited from its association with a similar, but far more threatening, nationalist phenomenon in Scotland.

The Commission on the Constitution undertook to examine attitudes to government and in 1969, sponsored a sample survey as part of their enquiry.[3] The results gathered by the Commission are significant in that they were concerned with attitudes in Britain as a whole and not just within Scotland and Wales. It is a salutory reminder to some to discover that the people of Yorkshire, East Anglia and even Greater London showed similar levels of dissatisfaction with government and expressed similar preferences for reform as those in Wales (see Table 10-2). It must be noted however that while such research related to a live issue in Wales, no such salience prevailed the English regions.[4] Irrespective of these findings, the published recommendations of the Royal Commission endorsed decentralisation for only Wales and Scotland. It was perhaps, the harder evidence of nationalism and its success at the general elections of 1974 that provided the more piquant expression of public opinion.

Acts I and II : 1975-1978

The publication of the Government's White Paper: *Our Changing Democracy : Devolution to Scotland and Wales* (Cmnd 6348) concluded the many months of speculation and introduced a long period of parliamentary infighting over the legislation (see Chap 3). The Labour government's initial majority of three was quickly eroded through by-election losses and steadily undermined until in March 1977 a pact with the Liberal party was concluded. Central to this accommodation was the passage of the devolution legislation.

The White Paper proposals provoked little reaction in Wales for the Government's thinking had been clearly outlined in the two earlier 'green' papers. The initial surprise produced by the decision to treat Scotland and Wales in different fashions had passed and Plaid Cymru's MPs even welcomed the White Paper — though they were quickly cautioned by their National Council for doing so.[5] In December 1975, the *Western Mail* commissioned an opinion poll to gauge reception of the plans and found 30 per cent in favour, 39 per cent against with 31 per cent undecided.[6] A new factor however quickly entered the discussion; following the precedent of the EEC referendum, a movement spread in Wales insisting that any forthcoming devolutionary legislation be submitted to a referendum.[7] The *Western Mail* poll found this a decidedly popular measure with nearly three-quarters of the sample agreeing that a referendum would be appropriate.

Public opinion at this stage of the devolution debate shifted from being a policy input and became more a response to coverage of, and matters arising from, the Parliamentary proceedings. Estimates of public opinion became important weapons for both proponents and opponents of devolution in verifying or countering the various postures struck in the debate. Tracing the movements of opinion over

Regional Preferences for Devolution

Question 23(a) "For running the region as a whole, which of these five alternatives would you prefer?"

	Total	North	York-shire	North West	West Midland	East Midland	East Anglia	South East	Greater London	South	South West	Wales	Scotland
							Area						
Weighted base: all informants	(4,892)	(230)	(496)	(612)	(512)	(224)	(231)	(628)	(753)	(213)	(284)	(244)	(465)
	%	%	%	%	%	%	%	%	%	%	%	%	%
(1) Leave things as they are at present	13	11	16	8	15	12	16	14	16	11	20	15	6
(2) Keep things much the same as they are now but make sure that the needs of the region are better understood by the government	24	27	23	19	23	23	24	29	24	23	28	27	19
(3) Keep the present system but allow more decisions to be made in the region	24	26	24	30	26	26	17	21	24	20	20	21	26
(4) Have a new system of governing the region so that as many decisions as possible are made in the area	21	20	20	24	18	21	21	20	19	25	17	23	24
(5) Let the region take over complete responsibility for running things in the region	16	16	16	15	17	18	20	16	14	21	12	12	23
Don't know	2	1	1	3	1	0	2	1	2	0	2	0	1
Unweighted numbers of informants	(4,892)	(159)	(506)	(447)	(508)	(164)	(169)	(461)	(495)	(156)	(209)	(726)	(892)

Royal Commission on the Constitution, Research paper 7, "Devolution and other Aspects of Government: An Attitudes Survey." London: HMSO, p.62.

time, it must be remembered that the use of a referendum was not conceded by the Government until late 1976 and that the text of the referendum question was not known until even later. The picture of Welsh opinion provided by successive polls is inconclusive (see Table 10-3). Throughout the period the number of voters replying 'Don't Know' to a question on their intentions remained between a fifth and a third of all those asked. Devolution appeared to have the stable support of around 30 per cent of the total.[8] Nevertheless, the publication of the first Abacus poll for BBC Wales in May 1978 gave rise to considerable speculation for, when adjusted for turnout, both the 'Yes' and the 'No' lobbies were shown to have the support of 41 per cent of the sample. In view of the eventual referendum result, this division of opinion appears remarkable but similar findings were recorded in private polling for the political parties. Such a division of opinion was not shown by the Scottish electorate; poll evidence there showed a consistent majority preparing to vote 'Yes',[9] and thus the issue remained very much alive and in the centre of British politics.

Table 10-3
Referendum Voting Intention in Wales, 1975-1978

Fieldwork date	Polling Organisation[a]	YES %	NO %	DK %
12 Dec. 1975	R and M	30	39	31
6 Dec. 1976	R and M	27	40	33
18 March 1977	R and M	27	53	21
5 May 1978	Abacus	34[b]	39	27
15 Sept. 1978	Abacus	27	41	31

a. R and M: Research and Marketing (Wales and the West) Ltd were commissioned by the *Western Mail* and *HTV Wales*. Abacus acted for *BBC Wales*.

b. Abacus figures are inferred from two questions; a turn-out filter preceded the voting intention question whilst intending non-voters or those who were uncertain were asked their intention 'if they *were* to vote'. The voting intention of committed voters were
(i) 41 : 41 : 18 and (ii) 38 : 49 : 14.

Source: Denis Balsom and Ian McAllister, 'The Scottish and Welsh Devolution Referenda', *Parliamentary Affairs*, 32, 1979.

The collapse of the combined Scotland and Wales Bill in 1977 and the introduction of individual country bills containing provisions for an advisory referendum is fully dealt with in Chapter 3. However one amendment moved by George Cunningham, MP for Islington South, had a significant impact on public opinion. It required that 40 per cent of the registered electorate vote 'Yes' in the referendum before the provisions of the Act could be implemented and played a major role in the campaign in Scotland. In Wales, its provisions were felt by many to effectively preclude a positive outcome to the referendum. The hope of the devolutionists was that, should a simple majority be secured in favour of devolution, the moral weight of this achievement would secure a reconsideration of the rule.[10]

The *Wales Act* received the Royal Assent on 31 July 1978, but the announcement of a date for the referendum was forestalled by speculation over the possibility of an October 1978 general election. Once the election scare was over, the referendum became scheduled for early 1979. By the conclusion of the Parliamentary discussion of the *Wales Act,* the essential battle lines for the coming campaign had been drawn up. The Conservative party had moved from an earlier commitment to some form of devolution to opposition to the *Wales Act per se.* The Liberals and Nationalists endorsed the Act with reservations, whilst the Labour Party remained deeply divided (see Chap. 2). The outcome remained dependent on whether issue or party loyalty would carry more weight with the electorate on polling day.

Finale : The Referendum Campaign

The formal referendum campaign began on 8 February 1979, three weeks before polling day. The BBC Wales poll published that day, based upon fieldwork carried out a week earlier, showed a 46 : 33 division of opinion in favour of the 'No' side, with 21 per cent of intending voters undecided (see Table 10-4). Closer analysis of these figures revealed the true battleground of the campaign — Labour party supporters were evenly split between 'Yes' and 'No'. Plaid Cymru supporters were heavily in favour of devolution, the Conservatives predominantly against, whilst the Liberals, rather confusingly, were two to one against but with a higher number of undecided voters. The detailed course of the campaign and the claims and counter claims of each side are discussed elsewhere (see Chap. 6). This chapter will restrict itself to evidence of change in public opinion during the campaign period.

Practical restraints of data collection meant that the polls published immediately prior to polling day were based upon opinions canvassed between the 19 and 22 February. These polls however, published in the *Western Mail, The Sun* and on BBC Wales, all showed a common trend — devolution was to be rejected massively in Wales. Reports from Scotland showed that opinion had appeared to close rapidly during the campaign leaving the outcome there very much in the balance.[11]

The breakdown of partisan opinion given in Table 10-4 gives a closer insight into the effect of the campaign. The Conservative position had hardened considerably, as had that of Plaid Cymru, with over 8 out of 10 of their respective supporters intending to follow party lines. For these two groups there appears to have been no conflict of issue and party loyalty. The decisive group in Wales, the Labour voters, clearly rejected the official position of their party and defected massively to the 'No' side.

Table 10-4

Referendum Voting Intention During the Campaign

| Fieldwork date | Referendum Voting Intention | General Election Voting Intention | | | | |
		Con %	Lab %	Lib %	PC %	All %
1st Feb. 1979	Yes	20	41	27	73	33
	No	63	40	50	9	46
	DK	17	19	23	18	21
21-22nd Feb. 1979	Yes	7	27	19	83	22
	No	87	58	67	12	65
	DK	6	14	13	6	13

Source: Abacus — BBC Wales polls, 1979.

The potential conflict induced by this preference for issue loyalty over partisanship was undoubtedly mitigated by the very prominent position adopted by the 'gang of six' Labour rebels. Labour voters did not have to wrestle with their consciences when electing to join, not the Conservatives, but the leading Welsh Labour backbench members in voting 'No'. The Liberal position remained ambiguous, in that although committed to a federal Britain, their supporters appeared overwhelmingly opposed to the *Wales Act* proposals. Whilst there is a distinct element of anti-nationalism in Welsh Liberalism, ideologically and in policy orientation the Liberals and Plaid Cymru are not too far removed from one another nor are their supporters too dissimilar.

The growing gap between the two sides that was recorded in the campaign polls appeared to have continued to polling day. The final result showed Wales rejecting the *Wales Act* by a margin of four to one. Detailed comment on the results has preceded this chapter but the magnitude and uniformity of the result in Wales gave rise to an immediate spate of questions and incriminations — how could the politicians have so misjudged the public mood? The data presented earlier has attempted to show that whilst public opinion was certainly divided about the course of constitutional reform in Wales, the commitment to the status quo was never of the proportion revealed by the referendum. In securing such a victory, against prevailing party lines, the leading anti-devolutionists appear to have tapped a deeply significant and potent cleavage in Welsh society.

Post-Mortem

In attempting to assess what happened during the referendum, certain general points need to be borne in mind. Within British political history, referendums have been used very sparingly and the direct consequences of such a poll are also unfamiliar to the British electorate. In 1975 no immediate change stemmed from the EEC referendum, but in 1979 the Scottish and Welsh electorates had the power to overturn an Act of Parliament, though few perhaps were conscious of this new responsibility. In contrast to a general election, a referendum should allow lengthy discussion of the one specific issue, though this debate may be as mystifying as it is enlightening, with both sides producing their facts, figures and experts. Other incidental issues are likely to intrude into the debate however, for when the public has the opportunity to express its opinion it may not want to restrict its comments to the issue in question. At a referendum the voter's decision may be affected by the absence of the normal points of reference common to a conventional election. Thus it seems likely that, as Graham Wallas suggests in another context, the electorate will seek to identify cues and points of focus to 'something simpler . . . something that can be loved and trusted, and which can be recognised . . . as [having been] . . . trusted before'.[12] In the referendum campaign these identifiable foci were diffused as political parties split or abstained. Some recognisable public bodies and groups did

205

Table 10-5

The Uniformity of Change in Attitudes to Devolution

	% of committed voters in favour of devolution on:		
	May 5th 1978	Feb 21/22 1979	Difference
Sex			
Male	45.1	26.0	– 19.1
Female	54.3	23.7	– 30.6
Age-Group			
18—34	59.4	32.6	– 26.8
35—54	44.9	21.9	– 23.0
55 +	46.0	23.8	– 22.2
Socio-Economic Group			
AB—middle class	30.0	25.2	– 4.8
C1—lower middle	37.7	17.4	– 20.3
C2—skilled working	56.0	26.2	– 29.8
DE—semi/unskilled working class	59.1	31.9	– 27.2
Language			
Welsh Speakers	62.8	38.8	– 24.0
Non Welsh Speakers	44.2	20.3	– 23.9
Region			
South Wales	44.6	26.0	– 23.6
NW & W Wales	53.0	27.1	– 25.9
NE & Mid Wales	45.0	19.9	– 25.1
Voting Intention			
Labour	64.7	31.8	– 32.9
Conservative	23.6	8.1	– 15.5
Liberal	30.0	21.4	– 8.6
Plaid Cymru	86.8	88.0	+ 1.2
Wales Total	50.0	25.6	– 24.4

Source: BBC Wales-Abacus polls 1978/1979.

campaign and well known individual opinion leaders made proportionately greater impact. The public's perception of, and response to, the referendum will be related to these cues and stimuli.

The rapid erosion of support for devolution prior to polling day has been noted above and, in seeking to explain this change, the social and demographic characteristics of those involved is of obvious relevance. By contrasting the profile of support for devolution found in the first BBC Wales poll with that found immediately before polling, the impact of the campaign and discussion of the issue over some ten months can be gauged (see Table 10-5). The remarkable level of uniformity shown in the net differences between the polls suggests that the coalition of support that rejected devolution was broadly based and did not depend upon a particular sectional appeal. The great turnover of opinion shows up when controlled for voting intention, but otherwise appears almost wholly unrelated to any significant socio-economic or demographic cleavage. Welsh speakers and non Welsh speakers deserted the 'Yes' side in equal proportions, as did residents in the various regional areas of Wales. Women appear to have shifted rather more than men on the issue, whilst opinion in the AB, middle class socio-economic category, remained fairly consistent. Elsewhere the degree of uniformity of change is remarkable. The reversal of opinion revealed by the polls appears related to party but not to any structural or objective dimension in society.

This analysis suggests deeper subjective reasoning behind the shifts in opinion. The data available allows this line of enquiry to be pursued in two directions, firstly, on reasons given for preferences on devolution, and secondly in perceptions of the relative positions of key campaign groups. Using a list of the potential advantages and disadvantages associated with devolution by the main campaign groups, respondents to the surveys were asked to identify reasons for their voting intention — the advantages of devolution for those intending to vote 'Yes' and the disadvantages for those intending to vote 'No' (see Table 10-6). The two polls compared cover the intensive campaign period of February 1979 and it must be taken as an indictment of the substance of the campaign that little change emerges in the relative preferences, although, it must be remembered, between the polls the size of sample proposing to vote 'No' grew considerably. Opinions as to the relative merits or demerits of the proposed Assembly were not, on this evidence, substantially altered by the arguments presented by the campaigners. It is possible however, that although these were the benefits and liabilities of devolution suggested by

207

Table 10-6

Advantages and Disadvantages of Devolution: Public Preferences from a Predefined List

Q.
Which of the items on this card represents to you the most important (advantage that an Assembly might bring to Wales?) (disadvantage an Assembly might create?) (up to three items coded)

	SURVEYS[a]	
YES VOTERS	I	II
A Welsh Assembly (Will):	%	%
help to reduce the excessive workload at the Westminster Parliament	8.6	8.1
have more time to consider the special needs of Wales	24.7	25.8
help to protect jobs and improve the standard of living	23.1	21.4
is necessary because every nation should have its own Parliament	8.6	10.6
could help protect Wales	15.0	11.5
improve democracy in Wales	7.1	11.8
DK	12.9	10.8
NO VOTERS		
A Welsh Assembly (Will):		
involve extra costs	23.5	26.2
reduce Welsh influence at Westminster	6.2	7.0
cause uncertainty and damage the economy	15.4	13.3
is the first step towards the breakup of the UK	18.4	19.4
might try to get special benefits for Wales at the expense of other areas in Britain	4.6	4.2
just create another tier of government bureaucracy	19.1	20.7
DK	12.8	9.2

[a]*Surveys:* I BBC Wales-Abacus Poll   February 1st 1979
           II BBC Wales-Abacus Poll February 21/22nd 1979

campaign rhetoric, the real underlying opinions of the electorate were not exposed by such a test. A later, more detailed survey sought their respondents' spontaneous and unstructured replies to a question probing the reasons for their vote in the referendum (see Table 10-7).[13]

The variety of such unstructured comments has, through coding, to be aggregated into a few key categories, but the value of such generalisation is immediately apparent and a different unprompted profile of public concerns emerges. Amongst 'Yes' voters the commonest reason given for the direction of their support was the prospect of some form of improvement in the quality of government in Wales. Responses in this category varied but included statements claiming more accountability, greater democracy and less remote government. A respondent from West Flint replied:

> I feel that Wales stands a better chance by government in Cardiff, monitor and listen to the people, have first hand knowledge of what is going on.

These issues formed a central part of the 'Yes' campaign platform and thus appear to have been in sympathy with an important range of concerns for the electorate. Amongst 'No' voters however, the outstanding response is a concern over nationality, nationhood and nationalism, coded here as a lack of national assertiveness and self-confidence. The sentiments engendered by these concepts can be illustrated by several respondents comments:

> There are no right people to handle Welsh affairs (Wrexham)
>
> Possible domination of a Welsh administration by the Taffia (Cardiff)
>
> Out of fear of the ultimate consequences — a foothold for the extremists (Merthyr)
>
> I don't see any point in Wales becoming a banana republic (Rhondda)

These issues were not the predominant themes of the 'No' campaign but are a prevailing undercurrent in Welsh politics and suggest considerable psychological factors at work within the Welsh electorate.

Table 10-7

Advantages and Disadvantages of Devolution:
Unprompted Public Responses

Q.
Did you vote Yes or No to the Government's devolution plans at the referendum? Why did you vote that way?
(up to three items coded)

Aggregated general categories	Yes Voters Positive values %	No Voters Negative values %
National assertiveness, self confidence	15.4	41.0
The Welsh language	0.6	4.6
Quality of government	37.7.	16.8
Specific gains/losses economic, financial, general	16.0	15.4
Following party discipline	2.5	2.8
General, unspecific, uncodable	27.8	19.4

Source: Welsh Election Study Survey 1979.

Central to this discussion is the concept of national identity. This complex characteristic can only be measured crudely, but even so produces suggestive results. The Welsh Election Study ascertained identity by asking their respondents whether they considered themselves to be British, Welsh, English or whatever. The sample divided into 58 per cent Welsh identifiers and 34 per cent British identifiers. Voting in the referendum was clearly affected by an element of national consciousness and this is reflected in the relative preferences of the national identity groups. 'Yes' voters were proportionately 76 per cent Welsh identifiers and 19 per cent British, whilst 'No' voters were 50 per cent Welsh and 45 per cent British identifiers. Amongst the crucial category of Labour voters however the effect is even greater. Labour voters divided into 66 per cent Welsh and 29 per cent British identifiers. Of these however, the Welsh identifiers voted 33 per cent 'Yes' and 67 per cent 'No' whilst the British identifiers voted only 14 per cent 'Yes' and 86 per cent 'No'.

The second principal dimension to analysing the internal processes of the referendum is to test the electorate's perceptions of the issue positions of the various campaigning groups. To establish the significance of these cues, the polls asked a number of questions requiring respondents to place participating groups on one or other side of the debate. From the results of these tests several factors appear significant (see Table 10-8). At the outset of the campaign only Plaid Cymru were identified by a majority of respondents as being in favour of devolution. Not a single group was identified as being against the proposal by a majority of the sample, though the Conservatives were 'correctly' placed by some 46 per cent. A high level of uncertainty is shown regarding all the groups, as illustrated by the size of the 'Don't Know' category. These data suggest that generally the issue positions of the key groups were not widely known nor were they widely understood. The campaign period might have been expected to clarify these perceptions and the data presented from the final poll demonstrates some campaign effects. By the last week in February a

Table 10-8

Referendum Campaign Effects

Q.   Which side of the referendum debate do you think the following groups support?

	Mainly For		Evenly Split		Mainly Against		Don't Know	
	%	%	%	%	%	%	%	%
Bus. & Industry	16.2	10.8	20.2	17.2	32.4	38.9	31.1	33.1
Trade Unions	21.9	26.8	19.5	19.9	22.8	17.6	35.8	35.8
The Gov'nt	36.4	53.6	20.5	17.2	20.0	14.0	23.1	15.1
Labour M.P.s	33.8	39.0	27.9	34.0	14.1	10.0	24.3	17.1
Liberal Party	19.4	21.0	18.1	20.5	19.4	16.5	43.0	42.1
Cons. Party	9.5	6.3	14.5	12.1	46.2	58.6	29.9	23.0
Plaid Cymru	74.7	79.2	3.1	3.7	3.3	2.6	18.9	14.5
Survey[a]	I	II	I	II	I	II	I	II

[a]*Surveys:*   I   BBC Wales-Abacus Poll February 1st 1979
          II   BBC Wales-Abacus Poll February 21/22nd 1979

Table 10-9

Referendum Position Perceptions of Labour Voters

Q. Which side of the referendum do you think the following groups support?

| | Referendum Voting Intention | | | | | |
| | ALL | | YES | | NO | |
The Government	%	%	%	%	%	%
Mainly for	35.2	51.6	48.5	64.4	34.7	45.3
Mainly against	18.6	14.5	16.8	9.6	22.4	19.5
Labour M.P.s						
Mainly for	39.1	40.0	49.5	54.9	38.8	34.3
Mainly against	13.6	10.0	5.9	7.5	20.4	12.6
The Trade Unions						
Mainly for	20.1	15.6	32.7	52.1	17.3	19.8
Mainly against	24.3	20.4	21.8	9.9	29.6	27.8
Plaid Cymru						
Mainly for	75.7	75.0	78.2	78.6	85.7	81.4
Mainly against	3.0	2.7	2.0	5.4	3.1	1.2
Survey[a]	I	II	I	II	I	II

[a]*Surveys:* I   BBC Wales-Abacus Poll   February 1st 1979
II   BBC Wales-Abacus Poll   February 21/22nd 1979

bare majority linked the Government with devolution, a slightly larger group placed the Conservatives with the anti-devolutionists but eight out of ten had no trouble in equating Plaid Cymru with the proposals. The Trade Unions, who led the 'Yes' campaign, appear to have made little impact, the stance of the Liberal party was overwhelmingly misunderstood and only the genuine confusion in placing the Labour MPs reflected the real situation accurately.

As has been noted earlier, the target group for the campaigners was the traditional Labour voting bloc of Wales. Similar data on perceptions of group locations for only the Labour section of the electorate can be calculated and controlled for referendum voting intention. In party versus issue conflicts, loyal partisans will often 'refuse' to accept that their opinion differs with that of their party. With the Labour Party at large genuinely split on the devolution issue, different levels of perception amongst Labour voters hint at potential explanatory factors. For Labour voters as a whole, the main features of the campaign was an increasing awareness that the Government was advocating a 'Yes' vote, otherwise campaign effects appear small (see Table 10-9). When adjusted for referendum vote however, the pattern is more conclusive. Labour 'Yes' voters were much more conscious of the Government's position and also believed far more, that the Labour MPs were on their side. Of equal significance perhaps, is the wide disparity of perceptions concerning the position of the Trade Unions – a key reference group in South Wales. Over half of Labour 'Yes' voters believed the Trade Unions were with them, whilst only a fifth of Labour 'No' voters recognised the conflict between their own position and that of the unions. Amongst both groups of Labour voters, acknowledgement of the nationalists' position was high. Thus two mutually exclusive profiles appear within the Labour party – 'Yes' voters who consciously recognised that they were voting with their traditional friends and allies, and Labour 'No' voters who failed to appreciate they were in opposition to their traditional friends and allies. Only on the question of the nationalist party is there a unity of opinion. It appears that some Labour voters could accommodate this alliance with the nationalists, whilst the remainder strove to reject the connection.

The public at large identified only Plaid Cymru clearly and unequivocally with the issue of devolution. The evidence from the earlier analysis of reasons for referendum voting also concluded with the prime significance of nationalism. Thus having identified the interests of the nationalists with devolution, the Welsh electorate would appear to have accorded the issue the same derisory level of support as that which the nationalists manage to secure at most elections.

Conclusions

The evidence and argument presented here has attempted to portray the role of public opinion in the formulation of policy and the impact upon public opinion of political campaigning. The picture that emerges is one of volatility, with expressions of willingness to see constitutional change in the 1966-70 period, culminating in the massive endorsement of the status quo in the 1979 referendum. Parallel developments in party fortunes also meant that Wales was a more

213

Conservative environment in 1979 than in 1966 and this is also likely to have affected devolution polling. The key referendum problem remained: would party loyalty take preference over issue loyalty?

For some there was perhaps a genuine difficulty in reconciling a commitment to the issue of devolution and decentralisation with the actual features of the *Wales Act*. In Scotland there is evidence that pro-devolutionist Conservatives voted 'No' on the grounds of the inadequacy of the legislation rather than rejecting the principle.[14] However no such evidence pertains in Wales and it must be concluded that the referendum result was attributable to the Labour Party's failure to maintain its ranks, from which an alarming defection took place.

Defeat in the referendum initiated a sequence of events which culminated with the election of Mrs Thatcher's Conservative administration.[15] The results of the May 1979 General Election in Wales recorded a spectacular increase in the Conservative vote and even a modest increase in the Labour poll. Thus a startling paradox remains: the Labour Party, hopelessly divided and defeated on devolution was still able, within a few weeks, to revive itself sufficiently to re-establish its traditional electoral superiority in Wales. This chapter has suggested that the concepts of national identity and national consciousness pose particular problems for the Labour Party, traditionally concerned with such issues as unemployment, the economy and inflation. The referendum, on an exclusively Welsh issue, was unfamiliar ground for both the electorate and the political parties. In this exceptional circumstance the normal vocabulary of politics tended to assert itself and in doing so revealed the inability of the Labour Party and to a lesser extent of the Conservatives and Liberals to cope with the wholly Welsh politics. Their structure and outlook has been moulded by the expediencies of participation in the wider British political system. The referendum result and the public opinion poll data indicate that the existing structure of politics in Wales failed to promote the generation of a new and specifically Welsh political system. Perhaps such a radical change will always lie beyond the capabilities of an essentially evolutionary and pragmatic political culture. Public opinion both fosters such a political system and is shaped by it. Involving the electorate in the debate of these less common aspects of politics generated responses both alarming and educative. The referendum exposed, but did not resolve, issues and conflicts that have underlain Welsh politics for many years.

NOTES

1. *Western Mail* 3.3.79.

2. For general background to this period see, Denis Balsom 'Plaid Cymru' in H.M. Drucker, *Multi-Party-Britain*, (London, 1979) and A. Butt Philip, *The Welsh Question*, (Cardiff, 1975).

3. Royal Commission on the Constitution, Research paper 7 'Devolution and other aspects of government: An attitude survey' (London, 1973).

4. cf. J. Brand, *The National Movement in Scotland*, (London, 1978).

5. Denis Balsom, 'Plaid Cymru', *op.cit*, p.147.

6. *Western Mail* 16.12.75.

7. P. Luke and D. Johnson, 'Devolution by Referendum? A look at the Welsh situation', *Parliamentary Affairs, 29,* 1975-6.

8. Denis Balsom and Ian McAllister, 'The Scottish and Welsh Devolution Referenda of 1979', *Parliamentary Affairs, 32,* 1979.

9. *ibid,* p.408.

10. On the mechanics and implications of the 40 per cent rule see, Denis Balsom and Ian McAllister, 'Whose vote counts? Electoral Registration and the 40 per cent rule', *Political Quarterly, 51,* 1980.

11. Denis Balsom and Ian McAllister, *Parliamentary Affairs, op cit,* p.408.

12. G. Wallas, *Human Nature in Politics,* (London, 1910), p.83.

13. The Welsh Election Study survey was carried out in the summer of 1979 by Gallup Poll Ltd, financed by the SSRC and directed by Denis Balsom and Peter Madgwick.

14. Denis Balsom and Ian McAllister, *Parliamentary Affairs, op cit.*

15. For a detailed account of the circumstances leading up to the general election see, D. Butler and D. Kavanagh, *The British General Election of 1979,* (London, 1980).

CHAPTER 11

Implications: Two Salient Issues

J. BARRY JONES, R. A. WILFORD

The experiences, both of the Welsh devolution debate and of the referendum campaign itself have a significance not only for Wales but for the political process of the United Kingdom. It provides evidence of the utility of the referendum as a decision-making tool and, together with the subsequent general election results, appears to suggest the emergence of a new, perhaps fluid, configuration of electoral support in Wales.

The Referendum: A Vote for the Status Quo?

The referendum runs counter to the basic principles of the British political system. Pre-eminently, Britain is a parliamentary democracy in which the cardinal principle of the supremacy of parliament is allied to a particular form of representative democracy not significantly different from that defined by Edmund Burke in this speech to the electors of Bristol, thus:

> Your representative owes you not his industry only but his judgement; and he betrays instead of serving you, if he sacrifices it to your opinion.[1]

However, early in the twentieth century demands were voiced from the right of the political spectrum for the introduction of a referendum in order to exploit populist attitudes and forestall radical changes. They provided compelling evidence that some politicians considered the existing parliamentary institutions either incapable of, or inappropriate for, resolving fundamental constitutional problems. In 1911 the leader of the Conservative opposition had moved an amendment to the Parliament Bill proposing that any bill affecting the crown, establishing national councils in Ireland, Scotland, England or Wales, or affecting the constitution or powers of either House of

Parliament, should not receive the Royal Assent 'unless and until it has been submitted to a poll of the electors and approved at such a poll in accordance with the schedule of the Act'.[2]

The early identificiation of the Conservative party with 'the people's veto' contributed to establishing the view amongst certain elements of the party that the referendum provided, to quote Balfour, 'our one hope of getting the sort of constitutional security every other country but our own enjoys'.[3] Since Balfour the Conservative party has exhibited a continuing, if intermittent preoccupation with the referendum. Baldwin wanted one on tariff reform in 1931 and in 1945 Churchill suggested that a referendum might be used to extend the life of Parliament until Japan had been defeated. Butler and Kitzinger writing in 1976 reported that of the last 9 Conservative Prime Ministers 6 had advocated or voted for the referendum.[4] Subsequently Mrs Thatcher indicated that the referendum could be used to resolve problems of industrial relations and the Conservative Research Department produced a discussion paper which seriously considered the referendum as a device for constitutional engineering.[5]

Despite the historic identification of the Conservative party with the referendum, it is the Labour party which, in practice, has revealed the greater willingness to adopt the procedure. The referendum held in Scotland and Wales on 1 March 1979 was the second occasion in less than four years that a Labour Government decided that an issue affecting the constitutional structure of the United Kingdom should be removed from the normal parliamentary process*.

However the decision to refer the devolution issue to the Welsh and Scottish electorates was not taken because it was a profound constitutional issue but because it fitted only imperfectly into the traditional, if simplistic, left-right mould of British party politics. In this respect it had much in common with the EEC Referendum which was employed not as a constitutional device but as a political expedient. But the cases are not perfectly parallel. The EEC Referendum was adopted on the Government's own initiative and then pushed through a hesitant and dubious House of Commons. By contrast, the devolution referendums were extracted by backbenchers from a reluctant Government whose Parliamentary authority was threatened by an unlikely alliance of Conservatives, Liberals, Nationalists and Labour backbenchers largely drawn from North-East

*The Conservative government was responsible for the Northern Ireland (Border Poll) Act 1972, and the referendum held under it on 8 March 1973.

constituencies. Nevertheless, neither experience appears to have fundamentally undermined the parliamentary system of Government; the artifice of designating referendums as merely 'advisory' is generally perceived as having safeguarded the central concept of parliamentary supremacy. Even the massive rejection of the *Wales Act,* approved by Parliament and in receipt of the Royal Assent, has conspicuously failed to precipitate any apprehensions that parliamentary sovereignty had been violated. Doubtless, the widely shared view that the government's Welsh devolution policy had been passed by an 'artificial' majority content to destroy the proposals at the subsequent referendum has much to do with that complacency. However, the bizarre precedent of the Commons endorsing legislation of which it fundamentally disapproved was a further indication of the growing compatibility of the referendum with the parliamentary representative system of government.

If the referendum is to become a more familiar feature in our political landscape it is necessary that its characteristics, particularly those which appear to expand political participation, should be fully assessed. The experience of the Welsh referendum raised, at the very least, substantial doubts as to the efficacy of the referendum as a satisfactory decision making device and revealed deficiencies in four distinct but inter-related areas.

(a)   *The referendum excited a conservative reaction inimical to institutional reform and stimulated the widespread hostility of organised interests.* Throughout the campaign the 'Yes' groups, with decreasing success sought to operate along the lines which Elystan Morgan the Chairman of WAC had described as 'the politics of hope' (*South Wales Echo,* 7-2-79). Disconcerted by the detailed arrangements implicit in the *Wales Act,* the 'Yes' groups increasingly purveyed the hope that the Assembly would revive Welsh self confidence, regenerate the Welsh economy and devise some agreeable procedure whereby the Welsh culture might be safeguarded. By contrast the 'No' campaigners were concerned to emphasise the dangers inherent in the proposed constitutional changes and progressively became associated with the popular apprehensions that devolution would lead to domination by a Welsh speaking elite and eventually to the break-up of the United Kingdom. Throughout the campaign there was a perceptible and pervasive feeling that no matter how difficult life was in the UK frying pan, it would be much worse in a Welsh Assembly fire. However, fear of change was not simply emotional. There was a powerful rationale which helps to explain the evident reluctance of the Welsh electorate to embark on additional institutional reforms. Wales was still attempting to digest the re-organisation of its local government and health service, but the assumed public exasperation with the reformed structure of local government, far from providing the momentum for devolution as had been expected by the pro-devolutionists expressed itself in a deep seated desire for a moratorium on re-organisation.

It was this natural reluctance for change which a variety of interests sought to harness and exploit. Those interest groups in Wales which were part of large UK organisations were fearful that the new administrative arrangements proposed for Wales would disrupt long established procedures and delicate relationships formed with central Government. They were not over-concerned with the actual proposals, which by common agreement gave little real power to the Assembly, but concentrated on what *might* ensue if the Assembly were established. The most active and partisan approach was adopted by the NFSE but the CBI, and the BMA and the NFU all prophesied dire consequences if the Welsh Assembly were established; that it would discourage investment, inhibit small businessmen and farmers and endanger the health services. But the most vigorous and decisive campaign was mounted by Welsh local authorities who saw themselves threatened by the government's devolution proposals. They had not always been hostile. In 1974, at a meeting of the newly established Welsh Counties Committee, county councillors from all parts of Wales had been in general support of 'some measure of legislative devolution' and, as they were mostly Labour councillors operating within the widely criticised Tory re-organised local government system, they did not exclude the possibility that a Welsh Assembly might take some of the powers exercised by local government. The majority supported Councillor Squire (Chairman of Mid Glamorgan CC) in his view that an Assembly was 'needed to control the growing bureaucratic power of the Welsh Office which was able to over-rule elected representatives in Wales' (*Western Mail*, 11-5-74). However, by 1979 two developments had taken place. In an attempt to counter the 'extra tier of government' argument of the anti-devolutionists, the Labour Party had unequivocally linked the establishment of a Welsh Assembly with a slimmed down local government structure. Furthermore, the 1973-74 local government re-organisation had 'bedded-down' and evolved new power relationships and interests amongst both councillors and officials. Consequently it is not altogether surprising that seven of the eight Welsh counties came out against the Assembly;

219

that NALGO, Gwent County Council and South Glamorgan County Council financed 'No' campaigns; and that influential local politicians such as Lord Heycock, Councillor Allison and Councillor Squire, who had supported devolution in 1974, were its implacable opponents five years later in the 1979 referendum campaign. The concerted opposition of important sectional interests in Welsh life, who expressed arguments in a functional and non-political frame-work and presented criticisms in a specialised guise, was of considerable significance in consolidating the mood of conservative caution which contributed to the maintenance of the *status quo.*

b)   *It polarised issues in a manner which far from clarifying tended to obscure the basic principles of the debate and confuse the electorate.* The limited nature of the choice presented by the referendum question created a unique set of political alliance structures. On the 'Yes' side Liberals and Communists who differed fundamentally on so many issues, both favoured an Assembly with legislative powers. But both were obliged to sacrifice this aspect of their policy in order to play a positive role in the campaign. Plaid Cymru faced a similar but more profound problem. As a party they were divided; a substantial minority was totally opposed to the limited executive devolution contained in the *Wales Act* and was unwilling to accept the incrementalism it implied. Yet they were fearful to be seen publicly opposing the creation of a new national institution in Welsh life. Ironically they were also reluctant to be seen pushing too strongly in support of the Act because they feared such an overt role would produce a backlash in English speaking Wales. Furthermore, all three parties in addition to resolving their internal problems, were required to work in harness with a Labour Party which was their natural political adversary. A similar problem existed within the ranks of the 'No' coalition. Many Labour Party members, such as Kinnock who opposed the government's proposals for a Welsh Assembly, were concerned by the spread of nominated bodies and wedded to the concept of democratic decentralisation.[6] They were in the difficult position of agreeing with the Labour Party's diagnosis but rejecting its prescription. However, the narrow logic of the referendum format decreed that they should operate in partnership with groups from the opposite end of the political spectrum who were unequivocal unionists and quite uncritical of the constitutional *status quo.*

Thus from the moment a referendum was conceded in February 1977 the Welsh devolution debate was forced into a procedural strait-jacket which artificially polarised the issues, arrested the momentum of creative dialogue which had been conducted since the late 1960s, distorted the debate and, on the basis of the findings published in an opinion poll (see Chap. 10) on the eve of the referendum, confused the electorate. The poll's evidence strongly suggests that large numbers of people had great difficulty in associating the parties with particular positions in the devolution debate. For example, the Liberal Party, which had advocated a form of British federalism for two decades and which might therefore be described as the original party of devolution, could not be placed on either the 'Yes' or 'No' side by 42.1 per cent of the sample. Even more surprising only 53.6 per cent believed the government supported devolution and this after the issue had dominated the parliamentary timetable for almost three years and despite the intervention of 15 government ministers during the three week campaign. The trade unions in Wales had followed a consistent pro-devolution policy since 1973 when the Wales TUC had been founded. Yet when asked which side of the referendum debate the trade unions supported only 26.8 per cent of the sample thought they were mainly for; 19.9 per cent thought they were evenly divided and 17.6 per cent actually thought they were mainly against. But the confusion over the respective positions in the referendum debate of the various groups and political parties was not evenly spread. The poll revealed that the attitudes of Plaid Cymru and the Conservatives were clearly perceived by a large majority; 79.2 per cent believed Plaid Cymru was mainly for and only 2.6 per cent thought it was against. In the case of the Conservatives 58.6 per cent perceived them as a mainly against compared with 6.3 per cent who considered them mainly for. Thus it would appear that though confusion clouded the devolution debate the differing degree of confusion across the political spectrum contributed significantly to the referendum result.

c) *It was not a single issue campaign but was inextricably linked with the current developments in British politics.* It proved even more difficult than was the case during the EEC referendum to isolate the campaign's central issue from developments and events taking place in the rest of the political system.[7] Clearly the fact that Wales, with a population of less than 3 million has to co-exist within a United Kingdom of more than 57 million contributed to the difficulties in focussing the attention of the Welsh electorate on the devolution issue. Furthermore, the penetration of the London based media (see Chap. 7) diverted people's attention away from the narrower confines of the Welsh political debate. But if devolution rarely attained that national coverage and attention obtained by the EEC Referendum, such coverage as was granted tended to be directed largely at Scotland. Thus the whole debate on Welsh devolution was coloured by the nationalist threat in Scotland but which had little relevance to Wales. A similar 'issue contamination' effect was produced by the series of public service strikes which forced their way on to the front pages of the press (both Welsh and London based) and helped to create the impression that Welsh devolution was peripheral to the fundamental issues of British politics.

It also became increasingly evident during the course of the campaign that an intrusive partisan element was exacerbating divisions between the two sides of the debate. In part, this was inevitable given the clear opposition of the Conservative party but it was accentuated by Labour's decision to fight the campaign on the basis of maintaining the Government in office. The tactic had been implicit from the outset but initially was employed only by George Wright (Secretary, Wales TUC). However, in the last week, it became quite explicit as the referendum's outcome was linked with the fate of the Labour government. The distinctive Welsh context within which the campaign had been fought was increasingly diluted by the emergence of traditional British party politics which confused the issue and limited the significance of the result on 1 March 1979.

d) *It failed to resolve finally the issue of Welsh devolution.* Although the referendum is flawed in several crucial areas, there is a conviction on the part of both politicians and general public that it alone is capable of deciding fundamental, i.e. constitutional, issues; that it alone can legitimise a policy which otherwise would divide the country.[8] The experience of the EEC Referendum is frequently cited in support of this assessment. If the 2:1 majority in the 1975 referendum confirming British membership settled the issue of the Common Market, how much more likely has the emphatic rejection by a 4:1 majority removed the Welsh devolution question from the political agenda. This assessment is deficient on two counts; first if the EEC Referendum decided anything it did so only for the short-term. The growing debate on the budgetary contributions to the EEC is eloquent testimony to the continuity of the 'Common Market issue' in British politics.

The second criticism raises the question: can a referendum resolve any problem either in the short-term or once and for all? The evidence from Wales suggests that the devolution issue has not been finally resolved. Following the referendum defeat, the Welsh Liberal Party and Plaid Cymru severed their links with the all-party alliance and reaffirmed their enthusiasm and support for devolution either with a federal flavour (in the case of the Liberals) or based on national independence. Both parties interpreted the referendum vote as a rejection of specific government proposals and neither conceded that the concept of devolution itself had been rejected. Although the Labour Party in Wales was in a more embarrassing situation, it also reasserted its belief in devolution in a statement issued by its Welsh Executive immediately after the result and subsequently confirmed by its annual Welsh Conference in May (*Western Mail,* 21-5-79). Similarly, the Wales TUC visibly chastened by the result of both the referendum and the general election in Wales, sought not to reject but to re-define its policy on devolution (*Western Mail,* 5-5-79). The attitudes of both the Labour Party and the Wales TUC continue to be shaped by the fact that the nominated bodies and the problem of public accountability remain and need to be resolved. Clearly, the executive devolution envisaged in the *Wales Act* is now inappropriate but the Welsh Labour party still supports democratic decentralisation. However, opinion seem to be hardening that such a reform should be comprehensive, incorporating all the United Kingdom and not just Wales and Scotland.

Table 11-1

Preferred Form of Government

Forgetting the Referendum, which of the items on this list would represent your ideal form of government for Wales?

	February 8	February 28
No Assembly at all, keeping the government of Wales much as it is now	49.3	62.7
An Assembly as currently proposed by the government	9.0	7.8
A stronger Assembly, similar to that proposed for Scotland with its own law-making powers	16.4	11.0
Complete self-government for Wales	13.9	8.0
Don't Know	11.3	10.6

Source: BBC Wales Polls 8 February and 28 February.

But the evidence which raises the most serious doubts as to whether the Welsh referendum produced any definitive resolution is not confined to the post-referendum period. Numerous indicators emerged in the final week of the campaign, indicating a continuation of the devolution debate beyond 1 March 1979. The series of polls commissioned by the BBC was published in January and February 1979 showed that while Wales was fairly evenly divided between those who favoured the *status quo* and those favouring devolution, the precise form of devolution offered by the Government's *Wales Act* was the least liked of all the options (Table 11-1). Even the final poll taken when the anti-devolution tide was running most strongly, revealed greater public support for both legislative devolution and complete self government than for the more limited government proposals. In the final stages of the referendum debate a rough consensus on the undesirability of nominated bodies emerged with sufficient clarity for John Morris to claim that both sides favoured devolution but disagreed over the appropriate form (*Western Mail,* 28-2-79). In the case of the Labour 'No' Assembly rebels the claim was quite justified but it was also true that the Conservative Party was not totally opposed to devolution *per se.* During the campaign the Conservative party announced itself in favour of a strengthened Welsh Office, possibly in receipt of further devolved administrative powers and the establishment of a Welsh Select Committee which might sit and take evidence in Cardiff from time to time. Indeed, on 26 June 1979, on the same day that the House of Commons approved the draft of an Order in Council to repeal the *Wales Act* by 191 votes to 8, the Conservative Welsh Secretary, Mr Nicholas Edwards, unveiled the plans for a new Welsh Select Committee which would be able to look at the full range of the Welsh Secretary's responsibilities and to scrutinise public bodies within the Principality. The establishment of the Select Committee on Welsh Affairs possessed of both departmental ('Welsh Office') and subject ('Wales') status, whilst substantially less ambitious than the proposals of the 1974-1979 Labour Government may be construed as another step on the road of political devolution, providing an additional means of Parliamentary scrutiny of the executive and ensuring that Welsh socio-economic interests are brought to the attention of Parliament as a whole. It is a road along which Wales has been discreetly moving since the end of the last war. The Select Committee may yet provide a context within which it can be manifestly evident that Welsh devolution was not emasculated by the referendum result on 1 March 1979.

A New Welsh Political Profile?

The unambiguous snub to the referendum proposals in Wales and indecisive nature of the Scottish results created the pretext for a joint Tory-SNP assault mounted through a 'no-confidence' motion in Parliament, thus precipitating the general election of 3 May 1979 and the return of a Conservative government. The fears manifested by the Labour pro-devolutionists during the latter stages of the referendum campaign in Wales thus were realised.

Confronted by a general election, the internecine conflict that had characterised the Labour Party during the Welsh and Scottish devolution campaign was swiftly resolved. The rapid closing of the ranks was particularly evident in Wales where the resounding defeat of the Assembly proposals had suggested that complacency on the part of the Labour Party might be somewhat misguided. The fact that the Labour Party-Wales TUC pro-devolutionists had eventually contrived to present a 'Yes' vote for the Assembly proposals as a vote of confidence in the Government was an added reason for a lack of complacency. For the first time in more than fifty years the Labour Party and its proposals — in the shape of the *Wales Act* — had been resoundingly rejected by the Welsh electorate, whilst the Conservative Party emerged as the victor.

There is some justification for the claim that the referendum result and the results of the general election in Wales witnessed the emergence of a new Welsh political profile. The persistent belief that Welsh radicalism still remained a potent force was undermined by both sets of results. This was certainly the case in the traditional heartland of radicalism, the rural counties of Gwynedd and Dyfed, both of which returned an overwhelming 'No' vote. The results confirmed the trend away from devolution and their conclusiveness appeared to presage an electoral realignment in Wales.

The referendum results also revealed the quintessential nature of Welsh nationalism: that of rural and regional protest, heavily dependent on the language issue. This certainly appears to have been the case in the county of Gwynedd which suffers from the twin problems of rural depopulation and declining industries. The general election results in the two Gwynedd seats held by Plaid Cymru tend to confirm this evaluation. Dafydd Elis Thomas and Dafydd Wigley not only retained their seats but increased their majorities. The fact that the Plaid Cymru MPs managed to exact legislation from the tottering Labour Government designed to compensate ex-slate quarry workers and their families, on the same or similar terms as those earlier accorded to coal miners, no doubt assisted Thomas and Wigley during the election campaign — even though the Parliamentary price for the legislation was Plaid Cymru's support for the Government in the division lobby.

The referendum resulted in a swingeing defeat for the Government proposals. There are a number of possible explanations for this occurrence: the astute Act-centred tactics of the anti-Assembly issue-coalition; the pragmatic exploitation of the North-South divide; the growing unpopularity of the Government after a winter of bitter industrial action; the misapprehension by the Labour Party that, to put it at its lowest, there was a subliminal 'we-feeling' among the Welsh that could be encouraged and marshalled into support for the Government's limited proposals. All no doubt played a role in precipitating a landslide vote against the *Wales Act*.

However, there was a rather more subtle process of acculturation at work that performed a vital role leading to the unequivocal rejection of the Assembly proposals and which was lent further credibility by the results of the general election. In respect of Welsh politics the concept is normally referred to as 'Anglicisation', betokening the continuing decline in the number of Welsh speakers. However, 'acculturation' is much broader, and implies the acquisition of politico-cultural characteristics of the wider, English political and social system. This suggests a widespread diffusion of 'English' values, techniques and institutions into Wales. Such diffusion can occasion culture conflict but the evidence of such conflict in the Welsh context, as manifested by both the referendum and general election results, is merely vestigial, at least in the political sense. Whilst there is evidence of a narrowly construed specifically Welsh cultural resistance — perhaps given its most overt expression in such diverse forms as rugby football and eisteddfodau — the diffusion of wider English political values has permeated the political consciousness of the vast majority of the Welsh electorate. On this assumption a general acceptance of even a token Welsh Assembly (as represented by the proposals of the *Wales Act*) was doubtful in the extreme. The anti-Assembly issue-coalition clearly perceived the political significance of this acculturation process by conducting their normative critique of the *Wales Act* against a persistent backcloth of the 'slippery-slope' scenario, a perspective common to both the Tory dominated and the Labour 'No-Assembly' campaigns.

The commitment to centralism shared by both the Labour and Conservative parties for most of this century proved to be irresistible for the great mass of the electorate. An eloquent demonstration of the permeation of the centralist strategy is provided by the voting behaviour of the electorate in those areas of Wales conventionally regarded as Labour Party strongholds — the industrial valleys of South Wales. The scale of rejection of the Labour Government's Assembly proposals in Gwent, South Glamorgan, Mid Glamorgan and West Glamorgan was staggering, averaging over 83 per cent of the votes cast. The overwhelming snub to the proposals gave some Labour Party stalwarts cause for concern with the prospect of an imminent general election, particularly as the Labour Party-Wales TUC Assembly campaign had sought to portray a 'Yes' vote not only in terms of a vote of confidence *for* the Government, but in terms of a vote *against* the Tory Party. However, the general election results in these areas just two months later saw the party faithful back in the Labour camp; the fears that the Labour Party fortress had become an open city thus proved groundless. But, the fact that the traditional Labour voters had broken ranks at the referendum to engage in tactical voting to defeat the Government's proposals, may prove to be of longer term significance. Once a habit of voting is broken, it becomes less traumatic on a second occasion and this could bode ill for the Labour Party in South and South East Wales. What is of perhaps more immediate significance is the fact that traditional, working-class Labour voters in these areas demonstrated in the referendum that they perceived their interests in a British context and as not capable of resolution within the narrower, Welsh confines. Their voting behaviour at the referendum was an eloquent demonstration of the fact that there is a widespread assimilation of political values wholly consistent with a centralist and predominantly English mentality.

The acculturation process is not merely the product of the commitment to centralism exhibited by the major political parties. It can, and does, take rather more discrete forms, chief among which is the cumulative Anglicising influence of the mass media in Wales. The penetration of Wales by London based daily newspapers must be balanced against the fact that there is no single indigenous daily newspaper that covers the whole of Wales (see Chap. 7). Thus, the London dailies tend to act as vehicles for the diffusion of a metropolitan culture and help to reinforce a centripetal perspective. This function was especially evident during the referendum campaign. Whilst the indigenous Welsh dailies sought to present the issues in a balanced manner, the London-based tabloids did little to contribute constructively to the debate.

The tendency of both *The Sun* and the *Daily Mirror* was to trivialise and sensationalise the devolution issue. *The Sun,* on 8 February ran a centre page spread that presented a cartoon depicting a manic, kilted Scotsman and an equally wild Welsh woman in national costume sawing the figure of Britannia in half. The spread headlined 'Disunited Kingdom: Danger Ahead', was written by the paper's political correspondent Walter Terry, who concluded his article thus: 'if the Assemblies are a success the break-up of the UK will be on its way. If they are a flop we are stuck with one more cumbersome heap of bureaucracy'. Although the *Daily Mirror* was not as unequivocally hostile, it also tended to trivialise the issue. On the eve of the referendum vote it published an exceedingly brief news report predicting the rejection of the Assembly proposals in Wales. However, the report was relegated to the corner of page seven which was dominated by a picture of two topless girls, one Scottish, the other Welsh. Thus at least the picture editor achieved a spurious balance!

With the exceptions of *The Guardian* (whose Welsh sales are negligible) and the *Western Mail,* the other daily newspapers, including those published in Wales, took either a hostile or an indifferent editorial position on the issue of Welsh devolution.* Although one must not over-emphasise the persuasive and pervasive influence of the London dailies, the cumulative effect of their hostility or indifference to Welsh devolution, compounded by their role as general vehicles of political acculturation, should not be ignored. Consequently, newspaper readers in Wales were faced with a Press almost unanimously united in its opposition.

The situation with regard to the other mass medium, television, is rather more complex (see Chapter 9). Many Welsh television viewers, particularly in populous areas of South and North Wales, can tune into both BBC and IBA English transmitters. Thus, whilst BBC Wales and HTV Wales-Cymru ran balanced coverage of the devolution debate in both English and Welsh it was possible for significant numbers of viewers either consciously or unconsciously to avoid the devolution coverage provided by Welsh television. If this were the case, and given that the devolution debate was essentially conducted through the mass media, then this would tend further to heighten the influential role performed by the press during the campaign.

* All the London dailies tended to regard the Welsh devolution debate as of less news value than that taking place in Scotland — perhaps a tacit recognition on their part that the process of acculturation rendered the prospect of an Assembly in Wales more remote than one in Scotland.

Besides the obvious effects of political centralism and the rather more subtle effects of the mass media in promoting acculturation, there are a number of other more or less discrete factors hastening the process. The rural heartland of Wales has experienced significant demographic changes[9] which have had an impact upon both the devolution referendum and the subsequent general election. Successive Governments have sought to regenerate Welsh speaking areas suffering depopulation through policies of regional economic aid. *Inter alia,* this has meant that North Wales, in particular, has experienced an influx of upwardly mobile workers from England, (particularly the West Midlands and Merseyside) who bring with them little tradition of either party loyalty or radicalism. This has complemented the traditional influx of retired English people subjected to the dominant political culture and socialised into the acceptance of centralised decision-making. Both forms of demographic change have thus contributed to the broad acculturation process and, more specifically, influenced the results of both the referendum and the general election. It is possible therefore that the Labour Government by encouraging the industrial regeneration of Anglesey suffered at the hands of its own policy of regional economic aid. Not only was its devolution policy crushingly rejected by North Wales in the referendum but for the first time this century Anglesey's electorate returned a Conservative MP at the subsequent general election.

The growth of the tertiary sector in South Wales, in part accelerated by the central Government's policy of re-locating Civil Service departments, with the consequent influx of professional white-collar workers, may also have a similar detrimental effect upon the Labour vote. To some extent this is already occurring. The general election results saw the Labour Party in Wales almost wholly confined to the enclave of the industrial valleys in the South. In North and West Wales the Conservatives emerged as the largest single party, whilst in Wales as a whole it secured 32.2 per cent of the poll in May 1979 as compared with 23.9 per cent in October 1974.

The substantial rise in the popular vote of the Conservative Party, and its acquisition of three additional seats at the general election, would appear to vindicate the stance it adopted during the devolution campaign. Although the Labour Party eventually sought to secure support for the *Wales Act* by projecting devolution as a 'Wales versus the Tories' issue, opinion polls published late in the campaign suggested that the electorate perceived the issue in terms of 'Nationalists versus the Rest' (see Chap. 10). It was the Conservative

229

Party which appeared to the electorate as the only Party displaying a clear and consistent anti-devolution stance. That the devolution debate would polarise along these lines had been predicted two years prior to the referendum by Ian Grist, Conservative MP for Cardiff North. Convinced that the Welsh electorate would reject the Government's policy, he declared:

> It is ironic that two expatriate Englishmen sitting for Welsh seats, namely Jim Callaghan and Michael Foot, should now be doing more to identify the Conservative Party with the people of Wales than any previous administration.[10]

It is difficult to avoid the conclusion that the referendum campaign represented a watershed in Welsh politics. The results of both the referendum and the general election would seem to confirm the dynamic nature of the acculturation process. The political ramifications of the process may in the long term include a further decline in support for the Labour Party from which possibly but not necessarily the Conservative Party might benefit. Whatever the precise nature of future political developments in Wales, the referendum appears to have acted as a catalyst: old combinations have been broken and new ones seem likely to be forged.

NOTES

1. Edmund Burke, 'Speech to the electors of Bristol', *Works: Vol. 1* Bohn's Standard Library, 1902, p. 447.
2. Quoted in P. Goodhart, *Full Hearted Consent,* 1976, p. 197.
3. *Ibid.,* p. 198.
4. D. Butler and Kitzinger, *The 1975 Referendum,* 1976, p. 10.
5. *Politics Today — The Referendum and the Constitution,* Conservative Research Department, 12 September 1978.
6. N. Kinnock, *Western Mail,* 22 February 1979.
7. See Table 7-2.
8. Butler and Kitzinger, *op. cit.* p. 279.
9. Table 1.08 Components of Population Change *Digest of Welsh Statistics* No. 23, HMSO. 1977, p. 5.
10. *Conservative Monthly News,* January 1977.

Epilogue

J. BARRY JONES, R.A. WILFORD

The St. David's Day referendum ensured that Welsh devolution, in the short term at least, was dead and probably would never reappear in the form envisaged by the *Wales Act* 1978, such were the constitutional anomalies and political problems exposed by its critics during the referendum campaign. But Welsh politics was not ossified by the result of the referendum despite the decisive nature of the vote. After 1 March 1979, Wales entered into a changed political environment and a deteriorating economic situation which combined to produce novel and potent factors in the political process.

The most obvious and immediate political change was in the attitudes of the major political parties who displayed less interest and invested less effort in specifically 'Welsh' political issues. The Conservative Party's posture was consistent with its earlier position in deliberately foregoing the opportunity to give evidence to the Royal Commission on the Constitution in 1970. Then it had rejected the case that Wales needed to be treated in a fundamentally different fashion from the rest of Britain and this was also a recurrent theme in the pronouncements of Conservative Party spokesmen during the referendum campaign. The formal and traumatic identification of the Labour Party with the *Wales Act* and the 'Yes' campaign obliged the party, in the interests of political self-preservation, to adopt a much lower profile on Welsh affairs, a policy shift which fortuitously coincided with the retirement of Emrys Jones, the party's Welsh Secretary and Regional Organiser, who had been an enthusiastic architect of the devolution policy. Despite the divisions evident in the referendum campaign, the party managed in the subsequent general election to retain its dominant role in Welsh politics. However, confronted by a government whose economic policies threatened a rapid and substantial de-industrialisation of Wales, Labour re-emerged as a party of territorial defence, a posture that may redound to the benefit of the de-centralisers within the party, albeit at some future date. Even the Liberals, for so long the party of 'Home Rule All Round' and federalism, were impressed by the scale of rejection reflected in the referendum vote and, in common with the other parties, found it prudent to say little if anything on the subject of devolution in the aftermath of the referendum.

During the course of the referendum campaign, one of the few points of common agreement to emerge was the desirability of establishing a framework of democratic accountability for the various nominated and *ad hoc* bodies in Wales. The pro-devolutionists had regarded the proposed Assembly as capable of fulfilling this role, whilst their opponents, particularly the Conservatives, had argued that the task would be more efficiently discharged by a House of Commons Select Committee. It was, therefore, not wholly unexpected that the new Conservative government used the occasion for the repeal of the *Wales Act* to announce the establishment of a Select Committee for Welsh Affairs. It was a centralist alternative to the policy of devolution; one which, although betokening a recognition of a distinctively Welsh dimension to British politics, also ensured the re-assertion of the primacy of Parliament at Westminster. The Committee's Conservative architects perceived it as a more efficient means of securing executive accountability; a view shared by the Committee's Labour membership, three of whom (including its first Chairman, Leo Abse) had constituted half of the renegade 'gang of six'. The Committee's members, especially the Labour anti-devolutionists, had a vested interest in demonstrating that Welsh interests could be properly safeguarded through this reform of the Westminster investigative machinery.

In the later stages of the referendum campaign the anti-devolutionists had assiduously catalogued Wales' heavy dependence upon central government subsidies. The election of a Conservative government committed to a monetarist strategy, the imposition of stringent cash limits and cuts in public expenditure, thus had a disproportionately negative impact upon Wales. Within twelve months of the referendum the Welsh economy was embarked upon a serious downward spiral. This was exacerbated by a series of government decisions including the ending of steel production at Shotton, the rundown to half capacity of the Llanwern and Port Talbot works with potentially disastrous implications for the Welsh coal industry, and the government's decision to cut-back substantially its support of regional development policies. Against this background the Select Committee predictably chose unemployment and the condition of the Welsh economy as its first subject for investigation.

The Committee's first report,[1] published on 31 July 1980, when unemployment in Wales was higher than any other area of the U.K. with the exception of Northern Ireland, unanimously recommended a vastly expanded regional aid programme for Wales, coupled with the warning of 'risks of serious social disorder if there were to be very high and chronic unemployment, particularly among the young'[2]. The government, in a considered response published in December 1980[3], rejected both the Committee's diagnosis and prescriptions; only two of the Committee's 38 recommendations proving generally acceptable to the Welsh Office.

The unanimity of the report suggested that Welsh interests could still win preference over partisanship. But the government's near total rejection of the Committee's recommendations revealed the stark realities of the political power structure in Westminster and raised doubts as to the political viability of the Select Committee; of its ability to present itself as a significant medium for representing and transmitting Welsh interests and concerns; and as a substitute for the proposed Welsh Assembly.

Perhaps the party whose *raison d'être* was most severely tested by the referendum was Plaid Cymru. The party had always doubted the advisability of participating in the campaign, doubts borne both of tactical considerations and matters of fundamental principle. Nevertheless, it had fought strenuously within the ranks of the all-party 'Wales for the Assembly' group. The massive popular rejection of the proposals, gave indications of an ominous shift in public support, subsequently confirmed at the May General Election when Plaid Cymru polled 8.1 per cent of the votes, thereby registering its worst electoral performance since 1966. The inevitable *post mortem* opened up serious divisions within the party of a 'left'/'right' nature and raised the possibility in the early spring of 1981 that the small, but voluble, Welsh Socialist Republican Movement might fight in parliamentary elections against Plaid Cymru. However, Plaid Cymru's internal problems were largely resolved as a result of the governments' decision to renege on a commitment to establish a Welsh language fourth television channel. This apparent snub to Welsh interests united Plaid Cymru in a campaign to reverse the government's policy, which culminated with a threat by Gwynfor Evans, Plaid Cymru's president, to fast to death unless the original commitment was honoured.

By the summer of 1980 the issue had became the most pressing in Welsh politics and as such was chosen by the Select Committee on Welsh Affairs for its second investigation. However the government, apprehensive of the political consequences of the fast, indulged in another policy switch and reaffirmed its support for a Welsh language television channel. The Select Committee's investigation thus lost much of its popular impact and the ease with which the government conceded to extra-parliamentary pressure, whilst not jeopardising the Committee's parliamentary status, raised doubts as to its political relevance.

In the wake of the referendum, Welsh devolution occupied only a marginal position on the political agenda. Yet, given a combination of factors, the issue could be propelled to a position of significance. A change in the attitude of the general public is not impossible. Public opinion in Wales has proved itself in the past to be mutable with respect to devolution. For example, in 1968 an ORC opinion poll revealed that 70 per cent of the sample was in favour of more devolution to Wales, though 73 per cent was opposed to the idea of an independent Welsh state (Western Mail, 25-9-68). Whether these figures are wholly controverted by the referendum result is a moot point, but clearly public opinion is dynamic both over time and issues. We suggested in Chapter I that the process of acculturation contributed to the scale of the rejection of the Assembly proposals by diminishing the elusive phenomenon of a distinctive Welsh identity but the process may not be incontrovertible. The adverse effects of the recession, the Labour Party's reaffirmation of its support for regional devolution (including the English regions), the emergence of the Social Democratic Party committed to some form of devolution; taken together, these could generate demands for a measure of regional, political and economic autonomy even greater than that so convincingly rejected on 1 March 1979. However, it is not always possible to anticipate how the public will interpret prevailing circumstances. For example, the process of industrial decline in Wales could generate a reactive centralism, a widespread desire to reinforce the links between the centre and the periphery, thereby enhancing Wales' dependence upon the economic intiatives of Westminster and Whitehall.

Whether the centripetal or centrifugal forces prevail, the *status quo* of St. David's Day 1979 is no longer an option. Wales will become either more closely integrated with the centre, or experience a renaissance of demands for greater autonomy. But the battles over the *Wales Act* would not be refought. Should any devolutionary proposals for Wales reappear they would take a different form. They would not be under the guise of a Wales v. England debate but rather in the context of a general appraisal of centre-periphery relations within the United Kingdom as a whole.

NOTES

1. First Report from the Committee on Welsh Affairs (1979-80), 'The Role of the Welsh Office and Associated Bodies in Developing Employment Opportunities in Wales', Vol.I. H.C. 731, July 1980.
2. *Ibid.* para 28.
3. Government Observations upon the First Report from the Committee on Welsh Affairs, Cmnd 8085, 1980.

INDEX

238